A Private View

Irene Mayer Selznick

A Private View

ALFRED A. KNOPF NEW YORK 1983

THIS IS A BORZOI BOOK
PUBLISHED BY ALFRED A. KNOPF, INC.

All photographs not otherwise credited are from the author's private collection.
Insert following page 154: David and Irene with Jeffrey and Danny—Johnny Florea,
Life Magazine © Time Inc.; David, 1929, and "Gone With the Wind" premiere—
courtesy of Ronald Haver.
Insert following page 282: "A Streetcar Named Desire"—courtesy of Bettmann Archive, Inc.;
"Chalk Garden" and "Bell, Book and Candle"—Irene Mayer Selznick Collection,
Boston University Library.

Library of Congress Cataloging in Publication Data
Selznick, Irene Mayer [dates]
A private view.
1. Selznick, Irene Mayer.
2. Theatrical producers and directors—United States—Biography.
I. Title.
PN2287.S348A36   1983   792'.0232'0924 [B]   82-49192
ISBN 0-394-40192-1

Manufactured in the United States of America
First Edition

A Private View

Haverhill

I HAD dreams of glory. Mind you, not every girl's dream, but mine. Back there in Brookline, Massachusetts, I could see no reason why with luck and perseverance I could not become a Girl Scout captain.

This was not too much to hope for, because, after all, fortune shone on our little family. "Upward mobility" was a term unheard then, but we were a shining example; I mean, my father was. This Boston exhibitor and distributor had already made two films. And now there was big news: we were going to Hollywood, where he was going to become a movie producer. My sister, Edith, was thrilled, but I really thought we were coming up in the world fast enough without this.

All I wanted was to keep everything just as it was . . . make time stand still. What was this talk about "get ahead"? To where? Why? Who could ask for more? The status quo suited me. We were not like other families. Other parents loved their children, but not with the deep concern and concentration, the dedication, which mine gave. Or so we were told and so I believed.

Things had always gotten steadily better with us, but then that was to be expected, because my father adhered to rules of life which he had set out, the inevitable outcome of which had to be success. He had programmed it. From earliest memory our status, however modest, was spectacular when compared to the rest of the family, otherwise known as "the relatives." He swelled with pride when he pointed out how fortunate was our lot. And he insisted we maintain awareness . . . and respect. Respect for his efforts. I overshot the mark and cultivated a superstition that lack of appreciation would disperse the favoring gods. I was as grateful as the poor relatives should have been, of whom we seemed to have an increasing number.

Early on, there didn't seem to be too many. My father's were, mercifully, in Canada. He not only didn't like them, he didn't like talking about them, with the exception of his mother, whom he adored. All four of my grandparents had come in that great wave of immigration in the early 1880's, from Vilna and Kovno on the Russian-Polish border. The goal was New York or, failing that, Boston, a day cheaper. The Mayer money must only have stretched as far as St. John, New Brunswick, which is where they got off the ship—the parents, one little girl, and my father, Louis, aged three. There were a daughter and two more sons to come.

Several of my grandmother Sarah's children had died in infancy, so she set special store by my father, her first surviving son, who remained her most cherished child. She tried to protect him against his father, which may well have made life even more rugged for him. Certainly the old man was easier on his two younger sons, whose good looks could hardly have accounted for this fact. In those days, by all accounts, Jacob Mayer was grasping and tyrannical. The harshness of St. John's climate was matched by this man's nature.

He dealt in scrap metal, to which was added a marine salvage business, as there were sunken ships to be raised in St. John harbor. This company was actually formed by my father, although because of his youth his father's name was attached to it. This did not endear the boy to his parent. He worked desperately hard even as a small boy, and full-time from the age of twelve, but still he couldn't satisfy the old man. Because he was undersized, his father found it advantageous to send him forth, sometimes well across Canada, to bid at auctions on discarded bridges and burned-down factories; a thin little boy in short pants could be safely ignored by other buyers, and hardly suspected of being able to pay cash. His mother feared for his safety and, as my father told it, wept as she sewed the money into the waistband of his pants. He received neither pay nor recognition.

When it was too late, the old man changed the company's name, unfairly at that, to Jacob Mayer and Sons.

At sixteen, with his mother's encouragement, my father cut out to find his opportunity in the USA, a country with which he had a lifelong love affair, with all the fervor unique to converts. He worked harder than ever, but at least he got ahead. There was no time for fun or companions any more than there had been in Canada. He developed a habit which lasted most of his life, that of seeking out older people because he could learn from them.

I don't remember how he met my mother's Aunt Annie, who lived in Chicago, but he found in her his first friend. He was so straitlaced that he had never even looked at a girl, and he confided to Aunt Annie that he was lonely and longing for a home of his own—ideally, one connected to her. Although he was only nineteen, Aunt Annie realized he was mature and serious beyond his years, and finally she spoke to him of a special niece of hers in Boston, a paragon of virtue. He became infatuated with Aunt Annie's niece without ever having met her; the more he heard of Margaret, the more his longing grew.

Margaret's father was a cantor, Rev. Hyman Shenberg, who had a congregation first in Pittsburgh, where she was born, and later in Boston. As a youth, my grandfather was called the Golden One, not merely for his voice, but for his beauty, of which he was even more proud. Tall, with a fair complexion, blue eyes, and golden hair, he surely deserved an appropriate bride, with either wealth or great beauty. He was foiled. His parents chose a girl for her family, who were noted for their learning, their character, and their good deeds. He was so appalled that his bride, Rachel, had an olive complexion, dark hair, and dark eyes, that he preferred her to walk a few paces behind him in public. That she had married beneath her never occurred to him. He looked like a blond George V and dressed like Prince Albert, and it was incumbent upon his bride to produce a blond child to commemorate his beauty. There was poetic justice: she produced three decidedly brunette children.

My mother shared my grandmother's way of life, which was giving and serving. They gave shelter to arriving immigrants, an endless succession of "landsmen," who usually brought their featherbeds with them, on which they would bed down in the "front room." Very often there were several families at a time, until others came to take their places.

My mother found it perfectly natural to undertake tasks for the strangers under her roof—mind the children, a job found, lodgings, a small stake temporarily advanced—to start them on their way in the new country. It was the good-neighbor policy, in the tradition of her family, and the word spread as though there were a chalk mark on the fence.

My grandfather was filled with disdain and chose, when possible, to absent himself for more lordly undertakings. Such modest acts of generosity were hardly suitable to a vain and rather shallow man. However, he put up with her good deeds and she put up with him. She indulged his whims and chose to be amused by his pretensions. That my mother longed for a fair skin and blue eyes was, I am sure, her way of wanting to make things up to him. Failing that, she would surely absolve her mother by giving him blond grandchildren.

He retained his splendid figure and sartorial elegance into old age. However, he did not welcome losing his golden look and resorted to what must have been a do-it-yourself job. I recall arriving in front of our apartment and being frightened by a figure coming toward me with a violet-colored mustache and beard. The poor man was dyed purple! He was offended that I noticed anything; such was his conceit. I didn't understand why he couldn't have stayed home until it mended or grew out. This was the man who insisted his wife walk ten paces behind him for esthetic reasons!

My father took himself to Boston, determined to marry Aunt Annie's niece, Margaret. He even rented a room across the street from her in order to lay siege. Margaret had never before encountered such ambition and vitality; she was astonished by his single-mindedness and ardor. He was certainly unlike anyone in her family.

They were both about twenty when they married. Winning the girl of his choice, one who found strong favor with his mother, made him feel truly blessed. His mother's benediction sealed his happiness.

His drive for success was now doubled. He could vindicate his mother's faith and shine in the eyes of his bride. He had the brains, the energy, and she had the intuition and the heart. He agreed with his mother that "God had brought them together." He was out to win laurels that he might lay them in the laps of his mother and his wife. Yes, he was intense and he was idealistic and, heaven knows, emotional.

What a strange pair my parents must have been—my mother so thirsting for knowledge and with an urge to give, so gay and friendly and dear and pretty; my father, so much the opposite.

They became a tight little unit. Given his background and nature, his wife and home meant everything to him, and no sacrifice was too great. This did, however, mean shutting out the world and all the people in it, none of whom he could trust.

They attached more importance to having a baby than any other people I have yet to hear of. It was a privilege, a miracle, and the most important thing that had ever happened. I can easily imagine how they marveled at their first child. Edith was born exactly fourteen months after their marriage, and my mother was not to have another free moment; nor would she have wanted one.

They had hoped for a little girl, which is apparently what they said again when the second child came along twenty months later. However, it just may have been a disappointment to my father. If it was, the disappointment was outweighed by the fact that at his first look at me (and he never tired of telling me of that first look) he was struck by a resemblance and said, "It's little Margaret," which is what he called me off and on in moments of greatest affection until I grew up. He claimed, and never came down off it, that he was better off with daughters. "Sons leave, but daughters stay." Furthermore, he could pick his own sons, as opposed to the sons that might have been born to him. He never gave me reason to doubt his preference.

And yet, and yet . . . There was that recurrent remark over the years: "If she'd been a boy!" Feminists, please look the other way; I was flattered. I had it both ways—all this, yet not having to deliver. No loss of face or faith. I was a girl—after his own heart. How lovely for him, how lovely for me. I was convinced that it was better to have a son than to be one.

I'm not sure what he did at that time, but one of his proudest boasts to me used to be, "I was president of the New England Wool Trust when I was twenty-one." I don't know what that meant, but it couldn't have been as imposing as it sounds.

Then disaster struck. He was wiped out in the depression of 1907, the year I was born, and was forced to put his pride in his pocket and move in with his in-laws in their crowded quarters in Boston. He never forgot the humiliation of those few months. Not only couldn't he support his little brood, he had nothing with which to get started again. When the chance came to lease a theatre in Haverhill, on which his heart was set, he had a desperate struggle to raise the necessary small sum. Instilled in him forever was the principle of conserving one's resources against a possible setback and of having something put by for future opportunity.

He managed finally to raise the $650 he needed, and we were off to Haverhill, a thriving manufacturing town on the banks of the Merrimack River, north of Boston. The enterprise was, alas, a burlesque house, which didn't suit at all; he did not want to be in a business which appealed to baser instincts. He considered himself conservative; others called him prudish. He was filled with moral uplift even then. He overhauled both the theatre and its policy, and called it the Orpheum. He made it wholesome, so one could bring the entire family, and set its tone by his first act of showmanship: he installed an all-woman orchestra, resplendent in white blouses. Thus his life's work began.

As his concepts took form and paid off, he raised his sights; he had a vision of how it ought to be. He began to practice what he later preached at MGM: "You can educate the public. Give them quality and they will learn about better things." He had vaudeville and films, and later, when he had theatres in adjacent towns, he was able to bring in important artists, stars, and successful legitimate plays from Broadway.

These were golden years of progress and happiness for my father. His mother was indeed proud of him. I recall her only from her last visit to Haverhill; a trip to St. John when I was three is memorable only for seasickness. She died quite suddenly from a botched gallbladder operation when my father was only twenty-eight. No kind of emotion in his life ever matched the grief he felt at her death. He was totally devastated and mourned her passing the rest of his days. From that time on until he died, a large portrait of her hung over his bed. Every victory of his brought with it a pang that she was not there to share it, and that his money had come too late to save her. (It was then that first-class medical care and the maintenance of health became priorities.) He talked of her a great deal and kept her memory alive with us girls by constantly recounting her wisdom and proverbs. He felt that everything good in him had come from his mother. Whoever knew him could not escape her central importance to him. My father's life and nature would have been quite different had she lived her proper span of years.

In emotional moments my father would tell my sister and me that his mother, his sainted mother, had knelt on the floor and kissed the hem of my mother's garment. Strange language and imagery for my father to use, most uncharacteristic, and it was not figurative, but literal, because I have known him to re-enact it. In only slightly less dramatic moods he was wont to say about my mother, "I do things in a day that maybe aren't right. I make mistakes. I come home tired. I look in her eyes. Whatever I think of myself, it comes out all right. I am forgiven everything. I start fresh. I am cleansed. If she loves me, I'm a good man. It's not that she's smart; I don't know what it is. She has intuition. Can you have intuition without being smart? It's her intuition that counts." I think he meant spiritual grace. My parents were so pleased with each other and with life; there was a pride and a zeal which was almost tangible. She held extraordinary power over him.

It is no wonder that as a little girl my ultimate ambition was to be a wife, for surely there was no more exalted position than the one my mother held; the gods had bestowed Louis B. upon her. Moreover, she had us. Despite the maid, she fed us, she bathed us, she put us to bed, she heard our prayers. She was always at the door when we left for school and when we returned. My father said she sacrificed for us, but she made us feel we did her a favor by being her children. Was ever a woman so lucky? She had a mission which filled her with delight, and we were it.

My father would often talk to my sister and me about her, about her golden heart and character. He should have said "tenderness" and "mercy," which are truly what characterized her. She had a healing spirit and a gentle nature. She seemed incapable of an impure thought, and she never spoke ill of anyone in her life that I can recall.

Although they were about the same age, my father seemed much older than my mother, so much so that during my teens people were astonished to learn they were not father and daughter. Unlike her neighbors, my mother had a high-school diploma and had had a "skilled job" as a secretary and bookkeeper. Her experience served my father well in his early years in Haverhill, as she kept the office books.

My father was sober, serious, and industrious. Normal social activity was of no interest to him; he considered it a waste of time, as was anything which did not concern his family or his business. He was a man of tremendous energies, which were used first as a protection against the world for his family, then in fighting to succeed. No other father worked as hard; that's what he said, Mother said, and we believed. I guess it was the truth after all.

He brought home his business and spoke freely of it. He believed in planning ahead, in building on a firm foundation. He would talk about the day when his ship would come in and there would be retirement and wonderful journeys with my mother. Meanwhile, conservatism was the motto: "Never mind now; this is short. It is the future that counts; the future is long."

As his fortunes increased, he didn't cash in. He said there was a choice: either to live it up now or hold to a dream. With that firm principle in mind, he took one rung at a time. Hang on to what you have; tend it carefully. With the other hand you build the next step. Still, the opening of his second theatre, the Colonial, when it was finally finished, dazzled me. I had my first premiere at four and a half! In addition, my very own father went out on the stage and made a rousing speech.

There were more speeches to come in Haverhill, at civic affairs, and along went his best audience, the tight little unit. As my father's status rose, my parents came to know some of the town's first citizens. Asked to dinner at the best houses, Mother was thrilled.

My sister went to school, and I couldn't wait for that glorious adventure. Meanwhile, life was free and lovely and I was bursting with delight, despite the defect of being left-handed. There were daily reminders at the table, but Mother thought that school would straighten it out. When the big day came, off I went, bright-eyed and eager, hand held much too firmly by my mother, dressed in her best. We had only just moved from our darling little house across the river in Bradford, so I was a few weeks late in entering, which made me conspicuous.

The day was memorable for my mother's behavior. There I was, tucked away in the front row at the far corner of the schoolroom, and after a long consultation with the teacher my mother simply wouldn't leave. I looked pleadingly at her; I looked away, I looked back. She was still there. Why was Mother so pleased I was finally in school and yet so emotional? Why doesn't she leave? Please go away so they'll stop looking at me. And don't stare at me so adoringly. She kept "making eyes" at me even from the door. Little did I know what a wrench it was for her.

What was really important that day didn't make a proper dent. As a result of Mother's discussions, use of my left hand was banned; it was even tied behind me for a while. It wasn't known in those days that the common practice of switching hands could be a prime cause of stuttering. Alas.

What impressed my mother that day was that I seemed puny. I was smaller than the others, not round and rosy. Her maternal ministrations increased, with emphasis on starting me off properly each morning. I was to eat, and eat was real and awful. I refer to breakfast, the requirements for which were rigid. Perhaps I should look back on those Haverhill breakfasts with gratitude; they were the only issue that fostered my capacity to rebel.

The torture began with the cereal. "A lump? What does a five-year-old know? There is no lump." But there was! I swallowed it and up it came. I would shoot an accusing look at my mother. A soft-boiled egg may be a lavishment of nature to some, but not to a stubborn and miserable kid. How vast and endless a watery egg is . . . to say nothing of that "slippery stuff" mixed up in there. Trapping a bit wasn't the solution because I knew that the rest of it was lying in wait for me. I was not swayed by reminders of the hordes of hungry children in the world. My mother pleaded, and, as my tears began to spill, resorted to feeding me the now-cold egg spoonful by spoonful.

The worst ordeal was coming, that warm drink that was called "your nourishment," ostensibly cocoa. No going to school without that. "Let me go, I'll be late." How could it be so revolting, when hot chocolate at Schrafft's was bliss? This pinky-beige stuff had a skin on top. Denying its existence by a quick stir of the spoon didn't fool me a bit; it was lurking. Each moment held the terror that it would slip down and gag me.

I was entitled to one perfectly good chocolate—one a day—which I was permitted to have after dinner if I finished everything on my plate. There certainly was nothing to look forward to at night if, as a reward for getting through that breakfast cup of stuff, the precious chocolate of the day was dropped to the bottom. The cocoa got no better, and my chocolate was ruined. I was thought to be unreasonable when I objected. And I wasn't really stubborn; I was prepared to eat anything, provided it wasn't breakfast.

On to school. I wanted to be on time; my mother thought it was more important to be careful crossing the streets. I was outraged; of course I was careful—I didn't want to get run over!

There was a new complaint against me: I stuttered. "Strange she didn't do it when she was little." "Why are you stuttering? Breathe deeply. Speak slowly." I soon learned to get over that repetition of consonants. Instead my mouth would open like a fish gasping for air, and nothing would come out. Gradually I learned to control this too, but I can't bear to think how large a part of my concentration and energies in life was devoted to concealing my affliction. That stutter was agony for me. And it irritated the hell out of my family. I believe only Marion Davies ever got any mileage out of a stutter.

Boston

I T W A S a whole new way of life when we moved to Boston, thirty-two miles and a world away. Boston meant Brookline, which Mother knew had the best environment and the superior schools. We lived at 501 Boylston Street opposite the reservoir, a location carefully chosen for its proximity to the John D. Runkle School. There we would make worthwhile friends.

The idea was for us to have friends, but not to become close; we were not to trust anyone except the family. I never quite comprehended what they meant about not trusting friends just because friends came under the heading of strangers. I thought a friend was a friend. But we were told not to confide in them because everything was private. Worse was to come: we were not to keep secrets. "You must tell your mother. It is a sin to keep a secret from your mother." The things my little friends told me weren't really secrets except by label; they only made me promise not to tell because that was the part that was fun. According to Mother, God said those promises didn't count—only the promises to her. Oh, the torment!

God saw, He knew everything. I didn't want anyone's secrets if I had to tell my mother. And in addition I desperately didn't want them because then I would have to give mine. No good would come of secrets. I complied as best I could, but drew the line at her statement that a thought was like a deed; enough was enough.

My mother had a hunger for culture, and we were to be given the advantages she had longed for. She wanted us to be "accomplished" and able to contribute. Edie had piano lessons, and I was condemned to the violin, but I couldn't see why, as I had no intention of performing. Mother thought it would be lovely if we played duets.

From the earliest age "the girls" were always presented to visitors, each time warned to "act like little ladies." But I didn't want to be a little lady and I certainly had no longing to be a big lady. I wanted to be a little girl. We were told that children should be seen but not heard, and when spoken to by company, I early learned to catch the flick of an eye from one of my parents as to whether I was to respond. Elocution lessons had already been imposed in Haverhill, not incidentally to help my stuttering, and of course the moment would always come when my mother would ask us to "speak your new piece." I wasn't bashful, just madly reluctant, and my problem was compounded by my stuttering. Despite a preliminary practice period of "Peter Piper picked a peck of pickled peppers" and other appropriate verses, my dilemma remained. From that time on, "accomplishments" was forever linked in my mind with hazard. Edie, on the other hand, did very well, as she enjoyed performing and displaying her feelings. She was considered very emotional, with an artistic temperament, and was applauded appropriately. And she had a real edge on me when it came to dancing. Dancing class was okay until the night of the recital, when a bit of dreadful miscasting occurred. Edie and a bunch of other big girls plus undersized me were out there on the stage, all of us dressed up in turquoise-blue tutus with lamé bodices. We were out there being the Blue Danube. I brought the house down with laughter and didn't know why. Apparently when I reached stage center, I looked out imploringly, hoping for rescue. Obviously, I was not an interpretive artist.

Mother had two standard introductions for us. One was "This is our little lady and this one, the baby, is our tomboy." Edie gloried in this, as well she might, with her dimples and her lovely curls, which my mother painstakingly rolled up every night in something called kid curlers. She tried curling my hair, but my father hit the roof. "Leave her alone!" I had a Dutch bob and my mother put a bowl on my head and cut my bangs. Edie didn't even mind all those different things Mother used on her hair to "keep it light"—everything short of peroxide. Rachel Shenberg's crime had almost been wiped out; Mother had had a baby girl with blond hair. What a relief! What a triumph! If only it had stayed that way. . . . Her alternate introduction, "This is my blonde and this is my brunette," stayed in use long after Edie's hair had turned brown.

Edie wore great satin bows in her hair and sashes on her ruffly dresses with lots of lace. Mother wouldn't have had a chance with me, because my father didn't like me dressed up. "Put her in something simple. I like her just as she is." Hardly a consolation to either child. What I really wanted, and very badly, was what the other girls wore.

But, clearly, we weren't like the other girls. We were special. No physical harm must come to us because we were more precious to our parents than other children to theirs. I wanted to learn caution through risk, but they said, "Why take a chance?" Open windows, matches, scissors (oh, my kingdom, such as it was, for a decent pair of sharp scissors that didn't have rounded ends!). Tricycle but no bicycle; skating rink but no frozen reservoir. "Why does she have to dive? Don't go in over your head!" And then later in California, when it came to horses, I couldn't join the three or four good riders in the jumping class because it was so dangerous. I yearned for hockey only when I discovered it might prove a shortcut to a broken arm. Not that I wanted the broken arm; what I wanted was the splint, most particularly hung in a large black silk handkerchief tied around my neck, which was standard. Nothing could have given me greater cachet.

I was a wiry, sturdy little girl, fleet of foot, very earnest, with an unsuitable look of mischief. Yes, there was plenty of mischief, but the lid was on. I was proud of being favored by requests. "Let *her* get it, she's fast." Thus the dispensation of getting my father's slippers. Fast but, ah, not quiet enough down the stairs . . . that took practice. Praise made me fair game for anything; I felt I was letting them down if I didn't come through. While it was satisfying to be called on, there were times when it was exhausting—up and down, up and down repeatedly, until I was panting. Edie finally tipped me off: how could I be such a chump? Edie wasn't envious, only disdainful. Taken for granted was my regular mission of up the stairs and turn off that light, no matter who left it on.

OUR FIRST years in Brookline we spent the summers at the beach. My mother longed for the sea forever after, but my father wanted country, space at last, so for a couple of summers we rented a large house on a hill overlooking a lovely lake. My father taught me how to row a boat and how to fish and drive a buggy. I even got to ride a two-wheel bike. It was there I learned to love lilac, my mother's favorite flower; and apple blossom, trailing arbutus, violets growing wild. I wanted us to go there every summer for the rest of our lives.

Yet there was one thing I wanted even more, which was to go to camp like all the other girls. The very thought showed ingratitude! Our welfare came first, and it was safer and healthier at home, with all the advantages and all the tender loving care. I listened to school friends and pored over camp catalogs, but it was not to be. Never mind, someday I would go to boarding school; I would be so trustworthy and self-reliant that I'd get to go like the other girls. When that dream faded, I could at least rely on college, my mother's fondest hope.

Mother also had high regard for book learning. She put money by to invest in a set called the *Golden Treasury,* which was a mistake because a set of the *Book of Knowledge* was more important, so important that each volume had a red morocco spine. Our reading anything but them or the proper childhood classics brought lament; the more we learned, the better our marks would be at school. Three A's and a B were not very good; why did I have the B? Three A's and one A plus still did not meet expectations. She would brag behind my back, but not a pat on the back lest it turn my head.

In seventh grade I learned the poem "Excelsior." I also learned what the word "excelsior" meant and I thought it a marvelous coincidence that Ralph Waldo Emerson's poetry had already expressed just what my family felt.

MOTHER had brief moments of solitary pleasure. With all tasks finished, she would indulge herself by sitting at the piano, a sure sign all was right with her world. She would pick out tunes from sheet music, one finger at a time, singing softly and not too well, her imagination letting her enjoy it. What I saw, peeking at her, made me catch my breath. She had the same kind of serenity I beheld when she blessed the candles at sunset each Friday night.

My father was her lord and master, yet he put her on a pedestal. She reciprocated by trying to meet his demands. Perhaps she felt she wasn't up to him and set herself inordinate goals. "Toe the mark" was her slogan.

Their only dissension seemed to be about money, because a realistic estimate of domestic financial needs wasn't possible; whatever he gave her seemed to disappear.

As far back as I can remember, Mother needed money. She needed it for the relatives. And for their relatives. How was it possible that so many of the relatives on both sides were poor and needy?

Despite vows of staying within limits, Mother kept on giving, and so had to resort to various economies at all times. Those who required a large sum, or who got money on a monthly basis, could obviously receive it only from my father. Everything else she did with the left hand on a quite secretive basis. A woman so truthful resorting to furtiveness! The poor thing sometimes got caught out by people stepping up and thanking my father, or writing him for a second bite. She was as hooked as any addict, there was no force that could have stopped her. "Who will do for you? Only your own." It seemed to me a one-way street. We would say, "Mother, again the relatives?" Nothing upset her more; in a different way, nothing upset my father more.

The relatives were the bane of my existence. There had to be a better way to spend Sunday afternoon; it spoiled the whole weekend.

Mother made Grandpa Mayer welcome on his visits, and between them I'm sure they arranged for his granddaughter Ruth, Ida Cummings' oldest child, to come and live with us, which she did for the year we lived on Beacon Street. Not too long afterward that entire family came to live in Boston.

I certainly never thought this importing of relatives was going to begin all over again in California, but there was no day of sunshine that my mother didn't feel guilty and think how much better it would be for the relatives.

Operation Rescue quite naturally began with her in-laws. My father resisted, saying, "Let's wait and see how it's going to work out for us here. They're happy where they are. We will take trips to see them, and we can bring them out here on visits." I think he was prepared to pay anything to keep them all where they were; to just keep increasing the allowances.

My mother couldn't bear that. Subtly, in ways we never fathomed, behind those closed doors she worked it. And they came, one by one, ostensibly only on a visit.

My father's father established a beachhead, as before. Then I suppose

Ida's son Jack came along. And then we had Ruth, and eventually Aunt Ida with her other two children. After they had all infiltrated, my mother's relatives began: her parents, then her sister with her husband, Nathan Hoffman, and their brood of children. It took a great deal of doing—first a house to be rented and then a job to be found, but certainly not in the studio! Well, only four or five.

The dole was one thing—helping out was extra. Teeth and tonsils (endless tonsils), violins and pianos, houses and cars, to say nothing of driving lessons. Of course there were further needs due to change of position. But enough was never enough. It wasn't entirely their fault; Mother's solicitude encouraged most of the family to take advantage of her. Certainly her parents didn't, nor her brother Victor and his wife Etta, who gave me my favorite cousins.

The aftermath was worse than anything my father predicted. Those for whom they did the most attempted to break their wills: the Hoffmans, my mother's, and the Cummingses, my father's.

I watched all these people; I witnessed what they did about money. My father explained how hard it was for people to make a living and what money meant to them and what people would do for it, and it came to me that money is what upset people most. What a relief to know! In that case, I didn't want any part of it. I vowed as a little girl that never in my life would I let money dictate what I did or what I felt. I would never want things I couldn't have. I would never buy anything I couldn't pay for then and there. I would never get in debt. At times I'm sure I was a pain in the neck, but I've lived by that vow and I'm grateful that I took it.

Edie, on the other hand, wanted money. And she knew what she wanted it for—she wanted to spend it. "When our ship comes in? It's in! Why not now?"

We were an inconsistent mix: my mother pinching but dishing it out; me leaning over backward; Edie determined to have it; and my father, who was earning the money, trying to maintain his values, deciding how much was to be spent how.

WHEN I wasn't my father's tomboy, I was his baby and sat on his lap. He called me "the baby" well into my teens. When we went driving on Sunday afternoons, I was put in the middle of the back seat between my parents, and Edie would protest, sending up a storm from the side. My father would settle it, not too equitably, by putting me back on his lap. Perhaps Edie was right. There was, after all, the fact that when my father was critically ill with appendicitis in New York, my mother had been sent back to fetch me because he wanted to see me. "The baby."

I was given marbles and tops instead of tea sets and dolls, and when Dad went fishing I sometimes went along. And then he bestowed on me the ultimate privilege of accompanying him to the World Series. Alas, with no preparation other than his enthusiasm, it turned out that I was not up to this big deal, and I failed him; I just didn't understand what was going on. I asked a few questions and he explained things only briefly. When I couldn't join in the excitement, he was disappointed and irritated; he was used to what he called my instant grasp. Well, he failed me too. There were hot dogs, peanuts, and cotton candy, the only possible reward for sitting through this thing, and I wasn't to have any of them. That ice-cream cone I was offered I could have had anyplace! When he got me home, he complained to my mother that it had been a mistake —the kid couldn't catch on, it was a dreadful waste. (It's easy to understand why I have never seen a baseball game since; if one is on television, I walk out of the room.)

I'm not sure I always liked my father, but I admired him and loved him. And I wanted desperately to please him.

Papa seemed unique, unparalleled even in fiction—that is, until someone slipped me my first Horatio Alger. It was a great relief to have my father's philosophy vindicated. Here was proof that virtue would triumph and justice prevail. Alger gave me a double sense of pleasure: I could weep and thrill to his stories, yet I didn't have to live up to them. Clearly, I was getting by with murder, and my gratitude for not being a boy took shape then.

Papa was not a book man, but he read his newspapers thoroughly. We even got the Hearst paper, the *Boston American,* because my father was crazy about Arthur Brisbane's daily column, "Today," and read it religiously. Brisbane had reverence for mothers; he even claimed that Abraham Lincoln owed his greatness to the traits he inherited from Nancy Hanks. My father's sense of himself was enhanced by the theory that a son inherited from the mother. Curiously enough, we were not kept from reading the Hearst Sunday Supplement called the *American Weekly,* where I learned about high life and low doings: archdukes and Siamese twins. I also learned about addiction and, translating dope into chocolate, felt deep sympathy.

THERE was nothing spartan about our lives, but strictness prevailed. Dad's was probably a standard attitude, only it was a generation or two late. He felt children could not only be formed, but molded. He thought that to be aware is to be appreciative and thus grateful; to be grateful is to be unspoiled; to be spoiled is to become unhappy. Surely normal appreciation should be compounded by all our added advantages?

For me an admonition was the same as an order and I wasn't about to start getting out of line. I was afraid to disobey, afraid of my father and of the powers which dispersed all those favors.

I didn't try to please as much as I tried not to displease. However cherished, I couldn't have enough loving and petting. The worst punishment was censure. I wanted to say that they could skip the praise, but, please, no criticism; I broke my neck to avoid it. Clearly, no good came of attention—scrutiny could bring disapproval—so ignore me, please! Excellence, on the other hand, held other risks: how had I done it? Could I repeat it? It might be too much to live up to.

Above all, we had to be kept simple. I remember all too well, at age four, the dazzling figure of my wicked Uncle Rudolph, this one exotic note in our otherwise humdrum family. Certainly a man from Mars, a tall, handsome prince, a relative unlike all other relatives, bearing rich gifts on an unexpected visit from Montreal, where he resided in splendor with a mistress named Vera, a valet, and a revolving statue in the drawing room.

I felt like fortune's child when he held me high in the air, set me down, and presented me with the only beautiful, extravagant possession I ever had as a child; he had brought his little nieces two very large china dolls, the kind one only sees behind glass, with eyelashes and real hair, and dressed with the greatest luxury, Edie's in blue velvet and mine in red. I couldn't believe it was for me, little me, who couldn't be trusted with anything beyond a rag doll with a celluloid head. The dolls were taken away because "we don't want you to be spoiled."

My father grew more successful, but our scale of living didn't change appreciably, which Edie felt was unreasonable. Things should be grander. My father said that part of the fun was anticipation and we must wait. I was already content; in any case, what came was always more than anticipated; what he prophesied came true. Actually, no, he understated; the accomplishment was always larger than the prophecy. I was impressed every time. I believed.

Believing was the thing I did best. I swallowed everything, hook, line, and sinker. I believed that all public servants were models of learning and justice long after I should have known better. I believed in my school and my city and my country. Above all, I believed in my home. My home did not have to be ideal; what was important was what I thought it was. I was just the luckiest girl in the world. And, of course, I believed that my parents were perfect.

I also believed in Santa Claus—implicitly. I believed he got my letters and believed every promise he made when I sat on his knee in the department store. This created some difficulty, because naturally my parents didn't celebrate Christmas. Nevertheless, each Christmas Eve we hung up our stockings and faithfully recited "'Twas the night before Christmas." But Christmas after Christmas he betrayed me; there was nothing in the morning but a ready-stuffed, coarse-mesh stocking. My mother explained it by saying Santa Claus was very busy and, knowing we had so much, had given our share to less fortunate children. The big problem was which Christmas songs a Jewish girl could properly join in at school. I pretended to sing but permitted no sound when they played "Christ is born," but sang lustily about sleigh bells and Kris Kringle. One somehow got past the day itself, what with the splendid New England Christmas feast and the parents so loving to us poor girls.

MY FATHER had extraordinary reflexes, mental and physical. Being volatile and impatient, more often than not it was "move" or "think," and he meant fast. It became a game I enjoyed. It's probably why I had a secret desire to become his secretary, be where the action was, anticipate him at every turn. But then, didn't every other little girl want the same?

My father was not only omnipotent, he was omniscient. In a curious way, I got him mixed up with God, because of the word Almighty.

Fortunately, I was saved by the Ten Commandments; many of them I didn't understand, but the first Commandment said, "Thou shalt have no other god before me," and I clung to it. If it hadn't been for that, I would have been afraid of my father.

If ever there was a master in his own home, Dad was it. Our day was geared to his homecoming. Excitement, eagerness, usually accompanied by a bit of suspense. What was his mood? Whatever it was, we met it. If he was upset, we girls made ourselves scarce. Other times he was full of play—too boisterous, in Mother's judgment, for that time of day, with much chasing and sliding down the banisters. Naturally, he was spared all domestic concerns, but occasionally Mother felt forced to make good her threat and recounted our shortcomings, something Edie and I dreaded. There was no court of appeal, because he always backed her up.

Quiet could mean either tension or fatigue, which, because of his extremely low blood pressure, would sometimes cause him to faint without warning. More often the sense of well-being in our home would triumph, and he would open up and out would pour problems or progress. Mother led the rapt admiration of this hero. He discussed his allies and enemies, outlining his strategy and future campaigns, which, if won, resulted in later references to his foresight. Whatever they were, they served as a launching pad for Sermons from the Mount. Never mind other people's standards, he intended his to prevail. Thus we were not only informed but indoctrinated.

When he wasn't holding forth on business, he was laying out his moral precepts. I didn't know they were clichés, I thought them gospel. "As ye sow, so shall ye reap, mark my words." I did. He harped on just rewards, cause and effect, and the laws of compensation. "There it all is. Listen to me and you won't go wrong." I listened and I believed.

We learned not to interrupt or comment—no spontaneous conversation out of us. Mother, of course, would recount what was appropriate for us to hear, but she tailored her reports according to the climate.

I marveled at how he bore his responsibilities. It never occurred to me that other men had equal pressures. However, if he had had a good day, his high spirits would animate our evening meal. He could be spellbinding and made the great world outside seem fascinating. We shared the excitement of his life—vicarious triumphs for us, with none of the responsibilities. Togetherness hadn't been invented yet, but rarely has it been practiced more intensively.

My father, being far from frivolous, was not given to small talk, so there was no idle chatter at our supper table. Often, late in the meal, he would throw me questions, because he liked my answers; in fact, the family enjoyed them so much they pretended not to understand. I would therefore explain with ever more sensible replies, but their amusement would mount. I couldn't see why; I somehow never sensed the dividing line between ordinary conversation and supplying entertainment. I wouldn't bat an eye—that was how I earned the nickname Deadpan. They watched my reactions: "Look, look, she's being so brave. Not a sign!" It was a duel, they hardly able to suppress their laughter, and me my tears. "Look, look, a quiver. Oh, so cute." "Cute" is a dirty word. It did me in, and I tried my level best not to be cute, but the harder I tried, the more delighted they were. "How long can she hold out?" Then suddenly they would say "Look, look, enough . . ." but too late. Meal unfinished, a rush from the table. Face down on the floor of my bedroom, sobbing my heart out and kicking my feet. The entreaties, the affectionate reassurances didn't help. I wouldn't relent and again they called me stubborn . . . well, they were making me stubborn. The good Lord was watching me, they were watching me, and I was watching me, while most of all what I wanted was not to be noticed. I promise you I'll do the right thing, just please take your eyes off me. I'll do anything. I'll do extra!

I'd like to rewind the reel right now and tell my family, "I'm just a little girl, you mustn't tease me. Stop it. I can't stand it." The game persisted, with minor variations, as I grew older. The net result was an absolute lack of self-humor. It has taken most of a lifetime to begin to mend that failing.

A P A R T from my passion for chocolate, all my tastes and traits were imposed on me. I just picked up whatever was left over, from outgrown clothes to those portions of the chicken not favored elsewhere, to an even disposition. "Not a nerve in her body; she doesn't know how to get mad." The truth was, there wasn't any room for temper; they had used it all up. Their approval egged me on, and I cultivated the qualities assigned me: the baby comes last. But even she must have been suspicious at meals, because my father went on serving me tidbits from his plate. Nevertheless, I came to like best, eventually, those parts of the chicken to which I was condemned.

Yes, there was plenty of temper around. My father's was terrifying and

I dreaded it. Mother's advice was, "Do not speak up when your father's angry. Let him get it off his chest." She herself was too tender-hearted for real anger; she got cross, but mostly if he was upset. The anger spilled down in a kind of pecking order.

My idea of heaven was no raised voices ever, nobody upset, peace, peace. If only no one would be high-strung! I mean temper, of which Edith had a goodly share. She said she had inherited it from her father and was therefore not to blame. Later she attributed it to her own emotional nature. Mother said all this emotion was bad for their health. I see now that these people were ventilating and were enjoying a luxury I knew nothing about. On the other hand, they seemed in such terrible shape after losing their tempers that my sympathy was misplaced and I pitied them instead of their victims. I would see to it that it didn't happen to me. I devised a very private system whereby I would always be in the wrong, otherwise I might get mad too. It was easier to blame myself; to find yourself at fault is a splendid technique for controlling anger. If I felt rage, I didn't know it, it just got swallowed. When I finally learned anger, it was too damned late for it to come out in temper.

Both parents pounded away at the doctrine of learn to share, which was as hard on my sister as on me. Edie had no interest in my junk, and she naturally didn't want me grubbing around with her doll clothes and tea sets. We shared a room, even a bed, but neither could understand "Mine is mine but also hers."

I had an early lesson in Haverhill when I was six. I would hustle along to school, my money for candy clutched in my hot little hand. One could make a more careful choice on the way home, but the selection was better in the morning (provided one was early for school). I didn't care for jelly beans, period; however, for sheer bulk they were the most for the money. On the other hand, Necco wafers lasted the longest. These things are important when you have the sum of one cent a day to spend. As it happens, that was also the price of a Tootsie Roll, which was the best of all; besides, it was chocolate, lovely chocolate. If ever I skipped a day, it was a temptation to try something else, like a marshmallow man, which cost two cents. They came in white and in pink. If you bought one of them, though, you missed a day of chocolate. I wanted both. I thought the contrast would be wonderful and I would enjoy my chocolate more.

So I figured it out. I saved up, not for a rainy day, but a sweet day, a feast. I abstained for two weeks; that was ten cents.

The great day dawned; I was filled with anticipation. Fortunately, my

class let out at a different hour from Edith's, and I went on my own to
the shop and did very careful purchasing—pink men, white men, and
Tootsie Rolls, more than one. I blew my whole wad.

I went home and quietly set about preparing for the orgy. Although
I would have preferred seclusion, I picked a clear spot visible from the
side of the house, carefully laid a white cloth on the grass, and spread out
my dainties, arranging them and rearranging them in preparation for the
feast. I planned how I was to alternate bites, and of which. I took my
first nip, the foot of the white marshmallow man. Out came my mother,
scurrying, indignant, and very cross. "What are you doing, you'll get
sick!" She took the marshmallow man right out of my hand; she scolded
me for being selfish and not sharing with my sister. That didn't make sense
to me, because it was my ten cents! I hadn't known it was wrong, how
could I? Nothing was ever more surely mine than what my penny bought
each school day.

My treasures were not only snatched up, they were confiscated; I didn't
get to have even one day's worth. Unfair, unfair. And I was accused of
being sneaky when obviously I wasn't sneaky enough! The total injustice
of not getting even my share for that one day rankled. It rankled along
with the charge of being selfish, of not sharing. The incident made me
wary forevermore.

Dad laid down the guidelines along with the proper values. He
thought in terms of right and wrong; he had no shades of gray. His
reaction was we should have known better. Do it right. Then it was up
to Mother to instill the right habits. She tried in her own way, stressing
what came naturally to her—good deeds and kind thoughts. She didn't
know she was noble; she didn't preach, but she abounded in her own form
of clichés, which I had to sort out. (Dad said, "Fast"; she said, "Haste
makes waste.") Self-improvement was very high on her list, so "Improve
each shining hour" was often heard. The children's disputes were settled,
not too suitably in my view, with: "Turn the other cheek" or "Set a good
example." I couldn't buy them all; I was square enough as it was. What
I did buy was that damned Golden Rule—"Do unto others . . ." Right?
I was righteousness rampant.

What worried me was that I had to *learn* these virtues. I couldn't be
as good as Mother because I had to try so hard; if you were really good,
you wouldn't have to try. Mother came that way, it was so unfair.

I was an odd bundle of contradictions, perceptive but obtuse where I
shouldn't have been—and cautious but bold in a strange combination. I

stayed just within the law, whatever the traffic would bear, although something about me gave people the impression I was a handful. Mother implied she had to keep her eye on me, which wasn't fair, as I didn't misbehave.

Mother with mottoes, Dad with the big basics, but me, I was left with a vacuum. I didn't know which to apply to what. I didn't know why the rules were there, but I was busy trying not to break them. I was looking for a tangible set of directives, a table of stated weights and measures: this misstep, that many demerits. I should have spoken up: "Give me the rules, I'll follow them," and added, "Please include the fine print, and no last-minute additions."

Mother, trying to shield us from disappointments, philosophized that everything happens for the best. I latched on to that because it suited me; with this formula, any setback became positive and I could stay contented. It made my system complete. Even so, it took a lot of work to keep this credo valid; I had a lot of rationalizing to do to make the facts suit the philosophy. When things didn't come out right, I would console myself that the final results were not yet in. In extremis I would decide that adversity was good for my character. In other words, I had a sure thing going for me. However, even I couldn't figure out how teasing could be for the best. I do see that it served me in one way: it gave me a shield; in my long years of self-imposed concealment, no one had any idea of what I knew and little of what I felt. I learned to withstand pressure with apparent equanimity.

Edith didn't think our home the paradise I did, and when she squawked about things, I would sometimes offer my convoluted reasoning. She would have none of it. Her comments were a child's equivalent of "Hogwash!" Much later on she dismissed my viewpoint by calling me brainwashed. I guess I was, but happily so. Edie not only spoke up for her rights (rights? I didn't know I had any), she felt a need to express herself. It never occurred to me that I had a self to express.

If one's energy is exceeded only by one's self-restraint, it can make for a very observant child. Everything was neatly stored in a data bank the family found useful: names, addresses, routes. But I didn't want to give answers, I wanted to ask questions. In despair, my mother would suggest the *Book of Knowledge,* which didn't fill the bill.

It was overkill all down the line. Dad says, Mom thinks, Sunday School, and all of God's wishes added up to a pretty big demand on a little girl, even though I didn't see how God could keep track of everything, even in a book.

It was the Girl Scouts who came to my rescue. I thought it a miracle that they existed. They encompassed everything that was being drilled into me at home, and their manual spelled it all out in black and white. There were no surprises; you knew where you were with the Scouts, all you had to do was keep trying. Fulfillment was in sight. Merit counted. Badges had to be earned. Tests were supervised. It was fairer than school —there, teachers had favorites, and kids cheated.

The Scouts had a "pledge," and that was very patriotic. Their motto was "Be prepared." Well, that's the same as "Look ahead," and foresight was what my father preached. The slogan was "Do a good turn daily." That seemed easy pickings to me. The promise was "On my honor I will try to be true to God and my country. To help others at all times, obey the Scout laws." Clear rules at last! I had found my haven.

There were other advantages: no speck of criticism, no secrets, no question of the suitability of my companions. After passing tests, you took an oath. My main concern was, would I take it on a day when I didn't stutter?

I was a pushover for hard-luck stories in print, most particularly before Christmas. I never supposed that any of them were fiction. I had a fantasy of giving; always surprise, surprise. There would be cash in an envelope with no clue to the sender. Even so, good deeds without the Scouts meant I was looking for rewards; with them, I was only obeying the law.

Each day I tried to get my good deed out of the way quickly, in case there wasn't time later. I remember most sharply standing at Coolidge Corner at dusk, the wind howling, and me frantically looking for somebody to help. Please, won't the blind, the halt come in time? I would settle for an old lady to help cross the street. Never mind, give a poor little girl my nickel and run. All because I had taken the oath. Naturally I assumed that the other Scouts were doing likewise.

THERE are inconsistencies I cannot fathom. How could a man of my father's innate conservatism have chosen show business? Had he not been as emotional as he was, I don't believe he would have been so drawn to, or have succeeded so well in, the picture business. Certainly he had the necessary gut instinct for it. If I had to use one word to describe my father in every way, I would use "intensity."

Even when I was a very little girl, my father spoke of the importance of what was shown to the public. He deplored the way show business was being run; he thought everyone in it had an obligation to help make it respectable and then keep it so. Everybody needed diversion and recreation, and if they'd all endeavor to make the business wholesome, it would bring an added advantage—increasing audiences. He became evangelistic about show business, most particularly movies. The public may have found films a novelty, but to him they were a potent force and an important weapon. He believed they would have a profound influence on the public, on his country, and eventually the world.

While he was running his theatres, my father became a founding officer of the original Metro Company, which later became part of MGM, and he had charge of distribution for New England. When he stopped agreeing with the New York office, he left 60 Church Street and went across to number 69 and took a similar position with Lewis J. Selznick, who owned the Selznick Company and Select Pictures. But that lasted only a month, because he distinctly disapproved of Mr. Selznick and the way he ran his business. Thereafter he used "Selznick" as an epithet, almost until the time it became my name.

He was only too glad to return to Metro. Then First National was organized, the first company to have the distinction of releasing pictures made by independent producers, the ranks of which my father was soon to join.

And he was just as passionate about America itself. He saluted the flag with such fervor. He was so proud to be an American. America the beautiful! He said Americans took it for granted—you had to be newly naturalized to appreciate the glories of the USA. Because of the wonderful USA the whole world was marching forward. He received his final citizenship papers, applied for many years before, shortly after the Colonial opened.*

The Colonial opened in December 1911, and the following year he gave them more than they expected. I'm surprised to discover from old ads and reviews that he offered such diverse attractions as George M. Cohan in *45 Minutes from Broadway,* Laurette Taylor in *Peg O' My Heart,* Maude Adams, John Drew. That same year he gave them the Boston Opera Company, with Alice Nielsen in *Madame Butterfly.* (From time to time through the ensuing years my father would burst into snatches of

*Like many immigrants, he had no birth records, so he chose the Fourth of July as a birthday.

"Un bel dì.") All this became possible for him as he leased legitimate theatres in other cities, such as Philadelphia. He even had his own stock company.

Until each new venture was secure, he maintained what he already had for a fall-back position, such as the distribution company in Boston. By the time he bought the New England rights to *Birth of a Nation,* which gave him immediate recognition, he had begun to acquire an interest in a chain of theatres in Boston. As movies began to improve, so did their appeal. When something special came along, it would outdraw anything else at high prices. But there were too few big pictures. A couple of years earlier the opportunity had arisen to buy the New England rights for *Cabiria,* an early Italian spectacle. It had been a bold move.

There never was a Boston Saturday that we didn't go either to the movies or to the theatre to see a touring play. We saw all the great stars of the day. I was keen on Ethel Barrymore, but Edie considered a stage career after seeing Ina Claire and Ruth Chatterton.

There seems a contradiction. We girls were so shielded that it is hard to comprehend how we were permitted to see so many mature plays. In movies the latitude was also enormous—in retrospect it seems completely unrestricted. For a man so hell-bent on a wholesome and conservative atmosphere for his daughters, I find it very peculiar.

Of course we read every movie magazine and pasted pictures of our favorites in books. I was assigned Alice Brady and Viola Dana, and they weren't my favorites at all. Elsie Ferguson became Edie's model of femininity; she could see herself as just such a star. We both wanted Norma Talmadge, the Selznick Company's second biggest star, but Edie got her. What impressed me about Alice Brady was that her father, William Brady, was both a Broadway impresario *and* a film producer.

Our lives began to have a tiny bit more glamour than the lives of other girls at school. By this time we sometimes were allowed to meet film stars who were making personal appearances at my father's theatres. Yet all that was minor stuff, because it was only shaking hands at the theatre. But one Sunday afternoon, on our own front porch at 74 Pleasant Street, an incredible thing was about to happen. My father had announced that the reigning male star, Francis X. Bushman, and his leading lady, Beverly Bayne, were coming to call. I didn't know whether it was real or not, I could only think of telling the girls in school the next day.

The four of us sat there waiting, Edie and I holding our breath with disbelief. Then, sure enough, they drew up in a big touring car with the top down. Bushman bounded up those stairs. I never before had seen such virility and good looks. All that big, lovely personality and magnetism beamed in directly on each of us separately, even me! I was thrilled by him and by the massive ring on his little finger, gold with an enormous amethyst, and for many years thereafter no man was exciting who did not wear a big ring on his little finger.

We escalated further when a company came briefly to Marblehead to film some scenes of *Barbara Frietchie,* with Mary Miles Minter, the new star who was certain to dethrone Mary Pickford. Mr. Mayer's two little girls were not only permitted to watch, they acted in the picture. To be precise, they were extras for a couple of hours, but at least in costume. There never was anything more exciting. It almost prepared us for Hollywood.

Then a different kind of movie star came to our house—Anita Stewart had signed a contract to make pictures for my father, who, we began to realize, was adding this activity to his business. He made one film, *Virtuous Wives,* with her in a studio close to New York, an event I found impressive but not earth-shaking. Actually, he had formed a motion-picture company bearing his name and was really embarking on a career as a film producer.

J. Robert Rubin, of New York, who had been his lawyer for some years, had given up his practice and joined the company, which proved fortunate for them both; he remained my father's lifelong partner. What impressed my sister and me most about the whole thing was Bob Rubin. He was tall, handsome, quietly elegant. He was our idea of a gentleman; our idol.

The first film was a success and suddenly my parents were going all the way to California for a more important film, *In Old Kentucky.* I found this quite thrilling. Mother put Edie in charge of the house and servants. I was told to obey her, and we both had to write a letter daily. It was Edie's big chance. Even at that tender age she had fancy ideas about housekeeping, and she ran the house as she saw fit. I was slightly intimidated.

We hung on Mother's letters, which were filled with the marvels of Southern California. What other girl's parents had been to California and made a movie, eaten fresh dates, and picked fresh figs? I was a little shaky on the fruit because I hadn't known they came other than packaged.

Meanwhile, there came a cloud over this big, bold new step in life. The year was 1918, the year of the lethal influenza epidemic that hit and killed hundreds of thousands of people, and to which Edie fell victim. When our parents returned, they were shocked by the ravages of her brief illness. She was spent and pale. They felt terribly threatened, and again we had all the emphasis on health. I remember Mother putting Edith in the sun on the upper porch, feeding her eggnog, and assuring us all that sunny California would soon bring the roses back to her cheeks.

What was that? California? The news emerged gradually. I thought a trip to California would be exciting if it was only a trip. Slowly it appeared that it just might be for the school year. Even that seemed a terrible wrench to me, and badly timed, because I had just passed the last of my tests to become a second-class Scout and the badge was about to be sewn on my uniform. How could I move? Mother said they had Scouts in California too. Well, not quite. They had the Campfire Girls, which she tried to tell me were just as good. Humph.

It must have been an explosive issue, because the Girl Scout uniform traveled West with us. I didn't seem to realize that the uniform would not grow in size. However, there was one consoling thought: I might be leaving the Girl Scouts, but at least we got to leave the relatives behind. Little did I know.

B O S T O N was big, compared to Haverhill, but New York was enormous, frightening, exciting. When we arrived there on our way to Hollywood, we stayed in the Hotel Astor on the Great White Way. Hicks that we were, my mother took us on a sightseeing bus, from Grant's Tomb on Riverside Drive to Chinatown. At long last, the Statue of Liberty, about which my father had such passionate feelings. Never mind Bunker Hill and the Washington Monument, this was it! And the best was yet to come! Mother took us to the Hippodrome. It is still the most dazzled I have ever been, seated in a theatre. When all those girls dived into the water and disappeared, it settled in my mind that the world was a place of infinite possibilities, and the theatre something to be reckoned with. California wasn't everything. I had had advance warning: don't underestimate New York.

California

IN THOSE days a trip to California was an adventure and there would be a great send-off. People came to the station bringing gifts and stayed until the train actually left. In Boston my father's partners, Mr. Levin and Mr. Grosberg, and their wives—and, naturally, the relatives —were in the crowd at the station. We felt like celebrities.

It would have been more dramatic to arrive in California in midwinter and feel the contrast as Mother had, but never was there a more wide-eyed passenger than me sitting in the open part of the observation car of the Chief, taking in every single sight as though it were going to disappear forever, the continuing and mounting wonder of it. We got off at the various stations, long stops where some of the passengers had their meals at the Fred Harvey Houses while we explored each town. By the time we got to Albuquerque, which was an hour stop, we were seasoned sightseers. I might never see those towns again, because they went by in the middle of the night when you were going East and I might never go to California again. I also spent a lot of the time playing cards with my father. There were no likely prospects around, so he decided he would make me into a worthy opponent at two-handed pinochle.

Some months earlier my father had signed a second star, a girl named Mildred Harris. As an "under-age" bride, she had just married a reluctant, even unwilling, Charlie Chaplin, and was therefore to be billed as Mildred Harris Chaplin, a name not to Mr. Chaplin's liking, for which I do not blame him. Mildred Harris was sending her car to welcome us to California.

When we got to the station, there was Mrs. Chaplin herself, and we were agog. Waiting was a Marmon tonneau limousine, the closed back of which was upholstered in a soft, pale fabric and boasted a cut-glass vase containing a single rose. This wasn't a make-believe world, this was fairyland.

As we neared our house, the splendor of which we could hardly imagine, I held my breath. Then there it was, our anticlimax—not too elegantly located, and with a most unprepossessing exterior of brown-stained shingle. It was called a bungalow. It didn't even have a front hall, and was furnished in a somewhat desolate fashion. Mother said it was probably splendid upstairs.

We soon retreated to the living room and Edie and I sat huddled in silence. We had read too many movie magazines. My father persuaded us outside in the back to marvel at the varied fruit trees, which lifted the gloom momentarily. So this was California! Pleasant Street had looked like a palace compared to this.

I never did know whether this house was the faulty judgment of whomever my father had delegated to choose it, or whether it deliberately reflected his determination that he would keep a low profile and that the family would not "go Hollywood"—an understatement that was to be further emphasized.

Obviously, charm was not a requisite. The house was simplicity itself and called for simple living, and so it would seem we were back to one maid. My father said people lost their heads in Hollywood, whether because of the movies or all the sunshine or all the freedom, or just being away from the customary restraints; they didn't seem to realize that their presence was very possibly temporary and their careers tentative, that they must be *cautious.* He intended us to lean over backward. The thing that saved our spirits was that we girls were movie-struck and had landed in filmland, and if we walked the one block down to Hollywood Boulevard, there was a chance of seeing a movie being made right there in the street.

Los Angeles then was a vast, endlessly stretched-out area, and there were countless studios scattered around it, large and small, substantial and flimsy, although the majority were in Hollywood. These were actually bunched together just beyond Sunset and Vine, which is where Paramount (then called Famous Players–Lasky), considering its eminence, was so suitably located.

Hollywood was far larger than people realized, because they thought only in terms of these studios and the adjacent few blocks of Hollywood Boulevard, on both sides of which were small, nondescript establishments, enterprises catering to the riffraff which floated or straggled by. The people who weren't small-town tourists appeared to be extras. But then everyone in Hollywood was a potential extra—after all, it was $5 a day for not doing anything, $10 a day if you furnished your own clothes, and up to $15 for a fancy-dress extra. There were outcasts, misfits, runaways; would-be character actors in sandals, with beard, staff, toga, and flowing locks; ambitious mothers holding the hands of tiny, peroxided kids; pretty girls with standard Mary Pickford curls.

But one could not shop in Hollywood any more than one could see one's lawyer or doctor or dentist there, because everything was in downtown Los Angeles, including the only really proper hotel to stay at, the Alexandria. (One didn't so flatter the ancient, rambling Hollywood Hotel.) Of course, way far out in the sticks, in a new development, there was something called the Beverly Hills Hotel, which was for rich winter residents as competition to Pasadena and Santa Barbara. A few film people had moved out there, but the only thing that could be said for it was that there was a lot of wide-open space and it was partway to the beach at Santa Monica.

O U R O N L Y grandeur was that we were to go to a private school, the Hollywood School for Girls. The Brookline schools had a long tradition of high standards, but the public schools of Hollywood made my parents uneasy. This school had no pretensions whatsoever; clearly it was a jerry-built place run on a shoestring. It had some rooms for boarders; everything else was ramshackle—some unlikely scattered shacks and a few oversized crates. The excuse was that it was an "outdoor" school. The entire high school was contained in a one-room building, one side of which folded out, but that did not make it an outdoor school. From time to time Mother reminded them that they were supposed to hold classes in the sunshine, which is where she intended Edith to be.

Nevertheless, it was only about a mile from our house, and besides it was the only private school in Hollywood. What impressed Mother was that there were trees and flowers, riding and tennis, and what gave it the seal of approval was the presence of the de Mille girls. Actually, the

school not only educated the de Mille children, it appeared to be dominated by their parents (William de Mille with a small "d," the intellectual
brother, and Cecil DeMille with a big "D," glamorous and more successful). Cecilia, to whom horses were all-important, seemed to account for
the riding class. Tennis was probably attributable to the William de
Milles.

Rarely can there have been a more heterogeneous group of girls than
those who had landed there. Most of them were new or temporary
residents (but then so was practically everybody else in Southern California), except for a few socialites-to-be. There was a small handful who later
recrossed my path, such as Jean Harlow and Joel McCrea, who was the only
boy in the high school apart from Harriet Beecher Stowe's nephew.
Douglas Fairbanks, Jr., in a long-standing joke, claims we were there at the
same time, but we both know better, because he was there much earlier.
We've adapted it to "We practically went to school together."

Then there was my art teacher, who also taught French, named Edith
Spare, a remarkably talented young woman whom I didn't meet again
for many decades, when she was the celebrated designer Edith Head. I
tried to reminisce with her about the old days, but she denied the whole
thing. Oh well. The only continuing relationship was with Agnes and
Margaret de Mille, even after they left to live in New York.

Other girls' fathers went to the office, but mine went to the studio.
That was a pretty stunning phrase, except for the fact that the studio
wasn't even in Hollywood. Where was it? It was at the Selig Zoo! Where
was the Selig Zoo? It was at Eastlake Park, near the wrong end of
Pasadena, of all places. Colonel Selig had a zoo because he had animals,
and he had animals because he had made movies with them, and there
had to be some use for these animals when he wasn't using them or renting
them out. And to use them he needed a small studio and considerable land,
which was cheaply available in a remote part of southeastern Los Angeles.
My father could lease space there because by this time it was more zoo
than studio.

The locality did not detract from the thrilling privilege of seeing a
movie being made in a real studio, though we were laden with prohibi-
tions. Children did not belong in studios. We were to be practically
invisible. Moreover, there was not to be a word out of us; even a sneeze
would have been reprehensible. It was as though sound pictures were
already in.

The new climate did have an effect on Dad after all, because one

Sunday we stopped at a rabbit farm and he bought me a pair of rabbits. I recall the elaborate hutch built at the studio, and I was to "take the responsibility." Feeding, cleaning. My mother was afraid we were going to be overrun with rabbits; my father couldn't wait for the litter. The excited expectancy was exceeded only by the growing disappointment when nothing happened. The explanation was simple: they were the same sex. All that big hutch for nothing.

About this time my father thought it would be nice for me to have a baby lamb. He knew it was unwise, but he said he found the image of me going to school followed by the lamb irresistible. Inasmuch as I already had rabbit duties in the back of the garden, I might as well take on the lamb, who was called Lammikin. The poor little thing was a couple of weeks old, of uncertain gender, and could hardly stand up. I had to warm milk and feed it from a bottle several times a day, including the middle of the night.

At first I adored the lamb, which promised a good deal more action than the rabbits, who were pretty dull. At least it sometimes followed me around in the garden. But there was no future in the lamb, which didn't enjoy going along Franklin Avenue to school. It was even more impractical for the neighbors, because as it got older its voice got lustier, and the baaa, baaa, baaa rent the air through the night until the police were sent for. Finally I tried making it a household pet; I took it upstairs onto my bed one morning, where it made a dubious contribution. In June we went East, and Lammikin spent the summer at the Selig Zoo. After that it couldn't be retrieved because it was indistinguishable from the other lambs, sheep by then!

We seemed all settled in Hollywood, yet still reading the *Boston Post;* there was a scramble each day for who got to read it first after Dad. We were tremendous tourists, going off each Sunday exploring all of Southern California. We tried to get in everything in one great gulp in case it was a one-shot deal. I saw every mission from San Juan Capistrano to Santa Barbara, and had a sense of real importance when we crossed the border south of San Diego, going to that terrible Tijuana and actually touching foreign soil.

Landmarks in Hollywood were celebrities' houses. Skipping along, I would pass the house of Robert Z. Leonard and Mae Murray; then that of Antonio Moreno; and finally, as I reached the school on La Brea, I had Sam Goldwyn and the impressive mansions of William Farnum and Jesse Lasky.

I even thought a certain celebrity had begun to attach itself to me, because my father wound up on the front pages of the Los Angeles papers. Moreover, the item connected him to Charlie Chaplin, no less.

The combination of front page and Chaplin had led me to overlook the fact that a fistfight in the Alexandria Hotel might be a dubious claim to fame. Mildred and Charlie were being divorced, and she was having not unexpected trouble with a financial settlement, which is what lay behind the immediate hostility. Charlie challenged my father and told him to take off his glasses. Unfortunately, from a publicity standpoint, they were in the lobby with its million-dollar carpet, so-called because of the importance of the deals consummated there. It was a one-blow fight which flattened Charlie out on the carpet. Well, that was pretty emphatic. Actually, if it had to happen, at least my father had a top cast and setting, and one hell of a wallop.

Celebrities abounded, but my father would have no part of them. Edie and I found this attitude disenchanting. Here we were in golden California, surrounded by tantalizing personalities, and my father said nothing doing. There were not as yet many substantial citizens in filmland, and he didn't approve at all of the kind the industry had attracted. Frowning on their ways, he hoped in time to find more serious film-makers from whom he could learn, and meanwhile he sought to make his connections with the downtown establishment. And he was as disinclined as ever to get involved socially, except for limited relationships with those people connected with his company, and with those he valued from the past when they came West to visit.

It was a quiet family life: early dinner and to bed. An hour of sleep before midnight. . . .

However, one social occasion in our first year there sticks in my memory for the wrong reasons.

We were invited to Sunday lunch at Anita Stewart's house. I now not only knew a movie star, I was about to eat at her table. And she lived right next door to Cecil DeMille himself! But a cloud hung over the event for me in the shape of four little words . . . and a gift. Mother felt we must bring something, not come empty-handed, and settled on a big box of chocolates. So far so good. But it had to be presented . . . presented by me. Me, why me? And I was to hand it to her on arrival with those four words. Something told me it was dead wrong.

The arrival was a mess. Amidst greetings and coats, I stood there holding a hot potato which no one seemed to notice. Lugging the candy, I couldn't shake hands or get out of my coat. Then silence, and all eyes were focused on me. Finally the dreaded words came out. With burning cheeks and downcast eyes, I mumbled, "Sweets to the sweet," and hoped nobody really heard it. I obeyed, but only just.

I'm still embarrassed.

Because I felt temporary in my new school, I used to talk of Brookline and of going home. At the end of the first school year we didn't go "home," we went to New York, lucky girls. We window-shopped with awe and drank in details of still another world. That tight little unit stayed intact. We went to show after show, restaurants where we didn't belong, with people Edie and I didn't know.

Part of me had stayed behind in Brookline, so I tremendously looked forward to the visit to our home town. We had a triumphant return, met at the station by a large group.

I was properly dressed for Boston, which meant a hat, a wide-brimmed navy straw with streamers down my back. It was miserably snug, but then a year had passed and girls' heads grow. It was killing me, but I didn't have to pop it on my head until the train pulled in.

Mother, Edie, and I rode in the limousine of rich Mrs. Coleman Levin, wife of one of my father's partners. The ladies sat in the back, and as I settled into the jump seat, Mrs. Levin cast a pall on my entire visit. I heard her say, "Margaret, that hat is too tight for Irene. I can see that from here. Why don't you get her a new hat?" Mother, cut to the quick, shrugged it off with an answer that became standard language in the family: "A child; June, July, and August, and the summer's over." I took off the hat, but didn't turn my head because I knew my face was scarlet, one of the few big blushes of a lifetime. My mother never quite forgave her.

I longed to see my school friends, but it didn't quite work; as Thomas Wolfe said, you can't go home again. I was at a loss; they all wanted to "know," and I was not one to hold forth. The gap was more than a year's worth. It was when we went West again in time for school that we really returned home.

Now we didn't have a house, and until we found one, we stayed at the Hollywood Hotel, just as though we were celebrities, in that spread-out three-story stucco building right out of *Photoplay* magazine. I couldn't believe that Dad would let us get that close to glamour. I thought it absolutely thrilling, yet it was a seedy, sleepy place with a goodly share of permanent guests. It had a wide wooden veranda on which I sat late afternoons, watching the famous and the not-so-famous come and go.

The big moment each evening came midway through dinner, when Elinor Glyn, then resident, resplendent in evening gown, would make her majestic entrance, with the young Cedric Gibbons in attendance. She had dazzling white skin, bright red hair, and itty-bitty green eyes, heavily blackened. She came to Hollywood often and it was a mutual gain. She was at the height of her fame as a respectably salacious novelist who, apart from vast provocative publicity and writing screenplays, undertook to teach Hollywood about high life. Actually, she was a wise and clever woman who mixed in the best London circles. Having used up the phrase "sex appeal," she created "It" as a synonym.

One night a week the hotel had a gala of sorts. I mean they had a few lazy musicians playing inexpert music. On these occasions Elinor Glyn would enlarge her table and entertain a few notables. My father loved to dance and took each of his ladies in turn out on the floor, meanwhile contributing occasional hints and comments to improve our ballroom skills. I have a feeling that this is not how other girls learned to dance, and certainly not with La Glyn looking on from the next table.

Those were giddy weeks, but not made more so by the proximity of the Hollywood High School one block away, which throughout my school years I tried to avoid passing. It was dangerous because there were boys there, and had I been seen, it might have altered my father's trust in me. (It dawns on me only now that the absence of boys was my father's main reason for putting us in private school!)

About this time I seemed very suddenly unwieldy and given to helpless giggles. No one told me this awkwardness was adolescence and would go away. Edie just as suddenly was grown-up. I have a snapshot of us aged fifteen and thirteen. She looks eighteen, I look ten; Edie in black satin slippers, flaring black dress, a hat with tiny ostrich plumes, I in socks, cotton dress with pleated skirt buttoned on, feet apart, Dutch bob, half a generation and a continent away. Not when, but would I ever get there? "Edith, what is a good complexion? Pink cheeks or white skin?" Apparently it was neither. "Edie, what do they mean when they say a good figure? Does that mean tall or is it thin?" She was not condescending, but surely in despair. No one ever told her—she just knew. And so did Margaret de Mille, younger than I. It comforts me that Agnes de Mille, the noble, gifted one I so admired, didn't have a clue either. For heaven's sake, her bosom (technically known as breasts) protruded shamelessly. I learned from Margaret, who was impatiently awaiting brassieres, that Agnes knew all about them and disdained them. When my time-for-brassieres arrived, I assisted what I conceived to be their purpose by tightening them with safety pins. Edith mercifully caught me out early and somehow conveyed to me that breasts were important, very important, and what I must do and mustn't do. Even if I didn't believe her, I would be grateful to her later on. Oh, I was.

THERE was much ado about horses in Southern California in those years, and I don't mean cowboys or Western pictures. Proper saddle horses and English riding habits were quite the thing. High-class stars were photographed in wonderfully tailored habits, always carrying a riding crop. It was also rather dashing to wear riding clothes for casual attire and just skip the horses.

My school had modest arrangements. A handful of us were taken to a little stable near Hollywood Boulevard and Cahuenga, where we would first ride around the ring under the eye of an instructor, who would then take us out to where we could ride in safety. Within a few minutes, after crossing risky Sunset Boulevard, we would be in flat, wide-open country with a dirt road and no buildings as far as the eye could see. It is hard to believe that road was Melrose Avenue, now so filled with traffic.

Still more surprising is the fact that my other athletic activity was to determine the course of my life. We played tennis twice a week at the Garden Court Apartments on Hollywood Boulevard. Being taught by Violet Sutton Doeg, the sister of a world champion and the mother of a future one, gave great importance to every single stroke. I didn't know I was taking my first lesson in how to find a husband.

Agnes de Mille was the best player. While all the de Mille girls gave cachet to the school, it was Agnes who had pre-eminence. She was elected to every post of responsibility, but was not too popular because she did not suffer us mere mortals gladly.

Edith and I seemed to go to ever more musical events. No need to look for a piano teacher, we'd go to the one the de Mille girls did. (My violin sentence had already been lifted.) Edith went to the dancing school Agnes went to, which I was spared. We saw all the plays, we heard all the touring artists, we saw Pavlova every year. It all furthered

Edie's ambition and need for artistic expression. I was in on a pass.

Cecil DeMille at that time was a magical name and a mythical figure. He owned a ranch named Paradise, which was legendary even to schoolgirls because of the hypothetical orgies practiced there. One day he was woven into our school history because several classes were to be taken to Paradise for a picnic. That he was to accompany us made it particularly exciting. He stood at the end of the driveway waiting as the twenty or so girls lined up for the teachers to settle which girls were to go with them in which cars. In the midst of the deliberations he intervened and said, "I will take this young lady with me." That was it. Off we went alone, and the others followed. I was thrilled. To be the chosen one so went to my head that I even thought I held up my end of the conversation during the drive. The fact that the ranch was prosaic, if lovely, did not detract from the glory I felt. The glow lasted for months.

IT WAS all too good to be true. California had not been quite up to those postcards and descriptions of Mother's, but to her it was a miracle place she found beautiful, a land of milk and honey and flowers everywhere. To my father it was not only progress, it was the Garden of Eden because of the boon of the climate. In Boston each winter brought severe sinus infections, and the necessary surgery brought complications. To both my parents California was synonymous with good health.

In the spring of our second year calamity struck: Edith had tuberculosis. It is still hard to credit the impact. In our home disease in a child was disaster. Moreover, it was the kind of disgrace more keenly felt in a home whose family had known poverty.

TB was a more rampant and more dangerous disease in those days. There was worry for her very life. If she was spared, there hung over her the threat of permanent invalidism—with luck, these patients lived out their days in the Swiss Alps or Saranac or perhaps Arizona. But even if she recovered, it was feared she would carry a stigma forever, and so it was a matter of greatest secrecy.

Denial set in and reality was postponed. Mother took us to the mountains so Edie could rest and breathe the fresh air. I was bewildered. My father interceded and secured the best obtainable specialist, who brought sterner measures. Edith became completely bedridden, partially quarantined and attended by trained nurses. A system of antisepsis was instituted of separate dishes, sterilized laundry, and sputum cups.

Fear pervaded. I remember the atmosphere of those first weeks, the hushed tones and bated breath. There would be silence as the sound of a cough ricocheted through the house. We needed a much larger place in order to cordon off part of it for an infirmary. We wound up in a conspicuous and enormous old-fashioned house with lots of gables, incongruously set on Sunset Boulevard, a spot no longer remembered as the first location of Schwab's drugstore.

This house contained lots of strange things, including a collection of polar-bear rugs and exotic lamps with gilt fringe. Its chief virtue, apart from size, was a windowed sleeping porch for Edith, with three exposures, which ran almost the full southern length of the house.

I had to undergo repeated examinations, for fear the contagion had spread to me. Despite the doctors' assurances, my parents' anxiety was so great that I was required to sleep in the absolute out-of-doors without even a roof over my head. Sprinkles were nothing, but when it began to rain, I mean really rain, I would scamper off my little porch through my parents' room to wind up not so safe with ordinary ventilation in my own bedroom.

A high-handed German nurse came to take care of Edie, and a mild reign of terror ensued. It was them versus us, a difficult and unnatural situation. Edie, already isolated, became alienated. There was continuing friction between her and my father over who was to dominate our home. Finally they were no longer speaking, and it was decided to send Edith to the desert and create for her a whole new environment.

The dragon lady was replaced by a darling Scottish nurse who appeared to be no more than a jolly companion, which indeed she was. Mother and I found them a bungalow at the Desert Inn in Palm Springs, then a remote and almost undiscovered spot, where Edie got not only desert air but a breath of freedom in which she reveled as she began to recover. Mother and I went to see her several times and found her very happy.

She was away a year or so, during which time my father bought a nice, sensible house on North Kenmore, at the opposite end of Hollywood, to which a sleeping porch, naturally, was added "for the girls." The fear of relapse was never mentioned, but it was ever-present.

The new house was a block or two from the William de Milles'. With Edie away, the practice of "keeping the girls together" was suspended, so I was allowed to sleep away from home at long last like other girls. I proudly accepted Margaret de Mille's invitation, although I didn't know if it included contact with her parents and whether I could measure up to it. I understood that Margaret's father was inclined to put down Hollywood, which, as it happened, impressed me. The de Mille brothers were in great contrast to each other. Cecil, once an actor, was the more successful—a charming man with considerable magnetism, who was considered synonymous with glamour and luxury. William, a former playwright, now a director, competed by living a literary and athletic life, which seemed his way of needling Cecil.

At the table the girls and I were treated like thinking people. The de Milles had intellectual and cultural standards new to me and talked about subjects beyond my ken. I remember looking up several definitions of the word "intellectual." I couldn't figure out how people got that way. It was quite a bracing climate, and I was relieved when I was asked back. Their living was simple and I found the fare frugal, but they had a brand-new, splendid tennis court, and more books than I had ever seen in one house in my life.

None of this prepared me for what lay ahead. We all got to sleep together! I had been denied camp and boarding school, so the closest I ever got to a dormitory was the long sleeping porch which the five of us shared—us girls and Mr. and Mrs. de Mille.

Again through Margaret I moved out a little bit. I went with her to see a Rex Ingram film being made. This was special. Margaret had a crush on Rex Ingram, who was devastating, so it was a sacred invitation. Besides, the film was an important one and they were doing some hush-hush location shots in the garden of an estate two hundred yards from my front door. When the guarded iron gates swung open, we both took a deep breath. This was high adventure; I hadn't gotten there through my father, but on my own. We were received like young ladies and not like somebody's little girls. Things were looking up.

THERE were economies, all right, but there were non-essentials as well. I had, not delusions, but actual grandeur, the only kind which meant something to me as a girl: I had my own horse.

In my last year or two at school I went riding with my father very early every morning. We would join a group of men, mostly bankers and lawyers, who were friends of his, and ride to the Hillcrest Club for breakfast. Then one morning my father had a horse demonstrated for me, a spectacular animal, white, black tail and mane, and blue eyes, who was high-schooled, so that on signal she could dance and could kneel, and when she did, my father said, "Get on. Her name is Marcheta. She's five-gaited. She's yours." He had given in to an unlikely impulse, just as he had with the lamb.

The only identity I had to some people was as the girl from the bridle path in Beverly Hills, which then ran the full length of Sunset Boulevard. "I know you, aren't you the girl on the white horse?"

One day a year later my father casually suggested I ride an attractive small chestnut mare. I didn't know on whose behalf, but just obeyed. As we rode along, he remarked that I seemed to be enjoying myself. Well, I was, because the horse had a lovely gait, which is what he had heard, and in that case she was mine. He said Dixie was a proper saddle horse, never mind novelties; that was all the explanation I ever got. What he got was a daughter who really loved her horse.

IT WAS a jolt for Edith to return to a life without a companion focused completely on her and to become reassimilated. She had a new personality, new standards. Mother and I were rather awed by the fastidiousness she had developed, through which I learned about the necessity of bath salts and hand lotion and sachet bags. Clearly, Edith had thoroughly enjoyed Palm Springs; I needn't have pitied her exile. Unfortunately, by now all her friends had graduated and gone away. She had to live a careful, restricted life and only gradually returned to normalcy. Back home, she was given a big front bedroom and permitted to order orchid taffeta curtains. She was determined to take the best possible care of herself; in fact, with her new requirements and rules, she considered herself a special person. Dad disagreed and thought it only a special situation and temporary at that, but made no reference to the trouble they had had. Mother, grateful that Edie was spared, was more sensitive to Edie's moods and was protective. I had survivor guilt. In addition, I had enjoyed being an only child and so I leaned over backward to mollify her. While Dad had an abiding respect for the discipline with which Edie maintained her regime, he wanted her to be more realistic and stop dramatizing herself; she had to learn to live with her family again.

But Edie now thought she was too good for us. She maintained her self-esteem by disparaging us. She told me what she didn't like about our home, but if I had tried to tell her why it suited me, I would have met with derision. Maybe I was made of sterner stuff. Well, she let me know she was made of finer stuff.

What had been simmering for quite some time between my father and Edie exploded. They matched tempers in a frightful row. Mother and I were terrified witnesses. It was a scene none of us ever forgot. More than ever, Mother told me to make allowances and not ruffle Edie's feathers. That was easy, because I was now afraid of her.

She also had a new role: she became our arbiter of taste and customs. What she really cared about with a passion was clothes, and she certainly knew more than we did; unlike Edie, Mother was no student of *Vogue* and *Harper's Bazaar*. We were so grateful to have some guidelines that we put up with a good deal of condescension. We didn't even understand that it was necessary to wear pure-silk underwear! Edie coveted French, but made do, provided hers had genuine lace and was all handmade. In extremis she took to making her own things, which were few but treasured and not to be touched by the likes of me.

Around this time I dared a pair of silk stockings and a dab of lipstick. The family didn't scoff, they hooted. They found my overdue attempt to be a "lady" hilarious. I had been "caught." My deadpan was unsuccessful, my confusion and conflict apparent. Damn, "cute" again. I heard the word "pathetic" and the laughter.

Mom and Edie took lots of steps about their appearance, why shouldn't I? I cared. I cared like everybody else. What I did was to make a decision and abide by it. I wouldn't care *much*. I would do minimum to look optimum. And I would do it fast. I didn't spend five minutes a week in front of a mirror. My father, of course, said that looks were not that important: looks don't last, it's character that counts. My looks were good enough, at least okay, and I had attributes which wouldn't wear out—my father said I had a good mind, my mother said I had good posture, Edie said I had good skin, and a cousin said I had good ankles. My father said a young man would be enchanted with my good qualities. He was absolutely wrong. Men did care about looks.

I paid too little attention. Edith paid too much. In the years that followed, my father would say, "What are you, a movie star?" I never did figure out what Edie did during those hours. I liked her looks better before her labors. Actually, the subject bored me; in proportion to possible results, it didn't justify the time, energy, hope.

Be that as it may, quite suddenly I went from tomboy to schoolgirl to, whammo, a woman. Full blown, a contradictory combination of maturity and innocence.

By the time I got to silk stockings, Edie had gone on to French, very expensive, so even she had only a few pair. "You can always tell them by their narrow seams." Confusion and despair overtook me. I was ready to give up.

The high fashion Edie favored was beyond our spending habits, so very important garments were made by an able but cozy seamstress named Belle Faye, who would "adapt" styles partway between fashion magazines and Edie's design. When the time came, however improbable, when I needed my first evening dress, it was Edie who guided me into the world of fashion. She had decreed a dress of Nile-green crepe. (It was not! It was pea green, a color I never again wore.) It was a large, broad dress whose armholes and safe neckline were bound with silver ribbon. It hung straight and had a bit of shirring several inches below the navel. Its only notable feature was a sizable bunch of silver grapes perched just above the pubic bone. I was miserable at the first fitting; I didn't know what I ought to have, only that this wasn't it. Confirmation came the night of its debut. After we came home my father said, "That won't do. Get her something decent."

I dealt with it myself, and it was ruby velvet, strikingly simple, made by Belle Faye but becoming to the figure. All he said this time was, "That's more like it."

That wasn't the only recognition I got. When I woke up on my seventeenth birthday, I was greeted by a tissue-paper package with satin ribbons and the happiest smile I had ever seen from Edith. She said to open it, and as I peeked, I burst into tears as though my heart would break. It was pink silk underwear, with real lace. I couldn't even take it out of its wrappings. She urged me to examine it and said she had done every stitch by hand. I couldn't thank her because I couldn't speak. I couldn't believe that it was mine, that Edie had done this for me. I wept and I wept. It was a gift of more than lingerie, and the gratitude I felt then has lasted. I am deeply moved even now at the memory.

W E   L E D a life of many contrasts and contradictions, but it was exactly as ordered by my father. During our teens there was a strange imbalance. We had more social life than other girls, depending on what one calls social life.

I had had intimations that something was missing in this super-life of ours when Edie had complained that she found herself at a disadvantage with girls at school, who exchanged confidences about boys and about, well, more boys. She said it was unnatural that she wasn't even allowed to go to other girls' houses when this dangerous species was present.

A couple of years later I found myself in the same spot and had to conceal the situation from the other girls. I had learned how, on Mondays, to handle my share of reporting the weekend's fun. I didn't misrepresent, I merely countered with something fascinating I'd done. I didn't want to be envied, I just wanted not to be pitied.

Of course I wanted boys too, but if I had been given a choice of my life as it was, with all its special features, or instead an average, happy-go-lucky existence with boy friends, I would have chosen what I had. But then, I *had* no choice. There were no boys, and there weren't going to be any. My father cared about his girls' reputations. He said no good came of being with boys. "Boys are a waste of time and lead to temptation." Boys took advantage. "Analyze: what is in a boy's mind? What is he after? If he gets the chance, he'll take liberties." To me, that meant he might put his arm around my waist. My father said a boy took a girl out to be alone with her and he would touch her if he could. "There's plenty of time when you grow up and there's a serious purpose, which is marriage." Edie and I wondered how he'd behave when we finally did have real sweethearts.

I might have liked the boys if I ever could have had at them. My one chance came in my last year of school, when they had to let me go to the party which Cecilia DeMille held at her house as the event marking the junior class giving the senior class its farewell. I was more experienced socially than any of the girls in either class, yet to my horror I discovered there was no one there more ill at ease than myself. I could have coped with Mr. DeMille, whose absence was a bitter disappointment—but I had nothing whatsoever to say to those boys. And my cherished school friends were perfect strangers I didn't like, with outlandish ways I couldn't fathom. I was a fish out of water.

Dreams of conquest had died quickly, and it was all I could do the next morning to conceal my abject misery from my mother. I think it was the single most humiliating social occasion of my life. It was just as well I had no notion of being a femme fatale.

B E F O R E we had gone East, new stages had been built and a very attractive Norman-style administration building rose at 3800 Mission Road. About that time B. P. Schulberg joined the ranks of independent producers and shared the space at the studio, so it was called the Mayer-Schulberg Studios. Gradually directors were added to the roster. Then, in 1923 Irving Thalberg joined the family. My father had a son without having to raise one—wise, loving, filial. Irving hadn't had an easy time at Universal, whence he had come, as they had "known him when." My father took him at face value, as of the present; he admired both his brain and his gentle nature. Irving was ambitious and yet unspoiled, but there was a flaw in this gift from the gods. Irving wasn't really his because he was borrowed. The gods would have him back, as he had a bad heart from an attack of rheumatic fever as a boy, and his doctors had warned my father that he could go at any time, and that there was no chance of his living beyond the age of thirty.

Irving's advent was a thunderbolt. How could a fellow of twenty-three possibly be much help at the studio? What was Dad so excited about? He was brilliant and Dad was so keen to get him that he'd promised him a partnership. That stunned us. Imagine, before he even started! Yet if he was all that wonderful, how come he'd leave a big studio like Universal and join a little company, and why didn't Carl Laemmle hang on to him? It seemed that he was underpaid there and he had been involved with the boss's daughter Rosabelle, and neither fact helped the other.

My father prepared us for the introduction of Irving into our lives, and he warned us we were going to see a great deal of him. "He's attractive. I don't want you girls to get any ideas in your heads, ever." The problem was minimized by the fact that, despite our years, we were not yet permitted to go out. He said he'd almost not signed Irving because of the romantic risk to one of us. He had advised Irving not to look on his daughters with favor. He didn't want to have to cure a problem, he wanted to prevent one, and we weren't warned once, twice; we were constantly admonished.

Irving very soon came to dinner. It was hard to believe that anyone that modest and boyish could be so important. He had a most engaging manner, but we had been totally unprepared for anyone that good-looking. Edie and I agreed that Dad was right: "If only he were healthy." Irving was the only charming man of the right age with whom we ever came in contact. My father said that if he sensed anything amiss for one moment, there would be no chance of ever seeing Irving again.

The evenings Irving came to dinner we found doubly exciting because at the table he and my father exchanged their opinions and ideas, exploring each other's reactions. The growing bond between them was evident. There was confidence, enthusiasm, and affection—all of it mutual. The more there was, the greater was my father's pain at the sentence which hung over Irving's head.

There seemed nothing in his background to account for his gifts or his personality. Irving was a throw-off, a mutant. The dominant force in the Thalberg family was his mother, Henrietta, shrewd and inclined to be harsh. Her situation couldn't have been worse if she had made a pact with the devil: "Give me a glowing, beautiful boy for a lesser time than that to which I am entitled." Sometime in the not too distant future the clock would strike and he would vanish. Surely he couldn't have survived as long as he did but for her vigilance. Her only partner in this was my father, and they relied upon one another.

Irving was a free agent unless either one of them caught him at it, Mama at home and my father at the studio. But he couldn't possibly live and function, either professionally or personally, constantly conscious of the threat to his life. He went blithely on, my father measuring his working hours and Henrietta trying to check the wiles of his friends, all of whom were leading him into "bad ways." Bad ways referred to a date, a drink, perhaps a dame. Irving's look of defiance when once, mildly and briefly, he tried to play tennis like the others, was poignant. He was closest to leading a normal life on the dance floor, an activity in which he could effectively compete with his peers. Even here there was no freedom: "they" watched him and watched him. Edie and I were told to feign fatigue and sit down any time the telltale flush became intense. Irving played no favorites: if he danced with one daughter, he danced with the other, on every occasion that was obligatory. Poor thing, he also had to dance with my mother, Mrs. Rapf, Mrs. Stromberg, but he was charming to us and even sweetly flirtatious.

Henrietta had to be wooed to a considerable degree, because of her pervasive influence with Irving. Dad reasoned with us that if we remembered that the burden was heaviest for her, we could understand her better. And by making Henrietta's life easier, we made Irving's life easier. She only appeared to be an over-protective mother; in truth, he needed her badly and depended on her. Mother, Edith, and I did everything we could to give all the Thalbergs a sense of family, of belonging.

My father's pride and delight in Irving were overwhelming. That was an aspect of him we never saw before or after. At times he bore him an aching love. The young man with the greatest future in the motion-picture business was a man without a future.

P E O P L E always seemed nice to the girls, but I had no way of knowing whether we were on sufferance. At last came a sign that we were not a total drag. Ad Schulberg, Ben's wife, discussing a forthcoming holiday she was planning with her children on Catalina, suddenly turned and said it would be fun to have us go with her. Saying it right in front of us meant it was spontaneous, and made it harder for our parents to refuse. Their permission seemed a miracle. Alone. Alone. Out in the world. Trusted.

Ad and Ben were friends of the family we really found charming and interesting. They were some years younger than my parents, so it made an easier group. They were friends for personal, not business reasons.

Ben Schulberg was a new breed of producer, well read and articulate. Little did anyone suspect that these two young fellows out on Mission Road were within a very few years to head up the two biggest and best studios in town.

Ad had a wonderfully attractive personality and was brimming with new ideas. She was "advanced." She was merrily leading Hollywood into child psychology and interior decoration (both almost as new to her as to us). She even flirted with Freud. Had she dabbled in fewer fields, she would have been more thorough, but she did found the only progressive school in town.

At the St. Catherine Hotel in Avalon, to us she was the fount of wisdom, and we grew up a lot in that week or two. It was such a success

that Ad said we would go to a different place each year. What praise!
We sat at her feet and didn't mind too much that we had to share her
with her son, Seymour, called Buddy, and her daughter, Sonia. She was
expecting her third child; I had never been with a pregnant woman
before, and her attitude of normality was a healthy thing for me.

I didn't have too much to say that first holiday, because Buddy had
a beaut of a stutter, the worst I'd ever encountered. As he stuttered and
stammered, I became increasingly silent; they never caught on, but for
a few weeks after I got home I had a terrible time getting unsnarled. It
didn't stop me, though, from looking forward to the following summer,
when we all went to Arrowhead Springs together.

AS FAR back as I can remember, I was going to make my mother
proud of me at college. It was taken for granted, except that the matter
was never discussed in front of my father.

Coming from Boston, of course my mother's heart was set on Welles-
ley. It was very unrealistic of her, but it was just as well, because she kept
my hopes alive.

I had no idea what was out there in that great world of scholars. I pored
over catalogs and thought, I've had history, I've had English and math;
I don't want them. What seemed tantalizing to me were things called
Philosophy, Psychology, Sociology, Ethics, and Logic. I didn't know
what they meant, yet I didn't understand why every girl wouldn't yearn
for such courses. What possible use did I have for them? Obviously, none,
except curiosity. I had no ambition of any kind; no, that isn't quite true.
All through my childhood, adults at a loss for conversation would say
to Edie and me, "What are you going to do when you grow up?"
Unequivocally and with deep conviction I would say, "I'm going to get
married and I'm going to have two little boys." Edie deplored my vision.
In the first place, she wanted two little girls and was horrified at the
thought of anything else. My future looked mundane; hers was going to
be filled with career and artistic conquest. The only thing I was dead
certain I wanted no more of was French. I can vouch for the fact that
without free-flowing speech, a foreign language is a booby trap. I found
French class almost the worst thing around. The tension would mount
as my turn approached. I would quickly take my "stutter-temperature"
and all too often shrug and sit down.

The only thing that ever came really easily to me, absolutely free, was spelling. I was the star of the high school, which held a monthly spelling bee. A silver cup was given annually to the girl who won the most matches; but for that second "s" in "supersede," I would have won three cups. There was agony attached, because one was required to pronounce the word as well as spell it. I don't recall ever being competitive about anything in life except those silver cups. I simply had to take the risk that I could get the word out.

Yet the debating team didn't give me a problem, because one had the choice of an alternative phrase, a gesture, or a pause. (Because of that tiny pause, to this day I am given credit for thinking before I speak. Not at all, it started as anticipatory stress and it has become part of my personality.) But there's no explanation at all of how I managed to act in the school plays. We did *The Forest Ring,* by William de Mille; Agnes naturally in the lead, Edie as the Fairy Queen, me the boy, and Joel McCrea playing the bear in a great furry suit complete with bear's head. I never did know what Joel was doing in that school, or why he rode a horse without a saddle at a clip no faster than a walk every afternoon along the residential stretch of Hollywood Boulevard, where he lived.

The big treat was the Mason Opera House, where Broadway stars appeared on tour. (When we went alone to a matinee, we naturally sat in the balcony.) Any offering served to re-ignite Edie's dreams. She had so many fantasies that they created a magic carpet for her which later furnished insulation for some difficult years. From time to time it was musical-comedy star, opera singer, ballet dancer, and, as a sideline, fashion designer. She was burning to set the world on fire.

Mother saw to it that she had outlets, carefully excluding anything physically taxing. She went to an art school and studied sketching for a few months. She had singing lessons because Mother thought they were good for her lungs. What she really wanted to do was to be an actress, and she blamed my father for standing in the way of her being a great star. One day she would show us! Meanwhile, I was as good an audience as she had.

She had the dedication necessary, but we never found out how deep her talents were. Had she not been so convinced of her frail health, she surely would have run away. Certainly she had the courage and the desire.

As it was, she had as much chance of a career as I had of going to college.

Careers were out and professions not considered, although it amused my father to picture me as a lawyer (please not). His lucky daughters would never have to work for a living. Heaven forbid! We had protection; even as a little girl I knew about all that life insurance. Work meant a job, a job with a terrible boss in the cold, cruel world.

Could be. On the other hand, I had been peeking in the classified columns from the age of eleven to have a look at what my chances were, "just in case." I don't know yet whether that was curiosity or deeply hidden anxiety.

College went by default. There was never a showdown, at least in front of me. When I would ask, Mother would say she was working on it. Poor Mother, how hard she must have tried. It was too bad. College was my chance for freedom. Then what had it all been about, gearing myself up, knocking myself out? I was ready to test myself. Now, gone too was the opportunity to show my parents how dependable I was.

I should have caught on sooner that there had been no possible chance, for the same reasons camp and boarding school were taboo. Away from home one would have been exposed to other girls' ways and "outside influences." College would put ideas in my head. "It doesn't make for happiness." He wanted me to have the good life. Besides, they wanted their daughters with them.

There was no battle out of me. It wouldn't have done any good anyway, I only *looked* like a rebel. However, Dad must have been bothered, because he kept bringing up the subject indirectly: " 'Those girls' *have* to go to college. They don't have your advantages."

Metro-Goldwyn-Mayer

THE FORMULA had been to lay down a good foundation in the formative years. Well, I had listened and learned, and now, having come through that twelve-year tunnel of school, I was poised for take-off into life. There had never been enough time, and suddenly I had nothing else but. My friends were going off to college. I was faced with a vacuum. I concealed even from myself the hint of boredom which threatened. I was superstitiously afraid to be discontented.

A bit of tennis and a bit of riding are not very fulfilling, yet I had no idea that I needed outlets for thinking and for feeling. What I got was piano lessons, singing lessons, and one hell of a lot of exercise. Swimming became particularly important because of the Santa Monica Swimming Club, to which we belonged. It was our social currency and enabled Edie and me to spend days at the beach with our girl friends. It was as close to normal as we ever got.

Without school to interfere, I had greater difficulty escaping the possibility of becoming a golf champion, which just might have happened if my desire had equaled my effort. I tried as hard as if my heart were in it, but the results proved otherwise. My father couldn't understand it. He kept changing the pros: each pro would change my grip; more blisters. The change that was needed was to the left hand, which was how I played tennis. I hadn't known there were left-handed clubs, but that's what I finally got, along with a whole new set of blisters.

One Sunday morning, after leaving the stable, my father drove me slowly through some of the small, unfamiliar back streets of Hollywood, chatting casually. He came to a low white building and went around that block several times. Then he asked what I thought of it, which was a pointless question. What was it?

It was the Metro studio, and someday he might be head of it, or some other studio like it. Did I believe him or not? I might have a surprise coming. "Just wait a year or two."

That's as much build-up or warning as I ever got about his becoming the head of the MGM studio. It was about a year before he made good his threat . . . and then some. This was big-time, all right: vice-president in charge of production, and not just of little old Metro with its minor buildings, but the imposing gates of the Goldwyn studio in Culver City. The whole thing was breathtaking. Talk about status!

There was no such talk out of my father. He said it meant he would have to work harder than ever, and we were going to have to be even more careful, because anything we did would reflect on him. We had accomplished nothing; we mustn't get too taken up with ourselves because he was getting on in the world.

That was certainly a come-uppance. And there wasn't even any glory at school, not a flicker. The merger happened in April 1924, a couple of months before graduation. Those girls seemed to have a time lag on recognition, but then they didn't read the film dailies as I did, and of course, apart from Pickford and Chaplin, nothing counted but Paramount. It was the best; it was indeed paramount.

Goldwyn and Metro were important companies, but doing poorly. Sam Goldwyn couldn't get along with anyone, and had been forced out of the company bearing his name, which had suffered further changes of regime in the next couple of years and was looking for a buyer. Metro had been acquired by Marcus Loew in 1919 to turn out product for his growing chain of theatres, a task it seemed unable to perform. In a casual conversation in Palm Beach, Marcus Loew told Lee Shubert he was thinking about folding Metro. Shubert, an investor in the debt-ridden Goldwyn company, thought Marcus would be better off buying that company and combining it with Metro. Metro's lawyer was my father's partner, Bob Rubin. As the prime asset of their little company was manpower, it was inevitable that Bob Rubin suggest a three-way merger.

Although his background had eminently prepared him for such a job, my father was an unexpected choice for this great opportunity. At the time it seemed to many people a great stroke of luck. I found it electrifying. Obviously, my impression that my father revealed everything at the dinner table was incorrect.

He was under forty and a strong, disciplined executive, the only one with experience in depth in all phases of the business, who by this time had also had lessons in running his own studio, with all the hopes and heartaches of making pictures. Reviewing it now, the choice seems logical, but it could hardly have been expected then that in working out the problems of a new company, this man would define and create the job of studio head, inventing a shape and pattern not only of how to run a studio, but of how to run the industry.

This was 1924, and there were many changes going on. The world had changed, Hollywood had changed, and the change in the Mayers' situation was the most incredible of all. It didn't become real until inauguration day, a day so gala I was certain that all else in life would be an anticlimax.

There was a large, square lawn between the actors' dressing rooms, which ran along Washington Boulevard, and a row of attached little one-room bungalows which served as offices for writers and directors. In the center of the grassy space a rostrum had been hastily erected out of two-by-fours; draped, not too unnaturally, in the American flag. I thought the turn-out splendid and enthusiastic: department heads, directors, writers, and actors. There were holdovers from Mission Road displaying their loyalty; others pledging allegiance to the new regime. The speeches were stirring and wound up on a religious note—with God's help and theirs, victory lay ahead. I had no idea that there were some cynics prepared to ride it out with a ho-hum, and I certainly didn't know that there were others who just didn't show up.

Heads would roll, but gradually. The grafters and the incompetents went first; then the trouble-makers and the uncooperatives. Strangely enough, out-and-out enemies were not fired, not if they were talented. My father and Irving had each had a scorching experience with a great director: Marshall Neilan had been my father's nemesis from Anita Stewart days, and Irving's was Erich von Stroheim, an enmity born of *Foolish Wives* at Universal; and there they both were, entrenched with contracts at MGM, which needed all the talent it could get. Both men were kept on until they became completely unproductive.

Two department heads survived the weed-out: Cedric Gibbons, the art director, and Joe Cohn, the production manager, had worked for Sam

Goldwyn back in New Jersey, and they were still at MGM long after my father left the studio.

Contract people and other personnel and equipment both from Metro and from Mission Road had to be assimilated. There were redundancies, yet many departments had to be staffed from scratch. They were short of shooting space, so Metro stages were cut up and carted across town. And meanwhile, despite the expansion with all its manifest pressures, production schedules had to be kept going. Current pictures had to be completed, some scrapped and others substituted.

Von Stroheim had finished his film *Greed;* he had reduced it to forty reels, and he dug his heels in against further cutting. We went to the studio early one morning to see it and sat through till evening of a very, very hot day, made no cooler by the final hours of endless footage shot in the blazing sun of Death Valley. It was masterful in ways, and parts of it were riveting, but it was an exhausting experience; the film in conception was a considerable exercise in self-indulgence, and a testament to the incompetence of the previous regime. When it was cut further, it still seemed over-length, except to certain critics who decried the desecration of a masterpiece—and the myth has been carried on by increasing numbers of people who, of course, never saw the original and who heard about it from others who also hadn't seen it. I was there— and, as it happens, on von Stroheim's side in advance and prepared to do battle. When it was over, nobody said a word—including me.

The most striking example of chaos was *Ben-Hur,* which was filming in Rome and had acquired a life of its own. In any case, it was not among Culver City's first problems. But as order began to prevail at the new studio, it became clear that *Ben-Hur* required a set of new decisions. The studio wanted the film brought back to California, but the home office in New York wanted to save face and hoped to salvage something of the millions of dollars already spent abroad on sets and a vast colosseum, as well as on a fleet of boats to be used for the battle of the galleys. Unfortunately, no aspect of the undertaking was sound other than the basic material. It needed a whole new deal: new script, new writers, new director, two new leading players, and, as it turned out, new galleys. Most of the work to date had to be scrapped.

Ben-Hur may have been a headache to the company, but to me it brought the biggest dividend that could be bestowed: my father had to go to Rome and straighten it out, and he was taking us with him. It was too glorious to believe.

Diary entry, eve of departure: "Sept. 10. I went to bed with a numb, pounding feeling, too excited to feel excited." The diary is filled with details of an enormous going-away party given at the Ambassador, and a send-off at the station that I found intoxicating. Spartan living was over; so was anonymity. We felt like heroines in a book.

It would be Paris first, so Edie got busy collecting shopping addresses and polishing her French. She was more confident than I was, and, knowing what that strange tongue did to me in the classroom, I didn't hope to shine in Paris. But at least I would be able to understand. Mother, slightly on the defensive, said there was only one language that was universal and that was Yiddish. Edie and I protested. She said, "You will see. In Paris there are Jews, and in Rome too, and Yiddish is spoken everywhere. I'm the only one who will get along just fine."

We sailed in splendor in the Imperial Suite on the *Majestic,* but the high times I expected on shipboard were not to be. We dressed for dinner every night and we had sips of champagne, but it was sedate, sedate, sedate. I walked the deck one afternoon with an interesting man and there was hell to pay.

Cherbourg was a nasty shock. They didn't know how to speak French! In Paris it didn't sound like our teacher either. We ladies went tearing off singly and together, dispersing and regrouping, sightseeing and shopping. Every moment counted; we might never be here again. I was awestruck and bewildered, and so were Mother and Edie, and not a little intimidated.

After that day of confusion Mother sought solace by trying to find the Jewish quarter. Obviously, she had a terrible time with the taxi drivers, who didn't know about synagogues. She went to one after another, hoping to find an Orthodox community nearby where Yiddish was spoken. She was frustrated. She said, "Wait till I get to Rome."

My father was not at his best in Paris, but I've never known a man who was. Before we ever left, he had warned us that he didn't want trouble with customs; he had a terror of smuggling. He had promised us each a Paris dress, and Edie knew just which collections we should see. Patou was where our hearts were, but Poiret was the only house able to accommodate us in time. (A few years later we discovered why, when they closed down.) Then he resumed his agitating about our shopping, lecturing us that everything was to be declared. He could think of nothing but his disgrace on the dock and could almost see his name on the front page.

He was glad to get out of Paris, but he didn't know about meal sittings on the train to Italy. To his astonishment, he had no authority at all in the dining car and could not get what he wanted, but was forced to submit to the menu of the day—foreign dishes, one slapped down right after the other! He punished them fine, he just didn't eat a thing. I hadn't seen him bested before.

Rome was not very racy. In fact, it was just like home, because we had brought home with us. There were new horizons, but the same old rules. Most of the social action centered around the Excelsior Hotel, so it was quite a blow to learn we were not to stay there with the others. It was hard, in fact impossible, for me to appreciate the advantage of living in a nice, quiet apartment far from everything. My father was in Rome for a stretch of demanding work and could not be in a hotel, but restful was not what I needed.

The building was very grand and the apartment enormous, with terrazzo floors and a very large staff, only a few of whom spoke English. They did not understand American cooking, or, as it turned out, Americans. We were equally unenlightened. The first night's dinner did not suit at all—it was Italian and "unhealthy," made up of endless courses, each the identical shade of pale gold. All of it went back to the kitchen. My father left it up to my mother to get some "wholesome food." Next day she sailed forth, with a sense of mission and her confidence restored, to go marketing.

In her search for a butcher shop where she could purchase Kosher meat, she first located a synagogue, but that was all, apparently, because when we queried her, she said, "Never mind." To her last day there she never disabused herself of the notion that there were Kosher butcher shops in Rome and Italians who spoke Yiddish, if she could only find them. Nevertheless, she had arrived home that first day laden with food, whereupon the major part of the staff walked out, including the only ones who spoke English. My father said, "It's just as well. We are not suited to them or them to us. The people left will be more willing." The next months I gave the orders with a hundred or so Italian words quickly acquired.

We lived pretty much as usual, which meant no pasta, no veal, no cheese, no wine. My father was not looking for adventure; he had a tough job to do. He wanted one tiny zone of sanity, comfort, and security to which he could return at night.

We ladies had the day to absorb as much of Rome as we liked. Armed with the cultural heritage of my senior year of high school, we stormed

Irene, age four

Margaret and Louis B. Mayer (right), along with Louis B.'s partners,
Mr. and Mrs. Coleman Levin, and friend, Massachusetts, c. 1910

Margaret and Louis B., New Hampshire, 1911

Mrs. Mayer with Irene and Edith

Irene and Louis B. playing checkers,
Sharon, Massachusetts

Irene, Louis B., and Edith,
Winthrop Beach, Massachusetts

Irene's second-grade class. She is the first one standing at the left.

A school production of *The Forest Ring* by William de Mille.
Irene is standing far left wearing a great deal of padding.
Agnes de Mille is second from left. Hollywood, 1921

Grandpa Shenberg (his beard is tinted)
and Lammikins, Hollywood, 1920

At dancing school,
Brookline, Massachusetts

Edith and Irene at home, 1927

Edith, Louis B., Margaret, and Irene with Assistant Attorney General Mable Walker Willebrandt, visiting President Coolidge at the White House, 1927

Paul Bern, Louis B., Aileen Pringle, H. L. Mencken, Norma Shearer, Irving Thalberg, and Harry Rapf at MGM, 1926

Edith and Irene at a neighbor's in Santa Monica, 1927

Irene and her mother

1925

Louis B. and Margaret Mayer

the churches. I had labored long and hard on a course I did not enjoy called Art History, which was misleading; it dealt exclusively with the churches in Rome and resulted in a large illustrated notebook, which at Mother's behest I lugged along.

The boldest thing we did was to visit our friends May McAvoy and Carmel Myers, who were in the picture, at the studio. These visits had to be strategically timed to avoid periods of crisis. We had come to Rome from Livorno, where the galley sequences had been filmed; this was going from the fire into the frying pan.

Fire had quite literally expedited us out of Livorno. It had broken out prematurely during the climax of the galley scenes, when the prow of one boat smashed the other amidships. The plan had been to stop short of actual collision, in order to make it possible to film the ravages of the battle and the men jumping overboard, but there was more impact than planned and the flames were more extensive. They didn't have to shoot the accompanying destruction and terror later, because as it was, the men poured enthusiastically over the sides of the boat. Pandemonium ensued, most of it caught by the camera; there was an investigation to discover whether anyone was lost. I think we left in rather a hurry for Rome. Later we got the all-clear signal, but I still wonder.

Livorno had been such a tremendous undertaking technically and physically, and so fraught with peril of all kinds, that it further handicapped the efforts in Rome. Scheduling had become next to impossible due to the worsening weather and political turmoil, and priority was given to shooting whatever couldn't economically be done in California. This trip hadn't persuaded my father that the film should be completed in Rome. What was important was not which scenes were shot where, but getting the whole thing right.

At that point the film represented nothing but grief and frustration. *Ben-Hur* was good copy, it had been for years. First the competition over the rights, then the casting, followed by continuing publicity of the progress of the great epic. Then the wheels had suddenly ground to a halt. When a big film spectacle changes directors, the omens do not augur well. It attracts lightning. There were hard feelings from those who had been deposed but lingered. The honor of the new company was at stake, and my father felt uncomfortable in the eye of the storm. He began to feel that his presence would shortly be bringing diminishing returns, and we moved on.

Well, my mother's Yiddish didn't work in Berlin either. Germany was a bonus; my father went there because the artistic level of picture-making was impressive and his studio's ranks of talent had to be expanded. His interest in European talent had been deepened by a Swedish director at MGM, Victor Seastrom, a man to whom he was devoted, and who had brought to his attention Mauritz Stiller, another Swedish director, who happened to be shooting a film in Germany with his young protégée, Greta Garbo.

We went on a Sunday afternoon to a projection room to see *The Atonement of Gösta Berling,* Stiller's most recent film. The only advance reservation my father had about him was the stipulation that he wouldn't come to Hollywood without his new leading lady, an obstacle my father thought he could overcome. Instead, Miss Garbo overcame him in the first reel. It was her eyes. He said, "She reminds me of Norma Talmadge." There was no resemblance, but what they had in common and what he must have meant was the capacity to convey feeling through their eyes. Dad said, "I'll take Stiller, all right. As for the girl, I want her even more than Stiller. I can make a star out of her. I'll take them both."

My father preceded us back to the Adlon, as Stiller was coming to talk. When we stepped into the elevator, a nice-looking but slightly heavy-set woman who looked faintly familiar also entered. She wore a large-brimmed black taffeta hat and a fairly long, dark, full skirt. No one could possibly have guessed that she was a girl between Edith and me in age. She got out at our floor, and as we stood together in front of the door to our suite, she smiled shyly at us and we smiled back, but no one introduced anyone.

The door opened and we all joined Dad and Mr. Stiller in the sitting room, and after the formalities the Mayer ladies withdrew. Stiller frightened the life out of me. He was an awesome physical sight. I likened him to the giant in "Jack and the Beanstalk"—enormously tall, with a very craggy face; a head, hands, and feet huge by comparison even with his height; his voice had the rumble of something from under a deep mountain. When he took my hand, it disappeared. The most striking feature of his face was his eyes—blue they were, and one was disfigured and teared. His personality was at odds with his appearance, as he was a quiet and very gentle man. He and the girl were an odd combination indeed.

The next I saw of Miss Garbo was many, many months later, in a publicity photograph taken on their arrival in New York, leaning against the ship's rail against the skyline of the city. She bore little resemblance to the girl from the Adlon Hotel. It was the face of the Garbo the world was to know. She was slender, smart, beautifully groomed. I've known her off and on ever since, but it was thirty-five years before she was to mention our first meeting.

Ben-Hur put MGM on the map; with *The Big Parade* it came of age. That picture clinched it for me. I was very proud. I thought that it gave new stature to the industry, and that the world would sit up and take notice. Paramount was doing fine, but MGM was doing better. Not long after, *The Merry Widow* came out and MGM drew up alongside of Paramount and, without pausing, pulled ahead.

Big Parade had started modestly. During the shooting my father caught the excitement of Irving and King Vidor, and agreed to a new budget. It was the beginning of the Thalberg legend and also of Irving's habit of retakes, and it proved to be a superb movie, making a big new star, John Gilbert, who exploded into a matinee idol as only Valentino had done before him.

Stars were thought vital to a film's success, and MGM had a slender list. My father's policy was to keep gathering talent, nurturing it, weeding and replenishing, slowly building individual strength. There was continuous flow, not as needed but as found. Infinitely more were dropped than retained. The salaries were meager, terms onerous; the minimum weeks guaranteed were few and the studio held long-term options. But it was this system that created the great stars and directors who made MGM what it was.

While Marcus Loew lived, there was no power struggle between the studio and the home office. Forever after, Nick Schenck was at the heart of the trouble.

The Schenck brothers, Joe and Nick, had both worked for Mr. Loew, but Joe, the elder, left to become an independent producer. (He married Norma Talmadge, the two of them becoming the first mogul–big-star couple, and produced her movies and those of her sister Constance for Selznick Pictures during my father's Boston days.) Joe, worldly and likable, was a smooth operator who wore an aura of power. He was big-time, generous, a sport. His contacts were widespread and he aided Nick whenever he could.

Nick, a trusted lieutenant, stayed behind in Marcus Loew's empire and bided his time. He led a modest, confined life, married to but separated from the former wife of a onetime Brooklyn cop.

When Marcus Loew died in 1927, his family inherited the stock, and Nick became president. They called him The General, but he was never the king like Marcus Loew. Mr. Loew had certainly not felt threatened by the indispensability of the studio team, because loyalty to him and to the company had been one and the same. It didn't work that way for Nick; he *did* feel threatened, and even though he had a more important job than Joe, I never heard Joe described as Nick's brother. Nick, having lived first in the shadow of Joe, then of Marcus Loew, now found himself unexpectedly in the shadow of my father. The glory and the money were now in Culver City, and in a sense Loew's was at the mercy of Irving and my father.

So it was up to Nick to "keep the boys happy," to which money was the key. I learned to dread the periods when negotiations with Nick for renewal of contracts took place. There were always violent battles, the most wrenching of which were over Irving's compensation. These struggles were accompanied by ultimatums, infighting, and a lot of divide-and-rule, Nick appearing to play Irving against my father and vice versa. (My father and Irving had further reason to distrust Nick. It is well known that in 1929 he attempted to sell the company out from under them to William Fox. My father was able to prevent the sale, but Nick ended up with nine million dollars and a bad image.) My father yielded repeatedly, if unhappily, by whittling down his share of the profits in Irving's behalf. It was never enough, and on one occasion Irving locked horns with Nick directly and got an enormous bonus, but only after a terrible fight.

I found Irving's demands understandable. No one else was a saint about money; there was no reason for him to be. He had a growing family, his life span was limited, but, above all, his value was incalculable. By the time of his death his share was larger than Dad's. To this day, fortunately, his family receives profits from MGM, thanks to TV.

Whenever Nick felt uneasy about what "they" were up to in Culver City, a trusted employee was sent to California "to help" on a temporary basis. When he became assimilated, another was sent. Although there were able men among them, most notably Eddie Mannix, those who remained were from time to time under suspicion of being double agents. And as more and more executives arrived from the East, upper echelons became top-heavy—and the uneasiness in New York increased.

I was relieved to see less and less of Nick. He was pleasant enough to the Mayer girls; he always asked solicitous questions, but he never bothered with the answers. The nicest part of Nick was Pansy, the good, sweet woman who became his second wife.

H A V I N G been to Europe, I felt altered, enhanced, decorated. After all, I was widely traveled, and it was a letdown to come back to where we had left off. Four people, four lives that boiled down to one life and that was my father's. What occupied him was what occupied us. When he talked, he wasn't intending to instruct, he was just thinking aloud. His own small company had been personal, and very much his and therefore ours. There was no cut-off when the merger came, life was just a little fuller. More names and more problems and, to tell the truth, more excitement. Just as well it was so stimulating, or the thinness of my personal life would have been apparent to me. Actually, it wasn't. I was still looking ahead.

We were completely wrapped up by what went on in filmland. What I didn't read or hear, I learned by osmosis. Movie news was all that counted; the rest of the world didn't exist. I was not alone in knowing who was doing what for which company, what films were being shot by each, and who was under contract where. What I did know, which others didn't, was certain things that went on at MGM. Mum was the word. "Be on your guard." (As if I wasn't!) "You can be used. Worse, you can hurt the company." Nothing got labeled "secret" as opposed to "top secret," thereby making *everything* top secret.

We were quietly at home more nights a week than we were out, if you don't count previews, of which there were many. There is always a lot riding on a first preview, but with a new company each was critical. In those days previews were really "sneak," because the films were quite unfinished and early guidance was needed for the vital decisions that could make or break the picture. The responsibility must have been fearsome. Silent films could be completely altered by recutting and a change of subtitles. I found it very illuminating to go to the second preview and see what they had accomplished.

One couldn't go to previews at all unless one knew how to behave. It was dinned into us to be cordial and pleasant to everyone . . . to enjoy the film and speak tactfully. What was not desired was any personal opinion because there were professionals present whose business it was. In the months ahead there would be critics' and audiences' views, but now and later I was to keep my opinion to myself.

My father's reactions were crystal clear. Walking away fast was a bad sign. Silence doubled that. On those nights a tense, uneasy ride home followed. If, however, he joined a pavement huddle, we learned to sense when to stand about and chat, or when to disappear into the car and wait for him, after which he would give us his views and tell us what had transpired. If he asked our opinions, he got pretty guarded answers, certainly from me. I never once said it was a bad picture; I would accentuate the positive and comment on a performance I had liked. In a pinch I resorted to "Perhaps a little cutting."

The big nights were when the picture looked great. There were no huddles then, everyone was on the sidewalk together. No one would ask the reflex question, "How did you like the picture?" There would be hand-shaking, back-slapping, and arms around shoulders. They would say, "See you in the morning, boys." When Dad's spirits were high like that, he really sought our opinions and, naturally, would be delighted by our enthusiasm. We'd even sit up to talk when we got home!

We had always been "taken along" more than other children, and now more than ever we went where the family went. Otherwise, we would have been isolated. I would have been quite lost had it not been for MGM coming along when it did. We trailed along, not on display, but we were in evidence, and I was always the youngest person around. We went to openings, to banquets, and to parties heavily laced with MGM people; they all knew the Mayer girls, and that did not seem inappropriate to me. Nevertheless, it was peculiar, certainly for Edie, who was past nineteen, and was being kept in an ivory tower.

By way of explanation, Dad said that, had we stayed in Brookline, things would have been more usual. I wonder. Anyhow, it was too late now for boys, which was fine with me, because it was men I liked. But according to Dad it was too early for them. In any case, we knew neither.

That was my life for two years. It varied only as our circle grew even wider and my social ease increased.

Men were divided into three groups: the older, married, quite interesting men; the glamorous ones, who were definitely taboo; and the third group, the most important, who were the great unknown: suitors. I worried whether I could get on as well with them. Would those who were worthy be interesting? And could they be integrated? Anyone tame enough to suit Louis B. could only be dullness personified. Edie was exasperated and said it wasn't Dad's conservatism, they just hadn't planned correctly; she could see no possible source of appropriate admirers, if and when the day ever came.

In desperation, Mother engineered our going to a few dinner parties with select civilians. As we went out the door, instead of saying, "Have a good time," Mother would say, "Have poise!" as though it were optional. I boiled it down to a technique: if you're self-conscious, don't show it.

Those evenings accustomed us to a degree of normal experience, but what was the use? Neither of us could go out with anyone we met, and we had to travel in solitary splendor via the chauffeur; besides, we didn't even vaguely resemble the "Our Crowd" kind of Jews, the old established families who were socially secure. My father said they were as alien to us as gentiles (also taboo), and to stick to our own kind. Our own kind? Where? How? Never mind who. Picture people were out. If the rich and/or social were also out, there began to be justice to Edie's remark, "They just don't want us to get married ever."

There were so many warnings we felt we were in a goldfish bowl. My father said that was true, we were. I couldn't believe that all eyes were on us. They weren't, but we were to behave as though they were.

Apart from "How does it look?" the important thing was discretion: don't be smart and step up with the answer; you may know everything, but don't show it. He said everybody talked too much. There he was absolutely right, and I still think so.

We were not told what to say, only what not to say and what not to do. We were told what to think, but no one told me how to feel. At least my feelings were free and private—and banked. No fluctuations or switches . . . they changed only with the degree of my convictions. I kept those feelings in as best I could; some escaped, but most got stashed.

Be yourself. That meant simplicity and no affectations, a tall order in that town. We must be sincere, and yet not take it for granted that anybody else was. What I couldn't understand was, if we were to avoid hypocrisy, how could we behave the same to those we didn't like as to those we did. Mother said, "If you know them, you'll like them." She said everyone has good qualities.

It was not enough that we be wholesome, we must also appear to be. Neatness counted for a lot (today it would be called quiet grooming). Nails had to be short and polished only with a buffer. The clear liquid polish was frowned on, while red, so new and glamorous, was used by women of easy virtue; it advertised one's morals like smoking a cigarette. Even the tone of one's lipstick and the height of one's heels were revealing. I didn't agree, but I didn't make an issue of it for two reasons: one, I didn't dare and, two, it wasn't for always.

If these were our practices, we would make the right impression and have good reputations. "A good reputation lasts forever."

M Y   F A T H E R didn't intend to be penalized whenever he took his family along. He said if you plan and you're organized, you don't need much luggage. Obviously, the girls shared a drawing room. And, naturally, one suitcase, barely large enough for Edith's things. But then, my parents did the same. If there's no porter around, who's going to carry the bags? We traveled light indeed, very poor practice for my days ahead with Mr. Selznick.

We were told in advance what was expected of us. The head of the family should not have to round us up and say, "We're leaving in ten minutes." He had more on his mind than we did; we were to be ready. "If I can, you can." He was dead right. We would get to a station so early there would not be a soul on the platform. And to think I was going to marry a man who "held" trains.

When we were going to a party (obviously, with our parents), we girls were to be downstairs in the front hall with our wraps on, purses in hand, ready to leave when they came down. My father came first, my mother next, and out the door we went, trailing them, not a word.

If I wanted to go someplace with him and he said fifteen minutes, I'd better be out front. If I got there a few minutes late, I saw him drive off. There was no complaint out of him, no grievance from me. Next time I'd know better.

Just as important as punctuality was economy, but since my father never stopped emphasizing that "nothing is more important than health," food was one area where economy was not practiced. He took pride when at last he could provide the very best. As in all else, the key word was "wholesome." There was nothing canned, nothing fried, no leftovers, no make-overs. Fresh. We ate well, but without variety. "Restricted" hardly describes our cuisine. We had chicken—roast, broiled, or boiled; beef—roast, broiled, or boiled. Occasionally lamb chops or fish—broiled.

When we ate out, all we ever got to taste was what Papa wanted. When we traveled, Mother's eyes sparkled at the adventures listed on menus, and hope sprang in us girls. We would tell him what we wanted;

then he ordered as though he hadn't heard. "Your mother doesn't realize what kind of junk these people serve."

He lectured us on food and housekeeping; it was good training for our futures as wives. "You can't run a house if you don't know how to cook. Your cook will have no respect for you."

As we got older, another program was added: "You have to play a good game of golf." "I don't want to play golf, Dad. I want to play tennis." "Only bums play tennis. Look ahead. Golf will last you your whole life. You can share it with your husband." "Perhaps my husband won't play golf." Papa: "You play a good game, you can play with me. But learn to cook."

Later on, upset with us over anything, he would, as a parting shot, turn back and say, "What's more, they don't know how to cook." Quite right.

No one asked me if I wanted singing lessons, but Edie did, so that automatically included me. Or was it Mother's old dream of parlor accomplishments (ye gods, in *Hollywood!*)? Every teacher Mother found had a magic method and a different theory. One of them had me singing arias—the Jewel Song from *Faust,* no less—in a matter of months.

My diary reflects some of the vicissitudes:

"Sept. 6, 1924: I sang a little better (thank God). I am a contralto."

"Jan. 13, 1925: new teacher . . . I sang my first high note (how memorable!) and was diagnosed as a coloratura.

"Jan. 14, 1925: Had voice tested. A new analysis—low.

"Feb. 6, 1925: I'm going to be a high soprano—but I'll *never* be really good."

I was right on the button there. Moreover, being disinclined to emotional interpretation, I sang deadpan; I didn't want to "give vent." Edie specialized in Mimi and Madame Butterfly. These lessons went on for years, and were the margin of difference to Edie; they were her lifeline and helped maintain her illusions.

A lot of me was wound up to go somewhere, and I landed in the library. Reading was at least private. The bookshelves in the Mayer family held impressive-looking sets of books, but "nothing to read." It was not exactly a bookish family. But now I read novels by the yard, and took out my vapors in poetry, with a higher regard for what I couldn't completely comprehend.

Before, reading for pleasure had been a reward for work done. Now, reading at random, I felt uneasy. There was no one to account to, so I accounted to myself. I wrote a short, very private report on each book for absolutely no purpose whatsoever, a make-work project.

My mother must surely have told my father about all this reading, because one day he suggested that if I came across any possible screen material, I should call the head of the story department. Mrs. Lee, however, was not exactly awaiting suggestions from the boss's daughter. I found her more courteous than interested, and, overawed as I was by professionals, I backed away. My one chance to speak my mind went for naught.

Social life revolved around the studio people—executives and directors, occasionally a few writers and actors. At the heart of it was the studio family, which by this time included, apart from the Thalbergs, the Harry Rapfs and the Hunt Strombergs. Hunt had only recently joined, but was an important part of the production team. Harry, who had been on Mission Road, was a warm-hearted, sentimental man with a great sense of showmanship. At one time he had worked for Lewis J. Selznick and later played a part in his life . . . and mine.

The social gatherings grew in size and number, and my pleasure accordingly. Our obligation was to protect the studio family. We were told that by helping to keep them happy we made a contribution. "Justify your presence by being useful." We were not to talk to someone we liked, but to someone neglected, usually a member of somebody's family. I never got good marks for it, only bad marks if I didn't; good training, but not much fun. My father said it was a fine way to keep humility.

It was also a kind of balancing act, not saying what you're not supposed to, and yet not being a bore . . . and trying to learn to like everyone. I was being myself, all right, but only a small part of myself. I wondered, when do I act on my convictions, embrace what I truly like without hurting anyone?

On and on he lectured about dignity and about bums . . . it was his way of neutralizing what he was exposing us to. If you have the right values, the *dignity,* none of this will touch you. If you're forewarned of the pitfalls and the problems, you don't have to wait for life to teach you. His puritanical instincts were being violated by his young female stars, who he thought needed protection and a guiding hand, and the more he gleaned of the lives of his young actresses, the more we got the backlash and the moralizing. He was a very unsophisticated man threatened by a sea of iniquity. The family was threatened, the studio was threatened, the industry was threatened!

At least he was consistent. When he hauled off at Jack Gilbert, then the number-one male star, it was because Jack had trodden on his most

sacred concept: motherhood. Jack came to my father's office one morning
to tell him about a story he was eager to do. My father pronounced the
material impossible, as the woman in the story was a whore and also a
mother, an inconceivable combination. Jack said not at all, *his* mother had
been a whore. My father demanded that he take that back. Jack not only
refused, he went further, whereupon Dad knocked him cold. No love was
lost between them from then on.

But Jack's career at MGM was not dependent on my father's good will,
because a big star is a big star, and anyhow he had Irving as a great friend.
When his popularity did not survive the advent of sound, however, Jack
decided that my father had set out to ruin him by having his voice come
over badly. Not even my father could have managed that while the other
people in the scenes with him sounded normal. The fact is that Jack had
been an idol and his voice just didn't match the public's vision of him.
Nevertheless, Jack remained my own personal screen hero, rather than
Valentino before him or Gable after. So I was particularly astonished
many years later, in my tennis house one Sunday afternoon, to be grabbed
in his arms and be told he had always been just a little in love with me
(his standard overture, I assumed). What a perfect revenge he might have
had on my father, if I hadn't been more flattered than tempted.

When we went to dinner parties, I was expected to hold up my end,
talking to my right and to my left, definitely not more. I obeyed, but
I didn't just listen passively to the general conversation, I maintained a
continuous dialogue—inside my head. What is odd is that I didn't think
that odd at all.

Larger parties gave more freedom. I was surrounded at these by
handsome young women with winning ways, asserting their personalities
and wooing favor. I badly needed a model, and there was none. I honestly
think I was without affectation, which gave me whatever individuality
I may have had. What I wanted was not being denied, only postponed.
In my mind stood the mathematical ratio: the greater the restraint, the
greater the reward. Besides, the sum total was so great, there was no point
in poisoning my paradise by concentrating on the single deprivation.

O N L Y a few in Hollywood owned their own houses, and at MGM no
one had yet "built." That would really mean you were there to stay. Still,
it was time now for us to move. Even my father knew our home was

too modest; besides, it was forty minutes from Culver City. Edie and I
had gone house-crazy and covered Beverly Hills. I would line them up,
and what didn't get vetoed by her was vetoed by my father, and when
our own house was sold, we rented an interim furnished house in Fremont
Place, a conservative neighborhood only half as far from the studio. It
was a distinguished, classic Italian house unlike any other in Los Angeles.
It was outside our ken, but we knew it was beautiful. I learned something
about quality there.

It was there I had my first gentleman caller, a brilliant young pianist
by the name of Mischa Levitzki, visiting Los Angeles on a concert tour.
He was quite handsome, and the hostesses and other ladies vied for his
time and attention. He, however, sought me out, and wanted to make
an engagement with me.

Consternation reigned. Obviously, I couldn't go out with him!
Mother suggested a compromise: that I ask him for tea, a meal not
customarily served in our home—in fact, I don't quite recall anyone ever
before being invited to tea. But my mother thought it a small enough
dividend to be permitted me.

I found his visit entrancing and had great difficulty with the ensuing
telephone calls, which wound up in still another tea invitation, some hurt
on his part, and the beginning of a tiny bit of female confidence in me.

With misgivings and against his will, my father widened his circle. The
social pressure increased with his position. He became, if not gregarious,
a little more outgoing. For example, we had Chaplin to dinner. Nary a
word of the past.

By this time Charlie had another child-bride, named Lita Grey, handsome and already heavily pregnant with her second child. Either the
signals got crossed or there hadn't been any, because Mrs. Chaplin arrived
at this little family meal in a white satin evening gown. It was short, bare,
and edged with beautiful crystal beading. Over this she wore white fox
furs, all quite stunning. The effect was heightened by the fact that Charlie
wore mufti. No one commented. Charlie was charming, Lita proved to
be very nice. It was an uneventful evening, memorable only for its
incongruity and because he was the first great celebrity to dine in our
house.

Not only did celebrities from the studio rarely visit us, but unlike
many children of Hollywood, Edie and I were not given the run of the
studio. In fact, we were rarely invited, so a visit became an occasion.
Once, though, before a trip to New York in 1925, my father contradicted

himself not only by ordering us several custom-made outfits, but by having them made at the studio. (He paid for them, needless to say.) The point was for the Mayer girls, then approaching marriageable age, to make a decent impression in New York.

Going to the wardrobe department for a fitting just happened to give us the opportunity of meeting a newcomer the very day she arrived on the lot. She was later named Joan Crawford. I thought she was preposterous—moon-faced, overweight, with frizzy hair, and she was wearing a tight black silk dress and an unfortunate pair of shiny black shoes, notable for the pompoms which adorned them. She caught on quickly and changed her style.

Joan tried harder than anyone else had ever tried. With increasing recognition, her determination became almost tangible. She blamed her overwhelming sense of rivalry on the preferred position Norma Shearer came to hold as Irving's wife, ignoring the fact that even Norma didn't always get the roles she wanted. She also overlooked the fact that Norma had been with the company since early Mission Road and had traveled a long way. The truth was that as the ever-growing group of MGM actresses reached stardom, each found the competition intense. Every one of them had come up through the ranks except Garbo; she began as a star.

E X P A N S I O N had begun, and in Beverly Hills houses were springing up like mushrooms. People were building, but Dad still said it was out of the question for us because people lost their heads; it was better to see what you're getting. When spring came and we hadn't been able to find the right house to buy, we thought of renting one near the Santa Monica Swimming Club for the summer while we went on looking. Renting for a few months would give Mother a chunk, if only for a brief time, of her heart's desire: the ultimate—to live with nothing between her home and the sea but sand.

There were slim pickings when we went to look, because the desirable beach ran less than a fifth of a mile from the Swimming Club and held then only about twenty houses. The steep cliffs of the palisades dropped to the Ocean Front road, along which were entrance gates and garages. Beyond them were the houses and the sea. It didn't seem very practical to me. If there was an earthquake, the palisades would tumble down; or if a tidal wave came, it would wash right over us. You got it coming and going.

The few available houses were either inadequate or wildly expensive for a short season. Now we were stymied and felt sunk; we discovered how much our hopes had rested on that idea. Our desperation propelled Dad into action. If the beach was so desirable, why bother about Beverly Hills? He knew it had always been in the back of Mother's mind; besides, it was closest to the studio. Find it and he'd buy it. There were none to buy? In that case, he'd build. Bombshell! Dream castles danced in the air. We could meanwhile take any old thing to be near the project.

My father said rent or build, not both. "You want to be in by summer? When we need a set at the studio, we build it overnight. We need a big village, we build it in weeks. Don't be at the mercy of those contractors. Don't start with the architects. With us, it's business, it gets done. I will talk to the people at the studio. If it can be done for the summer, we will have the beach house."

His momentum sounded far from ideal. This was not how we would do it. Besides, it meant really living there—we'd be practically marooned eight months a year. But he was in a take-it-or-leave-it mood. Mother was elated. The next day my father announced that the plans could be knocked out in a couple of weeks and the house built in six, provided that three shifts of workers were used. It was mind-boggling.

Cedric Gibbons would design the house, even though he wasn't an architect. He was trusted daily with far greater responsibilities than the Mayer beach house. Joe Cohn, the production manager, would know which key people could go on temporary leave to expedite the job. They would be scrupulous about charges lest a bad example be set; however, they would get outside labor, because studio workers' pay was prohibitive.

The lots were only thirty feet wide, at a fortune a foot, and 180 deep if anyone cared. A few houses had double lots, and so did we, and thirty feet as well between us and Jesse Lasky, which Dad prudently bought.

Dad said the beach houses were flimsy. If we built our home, it would be a house for all seasons. He got down to his basics: firm foundation. At last his philosophy could be applied literally. There was an inadequate breakwater then, and the seas could be very heavy, so the advice was to have a sea wall and to put the house on twenty-foot pilings; the pool too, if there was to be one. My father knew all about pilings from New Brunswick, and said, "We will have thirty-foot pilings for the house and the pool and then there will be give and there will be no cracking." It would cost money, but not money that showed. Conspicuous expenditure brought envy and bad luck. Extravagance should be put on the screen where it counted.

Enormous floodlights were installed (oh, the poor Laskys!). Three shifts seven days a week might seem excessive, but Dad said it would be cheaper in the end, because then there'd be no indecision or changes. He said it was self-evident which rooms would face the sea, and he would leave it to his three ladies to tell Gibbons what we needed. I am sure he saw the plans, but he delegated the authority. Mother yielded hers and said she would rely on "my girls. Just give me a balcony on the sea."

Six weeks is a tall story. Therefore I recently checked with Joe Cohn, who said, "Unlikely but true."

I can see there was a method in my father's madness. Life in Santa Monica would be informal. There was no risk of the grand living then starting up in Beverly Hills. He knew that building at the beach gave us more limitations than latitude and there couldn't be waste space; we would make every square foot count. He was pleased at the result, but his continuing pride was in the underpinnings of the structure.

There were four bedrooms and three servants, plus a chauffeur and a handyman, who also drove Grandpa around (a striking contrast to the seventeen employees next door at the Lasky house). Our scale of living stayed constant. We did not get grander with the years.

The beach was not entirely self-indulgence on Mother's part. She saw it as a way to open the door a little wider and to inch my father into having people at the house and giving us a slightly freer life. We were where everyone wanted to be, beginning with Mother; she loved that house, and she said she would as long as she lived. She left it to Edie and me when she died. It was sound, all right. It was so sound that, thirty years after it was built, we sold it to Pat Kennedy and Peter Lawford, and it became President Kennedy's base whenever he was in Los Angeles.

The irony of prosperity: my mother had her house at the beach, but her darling daughter was out there baking her skin to bronze when, in Mother's eyes, milk-white was the prime requisite for feminine beauty.

My father still thought learning to share would keep Edie and me close. It was important for our future, too, because a successful marriage meant sharing. Therefore start early, share with your sister. (Instead of making me easier to live with, I'm sure it had the reverse effect. When I got married, it was a different kind of togetherness I anticipated, one with a space I could call my own. I wanted a His and Hers; we could have Our bed—as long as he had one in his room too.)

As children we shared the same room and same bed until Edith took ill. Ocean Front is where sharing reached a fare-thee-well. Here we again shared a bedroom and we shared the desk—and we were supposed to share the big closet and the bathroom. We shared a car. When you share a car and live at the beach, you damn well learn to share activities. You put up with a lot you wouldn't otherwise, including those hopeless singing lessons. In any case, neither of us could get in too much trouble with a sister as chaperone.

However, parity didn't exist. How could it? I had rude good health. My life had not been interrupted, and I was having a fine time. My parents kept reminding me I was more fortunate than Edith. While "Learn to share" had once been the slogan, it later became "Sacrifice for your sister." Gradually added to that was "Your sister is your responsibility. Who will take care of her after we're gone?" Little did they know how strong she was. (Well, neither did I.) My mother told me to give in to her, even beyond her rights of seniority. I gave in to her, all right. I couldn't get out of bed until she woke, because her sleep was important. Nor could I use the bathroom until she was finished.

We never quarreled. Edie knew I wouldn't talk back and I wouldn't tattle. I went along with everything because she had been unlucky.

Apart from everything else, Edie preferred my face to her own. She was at pains to tell me which of my features she should have had, but then she also pointed out that her hands were prettier and that she was more graceful. Edie said eyes should be used to attract men, and she was not at all embarrassed to be found practicing in the mirror. Smiles were necessary and also practiced.

Edie advised me that men didn't like women to be clever; it wasn't feminine, and nothing was more important than femininity! Edie was just as clever as I was and then some, so she ought to know.

We stuck increasingly to our assigned roles. The more Edie cared about adornment, the more I shunned it. The more she lived in daydreams and gloried in illusion, the more down-to-earth and realistic I became. We must have polarized each other as the years went by. We took increasing pleasure in being distinctly unlike each other. The longer it took Edie to dress, the more I became the fireman's child.

Edie favored pastels, chiffon, and anything soft and lovely. I was tailored, crisp, and to the point.

There were other differences. I kept scraps of paper, snapshots, memorabilia, a habit Edie viewed with disdain. Her desk drawer was swept clean. I reminisced; Edie could not remember the names of our friends in Brookline. "Don't be ridiculous, always dragging the past along." In fact, when she got married, she took nothing—no article of clothing, no mementoes; a very streamlined operation.

There were, of course, certain attitudes and economies we had to share. For instance: it was better not to buy dark things because lighter things could be dyed and it doesn't work the other way around; make-over possibilities always had to be borne in mind when something was purchased. Above all, the color had to go with what shoes, purse, or coat one already had. A great education, that, learning to make do. Make do? I was practically done in by it. Not then, but later, when I had to learn to shake the habit.

I must say Edith and I were both very handy with our hats. I still insist no one could tell that it was the reblocked straw from last summer with a change of brim and trim, at the cost of only a few dollars.

With economies such as these, one could save up and buy clothes in New York, which, for reasons I have forgotten or didn't exist, were far superior. Once we got the hang of that, occasionally it was wholesale houses, the best wholesale houses, a privilege then rarely available. I hated it then and I hate it now. There are other ways to save money.

Edith, obsessed with clothes, said we ought to have an allowance from Dad. I thought that daring. Mother gave us pocket money and paid for our things, so she found the idea threatening; it would make her feel her "birdies were out of the nest." Her way kept us close. Also she was too tender-hearted to contemplate taking money from us when she checked her monthly bills.

Edie went ahead and made her case. My father was dubious. His girls were not going to learn to spend if he could help it. He said he was training us to be poor men's wives because what you haven't got you won't miss. If you married a man without money, he wouldn't complain about being married to a rich man's daughter. If the man had money, we would have things to look forward to.

I felt I had to speak up. I promised that the allowance would cover every single thing. In addition, it would teach us how to ration ourselves.

After consideration he announced that Edie was to have the princely sum of $100 a month, and $75 for me, but with the stipulation that we each save $25 a month. Edie said it was ridiculous "in our position." I have to admit that that time Edie was dead right. My father had overshot the mark. I really couldn't see how I was going to pay for presents, amusements, fan magazines, cosmetics, manicures, all my clothes, and still save. It was terrible. When it was raised to $125 and $100, I managed, but I became impossible. I was so anxious to keep my word that I tried to police Mother and Edie, but I couldn't make them hew the line. Would I let Mother pay for some little thing? No, not horrible me. It upset Mother terribly that her girls were paying her $3 for a large jar of Elizabeth Arden cleansing cream, which we then divided carefully in half. (Edie later upgraded her girlhood. Her daughter Barbara, who is a friend of mine, recently said: "But my mother was brought up as a princess." "Who told you that?" "My mother." "Well, *I* wasn't.")

However, there were some negotiations between Edie and Mother which I just didn't want to know about. I would leave the room and brood. But I began to see how Edie's money went so much further than mine. Also, she didn't save a red cent. She said it was impossible and Dad didn't expect us to, and, besides, the allowance wasn't enough as it was. She wasn't afraid of a showdown and I could be a martyr if I pleased. I was a damn fool in her view. She was right. As it turned out, Edie was more practical than I was. I was a stickler and did myself in. I started by being virtuous and ended by wanting to show Edie up. I waited years for the day of reckoning and my recognition, but it never came; no one knew or cared, and it served me right. Paragons can be a pain in the neck.

Our lives were an open book, and as there were no locks ("Young girls don't need locks if they have nothing to be ashamed of"), privacy was not invaded. It did not exist.

It never had. The family-proof pages of my 1924 diary reveal my whereabouts, but nothing I truly felt. The only significant line in it is that I would remember the thoughts which lay underneath. I kept it a few months and never again went on record. It is only now, reading it over, that I feel sorry for that girl. My family gave me everything except privacy and a sense of my own worth.

WE BEGAN going to more interesting parties. This period marked the beginning of what can only be called "wide acquaintance."

Joe Schenck had more than his share of influence with my father, or the family certainly wouldn't have been allowed to go to his parties. Joe was an unorthodox host; he casually had the great, and boldly had the raffish; his wife, Norma Talmadge, had whom she pleased, and neither of them cared about the mix. It was there I stood talking to Valentino, only half able to keep going for fear my father would walk into the room and discover me. He would have raised hell because I should have had better judgment. But I did think, oh, if those girls from school could see me now!

My father liked pinochle but not parties. If he couldn't avoid them, he could duck the small talk, at which he was not adept, by having a quiet little no-stakes game off in a corner, where he was less likely to be importuned. He did, after all, cope with careers all day long.

The only other thing he enjoyed evenings, apart from staying home, was dancing. He was a tireless, straightforward dancer who sat down at the tango, jumped up for the waltz, and deplored the Charleston when it came in. Dad was always the first out on the floor. He obeyed the protocol and danced first with whom he should, but from then on he took them all on, plain or fancy, old or young, provided they were light on their feet. Afterward he could be very funny, demonstrating how he suffered with the tugboats. He couldn't understand why they didn't want to relax and follow. They followed him, all right, after twice around the floor, right back to the table.

The best dance music in town was at the Cocoanut Grove, a great place to see everyone and be seen. You knew where you stood from where you sat. I would look enviously at those ringside tables for two, the beautiful people, particularly the young ones. There were two girls my age who were the belles: Jane Peters, who later became Carole Lombard, and Dorothy Hart, who first became Mrs. Jack Hearst, then Mrs. Bill Paley.

I was excited to be there at all, even though we were always at a long, narrow table which stretched back from the dance floor. My seating could make all the difference. The best seat, the most fun, would have been next to Irving. That never happened, ever, to Edie or me. One was, however, permitted to dance with him. There would be eyes on me hoping to catch a hint of something going on. No more went on than met the eye. He taught me to twirl, and twirl we did, around the Cocoanut Grove floor.

I don't know which Henrietta found more threatening, Irving's nights out with the "boys"—men-about-town who introduced him to "dissipation"—or when he dated various young women. I think she preferred the latter, provided none of it got serious. Flirtations were acceptable, but serious intentions were dangerous. She could not afford to put his fate in the hands of a wife; and no one could afford to let the whole truth of his health be known.

In the first flush of his success at Universal, it must have been thrilling for Henrietta that her son found favor with the great princess, Rosabelle Laemmle, whose father, Carl, owned the studio. However, this romance could not have been easy for Henrietta, because the Thalberg family would necessarily have had to show Rosabelle enormous deference. Rosabelle was used to authority. Henrietta was relieved when the alliance waned. He played around a bit, and then quite suddenly Constance Talmadge came into his life.

She scintillated. She was not only the toast of the town in New York, she was the only movie star who moved in the better circles of Europe and London. She was the first of the sophisticated comediennes, and her off-screen personality matched. She dressed in a style as suitable to the Continent as it was unknown to Hollywood, understated but irresistible. In the film world she had the additional prestige of being the youngest sister of Norma, still the top dramatic star of her day.

This was very heady wine for Irving. Constance brought out in him an even more charming personality than we had heretofore seen. They were a magical couple with an immense delight in each other. Irving behaved with her as he did with no other woman. Seeing him like this, one forgot there was any possible shadow over him.

Henrietta was alarmed. There were too many parties and too much dancing. To her relief, Constance would frequently slip off to New York and Europe, and in these periods Norma Shearer emerged as an occasional date. She said she'd keep Irving company while Constance was away and keep him out of trouble. However, during one of Connie's longer journeys we decided that Irving must be falling in love with Norma, because Henrietta began to praise Rosabelle Laemmle for the first time: how good a wife Rosabelle would be for Irving; how life-threatening Constance was. "She's frivolous, she's not concerned with his health, with his future. Rosabelle would understand." Then as Norma stood by and Rosabelle suddenly reappeared in Irving's life in quite a serious way, Henrietta praised Constance and told us how spoiled and imperious Rosabelle was. You knew which lady was up according to Henrietta's heated partisanship of the others.

Neither Rosabelle nor Constance was permanent in Los Angeles, but Norma Shearer was. Also, she was determined . . . but non-possessive. She would say, laughingly, "I'm Irving's spare tire. When Rosabelle and Constance are away, or someone stands him up, I'm always available, I'll break a date any time to be with him." She said she was biding her time. When Irving escorted Norma to parties to which Henrietta was invited, Norma would be dropped first and Henrietta would wait in the car while Irving said his goodnights. Norma made the best friends she could, under the circumstances, of Henrietta and of Sylvia, Irving's unmarried sister. When Irving began to see more of her, to spare him the exertion of taking her home, Norma spent the summer as a houseguest when Henrietta took a place at the beach. It was a sincere effort to become assimilated within the family, and it suited Henrietta, provided it went no further.

It took Norma four or five years to get him. The decision came quite suddenly. One night my father came home with a breathless bulletin: "Irving's decided to marry her! There's no risk—everything will go on as it was, Henrietta's accepted the situation." Norma agreed to move in with the family, as she didn't dare risk upsetting the conditions of his life. She didn't wish to rob him of his mother; she only wanted to add her own presence. Her visits would no longer be confined to summer at the beach.

There was to be a very small wedding within a few weeks. With the date only a week off, something amazing happened: Edie and I were asked to be bridesmaids! This was stupendous. Soon we were being fitted for dresses—simple organdy; organdy hats to match. They were to be all the same style, but we could pick our own pastel tints. It was frantic but thrilling. And there we were, along with Marion Davies and Bessie Love; Sylvia Thalberg, maid of honor; Norma's sister, Athole (now married to Irving's good friend Howard Hawks), matron of honor.

Norma became a live-in wife without too many prerogatives. It remained Henrietta's house; she sat at the head of the table. At the other end sat her husband, William, a pale man with pale blue eyes and a pale personality. Guests were invited by Henrietta, and she was the hostess who was thanked. The servants were hers, as were the menus. Norma and Henrietta managed, but there could never have been real peace between mother and wife; not because the wife could be held to be a rival, but because she would not be a watchdog, hardly a role for a bride. When Norma became pregnant four years later, she told Henrietta, "Alas, we will be too many; I just can't live here any more. Isn't that a pity!" To us she said, "It was the only way I could get out of there."

THE BEACH at Santa Monica had become a magnet. Those who longed for the sea joined the club and considered acquiring houses. The club had been the lure for us. Its membership was a cross-section of civilians with a sprinkling of film names banned from the adjoining club, a grander place called the Beach Club, which catered to Los Angeles society. (Ironically, it was a faster group.) Mother thought our proximity to the club would give us added opportunities to "reach out."

Now I was no longer limited in outlets—I had the most desirable front yard in town. It extended all the way to the club. It was great fun for me to run down the beach a couple of times a day with an extra swim at the club and a lovely run back. I became a familiar figure and I made friends with the people who lived between us and the club. I was no longer the girl on the white horse, I was the girl in the yellow bathing suit.

I acquired new habits, new ideas, and some unlikely new friends. There would be tantalizing tastes of the great world as I went by and either Mr. or Mrs. Lasky would call out to me to come and sit down and visit. Why not? After all, they were next-door neighbors, eminently respectable, and it was daylight and out-of-doors. . . . However, I always reported it at home so I would be trusted and not upset the apple cart.

Walter Wanger, who was a glamorous New York figure, an important executive at Paramount, stayed at the Laskys' on his frequent trips to California. I got to know him because he seemed to like to swim at the time I swam, a subtle approach wasted on me. He was too worldly and attractive for the likes of me, and I took his compliments as courtesies; that is, until later on.

I failed to recognize an even subtler approach along that same stretch of beach, at a house rented by *two* worldly and attractive bachelors named Richard Barthelmess and William Powell. They were gentlemanly to such a degree that I never suspected that any possible physical charms of mine had anything to do with the cordiality of their invitations to sit awhile on the sand. When they admired my tan, I thought they meant my *tan*. Years later they would retell these encounters in a very funny fashion.

Each summer there were delicious surprises over who was renting the still-rentable houses. Over the years the tenants included Arthur Hornblow, Anita Loos, Irving Thalberg, Sam Goldwyn, Jascha Heifetz and Florence Vidor, and Marion Davies. Those who bought or built were graduates of either the Swimming Club or a rented house. About five years later Irving built on that tiny stretch, and so did Sam Goldwyn, then Harold Lloyd. Much later so did my sister and the Zanucks. To my astonishment, I wound up there a couple of summers myself in a rented house shortly after my marriage.

The Laskys often had intriguing houseguests, and one morning they impulsively asked me to a party they were giving to introduce a radio man named William Paley to Hollywood. Of course I couldn't go. Then, longingly watching the dance floor being built over the swimming pool, I mentioned the invitation to my mother. She managed it with Dad, but unknowingly put a crimp in my pleasure by saying she was going to enjoy it too, by watching it all from her balcony. That was worse than being chaperoned; I was home by eleven. But I did get to go and I did meet the attractive guest of honor.

However, I did not report the Sam Goldwyns, who were often at the club. I longed to talk to them, but I didn't dare. Sam sensed this and shamed me into sitting down.

The Goldwyns, recently married, were forbidden fruit. My father detested Sam and Sam detested my father. My father thought Sam's wife, Frances, was a marvelous woman; her only defect was her lack of judgment in marrying Sam. The hostility dated back to my father's days in Haverhill. Sam Goldfish, before he became Sam Goldwyn, was attracted to show business. Although based in Gloversville and still selling gloves, he was also wooing Jesse Lasky's sister, Blanche, in New York. This worried Lasky. Jesse, a nice fellow who happened to know my father because he had sold him vaudeville acts, asked my father's opinion of Sam, whereupon my father said that if it were his sister, he'd stop the marriage. Jesse told Blanche and Blanche told her bridegroom. At least Sam's hostility was understandable. My father's feeling for Sam was more generalized: he just plain didn't like him. (Small-world department: twenty-five years later Sam, Jesse, and L.B. each had a house on Ocean Front, all within one hundred yards of each other.)

After he was ousted from the Goldwyn company in 1922, Sam couldn't call his name his own. Each time he used it, he was required to add: "Not now connected with Goldwyn Pictures." MGM at least let up on this stipulation. With a straight face Sam pretended to resent his name being used to advertise MGM films. Obviously, he had the last laugh: MGM still spreads Sam's name to the four corners of the earth, just as it does my father's. To this day people ask me about the long association between the two of them.

Frances had made a hit on the stage and won the lead in the film of *The Swan,* for which her aristocratic beauty was perfect, but she didn't care about acting. She had a mind of her own and was correct in thinking she would have her hands full as Sam's wife. She catered to him, but she also took him in hand and started to mend some of his broken fences, even to the point of inviting my parents to dinner, short-lived as those occasional truces would be. Frances treated me like a friend. Sam treated me like a bright kid, although I was only three years younger than his bride. He would tease me by asking if I'd defy my father when I got married and invite him to my wedding.

THE YEARS 1926 to 1930 were years of emergence, of learning by doing, for all of us. My mother, being sociable and gregarious, was absolutely delighted. It began when she started suggesting to people that they drop by and "look at the house" if they "happened" to be at the beach on Sunday. Having arrived, they were urged to stay on for supper and a movie or cards . . . "and next time bring your bathing suit." We began to stock assorted sizes of bathing suits.

After the first excitement wore off and our Sunday buffets became established, Edie and I were out to enlarge the cast, varying it and making things more interesting. If there weren't young people, then please could we have something more glamorous and fascinating? My father didn't want glamorous, fascinating, stimulating, or intellectual. He had enough challenge in the studio. The glamour people belonged on the screen and did not create the environment he wanted in his home. He didn't get things all his own way, which was just as well. When he had more demanding guests—such as Norma Talmadge and Joe Schenk, Mr. Hearst and Marion (and of course Irving when he became emancipated)—he found it useful, almost necessary, to produce some drawing cards to supplement the more conservative group. The most unexpected appearance was that of Garbo, heretofore not seen dressed up or at parties. She came in a feminine, chic, black velvet suit, on the arm of Jack Gilbert, in itself an unlikely event in our house. It was at the height of their romance and the gay mood of their evening brought them over. Our location had an impulse factor built in. It was not unheard of for people to stop by uninvited.

Only occasionally would Mother yield to temptation and sneak a relative in. One Sunday there was a reverse twist: a relative showed up, one who protested all the way. The poor fellow absolutely loathed the idea. Inasmuch as he was quite funny, it will not come as a surprise if I say it was Oscar Levant, my mother's cousin. He kept shaking his head and finally said, "If this ever gets out, I'm ruined!"

It was wonderful experience for Edie and me to handle the ever-changing array of guests and to assist with menus and arrangements. Mother said we were indispensable. However, for all her darling traits, my mother was enormously touchy about advice concerning her home. As if we would—or could—usurp her authority, poor little darling; well, "Little Darling" is exactly what we called her then. Yet at the same time, not boldly confident over "worldly" details, she would seek our counsel and place two observant growing girls in a constant dilemma of how to tactfully suggest and arrange.

These parties were large and extremely informal, but there were smaller ones, structured and more exacting—a small dinner on a Friday night, or a Saturday lunch for someone my father wished particularly to honor, such as distinguished political figures, his old favorite Arthur Brisbane whenever he came to town, and, obviously, Mr. Hearst.

Of all my father's friends, it was these two men, from far afield, who took the trouble to find out what I was thinking. Mr. Brisbane would come fifteen minutes earlier than he was bidden to "have a little talk with Irene." Extraordinary. He wanted to know what made me tick, and would interrogate me. I was immune to being "sounded out," but as Mr. Brisbane's questions had nothing to do with Hollywood and he wouldn't permit me to get away with my usual noncommittal answers, I spoke up. Almost the best part was watching my father's pleasure when he joined us.

But my stronger relationship, though less personal, was with Mr. Hearst, known to me as Uncle William. I got on with men in relation to their age, the older the better; which was fine, since Mr. Hearst mattered so much to my father. The fact that he was a yellow journalist and kept a mistress was far overshadowed for my father by what he considered Hearst's brilliance. For a man who had ever looked not to his peers but to older and wiser men, Mr. Hearst was a boon. That Hearst admired and respected him meant a great deal. They had many interests in common, films starring Marion Davies being but one of them. (Hearst's Cosmopolitan Pictures had come with the merger.) He seemed to consult my father on all kinds of matters—politics, finance, and even the Hearst Corporation. The two men would walk and talk and sit and talk . . . and the affection between them was clear. Towering above him, Hearst would place his hand on my father's head for emphasis and pat it as he spoke, calling him "Son." They were certainly an incongruous pair. Hearst tall, portly, a man with light blue eyes and a high-pitched voice who appeared not to have too much on his mind, and whose inner self never seemed to surface; my father stocky, compact, dynamic. Although they came to a parting of the ways in business, their friendship lasted until Hearst died. Considering Dad's propriety, I am at a loss to explain how he reconciled our being exposed to Marion.

We certainly must have bored the life out of her. When L.B. went to call, he was accompanied by a lady who had to be addressed as Mrs. Mayer and always those girls. I viewed us through her eyes as two inhibited little goody-goodies, way-down unsophisticated. She was a mischievous, gay companion to those she surrounded herself with— amusing people or celebrities, preferably both, plus some stooges and plenty of relatives.

I never heard my father either criticize or praise Marion, although he did remark more than once on how loyal she had been when W.R. met with reverses and she put up her jewelry and real estate to see him through. But she was neither gallant nor generous in his late years, and I felt almost justified in having been dubious about her.

But credit where credit is due. She was merry; she did have flashes of genuine talent—a lovely comic spirit and some charm. (She was more a hoyden than a heroine.) But that was it, that and Hearst's power. Maybe she was generous—she certainly was to her pals—but it was easy come, easy go, and she did have a fortune at her fingertips. As for her drinking, there was a lot of it—and a lot of jokes to do with smuggling drinks in for Marion. But I never saw her drunk, only what I would call tipsy; one degree less elfin, one degree closer to tawdry.

What was clearest was that Mr. Hearst loved her. I had not yet learned that imperfections can be endearing. He could have had his choice of beauties, but her gamine quality seemed to hold endless appeal. It didn't occur to me that *she* loved *him* until shortly after his death, when she married a not very prosperous or engaging fellow who bore an uncanny resemblance to him.

Hearst came often to our house because he liked seeing my father away from the distractions of his office, and because he loved to swim at the beach; we had a bathing suit put by for him. Then he decided that he would like to have still another house, a little one at the beach. He bought a broad, nondescript shingle place which Marion had rented for a summer, then bought a house nearby, and after that, the empty lot between. Then he bought still another lot, and then he merged the houses, as they were too small. As the new place began to take shape, he decided it was not really what he wanted, tore it all down, and bought considerably more footage at ever-escalating prices.

The great mansion began to assume its overpowering position on the beach and I became increasingly fascinated, and as it was on my turf, I was constantly drawn to have a look at what was going on. One day, to my embarrassment, I was discovered by Mr. Hearst. He had heard I'd been there and insisted on giving me the complete tour. He even said he hoped I'd come back. After that, whenever I went along the sand, I would keep my eye out for him. I didn't want to snoop; under these privileged circumstances I felt it right to go only when he was there.

Out of my experience with Cedric Gibbons, I had a frame of reference; at least Mr. Hearst treated me as if I had. My visits came to be almost definite appointments. As we parted, he would announce when he would be there next. He never said he expected me, but when I showed up, he'd say he'd been wondering where I was.

I learned about Georgian paneling, original brasses, and a lot more about mantels and overmantels than I ever had need to know. He had a pupil. More important for him, he had a companion in his house-building, since Marion never bothered to come, and he had a passion for building. I was more an accident than a choice.

The house became in a sense "our project." I was present when shipments from abroad were uncrated. He didn't let me feel in the way even when his consultant came from London for her periodic visits.

I learned not to flee in terror when he was angry, but to stand at a comfortable distance. He would then call out, "Come on, Irene." I would say, "Coming, Uncle William." We never discussed anything but details of the architecture, the imports, and what was to be done about the pool. The pool was begun several times; he increased its length, changed its depth. Once done, its interior surface was changed to an extraordinary design in mosaic.

With workmen here and there and crates everywhere, he said we were going to have a special event, a formal ceremony: he and I were going to baptize the pool. He set the date for the following week.

He was there before me on the appointed hour; the water in the pool sparkled—a perfect day, a perfect moment. But I didn't get the welcome I expected because he was upset, more upset than I had ever seen him. There was a problem which appeared minor (to me): Uncle William didn't have a bathing suit.

He covered all the rooms upstairs and I devoted myself to the base-ment, which was temporarily a supply depot. It was piled high with enormous cartons of bathing suits, every size except his. I regretted being present, but a graceful exit was no longer possible. He went upstairs to telephone. Someone must have gotten hell, because even standing by the pool I could hear his high-pitched voice. I closed my ears. When he returned, he was quiet and frightening. He declined my offer to run down the beach to get the suit we had for him. The moment had passed. Coldly, he asked me to conduct the so-called ceremony by myself; he would observe. It was no fun to mount the big board, swim the length, and come up to an unsmiling Uncle William. I fled down the beach, pained for the poor man who had been so humiliated.

There were many Hearsts, as contradictory as they were varied. I liked Uncle William the best, and I'm sure he liked us. There were presents to prove it, too. And the gifts were not only lavish, they were personal; and they were jewelry—always from Cartier. Mr. Hearst took the Mayer curse off Christmas. I thought the first year was a fluke, but it happened every Christmas until I married, and he shot the works. I still find it almost incredible, the amount of evident care he gave to every choice. He never gave my mother a piece of jewelry, yet every-thing was jeweled, whether it was a cigarette box or an evening purse; and my father's presents were also lavish. But it was the gifts he gave me and my sister I found extraordinary. They were related but different —cousins, not twins. Elegant but understated. First there were hat-pins, then fashionable. The next year we each got a narrow diamond watch on a black silken cord, with a face an eighth of an inch square. Then he gave us brooches—Edith's lapis lazuli with a few diamonds and mine onyx with a little red enamel and a few diamonds too; and we were actually allowed to wear them. I felt a woman of property, and it was no small thrill. Jewels! I was coming up in the world.

After the beach house opened, the parties were frequent and lavish. The house was so big that even after Marion had asked all her pals and Mr. Hearst everyone he wanted, there was still room for countless celebrities. The parties spread out through many rooms and I thought they were great—true galas. And I got attention from men, which pleased me as much as any girl, yet it still made me wonder whether I had done something wrong. I didn't think I had flirted, because I didn't know how to flirt. I wasn't shy, and if I wasn't poised, I seemed to give the impression of total assurance. Some men mistook this for sophistication and, coming closer, would say, "You're a baby! Remind me to look you up later on." Was this a compliment or an insult, and whom was I to ask?

Not Mr. Wanger. One night, on the long balcony facing the sea which ran the full width of the house, he approached me with a boldness I hadn't previously encountered from any man. He was so deliberately provocative that even Miss Innocence got the message. "Oh, Mr. Wanger, please. You musn't say such things to me. Please, Mr. Wanger." He went right on. I could feel myself going scarlet. Yet what I thought was, "What fun it would be to be truly grown up and sophisticated and able to handle a conversation like this one." I liked him. He was overt but beguiling. I've always felt the secret of his renowned success with the ladies was that he was truly crazy about them. He just liked women. I think it delighted him to make even the plainest woman feel irresistible.

He swam beside me the following morning and thereafter during that visit. Innocent but somehow forbidden. Definitely. It went on until my father spotted us.

HOWEVER active, we were still waiting for real life to begin. We musn't sit around—my mother said the devil found mischief for idle hands. I'd swim an eighth of a mile before breakfast in that sometimes cold and raging sea. I might play four sets of tennis or ride horseback or play golf, or all three, but there was a limit to exercise.

It must have been practical time, too. To keep me both busy and close at hand, Mother sent me off to business school, right there in Santa Monica. "Be useful." I hated it more than the singing, but I had a reprieve, because there was an unexpected trip to New York a week later. It was never mentioned again.

Then around noon one day, without warning, an ironing board and an electric iron showed up in our bedroom, followed soon after by Mother with an armful of damp linen. She told Edie and me to start ironing. We were baffled. Was she annoyed? Or had Dad said we were getting spoiled? Mother told us to start on handkerchiefs. We protested. "Do a couple of hand towels and then start on the handkerchiefs." Again we protested. "Why? What happened to the laundress?" "Iron. I'll be back." It was so completely unlike her. We ironed away. It was hard to get the edges even. After what seemed an endless time, she reappeared and said, "Fine, that's enough. Now that you know how hard it is and what time it takes, you girls will be more careful. You'll think twice about how you use handkerchiefs and towels." To tell the truth, for many, many years thereafter I started at the bottom of a hand towel and worked my way up. Only in a hotel would I presume to start with the middle of a hand towel.

In retrospect, it is deeply touching to realize how dedicated Mother was to each and every thing about us. She said that she could never get enough of us; she longed to know everything—our friends, our lessons. Her thirst for self-betterment was almost satisfied vicariously by our activities. Curiously, she was not possessive, yet she was more involved than was sensible for her.

My father emphasized to us girls that he set a good example of respecting one's parents. We had Honor Thy Mother and Father in living color.

My Grandfather Mayer lived with us off and on from the time we went to California. Considering the old man's cruelty when my father was young, this was a generous kind of revenge to take. It was a matter of continuing astonishment to me that the last five years of his life he spent in our Santa Monica home. His presence there reflected a virtue for which my father was admired, as well he might be. Grandpa would go on display at the dinner table with distinguished guests, his remarks studded with Talmudic lore, and he was thus considered a wise old man. Oh, how good my mother was to him. And she wouldn't hear a word against him, but I guessed a lot from her marveling at how he had mellowed.

The special role he played, which amused my father, was pleading for the relatives, most particularly for his daughter Ida Cummings, who had had two husbands and four children. Once Mother secured benefits for them, she'd let him be the hero. He would make an elaborate pitch, winding up with: "Louis, God made you the treasurer. Every family has one and that is why He gave you the brains and the strength. It is to earn money for the family."

I think he was fonder of Ida's children than of us. Ida had lived at home after she married, and her children had been to a degree under his control. In California he spent many afternoons at Ida's house, and as he was her envoy to my parents, he ruled there as he could not at ours.

He was a very cagey fellow, always looking for an opening, feigning benevolence, careful to be on his best behavior in front of Dad. I was respectful, but on guard. He used to say: "What is that look she gives? What is she thinking?" What I was thinking was that he was not very nice. Grandpa was the first person to sense there was a hint of the formidable in me. He watched his step too. How does a girl stir uneasiness in an old man?

I was a child who preferred grandmothers to grandfathers.

When I was a very little girl, my Grandmother Shenberg went on an unheard-of journey, which lasted six months. She traveled across the seas to Jerusalem in order to "take leave" of *her* mother, who had moved to the Holy Land to die so that she might be buried in sacred soil. Grandma brought back a towering, ivory-colored replica of the Temple of Jerusalem, about two feet square, which sat thereafter on her dining-room sideboard. More important, she brought back many sackfuls of earth, so that wherever she and her family were buried, there would be a token of this same sacred soil.

From time to time I went on missions for the relatives. There was one in which Edith was obliged to join me, and it was very special. My grandmother had suffered a severe stroke, which had resulted in total paralysis. As she gradually recovered, speech and movement on one side were restored; however, not a word of English was left; all that remained was her Yiddish. My sister and I would stop to see her on our way home from singing. I knew countless words and some phrases, learned before my parents caught on that both girls understood. Her embarrassment at her inability to communicate with us was so poignant that it actually enabled me to speak simple sentences in Yiddish, even translate for Edie. This temporary dispensation seemed to me a providential gift.

BUT EVEN with the occasional household responsibilities and the relatives and the endless exercise, it wasn't a very full life. What, for instance, was I supposed to do at dusk? I was caught all too often over a book. My mother said I would ruin my eyes, and my father said I knew too much already.

He had second thoughts. It was no small surprise to find him in our bedroom one morning, trying to smuggle in five large books and closing the door firmly behind him, very earnest, speaking in hushed tones. What he had to say was that we were of an age when we were being exposed to men, and harm could befall us unless we knew all there was to know. It was curiosity which made girls vulnerable; to know is to be forearmed. These books were to be our protection, and no harm would ever come to us if we but read these books.

He was in over his head, and I felt rather bad for him. He said he didn't know exactly what was in the volumes, but he didn't have to, because he would never come up against the kind of people that Edie and I would; we were living in different times and would be encountering more sophisticated people than he ever had. He thereupon presented us with all five volumes of *Studies in the Psychology of Sex* by Havelock Ellis. His parting remark was, "For heaven's sake, keep these away from your mother. She's as innocent as the day she was born."

That we already knew, because the year before we had gone to a matinee in New York of *The Captive,* starring Helen Menken, a distinguished play that became notorious when the cast landed in jail. One woman was crazy about another one and sent her violets. (Some years were to pass before violets could again be proposed by florists.) Mother was completely puzzled, shrugged when it was over, and said, "I don't know what that play's about. Do you?" We did, but we shrugged back.

Edie took a few dips into the books and found them absolutely disgusting. I read them one after the other, devouring every word, and dead certain Mr. Ellis was wrong about necrophilia: it couldn't be! I'm not sure whether this wasn't the beginning of my enormous interest in abnormal psychology. Those books were absolutely fascinating reading to me, however irrelevant to my life then or later. My father was the victim of bad advice, but he meant well, and I thought it was very brave of him.

OUR TRIPS to New York had a quite different pace and flavor from our lives in California. We were out with people every night, more often

than not at the theatre. And the Marcus Loews afforded us our first taste
of a fancy life. Mr. Loew was unassuming, with a personality far removed
from what one expected. His wife, Carrie, was warm-hearted, outgoing,
and towered over him. The only things pretentious about them were the
trappings, which had come about, one felt, out of direct competition with
Adolph Zukor and his wife, who did know their position. Zukor and
Loew had once been partners, but since then Zukor had the edge. Marcus's
son, Arthur, had married Zukor's daughter, Mildred, and now a new
rivalry was on.

The Zukors had a splendid estate with a private golf course; Marcus
Loew came through with the de la Marr estate in Glen Cove, which had
a two-story living room with a pipe organ. We felt as lost as they did
amid all that opulence. It was hard for Mrs. Loew to keep up with Mrs.
Zukor, who had more know-how in spending money. That was probably
why Marcus Loew had a private railroad car.

Marcus was very much a family man, although he liked to hang out
with his cronies. His homecomings would waken Carrie, who in the dark
would say, "Is that you, Marcus? What time is it?" Marcus invariably
said, "Plenty past twelve." Always the same time? One night she turned
on the light and a new regime began. At least she told the story on herself.

New York was more respectable than Los Angeles; there, to my
mother's relief, we were permitted occasionally to go out on dates in the
traditional way with vouched-for gentlemen, which didn't make it
greatly exciting. My tastes were not involved; it was all happenstance.

I decided to experiment, not joyously but clinically. Cool, curious,
determined. Did I say cool? I mean cold as ice. Heartless, but I didn't
know any better. It seemed to take courage on my part because of the
perils my father had painted. (Up to this time the only fellow to lay a
hand on me was on the Via Veneto, when I got a quick pinch.)

My virginity would be taken care of at marriage. Havelock Ellis had
taken care of my ignorance. It was up to me to get rid of my innocence.
I wanted to find out about kissing without risk of reputation or temptation. It wasn't as easy as it sounds.

The opportunity came with a very nice, solid citizen, a young col-
league of my father's. He was a decent, intelligent man whom I had met
a few times, and who was more than attentive. At the end of a long
evening, sitting in a very secluded booth in a restaurant on Park Avenue,
I yielded a little bit. Here was a man I could trust. I said he could kiss
me, but first I put my cards on the table, explained my goal, and made

clear my objectivity. Under these circumstances it was safe, as far as I was concerned, and almost justifiable, since I wasn't doing it out of attraction. Not that I didn't privately challenge it to be overwhelming.

He was ardent, in fact impassioned—just like the movies. I found it interesting and enjoyable and figured it could be pretty wonderful with the right man at the right time. Meanwhile, it was a relief to know that I could contain myself.

In the taxi there was a tussle which I found exciting but mortifying. I had lots of things to learn, and kissing didn't head the list.

But there were men to whom I was deeply attracted. Cedric Gibbons, who had designed our beach house, was one. He was the art director of the studio and the sweetheart of Aileen Pringle, the Elinor Glyn heroine. I had a secret crush on him. There had been unnecessary meetings, which I didn't connect with personal appeal. It would have been delusions of grandeur to think I intrigued him; that we were ever alone I attributed to lucky coincidence. Had he ever reached for my hand, I would have been speechless. A year or two later, during an unlikely gay party at our house, he caught me on the second-floor landing and attempted to kiss me. Terror and desire collided for the first time; I burst into tears and hid behind my slammed bedroom door. Years later, when I knew him well, he confessed he had contrived our meetings. Hadn't I realized? "What on earth was the matter with you?" He mercifully omitted mention of the explosion on the landing. I restored his masculine pride when I confessed how taken I had been with him.

Obviously, it was going to take a very peculiar fellow or off-beat situation to knock out my vigilance.

THE BLAZING issue was our lives; what was going to become of us? It was the only competition to Dad's world. How much better could things be? Well, they could be better, certainly for Edith. She was discontented and lonely and blamed my father. He wanted her to shape up and stop sulking. He told her her problems were her own fault. They had an armed truce.

How is it I didn't revolt? I didn't want to be called an ingrate. Besides, it was risky to force an issue; no good could come of it. My father had promised it would all work out, and look—everything else had! He had come through again, all right. Ocean Front was the threshold, and it was magically timed. We had done our part and he had done his. There we were, in a lovely house at the beach, with our father the head of a major studio, and we were meeting all kinds of fascinating people and going places other girls could only dream of. He couldn't have done better if he had conspired with the fates. My father's was a gradual, almost imperceptible rise in power, prestige, and importance. It was remarkable of him to so arrange it all for my last years at home.

David

"HOW DOES it look?"

That was the most oft-repeated phrase heard in the Mayer house when it came to "the girls." It was the question always to be borne in mind. It was the casual comment, the admonition, the rebuttal, the clinching remark. Appearances, appearances. Good manners, be refined. Don't be forward. Be quiet, but hold up your end. Poise, poise. It's only now it seems strange that the word "confidence" was never mentioned.

Above all, "unsophisticated"; unsophisticated meant purity, uncontaminated by Hollywood, untouched by man or boy.

The worthwhile young man who was to be my husband, for whom I was being trained and shaped, would be noble in character, pure in heart, and his past unsullied. A fellow like this would surely demand his equal in purity. My father had a fantasy, which was reduced to a yearning for what was surely the impossible: a male virgin. (Edie told me that this was a terrible thing and to be avoided at all costs. It would ruin our lives, she said.)

What counted in a man was brains and character. Health was taken for granted, and never mind the wrappings. He could have a good character only if he was poor. Money corrupted young men; if the parents had money, the boy was spoiled, he had played around (the word was "caroused"); in other families this was gratefully and euphemistically known as "sowing his wild oats."

My mother had other ideas. Her husband's hard work and success entitled her daughters to eligible young men; anyone's daughter could get a poor man, she wanted good family for us as well. Edie, on the other hand, had only romance in mind. She knew how he was to look: tall, blond, with long, tapering fingers, cultured and artistic.

I didn't go along with any of these attitudes. I wanted someone fascinating and very, very strong. At home everybody sat around discussing these all-important men who would soon be joining our family, but where were they? I was carried away by the thought that The Man actually existed. I knew he was tall, bright, and madly interesting—and four to eight years older than I. Edie said less than four years would not do; she actually preferred someone ten years older for herself.

We three ladies were very much concerned with love, an element my father said would arrive with the right kind of man. He assured us: "I will never tell you who to marry. Absolutely free, any choice you like. However, I reserve the right to say who you go out with. You can't know them if you don't see them; you don't see them if you don't go out with them." He said the right man would come at the right time, and I believed him; but Edie said, "How do we meet them? Time is passing. What are we going to do?" You never meet anyone when you're dragging along with your parents, which is where we always were. And you certainly didn't meet anyone at a Mayfair dance, those glittering affairs held periodically for the Hollywood elite in the Biltmore ballroom. We once had felt privileged and excited at participating, but now we were ashamed because we felt conspicuous without escorts. We never lacked for dancing partners, either studio people or glamorous escorts of the stars at our table, but that wasn't the same as walking in with a man of one's own. If an unattached male danced with us, we hoped others would think it was the man we came with. We would have settled for anyone who appeared presentable, even if we never saw him again. We felt everyone's eyes were focused on us and our sorry plight.

Actually, suitable young men were out of the question, because who could possibly not be at a disadvantage mixing with my parents' older, more successful group? The truth is there were no appropriate men for those occasions. What was inappropriate was girls like us being at the Mayfair dances.

The Mayfair held on New Year's Eve was the worst time of all to be caught unattended, and we had sworn never, never again. In 1926, mutiny at last was mounted; going with our parents would be too humiliating.

The morning conferences in Mother's room gained considerable heat, then suddenly the shoe was on the other foot. Someone had intervened; my father insisted we go. It seems we had to because Harry Rapf had invited two young men for us.

One of them was a new assistant of his who was very bright and very nice, despite the fact that his name was Selznick. Harry had assured him he was not like a Selznick at all. My father said, "This one got saved, the old man didn't have time to ruin him. Harry says he's a clean boy, has a good character."

The "old man" was Lewis J. Selznick, the once-powerful pioneer for whom my father had at one time worked for about a month. My father never forgot the experience, nor could he ever stop commenting on L.J. and his company. He prophesied doom: "Watch what I say, watch and see what happens to him. There is no firm foundation. Things must be built stone by stone."

He had also disapproved of the opulence and extravagance of the Selznick ménage at 270 Park Avenue: the Japanese butler, the tapestries, the statuary. He thought no good would come of those either. Highly unsuitable. He had predicted dire things for the Selznick boys, because one Sunday night he had seen the youngest son, twelve-year-old David, asking his father for money to go to the movies and his father had given him a $10 bill! On a Sunday night, too. That was not all: later L.J. had placed an older son, Myron, age nineteen, in charge of the studio, and given him limousines and charge accounts at all the night clubs in town. "Mark my words, no good will ever come of either of those boys."

The Selznick story remained in my father's repertoire, and when the Selznick Company finally went broke, even though it happened several years behind my father's schedule, he felt vindicated and continued to use it as justification for his own philosophy.

Myron had been precocious and had indeed been a man-about-town, with his name frequently in the columns, so his brother carried some of the glamour with him—that is, until I found him next to me at the Mayfair. To say I didn't like him is an understatement. He had no manners, which was immediately evident when he complained bitterly of his presence at our table. He had been hired for his working hours, not for his leisure time. Never again. Why the hell had he accepted the invitation? Was that part of the job, going to the MGM parties? He had never before been separated from his brother Myron on New Year's Eve, and he kept pointing to where his brother was sitting with a noisy, merry group, not like this one, full of stuffed shirts.

He also announced that the Selznicks were very independent, and that while he liked Harry Rapf, he should have told him to go to hell. He wasn't angry, just indignant with himself. He also was quietly getting drunk, a fact of which I soon accused him. He said, "Not drunk enough." At one point, to emphasize my disapproval, I changed my seat. He caught up with me. We got the one required dance out of the way and resumed our duel. I was reproving and superior. He finally said, "Listen, Miss Mayer, I have something to say to you. Once I was a much bigger prince than you are a princess. I know all about it, and let me tell you, there's nothing to it. Don't take it too seriously." It was the only remark that redeemed our first meeting. I only wished it had come from someone else.

My parents were pleased and expectant when we got into the car to go home, and my father was taken aback by the denunciation that followed; this was not what he had anticipated. On the other hand, we didn't expect him to come to the defense, as he did, of the maligned young man.

I didn't see David again until a couple of months later, one Sunday afternoon, when Mother took us to the housewarming of Eddie Goulding's new house overlooking the beach. Touring the house, I found myself tangled with David on the steps going down. I was on a circular staircase but he was on a flying trapeze; out of nowhere he had made a lunging, uncoordinated grapple at me. Who does he think he is, trying to kiss me! I said, "You don't even know who I am."

"Sure I do. You're the dame from New Year's Eve."

There he stood, bold, yet gauche and self-conscious . . . and suddenly ridiculous. He was like a huge, overgrown puppy with a too enthusiastic hello. Confusion overtook him. "What I really meant was, wouldn't you like to come next door where we all have that tennis court?" He meant the court Matt Moore had built on a piece of land he owned, to which David and his brother Myron and their friends went every Sunday. I still found him objectionable, but his eagerness was appealing. Besides, I was intrigued by the irreverence and unorthodox approach and thought I'd have a look at his famous brother and those friends of whom he had been bereft on New Year's Eve.

He was delighted with himself when he got me to the court, flashing looks at the others as though to say, "Look what I found." I was thinking exactly the same thing: a covey of men, and not a girl in sight. He wouldn't do, he had too much to atone for, but he had led me to the first concentration of unattached males I'd ever encountered. All this and tennis too.

He passed up the next set and devoted himself to his surprise package. He wasn't exactly penitent about New Year's Eve; in fact, he had a certain pride in the whole thing, and seemed to have forgotten I hadn't admired his indignation. What he did do was to fill me in on the eight or ten players present that day, among whom were the director Lewis (Millie) Milestone and, of course, his wonderful brother Myron.

They played serious tennis, accompanied by a considerable amount of badgering and bantering, and they spoke in a kind of idiom, full of half-finished sentences and inside jokes. The quality and the tempo of the talk were something I hadn't previously met up with.

Myron came over. He was accustomed to David fetching up girls; then, if there was one to Myron's liking, he would carry out a neat snatch. (Clever fellow, his brother—he'd gone next door and pulled out a girl!) He took a look and said, "Don't listen to my brother, he's a chump," decided I was a maiden and therefore useless, and walked away.

But I did listen to David, because he spoke with such zest and crackle. And his stories had humor and pertinence, and he told them with such relish. Did I enjoy watching tennis? Did I play? How wonderful! Next Sunday, then? Right then and there golf suffered a mortal blow.

Pretty slender invitation, that, but mighty tempting. Here was a whole new world, and I was going to have at it; I longed to be included at any cost. I sensed this was my chance, and Mother understood completely. I was not to worry—it would be okay even if there were guests; my father would be playing cards at the house and wouldn't know. Besides, he couldn't object: tennis was wholesome, and it was he who had approved David in the first place! The following Sunday along I went, armed with my racquet but with a sudden loss of confidence in my game.

Myron, tongue in cheek, baiting David, behaved as though it was he who'd invited me. "Come on, you play with me. Stay back, I'll take the net. Let David pick anyone he likes and we'll beat him." We certainly did, and that pleased me very much, and so did Myron. He went on piquing my interest for a few weeks, and then, against my will, my attention shifted. One brother had my eye, but the other got my ear and never did lose it. (Months later Myron boasted, "He's quite a fellow, you know." I did know, so I nodded; *now* he tells me! I wanted to tell Myron to go to hell, but really all he was saying was that I had passed muster. It was not unimportant, then or ever.)

The Selznicks were a loving pair, which was not evident at first sight. Myron was almost four years older, but a head shorter than his gangling brother, which is not why he tried to cut him down to size. He disparaged him just enough to keep everyone from suspecting that he completely adored him. David was tickled by Myron's taunts, roared at his barbs, and gave as good as he got. Each had a pride in the other that was close to immodest. They were almost inseparable; somehow Myron's act was incomplete without David.

Myron was compact, a man of few words, subtle yet cynical. He was balding at an early age and, what's more, wore glasses, an unlikely portrait of a Lothario and an athlete, both of which he was. David was quite the opposite, brimming with gusto and words, flailing around and forever bumping into things. They shared an air of defiance and a lack of conformity which both fascinated and frightened me. David was assertive, but Myron called the shots. Together they seemed to be the ringleaders, but Millie appeared to be the host. He was tolerant, wise, and amused; he was also a referee when needed, and sanctioned anything that made people happy. I never heard him object to anything or anybody; the proof is that he managed to live with the Selznick brothers when they first came to Hollywood. They lived a bohemian life in a couple of rooms in Hollywood, along with Bennie Zeidman, a Paramount producer. Whoever worked paid the rent and got to sleep in a bed.

The informality around the court was a blessing to me. The atmosphere of camaraderie and the indifference to status gave me a sense of release. They treated me just like any girl; it never occurred to any of them that I had been sheltered. I thought myself quite daring in this fast company I was keeping. The dialogue seemed racy, even at times risqué.

David was the exception. I found myself listening to him because the ideas which poured out had such originality and the opinions were so pungent. I didn't realize that a lot of it was for my benefit, even though, when he got off a good line or shot, he would look to see if I had caught it. That wasn't very suave. The only thing worse would have been if he had ignored me. I had to admit he was interesting, but I resented him. I liked him and I didn't like him. He upset me. I wouldn't go out with him if he asked me! Well, perhaps, but only to find out what he was like, because it seemed to me that every time David and I would start to talk, someone would interrupt our conversation, and the bits and pieces I got didn't give me a full idea.

I kept telling myself he was unattractive. He seemed intent on bringing me down a peg or two. In fact, there was a faint reprise of New Year's Eve, without either of us aware of it. However, it was he who each week would ask, "Will I see you next Sunday? Any chance?"

The court was crummy and had a short backstop, but I went every Sunday I could get away. It was the scene of my real social debut. I was the only girl regularly expected to play and I began to feel like a mascot. I could handle it because I was so at home on a tennis court and my form was good. I only hoped my lack of know-how wouldn't show. Between sets I studied the young, attractive women who would arrive and make up a small gallery as the afternoon wore on.

Fifty yards away was the house rented by Millie and Bennie. Everyone converged there at the end of the day. David would ask me to stop in when tennis was over and have a drink ("All right then, ginger ale"), but I was scared to go. I didn't know what went on in that house—I wasn't even sure who slept there. I sensed that dames had been around, and certainly there was liquor; the place could be raided! David might have been endorsed by Harry Rapf and accepted by my father, but he was not as safe and conservative as they thought he was; nothing tame about him, or his friends either. I didn't want to be caught with a wrong group or at a place I shouldn't be, for fear I blow the works. On the other hand, I didn't want to paint myself right out of the picture, and so I went in briefly a few times, despite the risk that my father would find out and I would have to listen again about reputation. (Secretly, I simply didn't agree about reputation. From my observation, inhibited young ladies were not the ones who made off with the best catches. Girls who had been divorced or, worse, girls who were thought to have had an affair seemed to do fine. And the squares got stuck with squares.)

They improvised their Sunday evenings, which was more than I could do. David kept asking me, "Why don't you hang around and see what's doing?" That certainly wasn't my idea of red carpet. I couldn't bear to reveal to my mother, after all those years of preparing and waiting, that I'd wound up with a last-minute invitation to "hang around." How do you say to someone, "If you want to see me, you plan it. You make a date. What's more, Sunday is impossible"? I simply said it was difficult on Sunday nights. That prompted him to ask about a night during the week. At last I was in a position to get even by declining. Instead, I went home to Mother and said I just might go out with that Selznick boy after all. At least I'd be out, and he was tall. And he'd said something about the Cocoanut Grove.

Mother was very pleased. She would handle it with Dad at the right moment. I didn't tell David "my problem," just suggested that, as I lived at the beach, I would meet him at the studio . . . no, outside the studio! I would explain some other time.

Surprisingly, he was late. (Unsurprisingly, he was perennially so.) As we drove east down Washington Boulevard, we passed what was once the Thomas H. Ince studio, a lovely colonial building with tall white columns I had long admired. It seemed that David admired it too; he said, "That's the kind of place I'd like to have." That sounded crazy from a fellow on his first job. Outlandish. But he wanted me to know that Selznicks didn't work for anyone; they were their own bosses. He was going to have his own company someday, small and special, and much sooner than anyone would think. It was a lot to spill not only on the first date but in the first mile.

Then at last I entered the portals of the Cocoanut Grove on the arm of a man of my own.

The fellow didn't make much money, so naturally I wasn't hungry. I turned down a first course and, with my eye on the right-hand column, settled on a modest dish. The captain then took David's order: lobster cocktail, soup, broiled steak, ad infinitum. On reconsideration, I relented and decided to join him in a little soup. He couldn't get through half of what he had ordered, never could. That was the beginning of my spendthrift days with the Selznicks.

It was also the beginning of my education. There had been no preamble or stilted prelude, we were off and running. I heard all about his family, his wonderful family; about coming to MGM and what had happened to his career since we first met. I learned the kind of pictures he'd like to make one day, why, and how. It was as though he were saying, "Know me, know me, know me quickly." I found him quite different alone: solicitous and responsive and totally engaging. I dropped my guard a bit and came clean about the difficulty of dates. "I don't see how you can stand it." I talked in a way I never had before, but then no one else had ever found me so bright. (I knew I wasn't, but if he thought I was, then perhaps he wasn't as bright as *I* thought *him*.) I wasn't sure he was my cup of tea, but the evening had whizzed by. I was riveted. So this is what it's like!

When I got home, my father was standing at the top of the stairway in the dark, waiting for me. At first I thought something awful had happened. It had. He was in a fury. He was shocked and disillusioned.

How right he had been never to let us out! How could he trust me? The questions were rhetorical; I was given no opportunity to say anything. I didn't comprehend at all. What had I done wrong? It was a quarter to two in the morning, that's what. Only bums are out until that hour. It was the single violent outburst of temper at me that I recall.

I had tried so hard all these years, and now look. How was I to know there was a curfew? Shades of the marshmallow men: there they go again with the retroactive fine print. I had never really displeased him before. It was a shattering experience. I worried about my future.

In the days that followed, negotiations ensued, and his grudging hour of midnight was moved to one A.M. and two o'clock on New Year's Eve. Other ground rules emerged as well, pretty rigid except for the likes of me. I couldn't go out two nights in a row—home alone with the family on alternate evenings; and no consecutive dates with anybody lest it appear I had a steady. In other words, if I wanted to go out with David, I'd have to find myself some other dates, which took considerable doing, starting from scratch as I was.

Already twenty, I hardly had a head start, except on Edie. I had some fellows put by who previously hadn't been worth the battle; now it would be a step backward if I didn't go forward, for Edie's sake as well. It wasn't important how much I liked them—if they were good dancers, that was velvet. They would do for dates, and dates led to beaux. After all, going out was the only way I was going to meet other men. I wanted romance, but I didn't want to fall in love. Above all, I didn't want anyone who would break my heart or me his. No scalps. I wanted to find my way first, so when *it* happened, I wouldn't be an ass and ruin everything. "Don't send the right man just yet, just some likelies." With alternate dates I could go on seeing David, and with any luck he would become the alternate date himself. I was banking on that.

Then, too, the right man meant love—and love meant marriage. But marriage would be out of the question, because the older daughter married first. In my family she certainly did. In that case, also "Please send Edie some dates." Now.

But David stayed the only permanent fixture in my nightlife; the others came and went. We were getting along famously, which might have been among the reasons my father decided to take his family to New York for a couple of months through the Christmas holidays. He had to go back to California during this period, and when he returned, he asked, "Have you heard from your friend Selznick lately?" No, I hadn't. He said, "That's right. He's left the studio. We kicked him out. I didn't think you'd be hearing from him."

When Christmas came, there was nothing but a printed card from Myron and David Selznick, addressed to Misses Edith and Irene Mayer. Christmas morning there was a basket as tall as I was, with enormous red roses, for my mother. My father beamed at this tribute, knowing it was from Nick Schenck or some such. He looked at the card and threw it down. Mother picked it up. On it was nothing more than David's name in his own handwriting. My mother glowed; she was his greatest ally. I thought there was a message in there for me, and it gave me quite a lift. There was a further one when I read in *Variety* that he had a job as assistant to Ben Schulberg, the head man at Paramount.

On my return to Ocean Front, outside my bedroom door was a magnificent bouquet to welcome me back; and we began in earnest.

For a long time he made me no pretty speeches, yet he tantalized me by the inscriptions he wrote in books he sent, chosen primarily for the opportunity the titles gave him. And by what he wrote on gift cards. In those days of the hideous, unwearable corsage, he sent, for special evenings, the only charming and original corsages I've ever seen. They put that florist on the map, and the cards put the flowers to shame. At least the flowers showed up on time.

A lot had happened in my absence. David had quarreled with Hunt Stromberg, for whom he was to produce his first big picture, *White Shadows in the South Seas*. David thought it an idyllic story; Hunt said he wanted lots of tits. They had words. When the problem reached Irving, David went too far. The next day Irving asked for an apology, or he would be forced to demand his resignation. David was willing to apologize, but refused to back down on his convictions and had already cleared out his desk. So his pride was intact, but he didn't have a job. My father said he was arrogant, but would be back "with his tail between his legs." However valuable he was, they had promoted him too quickly and too often. My view, on the other hand, is that if they hadn't, he would have been out of there sooner. David was part of a new breed in Hollywood. It was a good place to be aged twenty-four if one was talented, hard-working, and ambitious. The timing was right because he was just a few years ahead of talking pictures and the importation of the literate New York talent who were to put the old pioneers at a disadvantage.

Bennie Zeidman, Bernie Fineman, and Paul Bern helped him get that

Paramount job. By the time I got home, he had earned his first promotion there and was well ahead of where he had been at MGM. It had rankled that I had been the boss's daughter, and now it was quite different. However, he only half persuaded me that he would have behaved with more grace (and humility) at MGM if not for me. What is certain is that our days together would have been numbered had he stayed on in Culver City.

As we went along, I was learning the saga of the Selznicks, the splendor of their extravagance and their solidarity. I have never known another human being as fond of a parent as David was of his father. They made no demands of any kind on each other, nor was there ever from either direction the faintest criticism. There was nothing but delight. David emulated Pop's failings with pride. Pop thought big, earned big, spent big. He had made and lost several fortunes, but the biggest and the last was in the picture business, where he got himself up to fifteen or twenty million dollars. There was not only a common purse within the family, there had been, alas, a common purse between L.J. and his company. When the company went under, his health suffered a blow from which it never recovered, but his spirits were unflagging. He was the eternal optimist; to Pop, money was a stack of chips. He envisioned a bigger fortune in Florida, where he planned a studio city that would push Hollywood off the map (when that didn't work, it was back to New York and assorted hustling). Bankruptcy, by unanimous consent, was out of the question, and he turned a quiet deal now and then when he could. Now they were broke, and never a squawk out of one of them. There seemed no laments for the grandeur that had been or the luxuries lost. The boys just wanted Pop vindicated. They cared about his pride and his position, and since he could do no wrong, they felt he'd been done in. The rallying cry was Revenge. To David, it meant restoring the name; to Myron, it meant getting even. David wanted to build; Myron wanted to punish the big companies.

In New York there had been considerable hospitality at 270 Park Avenue—all comers, all hours. Mother Selznick had managed to find a Japanese major-domo who required no sleep. There were all-night poker parties over which Ishi presided, providing hot and cold running food until the sun came up. Those were nights when there could be a couple of hundred thousand dollars in the pot. Ishi got rich on the tips he made on poker nights, and he spent his days off gambling down in Chinatown, where he was a big shot. The Selznick spending extended to numerous imported cars, the most striking of which was a town car, in whose front seat rode a blue chow.

Restoration would be incomplete without redeeming the physical trappings—"redeem," because the Selznicks were, to put it bluntly, in hock. Yet to move from seventeen sumptuous rooms to a couple of furnished rooms was only a temporary setback. When I met David, he and Myron were living at the Villa Carlotta, an apartment house on Franklin Avenue, with their parents in another two-room apartment. They were certain that the unique sable coat, the costly rugs, the tapestries, and the furniture my father always described would soon be re-established in an even grander background. It took a couple of years and a lot of lawsuits—during one of the trials a leading Los Angeles banker was killed by a bullet in the head meant for a witness in another case. The litigation was endless, and when at last they won, I expected possessions worthy of Versailles. They weren't; but the stuff was so big that the boys had to rent a large Spanish house in Beverly Hills, which they could ill afford, to contain it. Even the Selznick optimism didn't stretch to the recapture of Mrs. Selznick's matching sets of jewelry. L.J. had had his fun in assembling the stones, and the pleasure of the memory seemed to suffice.

In 1926 Myron had been working on a deal of his father's, but there was no money coming in, so he told David he would have to get a job, even if he was a Selznick. He offered to drive him, studio by studio, and wait outside while David went in to seek his future. He said they'd start at MGM because they knew Harry Rapf. Harry was delighted, but was later forced to call up, abject, to say that it was out of the question: Mr. Mayer said that no Selznick could work in the studio, nor could one even cross the threshold. David claimed he could fix it. He'd read that Nick Schenck was in town, and he waited just by the automobile entrance to the Ambassador Hotel for a couple of days to catch him and remind him that Nick owed him a favor. After the MGM merger Nick had discovered, to his dismay, that he had inherited a prohibitive deal for the rights to *Ben-Hur,* one which provided fifty percent of the gross to the Erlanger interests. L.J., anticipating the situation, had, with the backing of a pal, bought up the Erlanger share for mischief or profit or both, and had Nick over a barrel. When the confrontation came, L.J. had David along with him and took pleasure in holding Nick up. When they reached an impasse, L.J., ever a double-or-nothing man, turned to David and asked him to decide. David told his father to sell the rights to Nick for exactly what he had paid. Nick, surprised and grateful, told David that if there was ever anything he could do for him, to let him know. David was now collecting.

Nick agreed that David was not out of line. David with audacity said he would settle for a two-week trial at $75 a week, a request modest only on the surface, at the end of which he was raised to $150. They were the busiest weeks he ever put in. He was tentatively placed as an assistant story editor, but was actually a glorified reader. Quietly he invaded the files and covered every literary property owned by the three companies. He salvaged countless stories, some expensive but largely forgotten, and overwhelmed Harry with memos on those which attracted him, complete with a new slant and proposed casting from the contract ranks. He titled or retitled a dozen new movies. He stuffed the suggestion box in the commissary so full that it had to be emptied daily instead of weekly, and Harry pleaded, "Enough, enough!" But David was given to excess. In a short time Harry took him out of the story department and made him an assistant with another hundred-percent raise and also turned over to him the supervision of some inexpensive Tim McCoy Westerns. David made them cheaper still, and by taking along on location a different script, another leading lady, and a few extra actors, he turned out two Westerns for slightly more than the cost of one. He was on his way. No wonder Harry had been able to persuade my father about New Year's Eve.

Myron stopped promoting and stepped into a slightly grander job with United Artists, where his talents were not appreciated as much as his independence was resented. Or do I mean his insolence?

Myron was both astute and talented. He was a big shot—at least he had been, and he still felt like one, which made it awkward. He knew a lot about making pictures and had produced a great many for his father, beginning in his late teens. His father had such inordinate confidence in him that he had turned over the entire production of films to him. Of course he couldn't get a job on that level, and he was damned if he would compromise much.

He became an agent, a decision that I believe ruined his life. He loathed every minute of it, even though he had a brilliant success. It had been inadvertent. His best friend in New York had been a Selznick star named Owen Moore, once married to Mary Pickford, and the best-dressed man in films. Owen, remarried, was now an MGM star and was having contract trouble, and Myron, an old hand, told him how to handle it. Owen could only carry out the first stage of the plan and appealed to

Myron, who went in and got all that Owen wanted—and plenty more. It was done in nothing flat, and Owen was floored.

Myron was giving advice increasingly to all his pals. When Howard Hughes wanted Milestone for *Two Arabian Knights* and he couldn't be found, Myron stepped in and closed the deal and made his first commission, the fastest money he had ever earned.

Myron and his mother were always very close, sharing a practical streak and even occasional misgivings. Given a chance, they worried, but the family was dominated by L.J.'s philosophy. On some level they must have known the score, but the parents denied reality even when faced with it; they chose escape and optimism. For instance, they finessed Howard, their firstborn; they simply ducked his problem—he had suffered a slight brain damage at birth—and when both brothers passed him in school, no one turned a hair. Howard had remarkable musical gifts which were not developed; the family felt he would "find himself." One evening at the dinner table his mother said, "How is it you always leave after the main course? Where do you go?" "I go to see my wife." "What wife? What do you mean?" "I've been married two years."

There had also been a little girl, born between Myron and David, who had died of blood poisoning when she was less than two, from a minor infection on her foot. As a result, they tended to undue alarm over possible physical mishaps. Had she lived, I'm sure the family could not have divided as neatly as they did—mother and Myron, father and David, with Howard the odd man out.

Stony as they were, I don't know where all the money came from. The boys supported that house, a home for their brother Howard, his wife and two daughters, lawyers' bills for the various lawsuits, and didn't seem to deny themselves very much. Mr. and Mrs. Selznick went on with their poker-playing, admittedly on a smaller scale, and the losses were always quietly taken care of. I raised my eyebrows once and only once, and never again asked or said a word about anything to do with finances and the Selznick parents.

Pop was a familiar figure in Myron's offices. He felt no compunction at all about reading the correspondence on Myron's desk or poking into other affairs of the agency. Myron didn't much like it, but never objected. He found it odd that the old man stayed completely clear of David's activities. It could be that Pop had no need to pry because David kept him so well informed. I'm not sure how often they talked on the telephone, but it was never as infrequent as once a day, and I was well aware that David called his father oftener than his father called him.

Until David got married, his father put him to bed every night, regardless of the hour. Pop would read with his ear cocked for David's return, whereupon he would descend to cover David up, stretched out on the couch in his study, instantly asleep. After an hour or two Pop would lead his comatose boy gently to his bed and undress him. This nightly ritual appeared commonplace to them both.

D A V I D was both poet and promoter. In addition, he was a rebel. He was not without contradictions, in fact he was a mass of conflicting impulses. One David thought of himself as a student. He cared about the English language; fulfillment would come only at Oxford University. He would write—no, he would publish. Another part of him had wanted to be one of the white-shoe boys at Yale, a big fellow at the proms. A third self led a solitary existence, wrote poems to imaginary damsels in distress. But then how could he also be an entrepreneur? I don't know how these various persons coexisted. Any role he would have chosen would have carried regrets for what he was missing. When he had risen to second from the top at Paramount, he was still weighing the merits of chucking the whole thing, going back to New York, and becoming a book publisher, which he thought more glamorous than films. He felt he would have become a publisher had he gone to Oxford; what he didn't face up to was the fact that he would have gone to Oxford had he gone to Yale, and he would have gone to Yale had he not been so involved with his father's business, where he worked afternoons after school. When it was time for college, he took extension courses at Columbia University and stuck with the movies. In short, he wanted all ends as well as the middle.

He had loved school, but couldn't get there when he was supposed to. Several schools had refused to put up with his tardiness. Finally his father found one on Park Avenue opposite where they lived, which agreed to let him check in for attendance, shoes unlaced, and then go home and eat his breakfast! He was glad to work more and stay later, but Monday mornings were such hell that the prospect poisoned Sunday afternoons. He dreaded sunsets on Sunday forevermore.

David prided himself on the diversity of his experience in the picture business. He told me that when he was a little boy, his father had taken him along when he went to Wall Street to arrange financing. His father had also given him a fling at exhibition and then distribution, with all its tricky contract clauses. While still in school he had been the editor of the Selznick newsreel, and then his father had let him loose in advertising, a field in which L.J. was already profligate. I suspect David was the culprit behind the mammoth electric signs which blanketed Broadway and so outraged the other companies.

No contemporary author had reached David as deeply as Scott Fitzgerald. He was a victim of both his books and his personal legend. Scott gave him a nostalgia for what neither had had, nor could have. He wanted to be Scott without the pain or penalties of his excesses. But I refused to be Zelda. We were both miscast.

Ours was a friendship that grew into an attachment, and an attachment that grew into a romance. No signals were flashed at the end of one reel or the beginning of a new chapter. However, I reached a point one evening when I made a remark not intended to be simple: "I like you." I meant it in a way apart from its common usage, as though I had just invented it. He understood in a flash. Between us the phrase always carried that special meaning.

I felt we were perfectly safe with each other because there was no chance of it ever getting serious between us. I had willed that we would be the exception. He was not only interesting, he was arresting. I had myself a fascinating friend, one I intended to keep, but I intended to keep him just that: friend. After all, he had had platonic friendships before. I had warned him before our first date that I didn't want to wrestle and would he please save his embraces for other girls. That's not quite the way it worked out, but then he would shrug and say, "There's no harm in trying."

He was quite uninhibited and, by way of understatement, he was articulate. The words poured out: anecdotes, reminiscences, opinions, fresh ideas, punctuated by witticisms and some fairly profound observations. Marvelous talk just for an audience of one. I was overawed by his erudition and bewailed my lack of education. He claimed there were a lot of educated fools, it was more important to think. He didn't tell me what to think, he *caused* me to think. He not only made me talk, he made me talk about what I thought. His candor shamed me into not weighing my words. With him I found my tongue, and everything unsaid throughout the years came out, the backlog of a lifetime. I don't know how there was time, because he was talking so much himself.

The counter-stimulation was enormous. There seemed to be layers and layers, an infinite peeling. No evening was ever long enough. We each had found the perfect audience. That was fatal.

How can two opposites be so congenial? The girl most disciplined and the man least constrained. He was reckless, I was cautious; he was unconventional, I was conservative. The thing was, right there in the middle where it counts, there was a big chunk of overlap. We had curiosity and we had appetite and an undue amount of energy. We were mad to know, to do, to see . . . and to listen. I discovered that underneath David's caustic tone there lurked an abashed idealism. All this and an idealist too—that was beyond my fondest hopes. His ideas were high-minded but not highfalutin. He was then, and for many years thereafter, filled with the aspiration of which heroes are made. I thought that man was marvelous. I still do.

We were friends, all right, but the platonic part began to get away from me. I inched involuntarily—and, I feared, unwisely—away from the role I had planned. Admire me, please, any which way, just so I see more of you. I didn't want anything to spoil our relationship, and I kept telling myself I had it all under control. I thought the rapport came from the conversation. Actually, we were always two stages ahead of what we conceded.

I tried not to give anything away in those morning sessions in Mother's room after an evening out. David had suddenly become Topic A to Mother and Edie. They watched me as if I were waiting for the telephone to ring, and if they didn't, I thought they were. Certainly when the phone rang during dinner, all eyes would turn to me. I hated the morning questions. I squirmed. The less I divulged, the less I would have to deny or defend. And I couldn't afford to say anything I might have to retract.

Edie, who had not had any dates yet except for a half-dozen with a good-looking obstetrician, ran David down badly and warned me about getting too involved. "Your children will be too Jewish-looking." My mother quite simply thought he was wonderful and always did, and he thought the same about her. My father said nothing. That was a good sign and it meant I was a good girl. At this point I had clear sailing.

The further apart I kept David and my family, the better off I was. When we had a date, I preferred him not to pick me up; he would attract too much interest and critical inspection. I didn't like to think of him running the gauntlet of the family or tussling with Mother's inevitable invitation to stay right there and have dinner. Besides, I didn't want them to see how late he was. I didn't need their help in finding out his flaws; I'd rather do it myself. And then I didn't want him to see me with my family, because I was different when I was alone with him and didn't want him to see me shifting gears.

A slight tension attached itself to Sunday evenings. Mother couldn't understand why I didn't want David to come to the Mayer weekly party. She had looked forward for so long to having "young people" around that she was sorely disappointed. But our place was a far cry from how those "fellows from the court" would like to spend their Sundays. If my presence was required at home, I would rather pass up seeing David. He had enormous resistance to those buffets, as he found the cast of characters absolutely awful. Some of them he liked individually, but the sight of studio people en masse at the boss's house got him down. Unfortunately, I began to see it through his eyes; it set up further conflicts within me. Mother wondered "how it looked" that David never came. We compromised: he made a token appearance now and then, which led to further problems. Prohibition or not, it was difficult but possible to get a drink at our house, despite my father's views. I had to warn Mother that David would expect one.

"You mean he drinks?"

"He takes a highball."

"A what?"

"Whiskey."

"Whiskey? That wouldn't be a very good idea. It would be better if he didn't."

I reminded her which foot the shoe was on; *we* were trying to get *him* to the house! "I will have to offer a drink. If he brings his brother, Myron will not only ask, he'll demand. Myron really drinks. He might even get drunk."

Actually, no one ever dared get drunk in that house, although Myron was tempted on the rare occasions he was there. Either David or I always hustled him out in time.

I THOUGHT it nice for David that his girl was preview-trained, but he neither appreciated nor understood. Paramount had a different huddle system that was less reverential, and I was included.

One night after a picture of his was previewed and we were alone, my trite little comments finally irritated him. Indignantly he asked: "Is this some kind of film manners you have?" Why was I so bright on everything else, so stupid about a movie? "It's just not possible that's all you have to say. I made the movie and I say it stinks. Now speak up; no one's going to hold it against you. If you're afraid, I promise you no one will ever know a word you've said."

Well, I *was* afraid. But I did gradually learn to speak up, presumptuous as it seemed, though to him alone. (David said he was undoing the damage my father had done.) He kept that promise to me and never quoted me about movies through all our years together.

It had amused my father to get my opinions and try to argue me around; I was never quite sure when we coincided. At least David would proclaim jackpot then and there, even for what I considered minor contributions. He developed a freedom in me so that I could say anything in the world I wanted to him. If he was going to ask me, I'd give food for thought. Over the years, when something important arose, an enjoyable game evolved. David would present his case and I would take the opposite side just long enough to persuade him. I would then reverse my views again and again. I became the devil's advocate and an expert on rebuttal. I didn't contradict myself, I merely spoke with equal passion and objectivity from a different vantage point and tried to conceal my real belief lest I prevail. It would appear I didn't want to be held responsible for a decision.

It was a curious feeling to skip a few grades and find myself dining at the Schulbergs' almost as a contemporary. I began to know the doings at Paramount as I did at MGM. To their credit, neither Ben nor David ever cautioned me against repeating anything. But then, I didn't report on MGM either. Nor, strangely enough, did my father warn me. You don't tell Paramount what MGM's doing and vice versa. I had my feet on two separate running boards.

Given the Selznick family tradition of hospitality, gradually Matt Moore wasn't playing as many sets of tennis on his own court as he should have been. David eyed a group of vacant 30-foot lots halfway between my house and the club. He had a notion that it would be lovely to have a tennis court, full-length at that, however impermanent, on a double lot, which happened to have precisely the right dimensions. He had just the pigeon to pull it off, too.

About ten of us got together and, gambling that the land wouldn't be built on too soon, anted up. They all left the driving to me. No one else wanted to be bothered. I got permission to use the land, picked the surface, and ordered the canvas windbreaks. In a matter of weeks we had a beautiful court at $200 a head. No one was more delighted than David. "See how simple it is?" That became a familiar pattern, though not all of his ideas had so few complications. They were entrancing to listen to, sometimes exhausting to carry out, and always in need of editing.

The court wasn't a chore or a favor, it was a project, my very first. I enjoyed it. What's more, I got to use the court during the week, which started my custom of giving all-day tennis parties "for the girls."

I now see that a joint venture (and close to home base!) was a dicey course. I have to admit it seems very contradictory, but there I was, knitting him into my life.

DAVID had always hungered for what he called a proper Christmas, meaning a great big wonderful tree. It was the only deprivation we had shared, and he was determined to make amends. The year after Mother's long-stemmed roses, the Selznicks were in their Whittier Drive house, and David was going to have the most beautiful tree ever. The build-up began. He had invited friends to drop by in the late afternoon on Christmas Day, but asked me to come early. Mid-afternoon I got a desperate call begging an hour's delay, he was behind schedule.

Edie came along. When we arrived, we were dismayed. At the end of the big story-and-a-half living room stood the biggest tree I had ever seen in a private house. The room was awash with ornaments, tinsel, strings of lights, and presents, scores of them. They were all unwrapped because he had not yet decided to whom they were going. The presents he had received were off in a corner, unopened. His enthusiasm for the gifts he was giving was enormous, and their number was enormous, many of them bought because he thought they would suit people who were not even on his list. It would be a full day's work to finish the tree and yet another to wrap the presents. The thing to do now was to wrap, at least for those people expected, then lend a hand with the tree. He alternated between panic that no one was coming and the realization that there were some friends he hadn't yet asked, so he started making telephone calls, stalling some guests and inviting others. Dusk came on and the mess was as bad as ever.

The family wasn't much in evidence, and no one seemed to be pitching in to help him. Myron wandered in and turned on his heel in disgust. He was not holiday-minded. I looked on in pity. David had so much poured in, he could never bail out. Less *is* sometimes more. The magnitude of his undertaking accentuated its doom.

Suddenly he was not to be found. I assumed he was off wrapping my gift. His mother came in and wondered where he was and how many guests he was expecting and when they were coming. I said I didn't know, but I would have to leave fairly soon. Edith gave me a look meaning, "Let's get out of here." I rapped on his study door, and there was silence. Could there have been indiscretion at the Yuletide board? Surely he couldn't have fallen asleep! I rapped again, and heard muffled sounds. "Give me a few minutes." Then the door opened a couple of inches.

He stood there without his glasses, tears streaming, eight years old. He said, "I can't stand it, forgive me, I'm so depressed. Christmas is almost over. Holidays are terrible, worse than Sundays, and Christmas is the worst of all. I get melancholia."

What salvaged his day was his gift to me. It was nice enough, a pretty carved soapstone box, but I was baffled. I couldn't understand why he looked at me so eagerly. He said, "Open it!" Within lay three beautiful carved necklaces: amber, white jade, and amethyst quartz. My delight was exceeded only by his. It was the year of the single gift—in a manner of speaking.

IN THE three and a half years between our meeting and our marriage, no two evenings we spent together were ever alike, formal or informal, planned or spontaneous, sometimes just prowling along with Myron, but often blessedly alone, because our time was rationed. Lots of invitations to David he left in limbo, saying, "We hope to stop by." He was keen about options, a glorious novelty in my programmed life; I took to them like a duck to water. I was learning what fun it was to be grown-up. I didn't know that I'd been grown-up for some time and that David was never going to be.

Our courtship days coincided with the beginning of the golden era in Hollywood. The transition period between silent and sound was a fascinating time. A different kind of talent and more interesting minds were coming West, because words became all-important. Small, smart dinner parties with stimulating new people, mostly sophisticated New Yorkers, began to take place, and I was enormously flattered to be invited. Naturally, it pleased David too that he didn't have to say, "May I bring . . . ?"

The house I liked best was that of producer Arthur Hornblow. It was just what I wanted without having known it existed. It was casual but assured. I liked the look of the rooms, the mixture of people, the kind of food; and I liked his wife. Crisp and debonair, Arthur was a man of taste in wine, women, and letters. Even when I became more sophisticated, he was still the ultimate cosmopolite.

The Mankiewicz house was a little earthier and very gemütlich. Herman was such a soft touch that in order to lend money he would have borrowed it. He had been with the drama section of the *New York Times* and had written a play with George Kaufman, then had been sent to Hollywood by Walter Wanger, with whom he collaborated in importing many of Manhattan's literary figures. His wit was spectacular, but he had as many faults as his wife, Sara, had virtues. Sara, no small draw on her own, was a good woman in almost a Biblical sense. In the goodness of her heart she reminded me of my mother. Herman adored her and she adored him back. Her faith in his talent was justified by his script of *Citizen Kane.*

I was still always the youngest person present, which was scarcely a novelty for me. But then so was David younger than the others. I needn't have marveled so at our inclusion, because later on I too always tried to find a fresh young couple, preferably in love, to give a little glow to an occasion. I didn't know we were lending any glow; I was just thrilled to be let in.

I began to have a wonderful time. David undertook to reverse my family's policy of looking forward and waiting to enjoy. The time was now. I latched on. David gave me one of his most important presents; it wasn't easy, but he taught me joy and the value of pleasure.

I had conformed to Dad's stipulations, so I had the peculiar notion that life would adapt to mine if I applied myself. I was so set in this belief that I couldn't see what was happening, except it was clear that things weren't on schedule. I thought, if David exists, there must be others. I wanted a batch of Davids. I wasn't going to let that four-eyed fellow foreclose my choices. Well, if you're looking for someone else and at the same time have to hang back until your sister has a fiancé in sight, it's bound to impede a romance. There's no other way to account for the absurdities which ran through our story.

I had been worrying for some time that the Selznick thing was getting out of hand. I had to immunize myself against getting in any deeper; David might really spoil things for me with The Man. I needed someone to consult, but I was not a confider. Instead I tried to concentrate on his shortcomings. I wanted to put the brakes on in a way quite different from what the Mayer rules allowed; I wanted one evening, just one, which went on and on until I got my fill of him. I wanted to be fed up . . . no, bored would have been more useful. Had they lifted the curfew once, I felt, I could be cured, just as by the overdose of chocolate I should have been permitted as a child. I longed for some bona-fide understudies, not the stalking horses I was using.

No one intervened. I had alternates but no contenders. I didn't dare explore my feelings . . . I was just trying to outrace them. When I was not with him, my thoughts were about him. I even had to watch myself not to compulsively bring up his name. I heard and saw everything in relation to him. This was an ominous sign and I tried to stop the habit as a means of self-protection, in case he cooled off or somehow disappeared. I already knew there was a part of him I would always miss . . . and that a piece of me was forever staked out. I didn't know David was the man I was looking for until I was in over my head. He was the right man at the wrong time. On my way to carte blanche at the candy store, I'd been waylaid by a fudge sundae—at Schrafft's—with almonds.

I still don't know whether the artificial restraints imposed on us impeded or ensured our relationship. As it turned out, my not being readily available helped to enhance me in his eyes. The intervening dates gave us each a breather, a false sense of security. David wasn't looking for a mate either; the more romances, the better. Because I gave him more leeway than he wanted, he didn't feel threatened; it wasn't when he wanted to see me, but when I was able to swing it. He had his cuties, so-called, whom he made jealous by his references to me. It didn't work the other way around because I didn't want to hear about them. I didn't care whom he saw, as long as nothing got in the paper which would lead my father to consider him a "Hollywood type." Besides, I didn't want to be equally frank and tell him which men I went out with. Nor could I afford to say that I wasn't keen on any of them, because I might be very taken with the next fellow, and then where would I be?

What he did those years on his nights off I have no idea. I desperately didn't want to know. He, on the other hand, wished to share. To me, that was either boasting or confessing. He liked to tell me of other girls' jealousy of me, and I wouldn't have that either. Had I been jealous, our romance never would have survived. If I couldn't compete then, I wouldn't be able to later on. What concerned me was my version of my own particular David, and the rest was none of my business.

He never did have a rival except in my daydreams; but I had one, as I discovered when we had been going out about six months. Her name was Jean Arthur, a girl in whose talents no one then believed but David. She was not one of the cuties who came and went, but a girl with whom he'd been in love and broken off. He couldn't bait me with her, and when I refused to listen to her reactions about me, he stopped talking about it. I never even knew when she left the scene and his thoughts. In my passion for privacy, I had given him, unwittingly, the gift of freedom.

I may as well reluctantly confess that I don't believe I have ever been jealous . . . normal as I think myself. I distrust the possibility of that trait being absent in anyone, so perhaps I have been jealous and just haven't recognized it as such, any more than I recognized anger when I was young. I have an undue amount of curiosity about everything except very personal matters, most easily explained by my desire not to have anyone intrude on mine; surely if someone is forthcoming with me, I must be no less. Never complain, never explain. I learned most about jealousy from listening to Myron, who was as suspicious and jealous as only a faithless man can be.

Even as we got in deeper, I never grumbled about David's freelancing. He was very unsophisticated and had a lot to learn. Besides, I felt he too had his share of fantasies, and other girls were good for him. He only stopped seeing them gradually—almost imperceptibly—as he began to spend quiet evenings home alone. It was becoming a ridiculous situation, David staying home because of me and me going out because of him. I had been taking the dating rules literally, as I had with my allowance, so uneasily I lapsed into simple prudence. One by one, I let my decoys slip away.

I found myself dressing to please him. He made suggestions, even though he realized the limitations of my allowance. He knew my skimpy wardrobe well, so sometimes I would have to ask him what I should wear. He embarrassed me by saying he really thought I ought to have a new dress. Could I please get out of those autumn colors? He would like something in black, I would look great in black. I said I couldn't: Edie had black. Okay, what about blue? Well, I couldn't have blue either; even navy blue was Edie's. I had brown. That made him mad. I reminded him I also had yellow, brick, orange, and thank heavens for beige. (I didn't tell him Mother thought me too dark for black.) He wanted black. "Why not please me?" I was a dove, but not a mouse, so I took courage and went to Magnin's, which to me was great for trying, not for buying. Those I liked were very elegant and too expensive. One day there I found it. It was black for his sake, but then it had a white cowl, which redeemed it with Mother, and even with its bit of white ermine edging the cowl, the price was $90. I went for broke.

I knew how he ought to look too, and he was most amenable. His collars were wrong, so off to Machin the shirtmaker. I picked Eddie Schmidt for his tailor, and we studied the swatches. Naturally, I changed his glasses; but the real metamorphosis was his hair. He looked in the mirror and said, "It's the new me." He was taken with himself.

A year earlier Myron had married, thereby making bachelorhood less enticing to David. His wife, Marjorie Daw, a former leading lady for Douglas Fairbanks, was a gentle, very pretty woman, almost the least assertive person I have ever known. There had been a sporadic romance between them over a period of many years. Six months previously she had gone East, touring in a play with Bill Tilden. Myron didn't seem to notice her absence until rumors reached his ears that she was dating Ronald Colman. That did it, and Myron was on the next train. No planning, no wooing, no nothing; he arrived indignant, married her within forty-eight hours, brought her back to his parents' home, and promptly neglected her. They lived there for a couple of years, until their daughter, Joan, was born.

Myron was cynical about women. He had made advances, some all too successful, to David's girls, disenchanting David about their purity. There was a reverse twist. Years before, in New York, Myron had had a fling with the stepdaughter of an important film executive, a chic young lady fresh out of a European finishing school who knew her way around. She announced she was pregnant and demanded marriage, a predicament he had not heretofore found himself in. In the midst of this dilemma David confessed that he himself had enjoyed ever so fleeting a conquest of the same lady, thereby resolving Myron's difficulties. He didn't know whether to be sore or grateful. Mostly he was relieved of his nagging suspicion that David was still a virgin.

I not only had a real beau, I had a proper girl friend, one I didn't have to share. Janet Gaynor showed up in my life at just the right moment, as though scheduled.

It's pathetic that this was the first time I'd ever confided in anyone; I was a late starter right down the line. I remember sitting with her on the sand facing the ocean, hidden by our sea wall. She was the one to whom I confessed my feelings about David. She never let me feel ridiculous when I asked her about dating etiquette, those fine points which came naturally to other girls as they grew up. She was deep without being complicated—and ever so wise. I learned to trust friends beginning with Janet.

My father, who disapproved of our having actress friends ("They're not after you, they're after me," among other failings), couldn't fault her. She wore low heels, no makeup, and was the symbol of wholesomeness. Moreover, she had a long-term contract with Fox, she had won the first Oscar, and she was number one at the box office. She didn't need my father.

Actually, Janet was the first star who gave glamour to simplicity, and niceness a new definition.

Some years later it was Janet's turn to confide in me. One day at lunch in 1939, Janet gave me tremendous news. She had found the love of her life, Gilbert Adrian, the celebrated costume designer at MGM, an urbane man of many talents. She said she was going to marry him.

I couldn't believe it. I liked Adrian, but they had nothing in common. That afternoon Adrian put it differently. "What am I going to do with these two chipmunks?" he asked, pointing to Janet and her mother, who had the same round brown eyes and merry look. They both found that delicious.

Later, when the three of us sat down over a drink, Adrian said it was his good fortune to have found Janet. "Just bad luck that she has no style. And no taste either. Doesn't even have a palate." He thought it funny. I thought they were both crazy. "You think you know her. Just wait and see the change. I'll have her trained in no time."

With consummate ease Janet became a fashion plate and hostess, a transformation one usually witnesses only on the screen. As she grew, essentially she remained the same, because she had absolute authenticity.

She and Adrian never looked back . . . or sideways. Until his death twenty
years later, the marriage was one of the best, if not the best, I've ever
encountered.

NOT THAT I have any idea exactly when David first proposed, but
I had been startled by very early intimations from him. When he got
trapped in Ocean Front at a couple of parties, he had said, "If and when
we get married, only a completely opposite system will prevail." Only
over his dead body would anyone cross the threshold of our house for
business reasons. It was to be fun, fun, and then more fun.

Even more premature and extreme were his declarations that "I will
never take anything from your father." This statement grew ever more
emphatic and superfluous.

David's rise at Paramount seemed fast to me, although entirely logical
to us both. David didn't think it was fast enough and periodically issued
ultimatums. My father thought it was too fast. He frowned on those
torn-up contracts and raises in salary. This escalation was not viewed as
an asset, but to my relief it tied him ever closer to Paramount, and I was
proud that he soon would be making $1,500 a week. No fortune-hunter,
he.

My father and David had many things in common: exceptional minds
and energy, as well as a passion for the picture business. That's a lot, but
only a patch on what they didn't share. However, David's strength was
equal to my father's, and strength was a quality I knew I would need for
emancipation and maturity. I knew it well and I knew it early.

David didn't seriously propose until long after we knew we were
going to get married. Once he started proposing, he never stopped. I
couldn't answer. I don't think David was so startled that he'd found his
girl, but he was shaken by the fact that he actually had proposed to one.
He couldn't get over it. I couldn't either. No evening we had was
complete without still another proposal, more original, more devastating
than the one before.

I didn't report any of that to the family because it seemed taken for
granted. Dad even started talking favorably about Lewis J. Selznick; he
said L.J. had mellowed. And he would refer to the good qualities of Mrs.
Selznick, "a fine lady, a good housekeeper, but then I always said that."
He even said we ought to have them over sometime, and I believe they

came one Sunday or two. (This somehow didn't end the misconception which still exists—one among many—that our two families were the Montagues and Capulets.) He even began affectionately calling me Selznick when in a teasing mood. Nothing had ever so startled me. What I had failed to notice was that for some time he had stopped calling people Selznick as a term of opprobrium.

I never felt anything but warmth and welcome from David's parents. The old man seemed well informed, pretty early, too. Standing in their front hall, he said to me, "When you are married to David, you will give me a grandson. Never mind my other daughters-in-law, you're the one I count on. There's just one thing worries me: will he be a Mayer or a Selznick? Tell me," he said, pointing to the grand piano at the end of the living room, "will you let my grandson dance on the top of that piano if he wants to? I never said no to a child of mine. You shouldn't either. I want him to be a Selznick." I didn't mention that to my father either.

What I did divulge was Pop's dictum about relatives, of which he had many. His sons were not to give them money; he forbade it. He said he had given heavily in his lifetime and then extra, with the proviso that it end with him. My father roared with laughter and my mother looked pained. There was almost a reproach in her eye at my indiscretion.

Around this time Bill Goetz showed up, and David and I desperately hoped he was a possible suitor for Edie. Life got considerably easier. But after a few months Bill disappeared.

Mine was a delicate situation and growing more difficult. I was going to marry David, but we were not engaged. Until Edie's life was settled, we were put on hold and the matter not discussed by my parents with me, or indicated by even a flicker between my father and David. Each wanted the other's esteem, yet when they met they were barely civil to each other, and each complained to me about the other's manner of greeting. Obviously, my father and David didn't really know each other. It was now too late for casual encounter and too early for acknowledgment. I had been congratulating myself that exposure in depth had been avoided. It wasn't my skill. More likely my father thought it premature and David wasn't looking for trouble. I don't believe they had one friendly talk from the New Year's Eve I met him till the fateful morning when David asked for my hand.

But my father talked to me a lot. He liked doing that best alone in his car, a sort of carry-over from our riding days. Some Sunday mornings he would drive me up the coast road, reminiscing, confiding, and getting what he called "my point of view." When he got around to the Selznicks, he would mostly praise David by criticizing Myron. If he mentioned David's virtues, he invariably added that he needed a balance wheel. He once asked me, "Are you serious about him?" "Yes, very." He didn't go further. Incredibly, he never did raise the $64 question about David, just made it clear I was to keep it under control, reminding me of my obligations to my sister. As we rode along, there would be increasing relaxation and he would then burst into song—ballads, of course. We found these rides reassuring and felt we understood each other. This couldn't have been more misleading, as we were both to discover.

For quite a while his tacit approval had no effect on the rule of alternate evenings at home, but if the family was out, I could have privacy on the phone with David, a rare treat in that house where the phones were fiendishly located to guard against it. It was a strange way of going steady. Well, if he was the right man for me and I was the right girl for him, we'd survive this peculiar LBM system.

What was incredible was that I found someone I was mad about who fell within my father's guidelines and yet was strong enough. That was more than I had bargained for. It was a bloody miracle.

Like any young lover, he had never loved as much before. Me, I had never loved at all.

We were it. Uniquely designed in all the world. We looked askance at other couples. We hadn't found love, it had found us. One day I went too far: I said I'd make him the perfect second wife; that I'd like him for my second husband. He looked crushed until I explained that there was such an inevitability about us that I would have left even my knight on a white horse for him. We were stuck with each other. There would be no exit.

There were other extremes. He didn't know how he could live up to me. I didn't know if I could catch up to him. Never were two people so persuaded that they were the chosen. We pitied everybody else. We even knew why others didn't get along and would have been happy to tell them how it was done. But I would have been even happier with less, because it frightened me. I sought relief in saying, "If there is no more, I've had my share." And I said it often.

When David and I were together, I was in a quite different realm, where values, ideas, language, habits steadily moved further away from everything I had known. It is unsettling when a stranger is more natural than one's own family and more real. Life was closing in on me fast.

Down deep, I knew it was him or no one. I could hold out no longer. The relief, oh, the blessed relief of at last saying, "I love you." I had never said it before; for me, those words were the equivalent of losing my virginity. I intended to say them to only one man in my life.

I had thought that when love came, a gong would ring, but no such thing happened. I had merely acknowledged my love with the right words. And there I was, in the ridiculous position of marrying my first sweetheart.

No whirlwind courtship, ours. But though the timing may have been off, the chemistry was right. Our lives were joined; we felt deeply wed. Well, not quite. In those days chastity was not unusual, even in Hollywood, except, I imagine, among the ranks of long-established sweethearts of important producers. A Mayer maiden I remained. Poor David!

Getting Married

THE TROUBLE that came with saying "Yes" was that then he kept asking, "When?" But it wasn't up to me. He knew that perfectly well. I begged him, "Don't go on about it." I used, "Are you really ready to give up your freedom?" Then I resorted to, "It's a test of our relationship."

Fortunately, Edie's former beau, Bill Goetz, reappeared on the scene six months later and Edie came into her own. There soon were stars in her eyes, and David's hopes rose. Without warning he presented me with an engagement ring, which I secretly wore on a chain around my neck and which was viewed singly and secretly by each member of the family. Mother showed it to Dad, who said nothing to me. In 1929 it was mandatory for a girl to have a ring when she became engaged, preferably a diamond, no matter how tiny. As one's fortunes improved, it could be traded up; one bought what one could afford. The Selznick family wasn't yet out of hock, but it was typical that I received a five-carat, square-cut solitaire. It didn't occur to David that the Goetz family was going to have to match it.

David kept after me. "Any news yet?" Finally in August I was able to say that Bill had proposed. They were getting married. At last! Wonderful, wonderful, but when? David guessed two months; I said four; it proved to be eight.

Bill was orphaned and had been brought up by two of his brothers,

Harry and Ben, both of whom were quite successful in the film industry. Bill was practical, with no pretensions, and he had an earthy sense of humor which was a big asset. He didn't have a job, which bothered him not at all, but then Edie had drive and ambition enough for two, and in time he grew to share them. His realism was a fortunate counterweight to Edie's dream world, which made them a well-suited pair. His brothers paid for the ring, and my father got him a job. The elders—his brothers and Dad—had conferences and made some kind of financial arrangements.

There had been no talk of costs, but since Dad had promised there would be "a time to spend," Edie assumed that this was it, and he'd better come through! It would be a way of redressing some of her grievances.

However, when no green light was given, Edie tackled him head-on one day in the library. Mother and I stood linked and quaking in the hall by the closed door. The pitch of their voices was alarming—one, then the other. Finally it was quieter and only Edie talking. Quieter still, and the door opened. Edie had won. She could buy a proper trousseau. Dad said he had been wrong. Not only that, he had apologized. Apologized!

She was going off in style, and I suspect that even he was relieved. He had not been supportive in her difficult years and she had this coming to her. While he was at it, he gave her a handsome diamond bracelet, redeeming an unstated promise when he had forbidden us jewelry. He also gave her an ermine coat and a Cadillac (then of course he had to repeat it all for me). But it was that trousseau that started Edie off being a luxury lady. She was never again going to be short-changed.

This was not only a turning point in her life, but also in her relationship with her father. It marked the suspension of her hostility to him. (Twenty years later she resumed it with a vengeance.)

At least now David and I could plan. It was to be Europe for our honeymoon. David would forego his two-week vacation that year, and as he hadn't had one at all the previous year, and counting 1930, he would have six weeks off, all on salary, and two weeks on our own. It was once in a lifetime, and I had agreed no holds barred, no stinting; I wouldn't mention economy. Since he wanted it lavish and I didn't want red ink, unbelievably, and for the first time in his life, the poor man began to save. Money was put away each week so there would be a bankroll for us to blow. Besides, he had that great big ring to pay for.

It is more difficult to schedule a studio program than a wedding. The production program was part of David's responsibility and in those assembly-line days at Paramount they planned six months ahead. David said April in Paris, the chestnut trees in bloom. I said perhaps, but if not, at least we'll make it by May. We got brochures from Cunard and the French Line. No harm done in studying them. David planned the studio's shooting schedule and kept pressing me for the date of Edie's and Bill's actual engagement—they were being inconsiderate. I said *he* was. Edie had waited a long time; she would not be hurried; she was making up for some terrible years. She called this "my period in the sun." David called it stalling.

The months dragged on. What kept me contained was the notion that I was "doing the right thing." I wasn't as noble as I was superstitious; I was just ensuring my happiness. I tried all my old formulas, but David refused to agree that everything was for the best. "How? Just how?" He was right—things turned out not to be for the best. No good deed goes unpunished.

Nothing ever shook our household like Edie's engagement and wedding. The merger and *Ben-Hur* were peanuts compared to it.

I had my initiation in big productions. Edie had regained her health, but it was important to all of us that it be protected. There was lots to be done, and I undertook the role of willing handmaiden and shopper extraordinaire for the great trousseau. I was entrusted with missions in search of chiffon, satin, and mousseline de soie. I became an expert on monogrammed sheets and towels. Given the need, Edie decided that I had taste after all, but she had to enlighten me on the fine points of the various kinds of handmade lace. I was indefatigable in my efforts, and when David complained that I seemed exhausted, I said the harder I worked, the sooner we could get married.

Then I was dispatched on a real-estate hunt, both for a house that my father would buy and for an interim apartment. As I wrote to David, who was briefly in New York on business, "I also went down to the Biltmore and alone made arrangements for foyer, ballroom, liquor, altar, private exits, camera room, three bedrooms, detectives, music, etc. Mother had pleaded with me to order my things with Edith's . . . what a terrific temptation it is."

David's letters to me from New York were filled with soul-searching about his future career. He had already told me not only the story of his life, but the travels of his heart. And beyond that, his amorous adventures. When he finished, he shamefacedly admitted: "That's all I have done."

He said he wished I had things to confess—he would forgive them all.

He wanted me to know still more. Since we never had enough time together and were too busy with the present and the future, he devised a plan by which, in his absence, I could deal with his past. He wanted to think of me sitting on the red sofa in his study reading his bundles of papers, letters, and verses. Knowing what he was and what he would be, I was also to know what he had been. His parents were away, the house was locked, and he gave me a key with instructions to light a fire, turn on our favorite music, and delve into his life. That way we would be together, although apart. While I had the car I stole some hours from my Edie chores and did as he asked. As I pored through the papers and letters of a lifetime, I was very moved by his openness.

My father, who was also in New York, did something peculiar. Although he had seen my ring, he still had never mentioned my marriage and I had never told him straight out that I was going to marry David, so I was astonished when David wrote, "He sent for me, for what I knew not. I arrived and he spread before me a collection of jewelry and he told me to pick something, preferably a formal dress set, as 'an engagement gift.' My protests . . . were in vain. . . . I'll do my level best to avoid it because it abashes me, because I think it unnecessary, and for general sake's sake."

David didn't wish to be bound by anything beyond marriage vows and copyright laws. Conventions were there to be flouted and rules to be broken. This obsession with freedom was to be with him all his life. It explains why he never had a job, a boss, until 1926, and then ten years later was driven to form his own company, and then, later still and unwisely, his own distribution company.

At that time he was the only man I'd ever known who felt that freedom was as necessary for his wife as for himself. He had always felt unfettered, and longed to emancipate me. But as someone who longed for an uninhibited wife, he had picked an unlikely candidate. The very traits and virtues my father believed would make me a great wife for the kind of man he had in mind were anathema to David. Adding to the perversity of fate, he didn't care to have an influential and rich father-in-law. It was all topsy-turvy. I was to tame David. He was to free me. I don't know whose task was greater, his or mine.

How was David going to have his freedom and also have me? He decided he didn't have his freedom anyhow, because I had happened to him and I was part of it. But our life was to be our own. Would my family's wishes undermine my capacity to go along with how he charted his course? Would I be willing to give up California? Would I promise not to hamper him if he wanted to return to New York, give up films, and become a publisher? That was a hard one. After much deliberation, I yielded. I came up with the corny truth, "anything for your happiness."

The shadow of my father loomed ever larger. David said, "He can't control me. How do I know you can withstand him?" He respected my father, he liked him, but he feared the power he suspected Dad had over me. He was out to slay the dragon in case he was a dragon. It was the only thing which could come between us, and about which we quarreled. I was forever having to prove I was my own person. Of course I wasn't, although I was getting there. I still had to be concerned with how things would look to my father, and to avoid his possible displeasure. I was on a tightrope with my fingers crossed; when I got safely to the other side, I would show David how unshackled and flexible I could be. Meanwhile, David said he would accept any opinions of mine as long as they were not controlled by Culver City. It was the only way in which he wished to dominate me.

THERE was an unexpected bonus from my Edie activities. I had the car, which permitted me to make an all-important appointment that required secrecy. I had to go and see a man about a stutter.

In the Hearst Sunday Supplement there had appeared a marvel; not in Oslo or darkest Africa, but right there in Los Angeles. There was a headline: "Stuttering Solved." A Professor Metfessel, at UCLA, stated that the right side of the brain controlled the motor functions of the left, and vice versa; and he had widely researched the damage resulting from switching left-handed people to the right hand. He claimed that this was the cause of stuttering and that he could undo the damage.

I waited for an opportunity. Two trips a week to town with Edie gave me no chance. I couldn't get away with a mysterious errand, nor could I bring myself to blurt out my ridiculous mission. That handicap of mine was the bane of my existence and I imagine of the family's as well, although they didn't discuss it openly. I had learned enough control for the most part to spare them, and by that point almost no one knew except David, who accepted it as a part of me. Accordingly, I didn't even mind stuttering in front of him, which was a mighty big relief. When the h's weren't working so a "Hello" was risky, I would answer the phone by saying, "25120." (When you meet someone and can't get "hello" out and you're too close for a wave, all that's left is an embrace. I've hugged some startled people in my day.) Failing that, it was "Yes?" Both were on tap. If there was a second or two of silence and it happened to be David, he would say, "If that's you, whistle." This brought such a laugh it made stuttering impossible.

I had hoarded my clipping for months, and now it was possible for me actually to make an appointment with this man, if he truly existed. I had been afraid even to inquire, in case I got caught in the act.

The big day came, and I went with head high and my hopes bursting.

I found Metfessel forthright and intelligent, and a man who gave generously of his thinking. He answered all my general questions. Suddenly he shifted and inquired of his rapt audience, "What is the age and sex of the patient?" I shattered like bits of crystal. I gasped, paled, and burst into tears. I not only wept, I sobbed. He could not console me. He knew in a flash what had happened and begged forgiveness for his lack of perception. He finally said, "I know you can't talk now. I will ask you questions. Just nod your head yes or no." A volley followed. Each question revealed an infinite comprehension. He had tests to determine the degree of left-handedness. He asked if the stuttering had begun when I went to school. "Do you switch words, phrases, topics, to accommodate your need? Do you have many alternate words at your disposal?" On and on he went. I nodded vigorously with gratitude and relief that there really was no mystery after all. Others had trod this path. This man knew and cared. He said, "Before I give you the blindfold tests, I want you to know that I have never seen a demonstration like yours. No one before has fooled me so completely. I find it heartbreaking." Whereupon I burst anew into tears. At last the self-pity for my plight was unpacked.

The blindfold tests began. A pencil in each hand, arms outstretched, I drew circles forward and back with each hand, my poor, helpless, untrained left hand adroit and smooth, the obedient right making a mess of things. He said, "Extreme. I can help you." There were further tests —one eye covered, then the other. He told me how many months it would take, how many visits per week.

With halting speech I explained it wasn't possible because I was too busy with my sister's wedding. I told him I was also going to be married shortly and was filled with terror because the ceremony required precise words, and what if I couldn't get them out? He said he didn't wish to add to my burdens, but gave some advice which would give me increasing relief. He suggested I use my left hand for all unobtrusive tasks such as a doorknob, a hairbrush, etc. "Most important, keep a pencil in your left hand and doodle whenever possible. Circles are a great help. I could have shifted you back completely to your left hand, but every single thing will help." He refused a fee because he said he had learned a lot. "If you need me, call me." I never saw the man again, and within a week I could write quite legibly with my left hand.

However fluent I appear, a part of me is never unaware that, as an alcoholic who doesn't drink is still an alcoholic, so a stutterer who doesn't stutter remains a stutterer. There is a tiny, secret enemy coiled up within, ready to spring.

N O T H I N G   was less characteristic of my father than the size and shape of my sister's wedding. His prominence had come so gradually I believe even he was unaware. It was emphasized by the space accorded the engagement in the newspapers. The lavishness of the gifts which poured in was princely—in tune certainly not with the times, but with his increasing position. The family was dazzled. The arrangements grew more splendid.

As they did, David's indignation came to the fore. He cringed. He proclaimed it grotesque. That stung. I spoke up: my father was conservative; it was *his* who stood for conspicuous consumption. Anyhow, what difference did it make to him? It wasn't his wedding.

Imagine solid-gold demitasse spoons from Tiffany in 1930! Given the state of the national economy, perhaps it was insensitive, but the Depression was not yet felt in Hollywood. This was the real beginning of film affluence. Films were in inverse ratio to other businesses and grew in popularity because they were an inexpensive way for people to forget their troubles.

Edith's wedding on March 19, 1930, was the event of the season. It came off huge, dignified, and quite formal. The custom tailors of Southern California were ecstatic and finally could take no more orders. The Biltmore ballroom had never seen so many penguins. For years thereafter, white tie and tails were commonplace at the Mayfair dances.

I was the maid of honor, and Edie's bridesmaids were Corinne Griffith,

Carmel Myers, Bessie Love, May McAvoy, and Marion Davies, who with Mr. Hearst had come through with a substantial diamond pin and bracelet from Cartier.

From the moment the ceremony began, I saw only Edie's face. She was a radiant bride; I couldn't believe how lovely she looked. I was caught up in a whirl of memory and emotion and was carried away publicly for the first time in my life. Apparently I'm doomed to weep through weddings. I wept through Edie's and I wept through mine, though for quite different reasons.

AT LAST, at last, the world was ours. Not a shadow anywhere. We thought it would be great as a lark for David to go and formally ask my father for my hand. He arranged a morning appointment at the studio. It would have been indecent the day after Edie's wedding, so he gave Dad the breather of an extra day. At the last moment we decided I ought to go along and not miss the fun. I couldn't resist watching them savor the best in each other. I only hoped my father wouldn't be too sentimental.

In we sailed to a warm welcome in that square mahogany office. I sat down next to my father and David stood against the desk, facing him. He began in ceremonious fashion. "My reason for being here can hardly come as a surprise to you." He made a noble speech about his love for me and his prospects and the promises of a glorious future. My father rose to the occasion and responded in kind. He too had looked forward to this happy day. Perfect. Did David know the kind of wonderful girl he was getting? Whereupon the full range of my glories reached my ears for the first time. And David was a splendid boy, Dad could ask for none finer. The son he had never had. That was followed by an inventory of his virtues. The testimonials over, out came the natural question. "What date do you have in mind?" April 29th.

That tore it. It was not only unsuitable, it was unthinkable. What was this, a fire sale of his daughters? A second wedding to take place in six weeks, like a shotgun marriage? Did David have no heart? This girl, his baby daughter, to be snatched from him? "Has Irene agreed to this date?" "Of course." "This is March 21st. What are you talking about, how can you get married on April 29th? Yes, of course you can get married. We'll talk, we'll arrange a date. What is this hurry?"

It was Paramount. David explained that there was no way of rearranging the studio production schedule, which he had had to lay out six months in advance to enable him to be gone those particular eight weeks. "Mr. Mayer, I cannot permit you to disrupt the Paramount schedule." As things now stood, David could get away at no other time; besides, we were going to Europe on our honeymoon and David had booked our suite months before. "You've made travel plans?" my father stormed. How could David arbitrarily assume he was going to marry me? Was David asking him or telling him?

David said, "She had a diamond ring hanging on a chain around her neck last summer. She told me you had seen it." But we had made plans behind his back. Could he no longer trust me? Should he rethink David's character and suitability? Was this the consideration he could expect from us in the future? He said, "Let's be practical. We just finished the biggest wedding that ever happened in this town. What do I look like, I give another one like that? The people haven't recovered yet. They went broke buying presents. You expect them to dig down again and buy presents like that? Give them time." David said we didn't want all those presents and we did not want a big wedding. That was an insult and another blow. Did we expect him to hide the wedding? This was a brilliant match. David said we wanted it intimate, only friends and people close. "Irene wants to be married at home."

We were selfish. There were others to be considered. Were David's parents not entitled to a splendid wedding? David's attitude about the gifts was cavalier. My father was being robbed. He had looked forward to lovely months ahead, having me at home and getting to know David.

On and on they went. It was turning into a nightmare, the single blackest day of my life! I sat silent and stunned. My big, brave men, my heroes, the two men who really cared most about me, they didn't even know I was there. That's wrong; it wouldn't have happened but for my presence. It should have turned me against men forever.

As the atmosphere worsened, my father reached for a compromise, a postponement; just a little one, just six weeks. He proposed that we be married in the traditional month of June, on his own wedding anniversary, June 14th. It would be a lovely thing to do. He offered David the sentimental prospect of celebrating our wedding anniversaries together in the years ahead. But David wanted his own anniversary; that way we'd have two to celebrate. Where was David's sentiment and reverence?

Against the tacit ultimatum of June 14th or else, David was adamant. My father asked whether he couldn't wait. "Wait? Do you realize how long I *have* waited? You cannot do this to me, Mr. Mayer." He spoke of the physical strain of a young man in love. "I cannot wait any longer. You're a man. What kind of hell do you think I go through? What do you suggest I do?"

However realistic, this was untimely. That sex was involved in marriage perhaps could be mentioned to my father, but certainly not in my presence. It only added fuel to the blazing fire. My father made it clear that this topic was offensive. He spoke of character and self-control.

I don't remember much else as they stormed at each other, but I can never forget the astonishing sight of David suddenly pounding the desk with his fist and saying, "I've had enough of this, Mr. Mayer." He turned on his heel, flung open the great mahogany door, paused on the threshold, and asked, "Irene, are you coming?" I was momentarily paralyzed. I could reason with David later, but not with my father. I managed, "I'd better stay for a bit." He slammed the door and departed, leaving me to deal with the old man. I felt that my father hadn't understood, that I could straighten it out. In explaining I made it worse.

"What do you have to say? You have planned this with someone else and then sprung it on me." Where was my judgment? Why had I not warned him? I said that he knew, had known for a long time. I thought he knew about Europe too. I said I didn't know what was going to happen. I meant I was fearful I had lost David. He said it was up to me. "What can I do? I must not manage his life." He said I would have to. "You saw what just happened. He's impulsive. You've got a head, you can steady him. It's what he needs, otherwise he'll be impossible. If you can't balance him now, how are you going to handle him later? Use your head. He will listen to you and I can guide you. Then we have a decent family." He assailed me, alternating appeals to my reason and my loyalties ("For Paramount you'd do this to me?").

Why didn't he understand that if I hadn't been so devoted to him, he wouldn't find me now so dedicated to David? To me, being a daughter had been an apprenticeship. Earnestly I outlined how I had adhered to the lessons he had instilled. I reminded him that he had raised me to be a good wife. Now he was landed with exactly the girl he had brought up so strictly: logical, literal, precise. In an attempt to convey my meaning, I said, "No man has ever had a more obedient and loving daughter. But when I tell a man I will marry him, in spirit I am his. I must begin the way I intend to continue. I cannot fly two flags. His flag must come first. Your flag will still fly, I will love you no less, but I must follow what he wants and feels is right for him."

That went through him like a knife. He felt betrayed. It was infamy. What had he been harboring in his home, in his heart, all these years? Why had I never told him I held such views? Why had I deceived him? I said I never had, and I had never lied to him. He said, "You've been thinking this." "Yes." "Why have you not told me?" I said, "You never gave me an opportunity. You never asked me what I thought about myself or my life. I thought I was doing exactly what you wanted. I thought I could please you both. I have tried very hard."

It went from bad to worse. I couldn't stand any more and fainted, for the only time in my life.

When I got out of there, what rang in my head was "Wrong, wrong, wrong." Who? What? Where? I didn't know, just wrong. If this was right, then I was wrong about everything, even my little philosophies. I had misunderstood everything back to Year One.

When I got home and opened the front door, I found my mother standing in the curve of the staircase, spread against the wall, waiting for me. When she saw me, she threw herself on me, protecting me as if I were a wounded animal, and half carried me up the stairs, sobbing, "I will stand behind you. I will defy him. For once in my life I will stand up to him." She spoke of my sacrifices; she called me her baby. "We will fight it together. I will not desert you." She asked no questions. Obviously, my father had called and told her what had happened.

It was a debacle. I lay huddled. I was wounded, numb. I would talk to no one, not even David. Looked at objectively half a century later, the episode doesn't seem earth-shaking, but it shook me to my roots. What is pathetic is the devastating effect it had on me. A few hours of psychotherapy then would have spared me extra years on the couch.

Late that night I heard voices from my parents' room. I had never heard my mother's raised before. The next day Mother said my father had left for New York.

A day or two later I told David I wasn't going to marry him; I would never marry anybody. The girl he loved was gone. I would never laugh again. I didn't ever want to feel again. I wished there were something like a Jewish nunnery. David said he would mend me, he would take what was left. He rescued me by pleading his own case. His feelings. What was to become of him? How could he now put his life together again? That brought me around. I sealed the whole sorry story up inside myself. A few days later Mother announced our engagement. She included my father's name.

There had been no need to ask why David had sailed out and left me to fend, or why I hadn't had the spirit to join him. We knew the answers. It was a no-win situation all around.

That it also took its toll of my father did not occur to me. It has taken me many many years to understand his behavior. I believe it seemed to him as though I had totally rejected him and any participation he might have in my future. It had never crossed my mind that he believed he could continue to have the major influence on me. As he had known from the beginning the extent of David's independent spirit, he must have assumed he could always control David through me, for I was his loving daughter whom he could count on. He could, but not for that. My love for him remained, although my faith in his infallibility was gone. He had made a tragic error in judgment which foreclosed what I see was his dream of becoming a patriarch. I later learned he had mourned on some trusted shoulders, grieving especially over the words "two flags."

I wonder whether, if not for that black episode, there wouldn't have been a showdown at some other point and my father wouldn't have tried to rule David through me.

It was my mother's will and courage which prevailed; she substituted hers for mine. This gentle, submissive woman turned lioness to protect her cub. She said, "When Edith comes back, she will stand with us; it will be three against one. Your father will have to do an about-face."

But when Edie returned from her honeymoon, she wanted no part of our trouble. She made it clear when she entered. I should have realized that Dad had already reached her and she did not intend to take sides against him, who had so recently made everything possible for her and from whom more blessings were to flow. She put her hands over her ears and said, "I mustn't listen. I've gotten away from all this. I have my own sweet little nest. I hate looking back." Anyhow, Billy wouldn't want her to get involved.

I swallowed that too. Not a peep out of me, damn fool that I was. It didn't dawn on Mother either, who bravely said we had gotten this far, we would go on without her. She said nobody could stop us now.

It's otherwise evident that I don't have amnesia, but I'm forced to note that I recall very little of what transpired in the weeks from then until my wedding. For the most part it isn't a blur, but a blank. I believe I was waiting for a miracle—for my wise, adoring father to see the error of his ways and magically restore my world. The miracle didn't happen. What appalls me is that Grandpa Mayer died during that period and I don't remember his death or anything about it, even the funeral. I know the invitations had already gone out, so his death wasn't the reason our wedding was at home, an interpretation I read somewhere not too long ago.

I don't know when my father returned from New York. I don't recall him at all until the wedding itself and my relief he was attending. I don't remember him giving me my diamond bracelet, or, for that matter, receiving the jewelry I did from Mr. Hearst. My father had arranged for us to have dinner at the White House on our way to New York, a favor David wanted to skip (it would be lovely under his own steam and at a different time). I don't know how I learned of it. There were lots of parties for us, but I remember only a fragment of the tremendous one the Schulbergs gave at the Beverly Wilshire. It was a brief social merger of Paramount and MGM, a command appearance. Midway in the evening there was a sudden hush, as though a cue had been given. Paramount's answer to MGM's Garbo, Marlene Dietrich, fresh from her triumph in *The Blue Angel,* made a spectacular entrance, followed by Josef von Sternberg. She strode across the full length of the enormous dance floor. The silence was broken by applause. She had arrived in Hollywood that day, and her debut caused such a flurry she practically seemed the guest of honor.

Mother told me Edie's trousseau had come to an impressive $5,000 and I was allowed the same. I had a lot to do. David said we were going to be footloose, so to please skip the hope-chest part of my trousseau. And not to worry if I didn't get all the clothes; we would finish it off in New York at Bergdorf Goodman. Apart from my going-away suit and the filmies, I don't remember any single garment I had. Under the circumstances I didn't get to spend all that much. I had $3,000 left over, and David insisted I keep it as a nest egg. It represented all the capital I was to have for many a year.

For the most part, I seemed to myself like a somnambulist. I was deeply touched by Mother and came alive only with David; there was no other reality. The rest of the time I went about my self-assigned tasks like an automaton. I don't remember performing them; I only remember watching this stranger as though from a hiding place. I watched her carefully about the lingerie because I knew she had planned it and would be sorry later if she didn't get it; by the time I got to wear all this, everything would be fine and right. My father would see to it, I didn't know how or when.

I was married right in the living room, where flowers transformed the fireplace into an altar. Adrian designed my gown and I wore Edie's veil, reduced to manageable proportions. I recall hearing voices, my father's amongst them, from his room, where David and his ushers had gathered. I waited, not for the strains of the wedding march, but for my father to come, take me in his arms, and give me his blessing. Then the music began and my bridesmaids started down; I hung back until I was told my father was waiting at the foot of the stairs. When I got there, instead of taking his arm, I tried to make peace. The procession was already in the living room by the time we started. Surely no one ever had a walk to the altar like mine. I marched down the aisle on his arm, still pleading with him, as he shushed me, all in full view of the guests. By the time I got to the altar, I had dried my tears, but I looked wan and grave. My vows weren't audible more than ten feet away.

The wedding was small and simple, despite the men being in white tie. It would have been smaller still if we could have omitted the relatives. The Selznicks at least contributed none except David's brother Howard and his family. Myron was David's best man and Edith was my matron of honor. Janet Gaynor, my best friend, was the only one of my brides-maids really close to me. There were tables outside on the terrace and a small orchestra. Naturally I danced with David first. Then my father asked for the next dance. If I'd had any guts I'd have said, "No, first let's go in the next room and talk this thing out." I didn't. I danced with him, as normal as apple pie.

The only stupendous part of the wedding was the size of the police force outside the house, doubtless arranged for by my father. An imperial touch was added by a double police escort to see our limousine speedily off to Santa Barbara. It took David several miles to shake them. All I felt was relief, relief. I had made it. I couldn't believe it.

I had not been a radiant bride, nor was I a joyous one now. I was simply exhausted by the accumulated misery and strain.

When we reached the Santa Barbara Biltmore, close to midnight, awaiting me there were the results of David's extravagant planning. Flowers and more flowers, all with notes. An elaborate supper, complete with candles and champagne and waiters in and out. It was a sequence out of a movie, and over-produced at that.

I furnished the next hurdle with my accoutrements. When I tackled my bags, I discovered that I was not used to their splendor either. They had been subjected to the same treatment as Edie's, everything packed in layers and layers of tissue paper, even pleated paper. Out came the bridal-night outfit with its clouds of tissue. I didn't know whether I was supposed to straighten up or leave it all strewn about, or how I'd ever get it all back in. My biggest effort had been the nightie and the flowing Grecian negligée, girdled with knotted fringe and tassels. With any sense I'd have worn it for supper. It was a knockout, but impractical; it had invisible openings fit for a Miss Houdini. David kept calling from the next room while I was struggling with that negligée. I couldn't much see the sense of it—why I had to get into this damn thing and then have to get out of it; it seemed so contrived. I suppose I'd had a scene from a movie in mind myself.

If nothing else, the trappings alone would have sunk us. Only David knew it was not a glorious night of love. He was strangely subdued the next day. By the following afternoon even I was only too willing to join his family for dinner in Pasadena, where we were boarding the Chief.

Myron sent his Duesenberg to bring us down to Pasadena with our six bags. The scenario turned to slapstick with elements of burlesque and thriller. When we all got into his parents' Cadillac to go to the station, Myron told his own driver to take our bags to the Santa Fe. He did, but he went to the Los Angeles station, from which the train had already departed. When it finally dawned on us, panic set in. Myron called the police, hoping to find the driver and turn him around; the car would be easy to spot, because it was the only Duesenberg in town. I banked on the driver to realize his mistake in the half-hour we had to spare. David stood there debating what to do—after all, it was a five-day trip. Myron assured us we'd have our bags by San Bernardino. We got on the train.

Uppermost in my mind was that we would look ridiculous if the story ever got out. Little did I know that Louella would get it right into print. I hoped for privacy, which was preposterous, because by San Bernardino the whole train knew that the honeymoon couple whose wedding had been all over the front page of the *Los Angeles Times* was aboard without any luggage.

Our fellow passengers were amused, faintly curious, and generous. David declined their offers for the time being, but stubble appeared before he could buy a razor. Telegrams flew back and forth. Our audience became embroiled in the suspense with which we awaited the luggage at each stop. They cheered us on: "Better luck at the next town." We made frantic scurries to buy emergency toilet articles. David got a big laugh when he walked into the dining car in a borrowed shirt three sizes too big. Then a definitive telegram came from Myron, saying we could count on Albuquerque. There were pools on the arrival. We bet against it, figuring to win either way. Well, we won. There were no bags.

Myron's next wire said the plane had been forced back by a storm; we'd have the bags in Washington. By that time I knew we were better off without them. Constraints had gone with the luggage; we were two happy runaways. Without the paraphernalia bogging us down, the real honeymoon began, with all the romantic advantages of an elopement. The only negligée I had was a sheet. Each improvisation brought gales of laughter.

We were aghast to get still another telegram advising us that a stunt flier who had never failed to get through had guaranteed delivery of the bags in Kansas City for $2,000. It was the last straw. Fortunately, that turned out to be a hoax.

We checked into the Washington Mayflower with a paper bag of items tagged with names and addresses, and our contingency plan for David to hire a dinner jacket and me to buy a dress at the last possible moment. But, lo, we found the air-flown luggage had arrived. No longer in awe of it, I ripped open what I needed, and off we went.

My actual White House memories begin about a year before with a startling visit. I mean startling. Seated around the Hoover dinner table was a handful of people. Midway through the meal appeared a perfect stranger, who had entered quietly and stood there about ten feet from the President. It was immediately obvious that the room was unguarded. We sat frozen in an awful silence. After "Who are you?" the thing uppermost in Hoover's mind was "How did you get in?" Equally unguarded, apparently, was the front door, through which the man had strolled; and, it would seem, so was the front gate as well. The man was quite polite; he had come a considerable distance to tell the President he needed a job because of the "terrible unemployment." Then the room filled with people. What is notable about that occasion is that from the next day on, March 13, 1929, the Secret Service was put in charge of the White House police by Presidential order.

That was no subject for me to mention at the White House that evening with David. Also taboo by agreement was the tale of our disreputable journey. At the table someone conventionally asked, "Did you have a nice trip?" whereupon David blurted out the entire saga, to the general merriment. I omitted that detail in a letter home, but I boldly mentioned that "we arrived back at the Sherry Netherland in full White House regalia at 6 A.M."

That certainly was the shape of things to come. We hit New York like two drunken sailors. We stayed up for the sake of staying up, a revenge on those hundreds of curfews. We wound up every evening by going back to the Casino in the Park to dance, then on to Reuben's or a ride through the park in a carriage. David got hold of some liquor, called his friends. We had a cocktail party for several days running in our suite. I couldn't mix a drink, I couldn't even swallow one, but I already had colored nail polish and was proudly smoking Chesterfields.

Men were occasionally seen at Bergdorf's, but the store was not used to a bridegroom on a binge. We turned the fourth floor upside down. David wanted to see "the smartest clothes you have," and thought he was paying for them. Mannequins paraded, attendants increased, David made me try on things I wouldn't dream of wearing—décolleté, slinky evening gowns, which we ended up buying.

We sailed on the *Olympic,* loaded down with gifts and flowers. We so impressed the Cunard Line that they added a third room to our suite. David produced a lady's maid—that was luxe in a hurry. There were even corsages, which David had planned for every evening, the only flowers for which I didn't have to write a note. Hanging over my head were not only the thank-you letters for the wedding presents, the bane of brides, but I had as well to say thanks for all those bon-voyage offerings. I'd have been twice as grateful if their cards had said, "You're on your honeymoon, don't bother to acknowledge this."

The most important letter I had to write was done in snatched moments. Like a little girl going off to camp, I had rashly promised my mother to write everything. Having made the promise, I had to keep it. We had been five in that house. Now they were two, and I was worried about my poor mother. In order to finish the letter in time for the pilot boat, I stupidly deserted David at the rail as our ship pulled away from the pier. I was wrong whatever I did.

The drama of writing home continued. The next scene was set in our hotel in Paris. While David had a nap one afternoon in the bedroom, I took my guilt to the sitting room and proceeded to write the family another installment. I laid out all my bits of scribble which I'd been hoarding. Suddenly David walked in, and I was caught in the act—or so it seemed to him, because I put my hands quickly over the letter and the scraps of paper. He reacted even more sharply than I had and demanded to know what was going on. I lost my cool and I lost my head. I said it was nothing at all; I was just writing a letter to my family. If that was so, why was I so guilty and frantic? "Let me see it." I said it was private; he said it was not. That's the only time I ever recall him losing his temper with me, or me with him. In fact, it's the only fight we ever had, more's the pity.

I grabbed the scraps in my hand and ran. We were both mad as hell. We knocked over the furniture, the lamps. We wrestled. He was bigger and stronger, but I was faster. We were equally determined. In the end, my notes were in ribbons and I was in tears.

It was not a lovers' quarrel, it was a shambles. Out of it came a big confession on my part and a concession on his. I told the full truth of my starvation for privacy, the feeling that no deed or thought went unobserved. He said he had no curiosity, actually, and it had only been my gesture of concealment; that he trusted me. Never again in the years ahead did he look at anything I had written. He had no such phobia, so it became terribly unfair—he'd leave things on his desk so that I *would* read them. In his room in the morning he'd *ask* me to read his mail; he loved sharing it. In all the years we were married, he never once opened my cupboards or desk. He claimed that my appreciation was out of proportion. It meant something to me, and it didn't mean anything to him; it was as simple as that.

Life with D.O.S.

THERE was no Prohibition on the boat, so it was there David undertook teaching me to drink. After trial and error he found a cocktail I liked, a magic potion called an Alexander (also known as the Virgin's Downfall), which had the attraction of a chocolate ice-cream soda and a kick to boot. They were wonderful. I had them before dinner and as an after-dinner drink, and, of course, had chocolate desserts twice a day.

When it came to wine, David's taste buds were on a par with mine. When we drank tokay with our entrees, the wine steward was tactful: "Is that perhaps too sweet?" He discreetly gave up.

I stood up to the cocktails, the tokay, and the desserts without turning a hair. The addition of foie gras in Paris did me in. When I got deathly ill in the middle of the night, it took a doctor to tell David that my cocktails contained equal portions of crème de cacao, brandy, and heavy cream.

David had never been to Europe, and he felt the discomfiture common to most American males in Europe. His boasted French yielded nothing more than a repeated "mais oui"—that is, until he got to the Italian border. The Italian phrases I taught him were used in Vienna. There I was sorry I had laughed at my mother in Berlin.

Our behavior was standard. In Paris we bought terrible champagne in the so-called brothels. Very daring we thought ourselves, and we "discovered" rue Blondel. Instant sophistication was ours. Hicks. We rode the canals of Venice at night, serenaded by musicians trailing us in a second gondola.

I had learned my lesson in Paris. It was David's turn when we got to Budapest. He had never cared much for foreign food, but something about the Hungarian cuisine carried him away. Literally. At a luncheon given for us by a friend well known for his table, David lost his head over the hors d'oeuvres, which were as rich as they were delicious. He wouldn't stop. My warnings went unheeded, and there was yet a meal to go. He was sick all afternoon.

In the middle of the night I thought *he* was dying and summoned a doctor. As the doctor didn't speak English, he wasn't much help. David was so uncomfortable he went to sleep. Days went by; he couldn't be roused for more than a minute at a time.

Finally I decided I'd better get him out of there, so early one morning, with the help of a couple of friends, I got him vertical, a zombie with a three-day beard. I put a pair of trousers and an overcoat over his pajamas, stuffed his hair, which had turned into a Harpo Marx wig, under a hat, put whatever belonged in his pockets into a purse I hung on his arm, and steered him into a taxi to the train station. Poor thing. I not only packed his bag, I packed *him*. There on the platform he was a standing piece of luggage. On the train he went back to sleep as soundly as though he were still in Budapest, and woke up as the train slowed down just outside Paris, fit as a fiddle, wondering where we were.

David had had enough of the Continent, quite apart from rich food and foreign languages. Being an Anglophile, he had looked forward to London; *there* he would show me what kind of cosmopolite he was. We had a fine time in London, buying David's trousseau and running out of money, and along the way we met some people who were to cross—and re-cross—our paths for the rest of our lives. One David already knew —Sidney Bernstein, a young bachelor a few years older than he was, who owned a chain of movie theatres. He asked us to dine, which didn't sound promising to me. However, Sidney turned out to be charming and cultured, and the evening at his townhouse was a remarkably well-put-together dinner party. It was delightful, but my praise irked David, who demanded to know what the hell I was so impressed with.

It was also in London, in our suite at the Savoy, that I had my first taste of being a producer's wife. An actor named Laurence Olivier and his fiancée, Jill Esmond, came to call; they had attracted some attention on the London stage and were considering Hollywood. David was enthusiastic, but their price proved too high for Paramount. Nevertheless, both the Selznicks were fated to play a part in Olivier's life.

Needless to say, we were broke when we boarded the *Ile de France* for the trip home. We had barely enough to see us across. David assured me that $3,000 from Myron would be waiting for us at the dock; at least we could pay customs.

Even the French Line indulged us by unexpectedly giving us a handsome suite. Awaiting me were beautiful red roses from Leland Hayward, a delight but not a surprise. He had begun the red roses the day my engagement was announced, and they went on appearing all through the honeymoon. It was an original wedding present, one of the happiest to remember.

A couple of days before docking, in the middle of a lovely afternoon, feeling exultant, David threw himself backward with abandon and fell spread-eagled on the bed, unaware of a low-jutting bedpost, on which he landed with cruel precision. He limped painfully off the boat. It took a surgeon in Los Angeles to mend the tender part of his bottom.

I had been bewildered by a cable from Mother announcing that she was meeting the boat. What might seem odd on a honeymoon proved a pleasure, because David was laid up during our day or two in New York and on the train. Mother had never traveled alone, and I couldn't imagine what could have induced her to undertake this journey. My father telephoned in confidence to explain. Since my marriage, her weeping in the middle of the night had been heartbreaking. He had been unable to console her, and so had proposed this solution. That shed new light on a line Mother had written me: "Dad tries to be tender and sweet; he does everything to please me." She was gay, once assured she was welcome. Yet it was a faint cause for worry.

Clearly, David had left quite a gap too, because his mother had cabled Budapest inviting us to stay with them on our return. We'd no more do that than my mother would join us on our honeymoon! Peculiar couple, one way without luggage, the other with a mother-in-law.

Both families sat around the Selznick dinner table that first night, having met us at Pasadena. (Not Myron. He got on the train at San Bernardino.) But the occasion did not recur. No extended family circle developed.

It was to be expected that the Selznick parents would be models of non-interference. Unexpectedly, so were the Mayers. As time went on, I couldn't help being aware how desperately my parents missed having their children under their roof, and the less said about it, the better. They seemed far more alone than the marriage of two daughters warranted.

Strangely enough, my father never referred to the awful session in his office, nor did I. I looked forward to talking it all over someday, but we never did. Not that it would have helped. It is remarkable that the incident didn't estrange us. For me, the only gain was an immediate rather than a gradual independence, but what had happened did not alter the fundamental bond. Nevertheless, that day in Dad's office cost him a certain latitude with me. I was not less devoted, but I became more vigilant. I must add, though, that from that day on he never again tried to run my life.

Without a roof, where does one go? With money, to a hotel, of course. Without money, a Selznick goes to the best hotel, at that time the Ambassador. I thought it incumbent upon me to find a furnished house quickly, the better to open and unpack that ever-threatening pile of damn presents.

No more remote areas for me, no canyons, just basic Beverly Hills streets, where houses were then not numerous. The bewildered real-estate agents were at a loss between this limitation and their clients' opposing ideas of scale. As the weeks went by, there was no compromise in sight, and as the hotel expenses mounted, I couldn't stand it. We moved into Whittier Drive with David's parents. I didn't know how to break the news to my parents, who had always spoken with horror and pity of people who lived with in-laws.

Well, that was the nicest holiday I ever had. Never before or since have I lived so without pressure or responsibility. My house-hunting was leisurely. I had to recover from the honeymoon, and we were out most nights having a high old time. Mother Selznick was a model of delicacy —never a comment or question beyond "Will you be in for a meal? How many guests?" For Pop, it was bliss. All he had lost was the privilege of undressing David and putting him to bed. On the other hand, he no longer had to worry about David falling asleep at the wheel driving home from Santa Monica.

Living there, I learned how really spoiled David had been. It seemed to go unnoticed when he was an hour or two late for dinner or brought home unexpected guests. I wondered—and then connected this to a conversation I had had with Mrs. Paine, the owner of the best domestic agency in town. Calling to offer best wishes on my engagement, she had added, "There will be a lot of trouble, Miss Irene. I will do everything for you that I can." It seems the Selznick name was anathema in her circles, although she explained that Mrs. Selznick was a wonderful woman and it wasn't her fault.

David yielded on the grandeur, and eventually we settled into a cozy little house on Camden Drive belonging to the silent screen star Blanche Sweet, who had lived there when she was married to Marshall Neilan. It boasted powder-blue handkerchief-linen sheets, which she hadn't entrusted to any previous tenant, as they were to be hand-ironed. She had the wrong Mayer girl as a tenant. Between Blanche's instructions and the taste David had acquired on his travels for fresh sheets every night, it was a struggle. My practical self re-emerged, and soon we were sleeping on Wamsutta percale.

All that was modest was the size of the house and our resources. Except for my nest egg, which was to be kept inviolate, we moved in without a dollar in the world other than David's salary—more than enough for anyone but David—and started off in life with a mere three servants. That was not all. A chauffeur was soon added for the recently bestowed Cadillac: David was a menace on the road, so, as he pointed out, this was a conservative move. If so, it was the only one.

I never cast a play with more loving care and precision than I assembled my first staff. Depression year or not, off they tootled after a couple of days. As Mrs. Paine had said, "It's a matter of the hours." I trembled lest my father hear of my humiliation. Here I was at the outset of my career and I was fumbling the ball. It wasn't all David's crazy schedule, because it developed that I didn't know how to interview. It seems I gave them the story of my life as I told them how I wanted things done. Finally Mrs. Paine sent me a remarkable Swedish woman, Mrs. Ides, as a personal maid, who arrived and took me over. There was nothing this woman did not know about the running of establishments far beyond mine. Having overheard me interviewing a butler, she offered some advice which, put less politely, boiled down to: "If you're talking, you can't hear. If you don't listen, you can't learn. Let *them* do the talking." Five years later, when we moved into the house we built, she departed, saying, "This is a new life. I've taught you all I can." She initiated my lifelong love of Scandinavians.

I didn't get to say a word when I interviewed the cook. Peder Pederson insisted on seeing me, although I told Mrs. Paine not to send a chef, even a Danish one, because it made me feel ridiculous. He told me firmly and benevolently that he was coming to work for me, however unsuitable I found it. In the Depression, he said, the large houses to which he was accustomed were cutting back on second chefs and kitchen maids, but not on their demands; he thought it would be refreshing to work for a bride. I explained the impracticality, the size of our house, and the miserable problem of our dinner hour. He smiled and said he would take care of everything. He requested only that he be permitted to wear his chef's hat and kerchief. "Little lady, I will start you out right. Your food will be the talk of the town. Your house will acquire a fine reputation." Pederson stayed long enough to cultivate my palate, and then went off to Pickfair, where he reigned for some years.

David suggested a six months' lease, "in case we don't really like it." What he really hankered for was the beach, but only in the summer. It would have meant moving every six months, and was out of the question, so David said, "Why don't you fix the place up?" and I set about the job as though we were going to live there forever.

I picked up a couple of secondhand upholstered chairs for $10 each and a sofa for $15, which I had inexpensively and cheerfully slipcovered, and some raw wood pieces I had sprayed. David's dowry consisted of books —stacks of them, his well-thumbed classics and the endless and ever-increasing number he hoped to read when he had time. They grew into an avalanche. Shelves had to be installed. So did a peculiar system of bells and telephones.

By the time I'd got Camden Drive the way we wanted it, it was time to go house-hunting—at the beach, of course. We had seven fixed residences in less than four years.

David had won the first financial round—the honeymoon—and now we had to square off about the future. He didn't believe in saving pennies; pennies were chicken feed and there were millions on the horizon. His only reluctance to spend centered on his concern for my independence in case something happened to him. He was determined I not look to my father for support, so he committed the un-Selznick act of taking out life-insurance policies. He wasn't moderate here either, as I was to live in a style to which he intended to accustom me. I couldn't accuse him of not saving money because, as he explained, it was a form of saving.

I never cared about having a lot of money; I could have lived at any level, even minimum, as long as I knew where I stood. Naturally, we couldn't agree on our living expenses. The only budget David understood related to a movie. But I could budget myself. When I couldn't get him below a walloping $500 a week for me, I succeeded in including the rent, auto expenses, gifts—in fact, everything except doctors, taxes, and insurance. I thought our affairs would soon be in good shape, because David had recently acquired a business manager, Rex Cole, who had him on a spending allowance. No one imagined he'd need an extra one for losses, loans, and debts.

Paramount had decided to invite David to join the fortunate few who acquired stock advantageously on a weekly basis. Flattered, he now availed himself of the privilege like the steady fellow he wasn't. But the rewards of virtue were not his. As his shares increased, the stock went down, and his enthusiasm for enforced saving sank accordingly. Wall Street was more than a little rocky. He said, "Look at the money I've saved by not saving. If I'd had some, I might have bought other stocks. I'm ahead of the game." All this only reinforced his feeling that we could have had a lot of fun with the money—and they couldn't have taken that away from us.

Yes, David was a hedonist. Not only the good life, but fun—the best and the most. He was a very poor man with a very big salary. All he wanted was quantity, quality, and variety.

I was used to direction, to limits. Now there was no one to say me nay. Had I embraced the freedom offered me, I would have got the bends. Having presumably settled down, we proceeded to knock ourselves out. David worked like a demon and I was busy matching his diligence. I worked to reinforce his view that everything was possible; it wasn't money I spent, but effort. So he had his way and, privately, I had mine. I shared his fun and had an easy conscience all in one. I was giddy with delight and usefulness.

Coming home one evening, David found me at my desk, bent over my checkbook. The image of his wife poring over figures offended him; it was depressing. He accused me of economizing. It showed a lack of faith. There had been a worse offense: I had darned a pair of socks. (Pretty damned well, too.) David was mortified. Oh, the insult to him! If I would just learn to be extravagant, even go into debt, it would prove my confidence in him. I, on the other hand, wanted to show him my checkbook; I thought he should know where his money went. I was mistaken; I must learn it wasn't *his,* it was *ours.* He was affronted at the notion of looking at my accounts, he didn't even want *me* looking at them. He wanted to picture me having fun, not paying bills. Turn it all over to Rex Cole. I wept, but I turned everything over except a new leaf. Old habits die hard, even good ones.

Our entertaining also took off on no ordinary level: Adolph Zukor, no less, the most powerful man in the industry. He was in town, and David proposed that we give a party for him. I thought that was presumptuous, an honor premature by several years. David said to invite him anyhow, he needn't accept. But he did. It was a quantum leap for me, but my first dinner party went so smoothly that David said once again, "See how easy it is?" David's motive for the invitation wasn't business but family. Zukor and Pop had at one time or other been rivals, partners, enemies. It must have given Pop odd satisfaction. In any case, David wasn't shining up to the big boss, inasmuch as he already had one foot out the door.

In his four years at Paramount he was unexpectedly an organization man, a passionate one. His proposals for productions, while put respectfully, were so bold, even audacious, that I don't know how he dared. I also don't know how he dared come in late as often as he did. They not only put up with him, they gave him a raise. They put him in charge of the studio for a few months when Ben Schulberg was in Europe, and when he got restive they gave him another $500 raise. Of course, they not only had in him an understudy to Ben, they had as well a possible Thalberg of their own, and in me, an unknown ally. I thought that some day in the far-off future he might be the head of that studio.

By this time the company was no longer at the top; MGM ranked first with a commanding lead. David had become increasingly critical over there on Marathon Avenue, disagreeing violently with how the pictures were being made. Ben's personal life and habits had undergone a marked change which seemed to affect his judgment. Repeatedly, David wanted out. I thought the impulse to leave was only a reflex, and each previous time I had dissuaded him. This was different. He thought the studio was on a disaster course and he didn't want to go down with the ship.

He stopped telling them how to run the place and got busy getting out of the contract he had signed a few months before with Lasky's promise of freedom if he was unhappy. Perhaps David was only a little too big for his britches, but he certainly was getting too big for his job. As freedom loomed, it reawakened his longing for independence and his own little company. His old pal Milestone, now at the top of the heap, was a kindred soul who listened to the point of joining up.

A young man in 1931 had to be either optimistic, courageous, or foolhardy to walk out on $2,000 a week. He was all three. Yet I was sorry to see David go, because Paramount's troubles worsened. And I was sorry about Schulberg too, who was judged only on his fall from grace and not given credit for his achievements, which had been enormous.

N O W   D A V I D had it all. A house on that strip of Santa Monica beach, albeit the tiniest, with a pool of matching size. He had a company called Selznick-Milestone. Most important, he had the offer from Jesse Lasky of a distribution release by Paramount, something no major company had yet granted an independent producer.

The company consisted of promises and plans. Millie would get half the profits of films he directed, which would attract other directors with similar deals. It could be the beginning of empire!

David went to New York to settle his own deal and arrange financing. There was no sense in my going because he would be there only a few days. Myron went with him, almost taking them back to their bachelor days. David wrote from the train: "Enjoying Myron immensely and he me, I'm sure. He seems so young and quaint somehow. I do love him so tremendously!" They spent the first weekend with the Wangers, where Myron had a nip-and-tuck with his appendix, which brought Sam Hirshfeld, a brilliant young surgeon friend of the Wangers, into our lives. It also brought Marjorie and me on the next train. In asking me to come, David had added, "Anyhow, it's going to take me a week or two longer here than I expected."

That week or two stretched into a long, hot summer. The Paramount release melted away. So did others, each just around the corner and each taking endless weeks to peter out. David shook off the rejections like a spaniel just out of the water and regrouped his forces. No two days were alike except for the degree of optimism, very little of which was warranted. His practical, realistic wife didn't face up either; I had more faith than qualms. We were always "on the verge"; these were not setbacks, only delays, as explained to Millie, who continued to string along.

Simultaneously, David was lining up backing. There was nothing he enjoyed professionally as much as promoting—he wasn't his father's son for nothing. Each new prospect was an adventure. I accused him of preferring the promoting to actually getting the funds.

Merian Cooper, something of a promoter himself, was in New York and at loose ends. He had recently directed *Four Feathers* at Paramount for David, a very successful film. He was an adventurous fellow who had been an explorer and a wartime flier; I believe there was even a statue erected to him in Poland. He had access to some impressive names who would love to invest in pictures, Depression or not. I scoffed, particularly when his last prospect, C. V. Whitney—well known as Sonny—didn't materialize until it was too late.

Coop would show up to follow the returns on strategic days. I'd ask him while I was waiting for David why he was hanging around, such an important fellow whose services were so in demand. What was in it for him? He told me to wait and see. He was the most farsighted of all.

No job, no money, no deals. It sounds abysmal, and anyone but David would have been suicidal. I had no idea we were having a terrible time because it was wonderful. From Saturday lunch with Otto Kahn at Cold Spring Harbor we proceeded to an exclusive Mayfair dance with Cary Grant when he was appearing as a leading man opposite Fay Wray in his first Broadway musical and was still called Archie Leach. Very nice I thought he was.

Meanwhile, we were back on Myron's bounty and never felt it. David and I were ensconced in a suite in the Pierre which had expanded to four rooms. After a while I thought we ought to move to a less expensive hotel, which only went to show how little I knew about promoting. It was chicken feed again and the most expensive economy imaginable! Besides, it lessened one's position in negotiating. The opening of this beautiful hotel had coincided with the Depression, and they didn't have many guests. They were so badly off they viewed our possible move with concern; they needed us and we needed them. And so we compromised with the Pierre and stayed on in style. It was a far cry from the days described by Ben Hecht as "Myron and David Selznick zigzagging through the town to throw creditors off the scent."

There was further proof that Myron's fortunes were definitely very high. One afternoon the doorbell rang and in came—surely in error— a set of the most luxurious pigskin luggage to be had. It was followed shortly by a squat Japanese gentleman, faultlessly groomed and attired. If Myron was back in the chips, Ishi was back in the fold. He was on his way to California. Ishi, who had long experience of listening to Mother Selznick, from then on had direct control of Myron's house, thereby putting it under Mother Selznick's guidance. Marjorie was a very tolerant woman.

Ishi had not taken any salary his last year with the family, but he was more prosperous than ever, judging from his custom-made clothes and shoes. There were rumors that he was the Baron Ishi and had money. Nothing was ever confirmed, yet Ishi departed for Japan the day after Pearl Harbor.

The summer passed. We lamented only the abandoned little house by the sea. When our lease ran out, Betty Ides sent me fall clothes and moved us into storage. What a distressing sight the van must have been for my mother, a few doors away.

I sensed her growing concern in her weekly calls. Finally one Sunday morning she burst out, "Why don't you both come back? I beg you. My heart aches for you." She began to weep, and I tried to reassure her. I couldn't understand her anxiety. I didn't realize she knew something I didn't know. However, her timing was fine; it was about a week before the breakthrough.

David was finally running out of major companies. Only MGM had not been approached, understandably, and wouldn't have been, even if my father had not strongly opposed David's plan. So there was none left but lowly RKO, whose only distinction was being owned by RCA. Therefore RKO was necessary, but then when David Sarnoff joined the meetings, RKO became infinitely desirable. Sarnoff, with his expansive personality and tremendous vision, completely bowled David Selznick over, the only person, I believe, who ever did. David found him a giant, yet it was like a homecoming.

When they got close to a deal, Millie suddenly was no longer available, which was awful. One couldn't blame him, though, for giving up, not after months of turning down other offers. He had no way of knowing the RKO talks wouldn't also turn out to be futile. Except for Sarnoff, they probably would have been. David sought an appointment with Sarnoff to break the sad news—a meeting that took an unexpected turn. Sarnoff asked David a lot of questions about himself, about the industry, and about RKO. The upshot was, he offered him the studio. A studio, a whole studio! Vice-president in charge of production!! I was staggered.

There was a flurry and a hurry and we whizzed home. To me, it was make-believe and only became a reality when we got to Pasadena and in time-honored custom were greeted by a row of photographers just as though he were the head of a studio.

It was a triumph for David; not the one he was after, nevertheless a big feather in his cap. There he was, about to sit in with the big boys, those chieftains, led by my father, who had doomed his hopes. I discovered this when my mother innocently blurted it out by telling me how overjoyed she was that we had returned in victory. She'd thought we knew—everybody did but us. David's plan had not been "in the best interests of the picture business," most particularly of the studios.

So David joined the meetings of that little group who had held the line against him. Incredibly, he felt no grievance, held no grudge. Deep inside, I was not that generous, even though my father presented a reasonable case. Obviously, his obligation was not to indulge the impulses of a son-in-law, but to protect his company and the industry.

I don't recall anger between them, even after the terrible morning in Dad's office. The clash I expected never came; nor did I ever learn where respect left off and affection began. Looking back, I'm reminded of how much weight ability carried with Dad, and that David had a hang-up about fathers. Or had they called a permanent truce after the pre-marital Culver City scene?

Of course, David understood Dad's weaknesses, for which he made allowances, and my father returned the courtesy. He made no attempt to control David; he may have wanted to, but he didn't try. Wise old owl. On the other hand, it can't have been as uncomplicated as it appears now; perhaps I have unwittingly drawn a merciful veil.

FROM the first, our life together was dominated by parties, gambling, and—most of all—work. For though David believed in fun, more fun, and still more fun, his chief priority always remained the job.

He didn't have to persuade me to take his work as seriously as he did —he got me that way, with a post-graduate degree from Louis B. I thought these men had it very hard; in fact, I pitied them. I didn't see how they could stand up under their burdens, because I found it hard to face even the responsibility of giving advice. I was chicken, but at least not domineering; after all, I gave opinions, not orders. I'm sure it was believed that I swayed his decisions. What I thought seemed to carry so much weight, I had to take utmost care. Not letting him know my bottom-line opinion made it a game. Sometimes just a simple question, lethal in effect, was enough to produce both decision and laughter.

He set so much store by what I thought that it made me feel a fake. I don't think it was what I said as much as what he distilled out of it. I couldn't believe that common sense could rate so high. By discounting a little of his version and putting myself in the other fellow's boots, I sometimes could come up with an aspect that hadn't occurred to him. He told people I had a crystal ball.

I don't know how, but I managed to resist his entreaties to read scripts. After a night of talk and still so much unsaid, I didn't want to add script discussion. I refused to speak up and be bright. (Or worse, be stupid.) And then have to read the rewrites. What's more, if I read scripts, I'd soon be watching rushes.

But though I stood back from the work itself, his striving for perfection was totally understandable to me. I was willing to sacrifice for that; in fact, it seemed perfectly natural. There were others as idealistic as he about the movies who perhaps lacked his opportunity or courage; he was in a position to act on his beliefs, and I subscribed to his crusading spirit and marveled at his capacity to bring about changes. Movies were like a great cause to us; to be pretentious, you could call it a sense of mission. I reinforced his aspirations. We had one romance with each other and another with the movies.

We gloried in the success of every fine film; every time a good movie succeeded, it helped everybody. We deeply resented the ballyhoo employed to put over an expensive flop, and we were bitter about the rip-off people who came in, did a bad job, took their money, and then gave interviews running Hollywood down. It was copy-cat land. David felt that if he made a fine picture others would think success lay in quality and compete in that area, and the word "Hollywood" would soon lose its pejorative connotations.

We were both idealistic about Hollywood, but it was better to think it and do it . . . just don't say it. That was for the fakes and the temperamentals. It was embarrassing to use the word "ideals," a word much bandied about and given lip-service. We thought every film made a difference, and David's caring extended to reaching for quality in each detail, every line of dialogue, every bit of casting. If we went to a movie theatre where the projection was poor, David followed up with letters to the exhibitor and to the distributor. "Excelsior" was being replayed for me. I couldn't understand why people in Hollywood

The tennis court on the sand, 1929: Felix and Martha Young, Sylvia and Irving Thalberg, Edith, Zion Myers, Norma Shearer, Benny Zeidman, David O. Selznick, Irene, Bernie Fineman

The Selznick boys,
Myron, David, and Howard

David, 1929

The wedding, 1930

David and Irene with Jeffrey and Dann[i]

Danny, Jeffrey, and Louis B.

At hon

Joan Payson, Irene, David, and Jock Whitney at Ocean Park Pier

At a costume party in 1931. Irene is dressed as Dolores
Del Rio in *Bird of Paradise*, David as Ed Wynn,
and Myron is just in costume.

David and Irene with George Cukor (right) leaving Los Angeles
for New York and then London to cast *David Copperfield*, 1933

David, Mary Pickford, Charlie Chaplin, and Irene, 1941

The Hollywood premiere of *Gone With the Wind*: Jock Whitney, Irene, Olivia de Havilland, David, Vivien Leigh, and Laurence Olivier

Carole Lombard, Clark Gable, and David

were not more protective of the picture business—*their* business.

David's intensity was not for success per se, but for the work itself. When the ignition switch mysteriously turned itself on, the wheels in his head would spin. Movies were as natural to him as swimming to a fish. They became his second language. Ideas were hatched at an incredible speed, yet they tumbled out so wonderfully structured. He had such a fertile brain that alternatives were endless. He just emptied his mind as he went. What he didn't say, he jotted down; once he got it down on paper, he felt it was already partly done. He left for the studio, his pockets jammed with endless bits of paper, convinced that half as many more had been thrown out. Then he found a gadget that held a huge roll of paper two inches wide that slid onto a writing surface. It enabled him to start his studio day with a single piece of paper, anywhere from six to sixty inches long. And from it memos flowed.

These, which had once been so effective, contributing largely to his early success, now became longer and more frequent. He became addicted. People groaned at the sight of them and took to calling him Meemo. He found that funny and told them they'd be getting still more—beware. His memos enabled him to get it all off his chest, to make what he was thinking a matter of record. Besides, he couldn't be interrupted. He said if he'd had time, he'd have edited them down. A fitting punishment was to occasionally make him read a whopper aloud.

But the talk, the memos, the obsession had only one goal—to make the work as good as possible. That gave him lots of leeway with me. To David, work was only real work if it was done at ungodly hours or under intense pressure. Whereas to me, it was not a question of when or how long you work, but, is it any good? I acknowledged no law saying that midnight oil, deadline, and overwork made up the essential formula for results.

I can't think of a more complicated life-work than keeping the engines running and wheels greased for a man like David. I had to compete for servants with normal households, eventually trying to get people before the grapevine got to them. There was no simple solution: David couldn't be expected to adapt his hours to what suited the servants and vice versa. I needed understanding from the staff and cooperation from agencies. Because I didn't believe there weren't possible cooks, dear Mrs. Paine permitted me to riffle through drawers of cards in her office after hours. I reached one box she hadn't intended me to see. Card after card said, "Not Selznick." Cooks in the know had mutinied in advance. David felt the sensible thing was simply to hire two shifts. Expense apart, I asked, which hours? Sleep where and administered by whom? David suggested an executive housekeeper (before Mrs. Danvers existed), but I had no place to put *her*.

Actually, our home was entitled to worse domestic troubles than it received. I marvel still that I was able to find and keep some remarkable people. My savior was a butler, James Farr. My luck was in getting him right off the train the day he arrived from New York. He was a tall, reserved Englishman with taste and wisdom who saved my sanity and stood by me—I don't know why—for almost twenty years. The one who topped even Farr was my maid Hildur Nordquist Pearson—Swedish, naturally—who put up with me for thirty-two years.

Mine was not only woman's work; it was a full-time job, increasingly demanding, but made possible by David's capacity to laugh at himself. He would do a résumé, starting with some small but unreasonable thing and recalling all his demands and contradictions until the entire structure appeared completely ridiculous to him. As his perspective returned his hilarious indictment of himself would clear the air.

He realized how illogical he really was. Sometimes in a memo to me he would recognize that the memo itself was preposterous and dictate his own reaction, in fact, tell me to forget the whole thing, but send it anyhow so I would acknowledge that he was also reasonable.

He was so damned grateful it gave him ever more license, and if it didn't, he took it anyway . . . with humor, and apologies. However, he kept saying, "Why do you knock yourself out? Take it easy." There was no way, because the demands remained and expectations escalated. "Wouldn't it be fun if we . . . ?" Eventually I said that "fun" was a dirty word.

But it wasn't thankless work. What woman can resist being called a Wonder Woman? I was the only wife I knew who complained of too much appreciation. It was overwhelming and addictive. The praise pleased me at the same time that it victimized me. I maintained the pattern instead of rebelling. I was even flattered by the challenge of a party at an hour's notice. "I knew you could handle it easily." The shops were closed, we didn't have freezers then, but I pulled it off and got good marks. I actually did have the sense to say, "Please don't try *that* again." He wanted the results, but at no cost to me. He wanted me to have freedom. I should have said, "Don't tell me to be free, help me."

But whenever I accomplished something he had considered impossible, it only furthered his belief in luck and magic.

D A V I D spent himself and his money with equal abandon. He was easy-going but not tranquil, endowed with high spirits and boundless energy. Containment wasn't his. He was all over the place; but then my energy would probably have swamped anyone else.

He granted me every conceivable latitude: "Do whatever you want to do." What I wanted to do most in the world was to look after his needs and pleasures, be admired and loved for it, to enjoy him and to share his life. If I hadn't been so accommodating and efficient, it might have served David better in the long run. But it wasn't his fault. I didn't feel imposed on. I was privileged! *This* was exactly what I wanted to do: be fully used; grow, learn; have his dreams come true. This was not unselfishness, it just happened to be the limit of my ambition. I was not only old-school, I was old-country.

He gave too much. Then he was able to say, "Bear with me, indulge me." I gave too much in return, and was as adoring, as believing as Pop, but, alas, with a critical eye. "How can you put up with me?" How indeed? Quite simply, he possessed a combination of qualities I couldn't resist. Besides, he was a big strong fascinating man.

We bribed each other, but not in the coin the other wanted, rather in the only coin each of us had. David bribed me by his good nature and his good talk. His spirits at dinner were almost unfailingly high. I wouldn't go to the studio, but he brought the studio to me. What there wasn't time to tell, he mailed me—even memos, including some one-liners about his perennial lack of handkerchiefs. I bribed him by doing the impossible: by making it possible for him to be impossible.

D A V I D may have had a wife and, eventually, children, but he was otherwise unencumbered. He carried no keys and knew no telephone numbers except the house and the studio. There was always someone around to help him—in a pinch he could call the studio switchboard.

Keys? We left the front door unlocked on the assumption that no one would believe that possible. He also didn't carry money, which was no inconvenience at all . . . to him. He couldn't read a road map. I never knew him to add up a hotel bill or restaurant check.

It so happened I carried the contents of my telephone book in my head, for instant retrieval. They blanked out when I got to New York; I woke up the following morning and New York addresses and telephone numbers had taken their place. David was not grateful but critical; he said it was a waste of good gray matter—why bother to carry around something you could look up? He, on the other hand, knew every screen credit of every movie he'd ever seen. That was his idea of practical, and he was right.

Accountability was never demanded, but I thought availability was a good idea: David might want to reach me. I left word at all times where I was. If I couldn't be reached, I checked in at the house every hour or so. Yes, it seems excessive, but I thought it necessary.

My luggage on trains still consisted of that one bag, but his grew and grew. When one drawing room became too small for David and me *and* his luggage, we took an adjoining compartment for it. Once the porter opened the connecting doors, some of his bags would slide in and we would soon be engulfed. (There were also the telegrams at every single stop. The porter would ring the bell during the night and I would answer while David slept soundly on.) It got so bad that eventually I would leave town a day or two ahead of him. It spared me the task of getting him up at Chicago before our car went to the yards. David never believed the Santa Fe would dare do it until we spent half an hour one cold morning out in the yards, crossing acres of track before breakfast, and no porters for the luggage. It was better traveling alone.

I CAN'T claim that David led me astray. He drove himself; I drove me. We were Jack Sprat and wife. I was methodical, disciplined, and organized; David was extravagant, disorganized, and the tardiest man in town. I don't believe there were a dozen nights in the fifteen years we lived together that he got home at the hour he said he would. It took the cooperation of all the girls in the office to "get him on the road." They looked to me in the morning and I looked to them in the evening. The first call announcing a fifteen-minute delay I considered thoughtful.

Then they called again to say he'd been delayed and was just leaving. When I'd get still another call saying, "He's just left," I would ask how much longer they really thought it would be before they got him out. I had to be careful not to send false signals to the kitchen; it was hell on wheels for the cook. My choice of menus depended on what I guessed his schedule would be and on the cook's temperament.

Sometimes he himself called: "Darling, really leaving this time. Have dinner ready," and he meant it, allowing time only for an instant, very cold cocktail. When dinner was announced, David always said, "Give me a minute, I'll just wash my hands." Why don't men "wash their hands" before they have their drink?

David looked eagerly to hostesses for commendation when he wasn't more than forty-five minutes late, and couldn't understand their lack of gratitude: after all, he had extended himself to get there when he did. Because he was so late, he had to ingratiate himself with notes of apology the next day, and flowers. He showered blandishments on the other guests, who were irritated by having to wait to eat because of him. He accepted invitations with pleasure, adding a postscript, "If you don't mind my being late." If he arrived so late that the party was petering out, he did have the capacity to pull it together.

To protect himself, he had figured out a way to deal with dinner partners who bored him, which was contrary to standard formula: don't listen to them or let them get a word in edgewise. Talk! Think aloud! They'll think they're stimulating. Just never let them catch up with you again, duck when you see them.

Cooks paled when they learned the Selznicks were coming. I would wait until I heard the car pull up, then jump in the tub and still be ready twenty minutes ahead of him. I finally took to showing up on time alone, sending his clothes to the studio. I reached an understanding with hostesses —if they were good enough to invite us, they must sit down at the table without waiting for David. If we finished the meal without him, he would take what he was given on a tray.

"What's-his-name" or "What's-her-name" was the fairly standard way to refer to the less interesting partner of any couple. On paper it goes: "and wife" (or "and husband"). Hollywood is second only to Washington in making a wife's identity clear by "and wife." I very often felt like "and wife," but I didn't mind, because that's precisely what I was. I preferred reflected glory. I assumed, I believe correctly, that people would rather listen to him than to me. At table he would try to get me to speak up. I explained to him that I was only good on a one-to-one basis. He couldn't understand that I didn't want to do a rise-and-shine. The fact was that David was such a good raconteur he was better value as a dinner guest than I was. Luckily I wasn't running a popularity contest.

It was hard to get him to parties, and almost as hard getting him out, as we were inclined to overstay our welcome. We returned this courtesy, although it was not always considered as such. David would spread-eagle himself across the front door, refusing to let anyone leave. Sometimes I would have to sneak them out.

It was gradually understood that reciprocity was not necessary. David reserved the right not to go to certain houses. On the other hand, we went to others, yet extended no hospitality in return. I kept a conscience list and would bring the names up with David, who agreed completely, but said, "Some other occasion."

As for our own entertaining, the policy was his, the choice of guests mine. They got invited because we liked them, no other reason ever. No invitation came with the contract, except for the Hitchcocks on arrival. No press, no guest lists given out, no photographers. It was considered okay not to entertain at all, but if you did, you damned well alternated Hedda and Louella for business reasons. Not us; we had neither.

David liked all our old friends, but he complained that if I didn't vary people, the group was just a traveling stock company. When we were out on the town or at a big party, we'd free-lance and not hang on to each other. We were like a couple of shills, looking not for pigeons but prospects for fun; we'd add them to our list. We were eager to explore new arrivals in town. I thought it was always going to be this way, forever new waves of fascinating people to combine with the old faithful.

Dinner parties during the week faced uncertainties not necessarily due to work. For instance, one night Merle Oberon called me at 7:35, very sorry, darling, terrible for a hostess at this hour, etc. Then: "I have a pimple on my chin." "Oh?" "It mars my beauty." End of story.

Saturday night was the night to howl, the most small-town aspect of Hollywood. We specialized in Sunday parties, a custom begun when we had rented the Colleen Moore house, which gave us a taste of having a pool, tennis court, and projection room. It was considered a showplace. David had talked me into it by persuading me that it was simpler and cheaper than again moving to the beach. At last we could say, "Come and play on *our* court. Stay for supper and see a movie." Serious tennis would start around two, there would be about thirty for supper, and the party could still be going on well after midnight. I agreed that these parties were wonderful, but dragging myself up the stairs after the festivities I would feel only despair when David would say, "I can hardly wait for next Sunday!" "Oh," I would moan, "please, David, not now."

D O N ' T let this day end, extend the evening. . . . I would warn him about the next morning. He said, "You'll see, I'll be up." "Could be. But if you get in the tub, everybody will be sunk." A tub put him promptly back to sleep. If he had a decent shower instead, would he be on time. It didn't happen, because he communed with himself in the shower. Bathing, shaving, and general morning stalling were thinking time. The shower of every house we lived in was too small and the water pressure was too low. Each time the possibility of building a house came up, David would immediately mention "a decent shower."

I made him a sporting proposition. When we built, I would give him a "gorgeous" shower—vast, marble, and capable of torrent. The catch was he wasn't to have a tub. The new house was going to help get him to the studio on time. He slept anyplace he was horizontal, it made no difference if it was filled with water. He fixed me—he had it both ways. After the thrill of his shower wore off, I would find him in my tub, happily reading, or on occasion sound asleep, a script partially submerged.

Most people are at their best as they start the day off, just as they're fresh at the beginning of the week. David reversed it. Six o'clock was the shank of the afternoon, and Monday was dreaded.

It was no minor feat to wake him. My maid would tiptoe in, shake him, then shake him again, trying to get him up without waking me. That was the first step. Once up, the burden rested on Farr, who had to watch for fear David would go right back to sleep. "Please, Farr, give me ten minutes more." When he occasionally slept in his own room, he was more resistant and had to be prodded, poked, and persuaded to get up. If he wasn't seated in a chair for his breakfast the battle was lost before the day had begun.

David's optimism embraced the notion that, once vertical, he could manage breakfast before conking out. If not, another one. He meant a fresh breakfast, no "kept-warm" for him. There might be quite a series. Poor Farr. Poor cook. Of course, there might be forty winks after breakfast. Poor studio. The car would be ordered for nine o'clock;

eventually the chauffeur would have to have his lunch. If, on occasion, he set forth at a reasonable hour after eating the first breakfast served up, he could be heard saying, "I don't think I'm going to do any good work this morning."

David couldn't regulate his time. The clock was his enemy and he defied it. He was unreasonably sleepy at unreasonable times. He couldn't help being sleepy. Unfortunately, David preferred being tardy. He had loved school and now he loved his work . . . if only he could infinitely postpone it each morning. He wanted to get to it when the mood suited him, without anyone put out or cross about it. I tried everything— pretending I was asleep, or getting on with my day with my doors closed and letting the penalties teach him as his day got fouled up. He preferred me to join him so that he could talk to me. Then he could say I had delayed him. He rationalized that he did his best thinking in the morning (never mind that he also said he did his best work at night).

He could distract me from the clock with his talk and with those phone calls he enjoyed having me overhear, and by his myriad undertakings. I couldn't imagine how it could take him so much time for what we came to call his "ablutions." Witnessing them, I was still bewildered. Piles of linen hand towels were heaped on the carpet along with handkerchiefs used for "dabbing," everything freely dusted with talcum powder. As he exhausted his great stack of handkerchiefs, he usually announced that someone was stealing them regularly. I replied they'd be of use only to Donald Ogden Stewart, and Don didn't need them.

When David was tired, he slept. Oh, did he sleep! Suddenly, unexpectedly, and sometimes inadvisedly. It's all that prevented him from overdoing as much as he really would have liked to. He decided the more sleep he had, the more he needed, so there was never enough. I didn't mind how much he slept, I just wanted him to do it on an earlier shift. I had the theory that he also slept when there was a fact he couldn't face or a task he wanted to shirk, or when he was sick.

I had once thought David's inordinate need of sleep came from his extraordinary output of energy, and I appealed to Sam Hirshfeld, who briefly considered narcolepsy until he discovered that David badly needed thyroid pills. When they didn't suffice, Sam found a noted endocrinologist in San Francisco who prescribed some tablets then still under evaluation. They were called Benzedrine. For David, they were the equivalent of unlocking the secrets of the universe. A few days later the endocrinologist phoned David to correct an error in his instructions: David was to take five milligrams, not five tablets. In other words, *one* tablet. David, who thought twice about an aspirin, was crestfallen at the revision. The doctor was incredulous that David had found the wrong dosage ideal. David's energy was natural, but that Benzedrine was the secret of his endurance.

It was also very much of a secret. I was stuck with still another matter over which I had to implore "less." These pills gave David what amounted to a couple of days extra a week. They also took years off his life, he later agreed. Much later.

David would fall asleep, nodding off the way a tired child does at the end of a picnic day, waking up charged with second wind, demanding the party go on and on. One night at a table which held down one end of Mocambo, the night club of the moment, David, after a couple of quick drinks and some hot soup, was suddenly a goner. It was a great party which he had been looking forward to; rather than leave, he lay down on the floor behind my chair, saying, "Keep an eye—just give me fifteen minutes." I woke him up after thirty, saying, "Let's go home." "No, not for anything. Give me fifteen more. Let me have a good time." No one seemed to notice except the waiters. The man was drunk, sick, or dead. I had to reassure more than one of them.

It also happened in his office. Poor Marcella Rabwin, first his secretary at RKO, later his assistant, knew the ropes well. What a marvel of tact she was if she found him sound asleep at his desk, the receiver resting on his shoulder, with someone out there suddenly given the compliment of David listening so patiently. A dynamo, but a tired one. Marcella covered by getting through on another line to explain there had been a disconnect.

David brought lots of work home, enough any evening for a week, then he complained that he didn't get to do it. He also didn't have time to do any optional reading, so just ordered the books instead. When we stayed home for a quiet evening, we stayed up later than when we went out to parties. Before beginning the evening's work, he wanted a little game with me—chess, backgammon, Russian bank, bezique. (Two-handed games were the only area in which we were competitive. High stakes? I'll say! Mostly satisfaction. When he lost, he was philosophical because he had beaten me so often. Oh, no, no, no. So he had a little green book made wherein I inscribed the precious scores as he watched, but he couldn't believe the record. His optimism was even retroactive.) A game also seemed a good idea when we came home not too late from a party. Just one game . . . When the games were over, he took to talking, sometimes through the night. His regrets, hopes, fears, hurts, doubts. Dawn would come up. Purged, he would say it was worth the hours. The next morning he would complain bitterly that I once again had kept him up.

I HADN'T thought that a woman might have a profound effect on a man's life, but I did believe that a woman's life depended completely on her choice of a husband. Very revealing of my view of women—no wonder I couldn't accept David's appreciation. We had a catalytic effect on each other. One and one didn't make two; David said in our case one and one made three. We were synergistic.

I always thought David dominated me. He thought I dominated him. However, I couldn't give him order and he couldn't give me devil-may-care. If I became more flexible and carefree, could he manage a little moderation? There would have been no sense in that. Yield and we'd have fun—no, more fun.

I edited his impulses, his rashness—at least partly. I never got him close to normal, but what a cutback. I knew I couldn't cure his faults; I tried to settle for reducing his more inconvenient tendencies, those which our friends found maddening, and those that caused servants to quit.

Go for broke applied to more than money, it meant no limit in hours or energy, whether for good times or gifts. It resulted in over-production that would then become the norm. Where do we go from there? I don't know what level I could have reached at which he would have said, "Enough." He would have liked me to be the best-dressed woman in town; he wanted me to knock them dead. I said, why? Sartorial elegance had never been my goal. Every party, every gift, every movie must be the best, then that would be the next starting point. I would be without a yardstick.

David had a gift for gift-giving and a passion to equal it. I can't imagine any recipient receiving pleasure greater than was his in the choosing and giving. It made no difference if the person had been out of his life for years, he or she was not forgotten when he espied something which seemed ideally suited.

The list for our Christmas giving got longer each year, and the sums expended made me dizzy. I was going at it in my orderly fashion, and I had a partner who was out on a spree; and where a $50 present might be appropriate, David arrived home with some glorious morsel for $300. I would be forced to say, "Are you sure you're not going to cause embarrassment?" Finally, between his extravagance and the pressures of work, it was agreed that I would do the buying, subject to his final approval before anything was wrapped.

David never wanted to decide presents ahead in case something caught his eye at the last moment. He even wanted to buy extras, in case someone dropped in. No one ever did, but no matter. The only things he bought early were for me, and when the proper Christmas-shopping time came, he felt deprived and started over. He was crazy about last-minute shopping; he made his secretary call stores and ask to keep them open. I complained that this gave him an obligation to buy. He went so crazy on what he bought for the boys that I had to take that over too. I took the fun out of Christmas by making order, but even so it was pandemonium.

Not only Christmas, but birthdays and anniversaries were punctuated by a staggering array of gifts. A film could almost have been produced with the equivalent of the time, effort, and imagination invested. The detail and perfectionism he was to employ in his movies had their first workout in these offerings to me. They were varied, often deliciously original and made to order; and they mounted in splendor. The minor gifts came first, accompanied by pertinent notes. The middle section was filled with items like a purse, the cost of which would exceed all my other purses for years, and lingerie, costing a couple of hundred dollars apiece, which had my name embroidered on it for protection. His excuse was, "If I don't give them to you, you're not going to have them."

As I opened each gift, I was moved, delighted, excited. It was intoxicating. But when the height of luxury and expense has been reached on the twentieth gift and there are five to go, panic sets in. I never came right out and said I'd be infinitely more grateful for some moderation. How could I complain?

At one point I did say, "Either gambling or presents, not both. We'll be in the poorhouse." I suppose they were both forms of self-indulgence. David used to get "gloriously drunk." In the same spirit, he never used the word "broke" except as in "go gloriously broke." To me, gambling and glory were not synonymous.

The first year, David, who was working one night, phoned to say he had had a tough session, hoped I didn't mind if he had a drink with the boys. Hours went by. I could only think of ambulances. In the wee hours he returned. My anxiety turned to shock and then disenchantment. He had been gambling, a family vice he did not share, or so I'd thought. (There had been an isolated instance before we married, which had happened because he "had to help Myron out.") Now, he blurted out what he had been up to. Moreover, he had lost and had lost a lot. I was horrified. Unable to control himself, he told me the amount, which was close to the total of what the servants earned in a year. While he was at it, he said he had misrepresented himself: he did have a weakness for gambling. He had deceived me because he had hoped it was over. I wept and I brooded and wept some more. He sought absolution, but there wasn't an ounce of forgiveness in me. What kind of protector had I chosen? I was as heartbroken as though I had discovered he no longer loved me; tragedy with all the stops out. It was a terrible drama for us both. David gradually rationalized that it was the best thing that could have happened. He had learned a lesson he wouldn't forget; I would never have to worry about gambling again. Not until the next time, as I discovered.

It had surprised me to learn soon after our wedding that the first debt that must be paid is a gambling debt. David resented having to tell people not to let me know he borrowed. I should accept him as he was without criticism.

The Selznicks were proud of the fact that they had never gone through bankruptcy; meanwhile, Pop and Mother Selznick had nothing in their own names. Someone brought a nuisance suit and attached whatever David had. I rashly said not to worry, I had some money. "Really?" "Yes." Big mistake—it was obvious I had been squirreling it away. David didn't know whether to condemn or congratulate me. It gave him the same wrong idea later when we moved into our new house.

There, of course, expenses were higher. I said I could manage, as there was no rent, and instead of saving a bit each week, I would put it into furnishing the bare house. It was preposterous to be living in that mansion, eking out a lamp here, a chair there; to eat meatloaf instead of roast beef, all because of his gambling. To be insolvent with David's income and my efforts was disgraceful. Fortunately, my father had trained me to marry a poor man. It proved to be more necessary with a husband who gambled.

This is what gave David his worst pangs. Nothing was spared on health or comfort for anyone living under our roof, and hospitality was lavish. Therefore, the economies could come from only one source. While my personal expenditures were many times beyond anything I had ever dreamed of, they weren't proportionate to our scale of living. I ache to think of the time and energy I spent. He could blow in a few hours more than I could save in two years.

The girl from New England, trying to be flexible, stupidly presented what seemed a sensible solution: gamble in a planned way. Make an evening of roulette, go in time for dinner, play at a leisurely pace for a few hours. I would play in my own little way. Companionable. So we tried it once. It was the only time gambling bored him. No hectic flush, no crowds, no risk. The employees were puzzled, and we passed some regulars coming in on our way out. The evening was a disaster.

What good is planning or saving? What good is a budget? None, unless there is a limit on gambling. I was prepared to see him blow any percentage of his salary. I would manage. He said I was so reasonable as to be unreasonable. What couldn't be got through my head was that it wasn't gambling or fun unless the potential loss hurt. (Yet he enjoyed bridge at puny stakes. Needless to add, he was quick at the re-double and then looked to me to bail him out, although I played no better than he. The rest of the evening would be devoted to getting even; gave it zest.)

Gambling is good when you've been to a dull party and left early. Gambling is good for celebration. Anything was an excuse: clear one's mind, terrible day, feeling lucky, feeling low—plus all the excuses that prompt an alcoholic, and we've all heard their excuses!

So unfair for me to be grimly silent when he needed solace, or to lie there crying my eyes out. He then managed to come up with a grievance: I gave him guilt. Some nerve! Was this the fellow who wanted me to learn to feel free, to spend? I used to think a wild streak of spending on my part might have cured him. Not true, it only would have given him relief. I don't know where we would have wound up.

After a catastrophic session his remorse was frightful. He, not I, pointed out what it was doing to his reputation, to his health. Still very young, he was advised he might not be able to get the increased life insurance he was seeking unless he cut back on his gambling. Apparently underwriters keep dossiers.

In a melodramatic letter of wretchedness he wrote, as the sun rose, "I try to think of Pop and how he'd have made me feel better about it. But all this does is sink me with memories of him, reawakening the depression over him I've been fighting to get over."

He took vows so sincere one couldn't doubt him, until the next time.

Occasionally he went on the gambling wagon and felt great about himself and had contempt for the weakling. "Look, it's three months and I don't miss it at all." That was a fool's paradise. In any case, when he didn't gamble for long stretches, the threat still hung over us. And when he did, he lost so consistently, regardless of the game, that I can only believe he wanted to gamble more than he wanted to win. No matter how far ahead he was, he stayed on until he lost.

There wasn't peace of mind even when the police would briefly close down the clubs. There were those friends who couldn't wait to get David into a poker game, in the middle of a party, "just for an hour at low stakes." Alas, David could explain poker, but not play it; he taught it to me, and even I could play better than he could. Poker is fun—for me, as much for matches as for money. I didn't want to lose any money of mine or win anyone else's, though I wouldn't have minded a quarter limit. David's poker was table stakes, no limit.

Constance Bennett never missed a chance to start a game if David was there. When I would see Joe Schenck enter the game, my heart would sink further because I knew the stakes would zoom still higher, though Joe, at least, was a generous and sporting player and, when far ahead, had been seen to deliberately help whoever was deepest in the hole, David included.

How these players must have been annoyed by the sight of my pale, drawn face peeking in hourly after midnight! When Bill Goetz, a shrewd player and sure winner, was present, I felt reassured. Perhaps unrealistically, I did assume he offered some protection. That notion vanished when I heard him raise uproarious laughter from a group by saying, "Hell! How do you think I afford my scale of living? I couldn't manage it without David Selznick!"

I don't think Edie knew that, but I did resent her sympathy over David's gambling. David resented that she filled me in on his losses. He tactfully told her to leave the reporting to him.

The greatest tribute I can pay our marriage is that it survived the gambling. But it definitely rocked the boat, and a couple of times I almost left him over it. And it certainly robbed me of my idealism about him. Fortunately, my illusions about so many of his other qualities were justified. But over the years the tax on my faith, hope, and charity took its toll. I trusted David in every area but this. It took the fine edge of happiness off my marriage. And it left me determined on one thing: I would prevent it being handed down to the boys like a gene.

Gambling undermined both his self-esteem and his independence. I couldn't see how he'd ever have enough put by to enjoy a sense of freedom professionally. There were times when he was running his own company that home, health, and children were being sacrificed to the business. But the business itself was jeopardized by gambling, and so was the fortune he might have had. He faced up to it all in his last years.

Mogul

R K O was the most minor of the major studios, lacking manpower, money, and prestige. But still it was a major studio, making about forty pictures a year, and in those days the appointment of a new studio chief was really big news. The announcement was greeted by cheers: "Just what RKO needs"; "The young punk might just pull it off." On the other hand, there were jeers from some people that the studio was going to fold in a few months anyhow. The challenge was to take advantage of the momentum and turn the studio around quickly.

There was a rueful acceptance by David that promoting was over for a while. It was back to work with a vengeance, plus the pent-up energies of months of unemployment. David was forced to ignore pictures already in progress, and he even allowed a few pictures which he deplored to go into production. The important thing was to get some decent ones started in a hurry. Above all, he needed to attract manpower and talent to replace the deadwood he was cutting out, always the most harrowing task.

David, being young and eager, created a refreshing informality which gave more direct access to the boss than other studios. Actually, there wasn't enough dough for a palace guard, and no one around there had the time or taste for pomp. The place acquired a good climate. Money isn't the only attraction.

Merian Cooper came aboard as David's executive assistant, but he had a project up his sleeve that I never took seriously because it was so preposterous. It was *King Kong.* I thought he was kidding. Anyone would but David, who promised to scrounge for funds if Coop could work out the problems.

David had to cut corners on the modest pictures in order to hoard for a few fine ones. Improvisation was in order. Fortunately, he had a pound of ideas he had dreamt up on the train (plus the backlog rejected by Schulberg), which included some long-cherished notions like *A Bill of Divorcement.* My contribution was slender. I was sick of the phony films about Hollywood and longed to see one with some reality. He tried with *What Price Hollywood?* and promised me someday he'd make a proper one. It turned out to be *A Star is Born.*

George Cukor's star rose with the performance he got from Constance Bennett in *What Price Hollywood?* Stories from the set wafted across Hollywood that he was vituperative in a way that was not only amusing but got results. Even his profanity was salutary. At Paramount, David had taken George in hand when he'd arrived fresh from the New York theatre, but George hadn't got properly launched, which made it possible to get him out of his Paramount contract. He had an invigorating viewpoint and an original personality—he was full of beans, taste, and humor; he had both warmth and bite. I doted on him. He also had a sharp eye and ear for style, which made him the natural choice to direct *Bill of Divorcement.*

David was obviously having success attracting people like Coop and George, but, however remarkable a job he might be doing, it wouldn't be evident quickly—as in any enterprise involving long-range products. Nevertheless, in his youthful fervor he really believed that, given a few years and enough leeway, he could take RKO to the very top. As it was, he had a one-year contract and he was a young man in a hurry.

T E M P O applied to me as well, and I quickly took the Lawrence Tibbett house on Rexford Drive and thought about getting on with the remaining third of my ambitions, those two little boys. With David deep in the salt mines, we were going to stay put for a while and this would be an ideal time. David wanted a baby, but not if it was going to change our life. He had also fancied two little boys, but he was not exactly in a hurry because he felt it would be the end of our honeymoon. Incredibly, marriage had not tied him down, and he was fearful that a baby would make him feel a "family man." The hints and the unspoken pleas in the eyes of the four grandparents had gone unheeded, but Sam Hirshfeld spoke out. He'd arrived soon after us and was our first houseguest. He said that even if we weren't quite ready, I'd better start trying, because one never knew how long it would take. What an entrancing idea!

I had three notions about having a baby: a child should be deliberately conceived; I would get pregnant on the first attempt; I knew exactly how to achieve a male baby. No matter how idiotic I was, all three happened. (Not once, but twice. After the second son I learned that my theories were cockeyed!) Within a couple of days I informed an astonished David that, sooner than hoped for, we had succeeded. By a coincidence Walter Winchell simultaneously announced our news. At that point not even a rabbit could have told him.

It was understood that this was not to be your usual pregnancy. I was to be slim as long as possible, young as ever—I take that back; *he* was to be as young as ever. By the advent of this child he would have reached the traumatic age of thirty, a doom he had dreaded for years. To him, thirty was "the end of my youth." "Promise me, promise me everything will be the same. The baby won't make any difference." Thinking about it today, I get sore at both of us.

Incredible that I was going to be a mother. It had never happened to anyone else, even though Edie had had a baby girl the year before. Yet it couldn't really be such a miracle—look at all the people in the streets: behind each one there had once been a pregnant woman!

I was superstitious that if I took things for granted, something might go wrong; there was no guarantee one would have a live, healthy child at the end of nine months, and I was undone by the possibility of walking back into my home with empty arms. I couldn't bear the thought of the pity. My susceptibility was such that a few years later, when I met John Garfield's wife, who had recently had a stillborn baby, I could say no more than, "Mrs. Garfield, I . . . " without breaking down. The good woman ended up comforting me.

I had to do something to fortify myself against possible disappointment. Let other women count chickens and air their blissful anticipation. Not me. I was cool. I never let on how desperately I cared. No one would catch me cooing over tiny garments. I bought one little jacket and a dozen of something sealed in a package, and left them on a shelf. No baby showers for me, nor did I wish to hear about baby presents. My mother was upset that the baby was not to have a proper nursery and claimed it as her gift. Lovely, if I heard no word of it and nothing was done before I went to the hospital. Mother and Edie turned it over to Adrian, no less, and as if by magic there existed a crisp, clean, charming nursery into which the crown prince was carried in triumph. Need I say, at a beach house.

I had decided long before I embarked on this mighty undertaking that I needed a positive approach. I would not be impatient, but would somehow value each day for itself. In this way the baby wouldn't owe me anything; we'd be quits. I reasoned that never again would the baby be this safe and never again could I live only for myself (that is, in the daytime). The most important thing I had to do was to do nothing. Self-centered was not the word for it. For someone so drilled in tasks and obligations, it was a revelation to have indolence as my proper goal and have it without guilt. I read novels and drank milk. A woman came every day and gave me a soothing massage after my nap. One-tenth the care would have produced the same results. I had been as cautious as ever.

The nights went on as usual, because David's wife was not like any other expectant mother. As the pregnancy progressed, he had worries, but not the usual ones. A promise was exacted for the future: we must go to New York after the baby was born and demonstrate that I would be able to leave it. The only penalty David was to pay was that I wanted him present in the delivery room. Poor thing, he was. Very modern for an old-fashioned girl.

As I came to, I heard them say it was a boy and all was well. In the wee hours, being wheeled down a corridor, I saw all the family flattened against the wall. I couldn't imagine what they were doing in a hospital in the middle of the night. They were misty-eyed but smiling. Pop was resplendent—his dreams had come true. First David's success, and now David's son. I understand he magnanimously promised Edie a boy next time, but Edie didn't need consolation because she didn't want a son. Weeks later she was still indignant.

Not until I was in my room and they had brought the morsel in for a brief glimpse did I dare think Mission Accomplished. So far, so good. But the ordeal wasn't over; it was actually about to begin.

David didn't show up in the morning as planned. Hours later, when he did arrive, he was in terrible shape. He had celebrated with Myron and had a beaut of a hangover. He was even unshaven. He rose above it all, though, and was apologetic only for bearing bad tidings—indeed, tragic ones. He had spent the last hour trying to spare me, but it must be faced: our baby was gone.

For a split second of horror I thought he meant kidnapped. No, he meant something worse: they were trying to palm off someone else's child on us. The baby I'd held in my arms that morning wasn't ours? That's right, it wasn't, they had shown him that child too, and it definitely wasn't the one he had seen being born. This was no mix-up, it was a plot! Ours was a prize baby; Pop had warned him something like this might happen. David was leaving no stone unturned.

That part at least was true: the hospital was in an uproar. But I wasn't. He couldn't understand my lack of response. I didn't believe him because I knew my own baby. That made him even more upset. I reminded him that he had watched them put a name necklace around the child's throat. That didn't count. Nor did the footprint he had seen taken. He wanted no part of my logic—there were ways around such precautions, and he had told the superintendent of the hospital as much. In fact, he, David, had an investigation already under way. He grew indignant with me. "Can't you tell the difference? How is it possible? How can you not care?" I cared, all right. The implication was that "his" child was superior. He was downgrading *my* baby. I wanted him to stop—I liked the baby just fine. That was his point: he was afraid I'd love this changeling and would reject ours when he recovered him. He demanded appreciation for his efforts and sympathy for all *he* was going through. I was not on his side; I wanted to keep the baby and send the father back.

The next day he didn't precisely back down, but he conceded that Jeffrey was the overall finest baby in the nursery. He arrived with a tender offering in his hand. There was a verse:

> *So we are three:*
> *My darling, and my darling's darling,*
> *And, humbly, me. . . .*
>
> *And where, before,*
> *We thought there were no more*
> *To add to Happiness,*
> *'Tis only now we know*
> *What Life . . . and Love . . . are for.*

My baby had become our baby.

The head nurse came in to take my emotional temperature. The superintendent came to reassure me and apologize. I reassured *him* and apologized.

However, there was another turbulence. "What kind of a name is Jeffrey? I'm a laughingstock all over town, I can't show my face." The name had been settled ages ago. Suddenly it was completely unsuitable. The "boys," whoever they were, said his wife was full of romantic notions. True, it hadn't been his choice, but he had acquiesced. He didn't want to upset me, but he did; I was miserable and so was he. Finally I reverted to Nicholas, which we hadn't used because of Nick Schenck. A few days later I offered Daniel. He fancied that, but said we'd save it for the next one. He would look ridiculous changing now. Besides, he had already been referring to him as Jeffrey. He had begun to accept the situation.

David couldn't get his hours synchronized with the hospital's. There seemed to be a conspiracy against him. David took childbirth hard. By the time he recovered, I was a wreck.

Los Angeles was a company town, so the press treated certain film babies importantly—they warranted an article and photographs of the mother, first as a coming event, then again at birth. It's a wonder anybody kept his head. The pressures had begun. There were more flowers than at a gangster's funeral. An avalanche of gifts and telegrams poured in. There were a couple of hundred notes to write.

We had imposed fancy rules: I was to be spared visitors outside of the family, except for my friend Paul Bern. Young Selznick held daily court through the plate glass of the nursery, and lists of his visitors were brought me.

Jeffrey was not born with a silver spoon. He had a gold spoon, more than one. In fact, this fellow actually had a gold cup. He even had a carriage robe of ermine, with tails, no less. It was a gift from George Cukor, an impulse of affection but surely in part a sardonic comment. A new kingdom, Hollywood.

There was calm and regulation the first weeks home because I was nursing the baby. Then the peace was shattered on Labor Day. Paul Bern, probably the single most beloved figure in Hollywood, had committed suicide. His death created a tremendous scandal. To me, it was a tragedy.

Paul Bern was special in many ways. He was the only person I ever knew who cherished people he loved as much for their frailties as for their virtues. He had compassion, erudition, and great generosity. He lived modestly, spending little on himself, yet at the end of each week he had not a dollar left; he had given it all away. He was worldly-wise and intellectual, European in manner and thought, but his chivalry was his own. He courted the town's most exotic sirens. He seemed always to have loved and lost, yet the lure didn't lessen. He was a writer who became a director, then a producer, but he was more concerned with nurturing the talent of others. He seemed to find David totally wonderful—he was almost as indulgent of him as was Pop. Paul had helped David get established at Paramount, and his friendship gave David stature and confidence.

When I entered David's life, Paul adopted me as well. No, he didn't adopt me, he adopted us as his favorite young couple and watched over us. I think he felt he had invented us. He smoothed out the misunderstandings, the quarrels. He always looked at those he cared for with such tenderness and mercy that one almost believed one partook of the qualities he attributed. He gave me a whole other image of myself: I wasn't a girl to him, I was a woman. It is easy for a man to make a woman feel desirable. He had a rarer gift, and one more impersonal: he had the capacity to make a woman feel glamorous.

Paul Bern lived in a tiny, austere room with a little alcove for his narrow bed, high up in the Ambassador Hotel. His friends worried that he had no home and for years tried to prevail on him to buy a house, which he could ill afford. Finally he found a half-finished place far up in a canyon, and everyone looked forward to his having a proper haven. The house was finished just before David and I got married. As Paul did not have the money to buy us the kind of gift he would like, we could make *him* a present if we would "bless his house" by living in it for the first two years, as he was quite happy at the Ambassador; he would enjoy having the house more if we had lived in it. When I protested, he tried to settle for a year. The day of the housewarming he lamented that it would have been a perfect day if only it were David and I who were moving in.

Paul was my first close male friend and I loved him dearly. My trust in him was infinite. However, I did not greatly admire his taste in ladies. Then suddenly he changed his style. He showed up with somebody young, somebody blonde. Not only that, she was from the Hollywood School for Girls!

It was a year or so before our marriage, when David decided to give his first big party since the days of 270 Park. Carried away, he had a dance floor built out in the garden. Paul wouldn't tell whom he was bringing, but promised us a wonderful surprise. I was waiting at the door with David to greet the guests and saw Paul with his surprise amongst the first to arrive. She sashayed up the walk on his arm. As they approached, I welcomed her with an extended hand and a "Hello, Harlean." She corrected me indignantly with a toss of her head: "Jean Harlow, if you please." The whole thing had fizzled. Paul, embarrassed, explained that he really had contemplated a more sentimental meeting of old school friends.

We hadn't been friends because she was several years younger than I. In any case, little Miss Harlean Carpenter was unforgettable. There had been something spectacular about her even in the school uniform, which was seductive only on her. No middy blouse but hers was cut so low, and, despite admonitions, her hips swayed under the ankle-length pleated skirt. Topping it all off was a mop of real tow hair, a color rarely seen beyond the age of three. She had been one of the school's few boarders, and on Friday afternoon we girls would huddle behind the shrubbery at the entrance to watch a big foreign car drive up, in which was hidden a veiled woman. A mysterious dark gentleman would emerge and usher Harlean into the car and off to places undisclosed. The rumors were that it was her mother with a lover of unknown origin. After a few years she dropped out of school without notice. We knew perfectly well we hadn't heard the last of her.

Four years later, on a back page of the *Los Angeles Examiner,* with the shipping news, I happened across a picture with a banner saying "A RECENT BRIDE." Something familiar caught my eye. Sitting on the ship's rail, skirt high, legs crossed in the manner of a Ziegfeld beauty, there she was. The description below the picture claimed that the bride, seventeen, was a debutante, an heiress from Kansas City. A likely tale.

Now the youthful bridegroom was gone, and she was going to be an actress; very soon, too. She and Paul were an illogical couple. Neither David nor I realized that they were a twosome; it seemed even less likely as the evening wore on. David got me aside and said, "Help, help! This dame keeps dragging me into the bushes. What's the matter with Paul? Keep your eye open, you may have to rescue me." Shortly thereafter I got a signal from the dance floor and I sent someone to cut in. The only moment which lived up to Paul's anticipation was her affectionate leave-taking of me.

They appeared only occasionally together and never around us. She was otherwise involved and so was he. She was signed by Howard Hughes for a small part in *Hell's Angels,* and cheesecake photos of her began to appear. She wound up as its leading lady, which did not put her in demand, but gave her a lot of publicity. Through Paul's efforts—he was now at MGM and very close to Irving—she secured the lead role in *Red-Headed Woman,* which made her a star.

Paul had been her benefactor and mentor, but it never crossed my mind he was a suitor until four or five months before Jeffrey was born. Then one day on his way home from the studio, Paul stopped by to visit me and said, "I've had a letter from Jean," who was off on a long personal-appearance tour. He said he was madly in love with her and what would I think if he married her? I didn't have to think, I just answered, "You'd blow your brains out." He knew I meant unsuitability, and I thought he was only romanticizing. When I suggested that he hadn't really seen very much of her, he explained that she had resisted his attentions until *Red-Headed Woman* opened and was a success; obviously, he wanted to impress me with her character by demonstrating how scrupulous she had been. He read me some snatches of her letter, which reflected a kind of affection. He'd like to bring her to dinner.

When she returned a couple of months later, they came, and after dinner Jean asked to go upstairs with me. She sat in the dressing room and said she envied me, that her greatest desire was to have a baby, and asked if she could put her hand on my stomach. I was taken aback, but she was serious and much moved. When we rejoined the men, she said to Paul, "Do you know, I may really marry you. I would like a home, like Irene." The next morning he phoned to tell me I was partly responsible for his incredible good fortune; he wanted me to be the first to know that Jean had accepted him.

Florence and Freddy March gave a party to honor the bridal couple. Paul was adamant about my coming, even though I didn't want to go out during the last weeks before the baby. He said I only had to do it twice—to that party and to his wedding.

Making the effort for the party had been pointless, because I saw Paul only to greet him. When I went to take an early leave, he was not to be found. I learned he was tired and had gone upstairs for a brief nap, a strange thing for the guest of honor to do. When he came down, I was in the entry looking back into the living room, where C. V. Whitney, whom we had brought, was playing the piano; Jean, in a skin-colored satin dress, was standing nestled into the curve of the piano, singing to him and moving her body in a most provocative way. I was embarrassed that Paul had found me watching this scene. He gripped me roughly by the arms, this gentle man, spun me around, shook me, and said, "Look at her, look at her! She is an angel from heaven. I want you to remember and never forget it. No matter what happens, you are to remember that she is an angel from heaven!"

I made it to the wedding, admittedly with mixed feelings. I never saw Paul again. He made appointments to come to the hospital which his secretary then canceled. Extraordinary for someone who had so eagerly anticipated the arrival of the baby. I was deeply hurt. But Jean came to gaze at the baby—as though an errand like that could be delegated. His flowers came with a card bearing an embossed silver profile of Jean, the message written by her; so did a gift. Then he broke the date he had made to come to Santa Monica. He was desolated, but assured me he could explain it all and I would forgive.

The dreadful news came on the day which marked the end of my confinement. The telephone rang. David picked it up. "Irving? My God! No! When? Oh, God, no!" I screamed out, "It's Paul, he's killed himself! I will kill her!" Irving and David flew to Paul's house. I went back to bed for another week.

The press pilloried Jean; she became a villainess, not a victim. The community's hostility ran high, there was conjecture and hysteria. My father bore the brunt of the aftermath, with all its ramifications. Despite the clear evidence of suicide, a murder indictment was drawn up against her. She was spared because my father's doctor, having had Paul as a patient, divulged to him physiological facts which should have prevented a marriage. Jean, sheltered in her mother's house, seemed willing to face murder charges rather than reveal anything against Paul. My father told me that at one point she ran from her bed to throw herself off the balcony which hung over a rocky chasm. Only by catching hold of her robe was my father able to save her. She would offer no explanation for Paul's deed. Hers had been a happy marriage. She accepted the fact that her career was over and did nothing to help herself. She protected Paul beyond the point of reason. Unbeknownst then to all but a few, she was truly a heroine. When I learned of her gallantry, I was ashamed of my violent feelings.

I didn't see Jean again until about six months later, when we were both dinner guests at the Thalbergs'. When I went to greet her, she stood up and said, "It's all right. You don't have to. I understand how you must feel." I was glad to be able to repeat Paul's words to me. There was peace between us, which was just as well, as she reappeared still again in my life through her last love, Bill Powell, Myron's best friend, to whom I was also devoted.

Paul's death had thrown Irving and David together again, and it was to Irving's house, almost next door, a few weeks later, that I went quietly to see *A Bill of Divorcement,* having missed the preview when I was in the hospital. I had followed this picture more closely than any other that David had made and was impatient to see it.

Bill of Divorcement was an English play by Clemence Dane which had made the young Katharine Cornell a star. It had been considered an unlikely prospect for the screen because it dealt with insanity. It could be made, of course, provided one had the right director and the right girl and it could be filmed with authenticity and delicacy. David aspired to do just that, but it was a gamble at best.

At least he had the girl—Jill Esmond, Larry Olivier's wife. RKO had met their price and they were there when David took over the studio. But Larry's luck hadn't been too good, so he persuaded Jill to pass up the role and return with him to England, thereby losing her chance at Hollywood.

Cukor was the ideal director, but the renewed problem of the young woman wasn't solved until Coop's friend Belle Roosevelt sent him a photo of a promising new girl, Katharine Hepburn, who was playing on Broadway in *The Warrior's Husband.* The critics had been unanimous only in praise of her legs, hardly a requisite for this particular movie.

Her first test was full of contradictions. She was gawky, yet graceful, like a colt. She seemed both cocksure and panicky. Her acting was uneven, a skilled moment followed by something amateurish. But she got my vote, for what it was worth, because her looks and personality were refreshing and there was something original about her.

She gave a mixed impression on arrival as well. She didn't seem a struggling young actress at all, judging by the expensive Elizabeth Hawes outfit she wore, which was more eccentric than becoming. The rumors were that she came from a very rich family, an error she did nothing to correct. Her behavior was not only unconventional, it was slightly whacky. It was as though California were just a lark; more likely this was an act so that if she failed in the role, she hadn't really wanted films anyhow. We had a wave of misgivings, but the girl had class and plenty of spunk. George was enthusiastic about her from the very first, and they hit it off marvelously well. For once I was glad to watch the early rushes, and I found it fascinating as she became less mannered and gradually her validity was established, thanks in no small part to George and the rapport between them. It would appear that Paramount had let a talented and valuable director slip through its fingers.

I adored the picture. Also, I was thrilled because at last here was the kind of quality David had been striving for. It had the stamp which came to characterize the best of his pictures; anyone in the business would have been proud of that film. And it was a picture which opened the door to other unorthodox stories requiring sensitive handling. In itself it gave promise that RKO would soon be an outfit to be reckoned with. Moreover, a star had been made.

The evening had a lot of meaning for me. I had never contemplated sitting in Irving's living room watching my husband's latest film and listening to Irving's praise. All things considered, it was a lovely moment.

Irving no longer wanted to work as hard as he had, so it shouldn't have come as a surprise that not too long after our evening at his house my father made David an offer that he couldn't refuse. But he did; he was flattered, but vehement against it, and so was I. He said as much and more in too long a letter, eloquently turning my father down, a letter which began, "Under no circumstances would it be right for me to go with MGM," and wound up with, "Irene shares my opinion." I winced at the forthrightness, not having put it that bluntly myself. But how could my father have thought that David would consider MGM even for an instant? He had his own little bailiwick and wondrous plans for it.

Our being invited to the Goldwyns' was another early sign that David's stock was rising. Sam liked to have successful people around him; we were surely on our way. He also cultivated sources of New York power and chose to entertain them when they came to California. Sam had the reach and Frances had the know-how. She also had courage and discipline—she did Sam out of many a first-class row. Sam, who couldn't get along with anyone, could not, in my opinion, have gotten along without her. On the whole, Frances did the best job of wifehood in Hollywood.

No one ever seemed to walk in Beverly Hills, so walkers were conspicuous. I frequently spotted Frances on Sunset Boulevard, walking Sam to the studio. She also walked by the old reservoir, joined occasionally by me, a place remote enough to seem off-limits. We had many viewpoints in common, so I could be as candid about Hollywood and life as I dared, our peculiar husbands included.

David admired Sam's work, if not his habits. He understood Sam's extravagant personality and was amused by his idiosyncrasies. In short, he had a weakness for Sam. Nevertheless, he didn't let him get away with much, apart from what he lost to him at gin rummy.

David was a connoisseur of Goldwynisms, and insisted he could spot a counterfeit, of which there were many. The best I ever heard were those David brought back, freshly minted, from producers' meetings. Meanwhile, I kept complaining that I had never heard a Goldwynism firsthand. David said I didn't listen carefully enough. I did listen. I waited. I yearned. It never happened.

T H E R E was no longer any doubt about David's position, so it was preposterous for him to remain stiff-necked about living in a house he hadn't paid for; my father had been determined to give each daughter a house when she married, and Edie was at work with her architect within weeks after her wedding, but I was sentenced to the burdens that constant moving entailed. In my mother's eyes this was David's only failing. She longed for that house. She said I lived like a gypsy and David should think of me. My father limited his comments to, "You like to live this way?" Mother kept dropping heavy hints to David and then finally pleaded with me. "With a family, a home is essential." She was right; he was penalizing me, the baby, and my parents, so we had a showdown. He agreed so readily one couldn't have guessed how unreasonable he'd been. I took him at his word and moved right ahead. Actually, it was four houses down and—little did I know it—three more to go before we finally got into our new manse.

I also moved on my promise to leave the baby and go to New York. A year had passed since we were there, an important one. It was high time we went. Also, David's contract had run out. To lessen my pangs about Jeffrey, David arranged to have professional movies shot of his young rival and shipped to New York. The only trouble with this, apart from the extravagance, was that it had the opposite effect on me.

We not only went, we went through the Canal, perversely enough; the long way around. David justified this sea voyage as a way to work more closely on a script. The time had come to indulge himself in a classic: he was going to make *Little Women* with Hepburn, George directing. He took several people along, naturally including George, whose presence guaranteed that the trip would be fun.

It *was* fun. So was New York. Hollywood people were being assimilated in certain Eastern circles and it was a period of barriers coming down everywhere. For me, it was unparalleled freedom. I was more pleasure-loving in New York and, unless I am mistaken, better company. I am certain I was less cautious. For David, it was novelty, fresh faces, and stimulation. We joined a large, ever-changing group that could be classified as somewhere between the Algonquin and café society—theatre people like the George Kaufmans, Philip Barry, Bob Sherwood; society people who were bored with society—including Jock Whitney, who was to become our closest friend; writers and journalists from Bob Benchley to Herbert Bayard Swope. These were all bright, interesting people, many of whom were delighted, in turn, to accept Hollywood's hospitality, which was considerable. Westerners are just more hospitable than New Yorkers. And the Santa Anita racetrack had restored Southern California as a winter resort. Within a year Los Angeles became the place to go—so much so that Elsa Maxwell pitched her tent there, or, rather, for several years she rented a mansion for one rich woman, then another, where she would reign as houseguest-hostess.

In the early Twenties, David had known a young man who had a crazy dream about starting a new kind of magazine; his name was Henry Luce and the magazine was *Time.* David couldn't wait for me to meet him.

When we first met, he and his wife, Lila, had just moved into their apartment at Fifth Avenue and 72nd Street, on the ground floor. I couldn't believe a young couple could live in such lugubrious surroundings. There were just the four of us in that vast, dark dining room with its heavy lace curtains. And there were heavy silences to match. I was dismayed to discover the reason: for heaven's sake, the man stuttered! He not only stuttered, he was having a hell of a struggle.

Needless to add, I said not a word. It was a bad start.

There were some further meetings that I've forgotten. I next remember him in 1935, when we attended a party in New York celebrating his marriage to Clare Boothe, whom David called "that glamorous dame from *Vanity Fair.*" In the middle of this glorious big evening at Condé Nast's, I slipped off to the powder room and stumbled by mistake into an exquisite little salon. Sitting there all by himself was a solemn-looking Harry Luce.

Embarrassed to catch a guest of honor hiding out, I made matters
worse. I blurted out: "What's the matter? Are you stuttering?" Only a
fellow sufferer could have thought that, let alone said it. I tried to explain,
but suddenly couldn't make a sound. By gesture I indicated that I was
a member of the club. He caught on instantly. We embraced, I dried my
tears, and so began our friendship.

Clare, having just had a play produced, was pleasantly surprised to
discover show-biz people among Harry's friends. And early Clare was a
delicious package. We found her witty, lively, and handsome, with better
legs than any Miss America to date. She and Harry seemed an odd match.

Before long the Luces were in California and staying with us. Chez
Selznick suited Clare so well she decided she'd stay no other place
whenever she came West. She was a splendid houseguest—considerate,
entertaining, and out for meals. It was fun to give a dinner party for her
because the talk would sparkle. Bon mots from men like Lubitsch or
Arthur Hornblow showed Clare at her best. She was never again as
lighthearted once she became a politico and a pundit.

Clare's ambition was so great she never stood a chance of satisfaction.
She did like a challenge and could rise to any that didn't include
housekeeping; she was allergic to servants and convinced they were her
enemies. She needed a wife more than any career lady I knew.

FOR A while in the early Thirties the Donald Ogden Stewart house
was the first port of call for New York intelligentsia and café society.
It was there I met up again with Bill Paley, by now Mr. CBS, and his
recent bride. I hadn't seen either since my wide-eyed days, Bill next door
at the Lasky party and Dorothy dancing at the Cocoanut Grove. They
were on their way to being the most glamorous young couple in New
York.

Somehow, within a year or two Dorothy and I were best friends. I
don't remember how or when. Let it be said: she picked me, I wouldn't
have presumed. Her taste in clothes, decor, food, was by then established.
She headed the best-dressed list, and the portraits of her in *Vogue* and
Harper's Bazaar scarcely did justice to her beauty. That is not why I loved
her. I thought she was all things wise and wonderful.

A most congenial foursome were the Selznicks and the Paleys. Dorothy
enjoyed David's company and was grateful for the challenge and pleasure

he gave Bill. Bill, also an over-achiever, did as much for David. The Paleys offered us an added window on the great world.

By coincidence their Long Island house adjoined Jock Whitney's (actually his mother's) estate, which became our other favorite weekend spot. But our visits remained mutually exclusive because even though the couples were acquainted, Liz and Dorothy were poles apart, so we never proposed joining up during a weekend. (It is interesting that much later the gentlemen in question married sisters and became not only related, but intimate friends. The two Mrs. Paleys couldn't have been more different. What they had in common, apart from celebrated looks and taste, was the monumental job of pleasing Bill. And I think because of Bill they both set the best table in town.)

The Paleys were innovative and stimulating and self-willed. They had advanced ideas on everything from paintings to politics. I knew nothing about politics and cared less; I had too much else to absorb. Dorothy was deep into child psychology, which suited me better. Both of them were logical and recent converts to psychoanalysis and freely admitted it. I would have kept mum for the sake of "appearances, appearances." People complained that Dorothy made everything psychoanalytic, but I drank it in, although it was quite over my head. I felt I was getting the benefits and insights the easy way. Anyhow, clear-headed as I was, I was the last person who would ever need analysis.

Dorothy lavished knowledge and affection on me. She let me feel that her time was at my disposal and raised my self-esteem a hundred points. I was so indebted I began to feel uncomfortable, so she put me down a few pegs and enlightened me at the same time. She said I enjoyed being a giver. I was being selfish. It so happened she also liked to give—I must learn to take. That was a new concept to me, unsettling and unwelcome. She said I should apply it to my sister too. She took a dim view of that relationship. She didn't criticize Edie, just me, which turned all my virtue into a fault. I didn't have to go on compensating for inequities of the past: Edie was now healthy, had a happy home, a good husband, and two lovely daughters; I was behaving as though she still needed me.

I even forgave her telling me that David was neurotic and, what was more, that I was too, for catering to him . . . I made life difficult for other wives. But then, she had no way of appreciating how wonderful David was to me. Bill did and objected; he called David president of the Spoilers' Club and begged him to desist.

NOVEMBER 1932 was in many other ways a completely different New York from any David or I had ever seen. He was now a studio head visiting the home office and making them look awfully good for having taken a chance on him. It was hardly surprising that, despite the hassles through the year for increased budgets and autonomy, they were talking a new contract which included a participation in profits. They were pretty pleased with themselves and with him, and they rolled out the red carpet.

However, this trip David had his father on his mind. Pop was not well. The old man had long had severe diabetes, but held the theory that only food eaten at table could harm him. Mother Selznick resorted to padlocks on the icebox, but in vain. I was on her side. David, in the firm conviction that his father would live forever, said he would rather Pop had anything he wanted and lived less long. "Pop would not want to live with restrictions."

When Pop had become bedridden, he was deprived of his new grandson, which was a pity, so I had gathered Jeffrey up and taken him for a surprise visit. I could think of nothing that would do Pop more good.

That was a period when certain children led sheltered lives—children like Jeffrey, whose pediatrician visited him at the beach for a monthly inspection; that boy was no more going to be exposed to the germs of a doctor's office than to the hazards of the road. However, he had made his debut into the outside world when he was three months old. I had outfitted him in finery suitable only to a royal christening, appeared out of nowhere, propped the infant up at the foot of Pop's bed, and said, "Look who's come to see you." Well, *that* was a good idea.

In our absence my father had visited Pop at the Selznick penthouse in the Sunset Towers. They talked of more than their mutual grandson. L.J. decided that L.B. was not a bad sort after all. It must have been music to Pop's ears to hear my father's lament at having failed to lure David to MGM. Those two finally had things in common.

The only person I ever met more optimistic than David was his father. In the face of disaster and then mortal illness he never blinked an eye, nor did he complain. Yet there was something in David's daily telephone calls to his father which worried him and made him anxious to get back. On our return in December the old man did not improve, despite David's presence. He was sicker than we knew.

As he became more and more gravely ill, no one admitted the fact, although Ishi moved in, nurses were added, and Sam Hirshfeld spent all his spare time there. We visited oftener and stayed longer. One night late in January, David, Myron, and I never left at all. In the morning the nurse sent for Sam, who closed the double doors between the bedroom and the living room, where we were waiting. Suddenly he flung the doors open and made a gesture indicating that all was over.

David screamed, "No!" Sam grappled with him as he rushed forward, but he couldn't hold him. The three of us watched, stunned, as David, totally out of control, stood at the foot of the bed, arms outstretched, beseeching his father to hear him. "Pop, it's David, speak to me! It's David asking you. Do it for me. Pop, it's David!" His voice rose as he implored his father. He was defying death, willing him to live. It was the most dramatic scene I've ever witnessed. He had never believed Pop would leave him, but for once his father failed him.

A few minutes later that family did something very odd. They up and left. David and Myron escorted their mother out of there to Myron's apartment at the Beverly Wilshire with scarcely a backward glance. David said, "Take care of things. Ishi will help you."

I was alone except for Ishi and Pop. I had never before seen a dead person. I didn't know what David meant or what to do, so I phoned my mother. I was afraid the prospect of a long period before the funeral might be unendurable for the family, especially David.

Mother could advise. She suggested I could take advantage of the Orthodox law, which decrees funerals within twenty-four hours. I spent the rest of the day making it possible. I called the undertaker, then Ishi and I picked the clothes to give him when he came. I phoned my family's rabbi, who took this occasion to scold me for not having become a member of the Temple and complained that the elder Selznicks were not members of his congregation either. I picked the pallbearers; I arranged for flowers, transportation, dealt with the newspapers, chose the cemetery and bought a plot. I was fine until I got to the undertaker's at the other end of town to pick a casket. That vast room filled with endless coffins was surrealistic and it terrified me. I almost folded.

At the end of that long, hard day I arrived at Myron's apartment to find the family surrounded by Lewis Milestone, Ernst Lubitsch, and a dozen others having drinks and laughing. I had expected a harrowing spectacle, complete with prostrate bodies and smelling salts. I hadn't anticipated the perfectly natural scene of friends offering sympathy and condolences. This was very Selznick, just not the Mayer way. I was bedraggled, woebegone, ever so slightly martyred because of my heroic efforts on their behalf.

David greeted me with, "Where have you been all this time?" He'd been worried about me for hours. Apparently I had taken him too literally and I needn't have done so much. I also had made the funeral too soon; its timing was as close as David ever came to being Orthodox.

Mother Selznick took an apartment then and there in the Beverly Wilshire, where she lived for the next fifteen or twenty years. The penthouse opposite to Myron's happened to be available, and David and I slept there that night; the following day, after the funeral, I moved Jeffrey and the staff in from the beach, and we stayed for the next six months. It was a time to huddle close.

The day I had dreaded for years had come. David was unprepared to live in a world without Pop. He was inconsolable. The months that followed were horrendous. He cried out in his sleep, which was beset by nightmares. Time didn't help him, and circumstances less. When Pop died, David had been on the verge of closing his deal with RKO. Everything he had done to date had been out of conviction. Now his most vital decision was taken on impulse. Almost without deliberation he agreed to go back to MGM. In the space of a few days he had lost his father, given up his little kingdom, and taken a job where he least wanted to be. He could have taken no step better calculated to compound his misery.

I found it incomprehensible, having listened for five years to how fortunate he was to be out of MGM. When they had made their offer in November, I had done my share of discussing the pros and cons and had supported David's decision. I knew by heart all the reasons he had outlined in his letter to my father for not wanting to return; they were compelling, in fact irrefutable. But Dad hadn't really given up in November. I couldn't understand his persistence in view of the finality of David's refusal; I could have told him that nothing would induce David to reconsider, not even when an impasse with RKO arose a few weeks after our return. Although David issued a couple of resignation statements, he kept working away and had the sense to go right on negotiating. However, he kept that MGM door open a crack because Pop's last advice just happened to have been pro-MGM. Shortly before he died, he had said, "Blood is thicker than water." These words were not a directive, but apparently David took them to heart. Louis B.

wasn't Mr. MGM, he was family, and David was Little Boy Lost.

Quite suddenly it was all over. There was no gradual drawing nearer a decision, he capitulated without warning. It took him a day or two to realize what he'd done. He was in no position to say, "Why did you let me do it?" His despair was so great that I didn't tell him he had done it with his own little hatchet. I was silent. He tried to justify it to me by saying he hadn't been fully appreciated at RKO, whereas a bigger and better studio had been ardent and sustained in its courtship. "I find it ironic that what I am trying to achieve is better known in Culver City than in Radio City." And, after all, MGM had offered him his heart's desire: his own unit, with complete independence and the opportunity of making a limited number of quality pictures with unlimited budget.

Now at last my father had what he really wanted. How sensible it had been of him to do it without involving me. Had he tried in the manner he had earlier fondly imagined, I couldn't have stayed married, nor could he ever have gotten David. It was quite a coup, and I wonder whether he was surprised. Of course he was pleased and proud. He'd done a lot for his company, for himself, for David, and certainly for me. Or so it seemed to him.

Where but in the movies does a discharged employee come back five years later at twenty times the pay? David was to get $4,000 a week. The time was a month before FDR closed down the banks, and the studios were asking even contract people to take drastic pay cuts. Actually, his share of profits at RKO would have been larger, but resentment ran high when word of that salary got around. It created shock waves. Before they had subsided, the press came up with good old nepotism: "The Son-in-Law Also Rises." Unfair or not, that line dogged him for many a year. For a man who boasted of his reputation as a free spirit, it was devastating.

David had been premature. He had misjudged his position, because recognition had not caught up with what he had accomplished. He was made to seem a relative and an opportunist. To make matters worse, the trade papers hinted of political warfare and of Irving being outmaneuvered. Rumor spread through the studio that Irving might be replaced as head of production—rumor that was given credence because Irving wasn't at the studio and hadn't been for weeks. He had been incommunicado at home, ostensibly with influenza. For obvious reasons, it was a tightly held secret that he had had a severe heart attack on Christmas Eve and might never work again. His continued absence was demoralizing. Factions formed, and the Thalberg loyalists looked upon David as an interloper who was about to usurp Irving's throne. Predictably, David met with enormous hostility on that lot. He found increasing resistance to working with him, even from people recently well disposed. This was the worst penalty. His bitterness grew. I couldn't believe it was quite as bad as David imagined, but I respected then, as I do now, that it was his truth and his pain. He became distraught and despondent. Apparently he controlled his feelings during the work day, but he fell apart at night. My job was to put him back together and send him forth again each morning.

Along with the sniping, the press was devoting enormous space—thanks to the good publicity department David had built—to Coop, who had taken over RKO.

While David was preparing his first script for MGM, he was still tending to RKO, shaping their program and editing his last film. By the time it was full-time in Culver City, he dreaded going to the studio each day. He said he was "wanting in moral courage." Late one morning I was heartsick to find him in his study hunched on the daybed in sobs, hat and briefcase by his side. "I can't go on with it. I can't face it. Not another day." This was it. His statement would be brief: "I have made a mistake and I hereby resign." I hadn't known my full strength until I used it then and there. For once I didn't argue both sides. I was clear-cut. My attitude was, you've done it, live with it. To me the only thing more humiliating than staying was leaving. To be driven out would worsen his position, he'd look a double fool. He claimed I was sentencing him to serve time. Not at all! I wanted him to work out his two years. "Fight, fight back." He ought to fix his detractors by doing what he had been hired to do: make some great pictures. I thought he should use the very thing that had enticed him, the freedom to make whatever he wanted, the time to prepare, his call on the company's best people. I said good work would cure him. It was also the only way to salvage his reputation, which he felt was in ribbons.

The antagonism at MGM did not lessen as his successful RKO pictures went into release; it only made the other studios realize how clever MGM had been to grab him up. It took his first MGM success, *Dinner at Eight,* shot in three and a half weeks, to alter the climate.

He continued to be miserable. He found relief in writing endless letters on midnight oil to my father and Nick, begging to be let out. I was his reader and he didn't much mind not sending them. After he had made a couple of pictures and regained a little self-esteem, he finally sent a letter to my father. It was really long (even for him) and very passionate. Nothing came of it except that it quieted him down. It was easier when Irving came back in August, after an open-ended leave of absence in Europe, his health relatively restored. He cautiously decided not to take back his big studio job from my father who had been more or less been handling it during his absence, and to confine himself, like David, to a handful of quality pictures. In fact, he acquired a "bungalow" right next to David's. The most marked difference between them was that Irving kept his hiked share of MGM profits, which I don't think anyone minded. Much has been made of my father taking over the studio completely at this time, as though he had been in a tug-of-war with Irving. The truth of the matter is that the crisis of Irving's health had created a vacuum.

As David continued to search for an explanation of his folly, he decided it was an aberration committed during his grief. But almost the worst pain was having to attribute any part of his error to Pop. On the other hand, if he hadn't been married to me, admittedly he wouldn't have been in this spot. He didn't say so. He didn't have to. I felt it.

During this period I had proof that there was actually something more earth-shaking than David's troubles. To put it literally, an earthquake. Late one afternoon I had either lost my balance or the room was lurching. I looked out the window and things seemed crazy. It wasn't me, it wasn't the hotel, but, outside, the telegraph poles were swinging and swaying; I picked up the baby, threw a shawl around him, and ran down the ten flights of stairs to outrace the next tremor. That apparently used up all my common sense, for I then stupidly chose to stand in the riskiest spot available, on Wilshire Boulevard in front of the hotel, so that bits and pieces of its elaborate ornamentation could fall off and hit us. Only slightly less foolish were the people standing in the lobby under the chandeliers. I don't know what the other refugees and I were standing in the street waiting for, but I must have appeared to know, because very soon a limousine drew up and my father jumped out with "Hurry up, get in. What's the matter with you?" He behaved as though this had been prearranged, and he was disinclined to discuss his impulse.

That was a bad earthquake, and the experience gave me a need for a new perspective. I fled to the desert. I couldn't sleep and was near the end of my rope. My absence brought a letter from David signed "The Man Who Hates Himself." In it he swore he wouldn't again subject me to even the suspicion of blame. He felt guilty enough about what he was putting me through to say "when you very properly ran away from me."

The only thing guaranteed to lift David's spirits was a party, particularly if he gave it. The lower he felt, the more he wanted one. We had had a rough few months, and with an anniversary looming, I couldn't say no. But we couldn't afford it *and* gambling; in fact, we couldn't afford either, due to the latter. David said that a party was cheap, and to think of how many people we would be giving pleasure to. More than I bargained for, it turned out. We ended up hiring a ballroom in the Beverly Wilshire Hotel, where we still were living. David was quite proud of our economizing: it was the *smaller* ballroom.

IT SEEMED to me everyone was always after my father for something, yet I kept resisting his attempts to give me money. He knew we didn't have any and he would drop heavy hints that it was mine for the asking. When I didn't ask, he offered. I declined, because I was afraid it might affect our relationship. To say that would hurt his feelings, so I deliberately made it obscure: "I can't afford money." This maddened him, for which I don't blame him. (After *Gone With the Wind,* when he tried again, I said, "I have money, Dad, I don't need it." He recalled my earlier answer about not affording it; how could I reconcile that with the fact that I now had it? And just exactly what had I meant?)

However, in the summer of 1933, a few months after David returned to MGM, Dad offered me something specific. From time to time he invited me to lunch at the studio, but never when he had something serious to discuss; at those times he just came to see me. This time it was to explain about a new company called 20th Century that was being formed for Darryl Zanuck (who was ending his stint at Warner), with Joe Schenck as president and a release through United Artists. The company was to be financed by the Schenck brothers and my father, who had made a provision that Bill Goetz, then out of a job, be made an officer. My father thought to divide his large share of 20th Century stock by giving some of it to the Goetzes and some to the Selznicks.

We had trouble from the start. He couldn't understand why I didn't think the entire plan was proper, and I backed down when he suggested that perhaps my judgment wasn't equal to that of Joe and Nick Schenck, plus all their lawyers. Besides, he wasn't seeking my advice, what he was doing was offering David and me a piece of this company so that we would have some outside funds the way the Goetzes would.

I couldn't speak for David, but I myself—though very touched—was disinclined. In fact, my resistance was enormous. I tried to explain to my father that it wasn't that I didn't wish to be beholden to him, because I felt I already was and hoped I always would be. But accepting the stock would not increase this feeling, even though he might think it ought to. This time, however, I spared him my remarks about not affording money.

He said I had not reasoned it out and asked me to think it over. His plan was to lend me the money to buy the stock; all I had to do was sign a note, which would be in his safety-deposit box, and which he would reduce at the tax-free amount permissible each year. I demurred. He told me that this arrangement shouldn't worry me because if he died in the interim, the note would carry the stipulation that the debt be forgiven. Then I *really* knew I didn't want it. He said I was being a damn fool and to be practical. I said I *was* being practical: I had never owed money and didn't want to start now.

He called David and made him the same offer, which David absolutely refused. However, David agreed to reason with me about my stubbornness. David told me that I mustn't be penalized for his attitude. But even he couldn't change my feeling that I would rather do without profits than owe money. Finally my father gave David's share to the Goetzes. The Goetzes would sign notes.

As for me, in the end I proposed a compromise to my father—a difficult one, to be sure. If he was that determined on my having a share, he should give me the stock and pay the gift tax; nor would I mind if he reduced my share to compensate for paying the tax.

It disappointed my father to find me such a stickler, but it was he who had instilled it in me. And although it was wounding to him, he took it with grace, his only comment being: "You have a very good character, but you are not flexible. I'm not sure I want to do business with you in the future." We didn't.

20th Century proved a success, and as the dividends came in, I grew very troubled. I thought what he had done for Bill Goetz was fine, and it was fine that Edie and Bill should keep their stock. But I asked my father to give up his stock and interest in the company. He had enough without it, and so had I; I would give up my stock with his. The whole thing made me very uncomfortable, particularly since MGM was lending its stars to 20th Century, thus helping that company get on its feet more quickly than it could have otherwise. I felt it ought to build its roster the way other companies did—and what must the MGM stockholders be thinking? I fantasized dire consequences. (In the actual event, 20th Century did so well that it took over the Fox Company.)

The new company was indeed timely. By then the Goetzes were living in the lovely French Provincial house Edie had built in Bel-Air. She had started off married life with style. A four-room apartment or no, within the year there was a butler serving dinner. (Actually, he was a chauffeur, courtesy of my father, whom Edie felt she required because she was pregnant.)

Edie moved fast. After a few years she sold the Bel-Air house and everything in it, and built another on the Santa Monica strip, this time Early American, with furniture to match. She soon outgrew that one and bought a splendid mansion in Holmby Hills, as well as brand-new furniture, all designed by Billy Haines. Later on they added French Impressionist paintings to the new house, which lent itself admirably to an ever-growing collection that was first-rate by any standards. No throwaway opulence for Edie; she believed expenditure should be conspicuous. Her artistic ambitions were replaced by social aspirations. In fact, entertaining became her career.

Edie went in for elegance in a big way and got grander with the years. With this went a determination that everything she had and wore be the last word, giving a literal meaning to the family expression, "How does it look?" Bill made the ongoing luxury seem an amusing foible of Edie's. His comments were blunt, but made with humor and affection, which made her laugh even when they contained nuggets of unvarnished truth.

Bill boasted that he didn't particularly want a fine home. He said that he really liked hotels and preferred the food at Lindy's. He'd been a friend of Al Jolson's, and loved former vaudevillians like Jack Benny and George Burns. They considered Bill their greatest audience, and he himself excelled in deadpan one-liners. His humor was borderline in taste, but not lacking in shock value.

I liked Bill because he made Edie happy, and I think he liked me all right, even though I couldn't fully appreciate his gags and comedy routines. I had no idea what he felt or really thought. He was amiable and cheerful, yet I never felt any man could be as uncomplicated as Bill seemed.

Edie called the shots, but Bill was hardly henpecked. In any case, she had her way more than most wives. I admired her single-mindedness and the skills she developed. As she achieved her goals, she set them anew. As a gifted hostess she was infinitely helpful in Bill's career. She had the instinct to push him high and quick, and, with my father's assistance, did so. Bill made no bones about my father's help; he was glad to have it and said as much.

Years later Dad came to his rescue again when Bill, unwilling to go back to his old job after Zanuck returned from the war, was eased out of 20th Century–Fox. Dad set him up with a friend as an independent. The company was called International Pictures, much to David's indignation—this, of course, was after Selznick International Pictures. When it was later merged with Universal and called Universal-International, David was no less angry. By now the Goetzes were riding high and didn't much care. Bill was getting laughs by boldly announcing that he didn't need Dad any more.

When 20th Century began to pay dividends, my father gleefully questioned me about the extent of my new fortune. What he was really after was more appreciation. I didn't refer to his gift as often or as warmly as he hoped I would. He was crestfallen at its modest size and upset to discover the reason: I had not taken my share of tax deduction but had let our tax people put my income into the highest bracket so as not to penalize David. I thought it only fair; Dad thought it stupid.

Edith, on the other hand, was catering to him extravagantly. It suited her and it suited him; in fact he adored it. He wanted me to make more fuss over him, as she did, always adding "whether she means it or not." I told him it was not my nature to be demonstrative. I didn't love him more because he'd given me the stock—what was allotted was his, come what may. Didn't he feel my affection? Yes he did, and he trusted it. He just wanted me to show it more in front of people.

I WAS about to follow in Edie's footsteps: I was going to build that house. The infinite possibilities frightened me, the margin for error was so vast. One wrong decision at the outset, such as land or architect, and nothing would bail me out. It was certainly no time for impulse buying; I didn't want to learn to live with mistakes or waste money on retakes. Nothing was too much trouble because it was going to be our home forever—no June, July, and August situation. I had to plan for now and the future; I had to estimate David's further success. He told me to raise my sights and to think big.

I was out to achieve the impossible. It was going to be a house in the country and yet in the city. It was going to be luxurious and at the same time not extravagant. Moreover, it was going to be unique—it would have to be, to please us both.

Naturally, the perfect piece of land did not exist for a mansion that was going to be modest. David had something spectacular in mind with a wonderful view for the weekends, which meant it would be too high. I was to have from my father a sum equal to what Edith had spent on everything from land to the last lamp. Given David's ideas, I couldn't see how we were going to manage a house, let alone furnishings. I wasn't for being mingy, but I was concerned about bad weather, accessibility, servants, and children's activities. The compromise, so called, was the foothills—walking distance from the Beverly Hills Hotel. That was no mountaintop, but just down the road from Pickfair and across from Chaplin would not exactly be slumming. And I still maintain that two and a half acres with road on three sides and no sidewalks is an estate.

After looking over the portfolios of the most successful men, I decided the perfect architect didn't exist either. I had to go shopping street by street in the better residential areas of the city and even out to respectable Pasadena, which yielded half a dozen lovely houses, each quite different from the others. They all turned out to have been designed by a youngish man named Roland Coate.

I was a rare bird in that Depression year; no one else was building a house. Mr. Coate looked at me in despair. How welcome I would have been months before! Now it was too late, he was closing down his office. Here I was, wanting a proper house—a whitewashed brick, Georgian in feeling—but he had already let most of his staff go. Well, I was prepared to start immediately. He was adamant. My ultimate weapon turned out to be my method of choosing him—the fact that I had admired the very houses he most prided himself on. Mr. Coate liked our piece of land and David liked Mr. Coate, except that he found him stubborn because he insisted on slicing off the top of our hill to make room for our house.

I'd already had a lot to do with houses, apart from having lived in so many. (Thirteen in thirteen years is many miles of house-looking.) I had pored over a lot of books and magazines and had amassed a hope chest of clippings which I now offered up to Mr. Coate. There were limits to what could be demanded professionally. We made many a trade-off.

One request was made to maintain harmony in the home. David would never get out of bed for anything, certainly not to close windows. If it was raining in, let it rain. If there were gusts of wind that might knock over the lamps, he said get new ones, anything but get up. That was it until we had our own home. Now, rather than be spartan, I opted for electric-opening windows for our bedroom.

Mr. Coate couldn't get back the woman who had done his kitchens and bathrooms; for designing these he had neither the patience nor the aptitude. I had both, along with some unorthodox ideas. Sensing his resistance, I took the job on and laid out the bathrooms and the entire service area. I learned how to use a scale rule and do elevations. Over the years my friends didn't know they were flattering me when they asked to bring their architects to see our pantry and bathrooms. Even Roland Coate was amused.

The set-up we had had at the Colleen Moore house was so attractive for entertaining that we copied the idea of separating the pool area and the court by what we called the tennis house. But the new pool was conspicuous by its absence. Grass grew where it was destined to be. (Underneath, the pipes had been laid expectantly.) Even without a pool we were over budget before we started. However, there were no holds barred on the tennis court, which David considered more important than the house; it had to be the best, though, fortunately, not the largest, inasmuch as courts were standard size. Cedric Gibbons had a sunken court which made any player feel a champion because of the way the shots resounded. We could have no less. And ours had lights. Only once were they turned on at night, and that was for Garbo, who had an urge to play after the preview of *Anna Karenina*. I don't know whose tennis shoes she wore, but I do know that never before or since have I seen her in such high spirits. (We never knew each other well, but more than twenty years later she gave me another surprise. Our mutual friend Sam Spiegel, who occasionally had lunch with us on Christmas Day, one year proposed bringing Garbo, but on second thought he came alone and asked us to join her and him at his place later in the day. Jeff and Danny, well into their twenties, were beside themselves with delight. Assuming she might be less delighted, I said that we'd better make it brief and not impose.

I underestimated Garbo, who put me to shame. She came forward eagerly to greet the boys, saying, "Did you know I knew your mother before you did?" She made it sound an astonishing treat as she told all about the Adlon Hotel in 1924. I was pretty fascinated myself, because she had never before given any hint that she remembered. She was charm itself as she linked them not only with me, but with my father and with their father. They were bowled over.

Christmas gets to everyone, even Garbo. As I was leaving, she took me aside and said what, at least for the moment, she clearly felt: she wished she had children. "You have everything," she said. "I have nothing. I envy you.")

Our landscape architect was the admirable Florence Yoch. Southern California may be a garden spot, but not a blade of grass grows without being provided with that costly commodity, topsoil. Miss Yoch didn't stint there or on any of the sensible priorities. Money was sunk where it didn't show, so we had a grand new house, a splendid tennis court, a few nice trees, and many tiny plants. Miss Yoch said we were to practice patience and let them grow—a big order in that overnight town.

Nothing was being omitted; some things were being postponed. It was basics now and frills later, and just as well, since David had to pick up the remaining costs, which he couldn't afford because we didn't have any money. (That we had no money was something nobody would have believed.) The situation was aggravated when our almost completed projection booth had to be ripped out. One night there had been a small fire at the studio and David had practically hurled me into the street, screaming, "Run for your life!" In those days film was made of highly inflammable celluloid, which gave off lethal fumes. As a consequence, the booth in our house had to be made explosion-proof, with a deep reinforced-concrete base and a sprinkler system. That scared a pretty penny out of David.

The house was going to be rather bare at first because obviously the allotment for furniture had to be whittled down. We still had nothing but wedding presents and David's books. However, I had something which antedated everything: when I got married, I had packed my past into an old straw suitcase, and it had traveled unopened to all our various other houses. It finally got unpacked when we moved into 1050 Summit Drive. Among the treasures I had tucked away were some marbles in a pink bag I had made in sewing class, a small, battered doll, and my Girl Scout uniform, with the last badge still unsewed.

The film of *David Copperfield* came to my rescue, because it required a trip to England. It was beautifully timed. Antiques in Los Angeles were in short supply, expensive, and dubious in origin. Good furniture could be bought in England for a fraction of the price. I left town with blueprints under my arm. I didn't know much, just enough to make me anxious.

In New York I met a man who tried to help me by offering to take me to the top dealers in town. He didn't seem to understand that I wasn't in their league, that I got qualms just looking in their windows. He said one learns from seeing the best. The first day went so well we went again the following one. He taught me what to look for and how to do it. It was walk, look, and listen. He gave me just enough confidence to go it alone, and not too badly, when I got to London. That man was David Bruce. I marvel still at his patience and kindness.

It was rewarding all around. I had the house I wanted, Coate received awards, and there was more coming. Jack Warner phoned David with a request that was, he said, neither business nor social, but a personal favor. He had recently remarried and his new bride was unhappy with his old house. Might he bring her that very night to see our place? Five minutes after they arrived, Mr. Coate and Miss Yoch had a new client and an immense job; ours was minor in comparison. Fortunately, the results were beautiful. Miss Yoch's efforts with me also yielded her George Cukor, and her future credits were to include *Gone With the Wind*. She landscaped Tara.

IT SEEMS consistent that I was not interested in how much money people had. However, it was downright unnatural that I never inquired what *we* had. Not that David wouldn't have told me. It was simply self-preservation: any specific information would be misleading, since, like a fever chart, it would be accurate only at the moment of reading.

By this time we had a different personal business manager, Morgan Maree, who sometimes acted as a surrogate parent. He spared me David's gambling confessions and juggled funds accordingly. Less frequently he made investments for him. Morgan took seriously my need for accountability. He gave me the good marks I craved and didn't let me feel pathetic. On the other hand, when I sold my 20th Century stock, he turned the proceeds into what he called my portfolio, and educated me enough to deal myself with the stockbroker when I chose. He was amused that I learned to be pound foolish on occasion, at least with this money.

To show David I was capable of a bold gesture, I decided to splurge and give him a proper present. A painting, no less.

Qualifying myself to make the big decision by touring the museums in New York, I could see that French paintings were still beyond me, Americans were safer. I settled on George Bellows and found a landscape I didn't have to think twice about. There would now be an indication of what we someday hoped would be on our walls. But my panic grew with each succeeding week. Would he like it? Had I done the right thing?

Toward the end of our Christmas festivities I asked Farr to please bring in an ax. David paled. Of course I also meant the large wooden box which had been kept out of sight.

David was bowled over by my gumption. And the picture. However well it suited his room, he decided it should be hung on the overmantel of the projection room for all to see.

M G M had found David hard to get and hard to quiet down, but he was worth it. He had turned out some exceptionally successful films one after the other—just what they had wanted, and which enhanced David's reputation: *Dinner at Eight*, *David Copperfield*, *Anna Karenina*, *Tale of Two Cities*. By 1935 his old dreams had revived and he began planning for the future. So did MGM, but in an opposite direction; he was their man and they were in an ideal position to hold on to him. They cooked up quite a proposal. More than straight money was offered; it was unprecedented. My father, Bob Rubin, and even Irving actually planned to redivide their share of the profits and cut David in. Not only would it give the studio strength in depth, but my father's position would be impregnable. David felt obliged to tell them his hopes lay elsewhere; he wanted to go out on his own. Yes, still again. No more detours. RKO and MGM had delayed him, but, ironically, had qualified him still further. It was now or never.

I only cared that the decision be his; I could see both sides. But I was going to live with him, not his job. If he was tempted by MGM, fine, but please no sacrifices for my sake. There couldn't be security anyhow, as long as he gambled.

I was grateful my father hadn't embroiled me when he had lured David to MGM two years before. Nor had he this time; therefore I was totally unprepared when one afternoon without warning he arrived in my front hall. He came in at quite a clip, and he was there to ask me why he was having so much trouble reaching an arrangement with David. I never even got to the bottom of the stairs. Did I know what was going on? I said he knew better than I. My father didn't buy that. "Do you know what a partnership means? We talk to that boy every day. He listens, he's interested. The next morning we have to begin again. Something happens overnight. Is this where my opposition is, right here in my own family? I happen to know you people are broke. Are you aware of that?" I knew all too well. He went on: "I know just how much he gambles. Furthermore, I know he has taken out a loan on the insurance and on this house." I didn't know that, so it was a jolt, a nasty one. It was all I could do not to flinch. "Are you in a position to turn down a million dollars a year?" Put that way, it was pretty staggering, but I still didn't react.

I didn't like the spot I was in; still less what had to be said. But there could be no misunderstanding; I had to be clear. I stood there, on the steps, took a deep breath, and sanctimoniously told him that I wanted to be happy and I couldn't be if David was unhappy. I was not persuading David in either direction. I reminded my father that David was the only person I had ever met in my life who knew exactly what he wanted. My father cut in. "Don't be a fool. Who knows, with Irving's health as it is, David might be called on to step into Irving's shoes. There is no one else. I don't intend to work forever. In time he will step into mine. He has his chance now. Give it a few years; then he can always do the other, with his fortune made."

"He might not have the courage then. He's still young enough to try and to fail. If he does, you could have him back, as you once said, 'with his tail between his legs,' and he won't have been denied. On the other hand, has it ever occurred to you that he might succeed?" That was consistent with my stand that terrible morning in his office, but now there was more at stake for my father than the date of a wedding.

There was no end to the surprises of that day. Quietly he said, "I understand." Adding, "Thank you," he turned on his heel and walked out. It can't have been easy for him, but he never said another word about the matter.

My father seemed to avoid discussion of things he preferred to forget. Included was a particularly ugly incident from the previous year, when Joe and Nick Schenck had tried to pull one of the most unattractive corporate maneuvers I ever encountered. Joe, who was then heading 20th Century–Fox, approached David about taking over my father's job at MGM.

I was stunned. How could they dare? And how could they think David venal enough to listen?

Naturally, David said no, but that was not enough; he felt my father should know. Everything considered, we decided it was better I tell him. For one thing, I could be as circuitous as my father, if need be. But I was to judge for myself how far to go.

I was in New York and so was my father, who was going to Nick's for the weekend, apparently to talk contract. I can't remember where David was, but there's no way I could forget the essential story.

Giving as my excuse that it was my only chance to see Dad, I suggested I ride out to Long Island with him and spend Friday night at Nick's. On the way out I tried to feel my way by dropping hints about the Schencks, but only succeeded in annoying my father with my double-talk. "If you have something to say, say it." I decided that this was not the moment; besides, it was Nick's car.

I had second thoughts during the evening, when I witnessed the apparent warmth between the men and heard them agree to talk seriously in the morning.

After I went to bed, the enormity of the situation really hit me. Not daring to turn on the light, I tiptoed barefoot down the dark hall, scared to death, then turned the knob of my father's door, hoping I had the right room. Crouching beside him in the dark, I told him the story in whispers. He heard me out, saying little. In the morning I took myself back to town. I don't know what use, if any, my father made of my information, but I breathed a sigh of relief when the next contract was signed. (Some sixteen years later Nick finally did get rid of my father, and not too many years later he found himself out as well.)

C L E A R L Y, in the matter of MGM, the strength of David's dream won out over his presumed thirst for power. We never even learned the percentage they had in mind. Surely there was no one else in the picture business who would have turned down that deal. But then, only David would have considered it an odds-on bet that his own company would turn out equally profitable for him.

It was called Selznick International Pictures, and, not unnaturally, it was located in that lovely Colonial building with tall white columns that we had passed on our first date. One morning I happened to drive David to work. When we got there, he said, "Look, see what they're doing." I'd already seen and was undone. By a fluke it turned out to be the day they were painting the name on the studio. They had just reached the letter Z. There it was: his heart's desire, and in his favorite typeface.

The scene was corny, but I thought it was all wonderful and said so with the tears pouring down. I also said I was frightened—it was too much and much too soon. Yet it was a distilled moment; romantically, the climax of David's career. It could never be again. I wanted to make a burnt offering.

I was a child of Hollywood. To me, this was history.

Selznick International and "Gone With the Wind"

AT LAST, at last, and the sweeter for the waiting. David's company was as easy to form as it had been difficult four years before. It simply fell into place. He was now his own boss and he was out to demonstrate MGM quality at RKO costs with the Paramount system. Was ever anyone less frustrated! Here was proof a man could have what he wanted. Indeed, more: John Hay Whitney (Jock), who had become his closest friend, was his major partner.

Coop had been right when he figured the Whitneys to back David's company, before David went to RKO. Later on, when Coop got involved with Technicolor, the Whitneys backed him, investing heavily in that stock. They made some movies, not too successful, for a company they called Pioneer.

In a sense Selznick International Pictures had begun in our Hotel Pierre days. The last potential backer Coop had come up with had been Sonny Whitney; the Whitneys were prospects Coop had been nursing for some time. Sonny, an attractive fellow, found movies tempting, and so did his cousin John Hay Whitney, whom he longed for us to meet. In fact, he gave a cocktail party expressly to bring that about on our next visit the following year. Nice party, but we were not any more taken with Jock than he with us. However, his wife, Liz, a handsome, high-spirited young woman, persuaded us to meet them for a drink at "21" later in the evening. From then on, nothing could stop us.

Jock was an athlete, a sport, and a gentleman, not necessarily in that order—and a man of letters. He seemed to have it all: an unassailable position, an excellent Groton-Yale-Oxford education, and a host of friends and interests. He led a lusty, strenuous, swashbuckling life with seven-league boots on that gave him extraordinary variety and freedom, shadowed only by the obligations which surely lay ahead. His appetite exceeded even David's, and he shared David's feeling for quality.

Jock went to England frequently, where he had another world of friends, as well as his own racing and breeding stable. In New York he had his own polo team and a far more extensive racing set-up together with his mother and sister. His more serious interests were Yale, New York Hospital, and the Museum of Modern Art, and he eventually became top man on all their boards. He sat on other boards as well. And then—not surprisingly, given his kind of enterprise—he was a gambler in show business. There were lots of men under that one hat.

As he grew older, his conscience grew too. His sense of social responsibility increasingly emerged; his bottled-up respectability crept out. Now I see that he was packing the pleasures in against the day when he would have to assume the responsibilities destined for him. I find myself a little startled to realize that at the time of Selznick International Pictures he was only thirty-one. It's only now that I realize the opposition he must have met in putting that much money into something as chancy as the movie business. And in partnership with a fellow only two years older. No wonder eyebrows were raised. Jock hadn't even come into his inheritance then.

But the vast amount of money he was to inherit was not the notable thing about him—in fact, we thought it a handicap, because as a result of it he had been trained always to trust wiser heads. He defied them on the movies, though, and in irreverent undertakings as diverse as Billy Rose's *Jumbo* at the old Hippodrome and the newspaper *PM*. From the start we found him a man made up of contrasting and changing parts. What was constant was his perception, his consideration, and his taste. And his respect for the written word.

There was nothing mingy about Jock. He was big in size, spirit, and energy. "Lively" is a mild description of him at that time. In truth, neither he nor Liz worked hard enough at keeping the home fires burning; she was more interested in foals and puppies than in babies. But, oh, they were a handsome pair. When they danced up a storm at El Morocco, all eyes

were on them. He was catnip for ladies (or was it vice versa?). Liz had
a daredevil quality and she was natural—not to a fault but, oddly, to a
charm. Llangollen, her house in Virginia, ran helter-skelter, harum-
scarum, al fresco. Liz was utterly unpredictable. Item: I once saw a horse
casually led into the living room.

Burned by Billy Rose, more than rewarded by *Life with Father,* Jock
continued to back a great many Broadway plays during the 1930's. And
his friends were far from conventional. When he married, Robert Benchley was his best man, and among the ushers, not too traditionally, were
Donald Ogden Stewart and Fred Astaire. The stage would always remain
for him a minor but genuine interest. (His sister, Joan Payson, as good
a sport as he, here matched him dollar for dollar.)

Our acquisition of Jock didn't impress people in Hollywood as much
as it made them critical. That is, until they met him. They assumed he
was spoiled, stupid, or a stuffed shirt. When Jock had been with us at
someone's house, I would later hear, "That can't be Jock Whitney—why,
he's wonderful!"

I found his give-and-take with the earthier men in the New York end
of movies hilarious. They forgot their preconceived notion of him and
accepted him as he was. I fixed him up with a handful of Yiddish words
—nothing remarkable about that except his ability to use them for
punctuation at the appropriate moment.

In 1935 when David decided to leave MGM to form his own company,
his position was well established in filmland, but not in Whitney-land.
There were rumors and suspicions. To those in New York, it seemed clear
that Jock was being taken for a ride. Jock paid no heed. His friends in
London took a still dimmer view; they gave neither Jock nor David the
benefit of the doubt. But Jock had the largest investment in the company
and was the most enthusiastic, and it seemed not inappropriate for him to
accept the title of chairman if he was willing. On paper it gave the
company added luster, and until things got going he dealt with all the New
York end—worked, kibitzed, and advised. In other words, he had a job.

He did the job—efficiently, effortlessly, and effectively. It went from
a pastime to an involvement to a preoccupation to practically full-time
work. He worked hard, harder than he knew. It was interim, but an
important transition in Jock's life—fascination and responsibility combined. He made millions out of it, but his satisfaction couldn't be measured in the money. And, indeed, he had more than money on the line.
He really stuck his neck out. When the chips were down, Jock was

valiant, and David never forgot it. There was a chance to end the risk on *Gone With the Wind*—sell the rights with a profit of a million dollars and get on with the company. Jock said no and put up additional money for SIP. He was a true believer. There was no show of nerves, nor did he ever let us know what kind of flak he was taking in New York.

David had been all for Jock's being the main backer, but I was dubious about it, and also about his being chairman; I was afraid it might spell the end of a beautiful friendship. I was mistaken. He and David were as compatible by day as they were by night. Neither threw his weight around, which helped protect the relationship. I don't think it was good disposition or good manners, just prudence. They might argue a lot, but the pleasure would always be renewed. I didn't have to be the balance wheel because poor John Wharton, Jock's theatrical lawyer, was forced into that role. I was used otherwise: "Don't let on that I said anything, but if you get the chance, do explain." (Or persuade.) I got the same line from both of them—I don't know if either ever caught on that I was emissary to both sides. They must have approved of my services because they went on using me.

The relationship with Jock had continuity and content. We would seem to have had little in common, yet we had entered into each other's lives with a minimum of preliminaries. Formalities didn't exist. Jock's friends became ours and our friends became his. He had a home away from home. He rarely stayed with us, but thought nothing of changing the menu, which Farr would explain as I came home: "Mr. Whitney thought you wouldn't mind." All the scene lacked for him was his bosom pal, Bob Benchley; therefore when Bob was in town Jock brought him and made the circle complete. Jock loved me because he loved David, and then he loved David even more because he loved me. Jock had three relationships going—one with David, one with me, and one with the Selznicks.

We had the essentials of any friendship—trust and communication.

David hadn't known he needed Jock, but, once had, always missed. He came like an unexpected gift and gave pleasure and affection and fulfillment to David's dreams. In fact, Jock brought so much with him that he gave David a false clue as to what life could provide.

D A V I D ' S new company boasted no names other than his list of investors, and mighty impressive it was: of course Jock's sister, Joan,

Sonny Whitney and his two sisters, Arthur Lehman, Robert Lehman, and John Hertz. And Hollywood prestige: Irving Thalberg. One evening David came home absolutely agog. Irving was investing in the new company and, what's more, of his own accord; he himself had asked to be included. Of course the shares would be in Norma's name, but he was aboard. I found that intoxicating and hoped my father didn't know.

Myron, unasked, came in last but handsomely. At that time he had practically a monopoly on the best talent, so he gave warning not to expect favors. His clients came first. He was kidding, but on the square —not a dollar off, ever. In fact, David claimed it worked the other way.

The plan was to make six pictures a year, and the trouble with SIP from start to finish was too few pictures in proportion to the overhead. David's standards and work habits aggravated his ever-losing battle with the clock . . . and calendar. Perfectionism brings delay, disorder, and (naturally) expense. Each picture made money, but I suspect the company lost every year. Certainly David was on the defensive about not being more methodical. When *Gone With the Wind* was incorporated into the schedule, long-range planning came into his life. The company would simply have to maintain a flow of pictures in order to have ample time to develop his super-picture. Weighty resolutions were made.

He somewhat mended his ways. After the first year or two he really tried to step up the number of pictures. However, *A Star is Born,* which he called "the movie I promised you," monopolized his time. That was one movie I got to know in advance, scene by scene, because David used me as a sounding board. Contrary to myths and credits, the story was largely his; it was stylish and unexpected of Bill Wellman to say, when he accepted the writing award, that the Oscar really belonged to David.

NEW HOURS, new company, new son. Jeff's third birthday was a sharp reminder that time was passing. Daniel Mayer Selznick was born May 18, 1936, nine months and one week later. No fancy pregnancy and not all that fuss either about his birth. He just showed up in the middle of the afternoon, fat, placid, and laughing. He wasn't the crown prince; he quite sensibly just fitted in.

David didn't burst with pride, and this time he didn't get drunk. He was pleased, mighty pleased. This baby was eminently and enormously satisfactory. Unlike Jeff, he was no threat, no competition. There was acceptance on sight; an ally had arrived. The enemy of his enemy was his friend, as I was to learn.

Myron was sore. Two sons! He said David didn't deserve boys, *he* did. "You better turn Jeffrey over to me." Jeffrey got the message and returned the interest. At Running Springs, Myron's place in the mountains, Jeff could be found outside, faithfully trudging behind Myron, imitating his gestures. Myron claimed there was a resemblance. Mother Selznick agreed and adored him forever.

Naturally, after the birth, a sea voyage ensued. This time I looked forward to the trip, because the baby was older and it was only for three weeks. We went to Honolulu with the Averell Harrimans. Did we play bridge? We thought we did, until we played with them. I was Averell's partner; he soon made me his pupil as well. He was as good a teacher as he was a player, but he was tenacious; two nights later I was in tears. The poor man had been misled by my composure, and I had tried too hard, which is the story of my life. Thereafter moderation set in. I gave him an easier time with the surfboard at Waikiki. David's efforts drew a fascinated audience, but he swore off ten minutes later while he was still in one piece.

Then back to Summit Drive, where we settled in again, now a family of four.

David and I never saw eye-to-eye on the children. He just didn't turn out to be the kind of father both of us had anticipated. He was prepared to be a loving parent, but in his own way, on his own clock. Children were an ornament and a pleasure—at his convenience; he had trouble finding time for them. In the morning he had overslept, or he was late, or they had left for school. In the evening they were in bed and asleep by the time he got home. In their preschool days he wanted me to change their hours to conform to his. If artificial light can alter when hens lay eggs, you can outwit children's natural schedules! He didn't know why I couldn't either keep them up or wake them up. The boys saw David when he was getting dressed, or on the phone, or surrounded by guests. There was no time carved out or given over to them. On matters already settled between us, he said, "Ask Mother." When I insisted that this was bad for them, David's instant defense was that he couldn't afford to say no because he didn't spend enough time with them.

Children belonged—oh, very much so—but they weren't included. We didn't take them places *en famille*. Essentially, I tend to think he felt that doing so would be rather middle-class, certainly not chic or gay. They never had meals with us except Christmas and Thanksgiving, when of course there were guests. I must say, though, that he never missed a birthday party. He'd arrive when it was at full tilt, followed by a film cameraman with standard equipment.

He would have done anything for the boys except what they needed. Participation didn't occur to him. Presents and unexpected treats don't make up for broken promises; they lead to an unspoken game of "I'll-indulge-you-if-you'll-indulge-me," and "Don't tell Mother, you know how she is." This behavior shed a false light on me, him, and what parents are. It was hard enough being a mother; I objected to being a father as well. But my objections got me nowhere.

David had a Norman Rockwell vision of fathers and sons enjoying electric trains together. The idea was fine, just years premature. A boy should first know what an electric train was, and yearn quite a while. Jeff's trains were too early, too grand, and his father was miscast.

When at seven Danny wrote charming little poems, David gave him a book about iambic pentameter. End of verses. The following year when Danny improvised some attractive melodies on the piano, a book about solfeggio and harmony turned up. End of tunes. David insisted this was only coincidence.

David's program for the children's future was equally unrealistic. They were still small when he was deep in plans for their education: Yale or Harvard, followed by a combination of Oxford, the Sorbonne, and perhaps Heidelberg.

David preferred to imagine that everything at home was a snap. His advice remained, "Hire, delegate, then go out and enjoy," and he didn't like it a bit when I worried, particularly if I was concerned over Jeffrey, who as time passed did not seem as gloriously happy as I wanted a child of mine to be. David decided that the only thing wrong with Jeff was over-solicitude on my part, and his prescription, once again, was to get me out of town. It was worth a trip to New York just to stop me worrying; on our return, Jeffrey would be fine. I agreed when he gave me permission to consult someone to learn what I was doing wrong.

Dorothy Paley recommended David Levy, the most eminent child psychiatrist in America. I went for helpful hints, but they were not forthcoming. Nor was he—he made me do all the talking. I answered questions which I felt could be of no possible relevance—our days, our nights, our weekends, our habits; he was particularly fascinated by the story of Jeffrey's birth and the trip which followed it. He asked me to return the next day. Again I held forth and still he didn't come up with any answers;

instead, he would have to see David. I apologized for my inability to give him sufficient information. On the contrary, I had given him a remarkably meticulous case history, and the only fault he had to find with me was that possibly I was over-conscientious. (That didn't seem so bright—I had heard it before!) However, he could be of no use unless he saw David. I explained that that was impossible—David was too busy. Correct: that was exactly David's response. He protested, he thought it was ridiculous, but at last he gave in, provided the appointment would not interfere with his day. Levy saw to it. David came back to the Waldorf just before dinner, in the only total rage I had ever seen him in or ever would. He was beside himself, violent and profane. I couldn't make head or tail of it. Apparently my only crime was being taken in by a fraud like that. His fury mounted until he reached the climax of the terrible things David Levy had told him: "Can you believe it? It's incredible. Me, of all people. And when you think of Pop, it's not possible. He said to me that I have rejected Jeffrey. Imagine me rejecting our son! God damn him!"

I thought both men were wrong, or at least too extreme, but I went back to see Levy anyhow. The doctor was aware that he had mortally offended David; he had rarely seen such an intense reaction. For all his praise, Levy gave me bad marks on David. He found him completely opposite to the man I had described. I yearned for help. He assured me that his door was open whenever he had the cooperation of both parents.

I recalled that David didn't want Jeff in the room mornings when he was getting dressed and we were talking; he would sign-language me to get him out. Odd he didn't mind Danny puttering around, and if absolutely necessary he himself could manage to ask Danny to leave. Not Jeff; that was up to me. David said, "He's listening." In other words, this fellow was an interloper. Always had been. David needed Mama all to himself.

It had to be faced that he was pretty damn competitive with that little boy. When he played a game with him, no holds were barred. He defended himself by telling me how quick-thinking Jeff was. So determined was David to win, one would think he was playing with Myron. It was all pretty elementary.

THE COMPANY was less than a year old when David asked me if I wanted to see a movie of a Civil War story. Of course I didn't. *He* didn't. No one did, not conceivably. David's story department in New York was headed by Kay Brown, who was putting pressure on him about a book that wasn't even published yet. He complained that she was giving him the rush act, and he was full of resistance. It was a first novel, carrying a stiff price and a terrible title. All that and the Civil War besides.

The first synopsis only convinced David that it would be expensive to make. And the price was foolish to pay if the book didn't turn out to be really big. On the other hand, if it were to be a huge success, he couldn't afford to pass it up, but then again he would have to be faithful to a wide readership. It was so long he said it would make twenty movies, not one. For a fellow who himself was over-length, he particularly dreaded the job of having to compress it. He stalled by asking for a long, detailed synopsis. Jock had the edge because he had read the book. He didn't push David the way Kay did, he just said he was going to buy it if David didn't. That clinched it.

David read *Gone With the Wind* some weeks later, on the way to Honolulu and back, as did half the passengers on the boat. The only difference was that he was reading it more slowly and he owned the picture rights. He decided that if he edited, omitted, and telescoped chunks of the book, he might get it down to gargantuan proportions. But its size and the challenge were about equal and they suited his temperament.

What usually held films up was the shooting script, so David started far in advance on *GWTW*. To counteract his own tendencies, he chose as writer an eminent playwright, Sidney Howard, who was a figure of considerable authority as well as strict about time and methods. But no amount of time would have sufficed. Later there were other writers, and in the end the script often came hot from the typewriter to the set, sometimes from David. But the script was essentially Sidney Howard's.

At first it was exciting to have an important property lined up, instead of being caught short without material. But there sprang up a nostalgia for the wonderful little company that had been and which was now threatened by the good fortune of owning the book. Everything escalated: interest, scope, expectation. David had a tiger by the tail. Failure would mean the end of his company and his career.

My father used to say everyone had two businesses: his own and show business. Everyone in America was a casting expert on *GWTW*. It was not a national pastime, it was an obsession. David was assailed about the casting in print and inundated by mail as though it was all to be settled by public vote. Had there been a contest for Rhett Butler, Gable would have won unanimously, but there was no logical choice for Scarlett O'Hara. As is already too well documented elsewhere, David undertook to find a new girl.

The search for Scarlett made Russell Birdwell, the publicity director, look good, but even he couldn't engender the kind of publicity that project created; nobody is *that* good. When Birdwell could no longer control it, he quite sensibly took credit for it. As the book caught fire, anything about the film became news. David was beside himself trying to contain the ballyhoo because it could boomerang against the picture, himself, and Scarlett, whoever she turned out to be.

The role of Scarlett inspired many a young woman with the conviction that she had been born to play the part. Liz Whitney, of all people, pretended she was among them and even managed to have a test of herself made. One young hopeful went to extreme lengths: she arrived in our courtyard one Sunday morning on the open back of a truck which carried a very tall volume with a *GWTW* cover. In its open pages stood the would-be heroine, dressed in a Scarlett costume, ready to step into the house and the role. She only landed in the papers.

After a couple of years and still no Scarlett, discouragement set in. For protection David began to consider certain well-known actresses. The press jumped on him and cried fraud; the search had been a stunt! By the time the final tests were being scheduled, it had to be faced that there still was no girl.

Oddly enough, one of the finalists turned out to be our nearest neighbor, Paulette Goddard. She and Charlie Chaplin lived right across the road, in fact our driveways faced each other, so naturally we became friends—though not close friends, since David and Charlie were not a match made in heaven. The real link was Paulette, of whom I grew fond —a woman of considerable looks, charm, and resourcefulness, who was giving Charlie a rather happy life. I had noticed her when she was a dashing blonde in New York during the more adventurous days of her first marriage, and it was hard to believe she could ever have turned into this ever-so-studious young woman, however playful.

Somehow I never put anything past Paulette. For instance: I had a hand-knit wool bathing suit, the color of lightly tanned skin—my favorite suit—which Paulette greatly admired; to be blunt, she coveted it. When that suit was missing one day, I called up Paulette and said not a word except, "Send it back, girl!" Back it came, only to disappear again shortly thereafter, right out of the pool house. She offered me certain swaps: no dice. We negotiated. Finally we compromised: Paulette was permitted to borrow it for very special occasions provided she returned it on her own. That would be the day!

Meanwhile, she had been acquiring professional skill through the coaching of the wise Constance Collier, and was beginning to achieve a place for herself as an actress. Now, quite unexpectedly, she was being considered as a possible Scarlett. At first we treated it as a joke. But her tests were good, and she was still in the running when the ranks had sifted down to the last half-dozen.

David called her in one day and told her it was no longer a joke. "My God, I may really be stuck with you!" (They were rather inclined to bait each other.) But he said he had to clarify her legal status; was she actually married to Charlie? She turned quite haughty: how dare David ask her a question like that? He said he had to, because he couldn't afford to jeopardize an investment like *GWTW* because of an irregularity in someone's personal life. She said she had been married on a boat off the China coast. He said that was clearly nonsense, although he had read it somewhere too. Then she declared that no one else had ever dared to talk to her that way. But David had the perfect answer: no one else had ever almost offered her a part like Scarlett O'Hara. Then, bursting into tears, Paulette told him that he was about to hear something that she had sworn never to reveal: actually, she and Charlie had been married by the mayor of Catalina.

Eventually it emerged from an attempt to check the records that Catalina was an unincorporated part of Los Angeles. No mayor. No soap . . .

Sugar (as I called her) was a handful, but I never saw her in a difficult mood. Extraordinary that when she and Charlie split up, this number-one gimme girl parted from that number-one non-giver without a ripple. And years later, when she next got married (to Burgess Meredith), there could be no doubts—Jeff and Danny were witnesses.

Alas, Paulette or no Paulette, not one of the candidates was exactly right; if you have half a dozen, it means you don't have one. David still had hope, not because it would be humiliating to back down, but because his need was so great. He declared that his luck wouldn't desert him and pleaded with me to share his belief. At deadline, Vivien appeared. There had been magical intervention. David said, "See, I told you."

It seems so far-fetched that a dark horse could show up at the last moment that occasional tales still surface to challenge this fact. Vivien Leigh, a relatively minor actress under contract to Alexander Korda in England, came to town apparently to see her sweetheart, Laurence Olivier, who was making *Wuthering Heights*. Ten years later in London I learned that her timing was not coincidental. Vivien was as determined as she was beautiful. What she desperately wanted was Larry and Scarlett, in that order; they were both in California, and each made the other more possible. Moreover, Larry's agent was Myron. Myron was so rocked by her looks that he invited them both to watch the burning of Atlanta, which was being filmed some weeks before the rest of the picture was to start. As has oft been told, Myron brought Vivien to the back lot, and with the light of the flames reflected on her face, said to David, "Meet Scarlett O'Hara." David was flabbergasted.

The conclusive tests were a week off. David turned superstitious and told me to try not to think too much about Vivien. "The others are still in contention." That was technically true, and as much trouble was taken with the other actresses as though there were no Vivien. We watched the tests at home on successive evenings. The suspense was killing. Vivien was last and incomparable.

Now David had the perfect Scarlett and obviously an important star for his company, even though he would have to share her with Korda; half a new star is better than none. But none is what he got. Ironically, Vivien never made another picture for David.

The anticipation about *Gone With the Wind* was, not to bandy the word, colossal. A vast, ready-made audience is always desirable, but this one was also demanding, and exasperated by what it considered unwarranted delay. It was not the publicity which was damaging, but the scrutiny it brought. David's decisions and procedures were analyzed and criticized in print, the picture's faults were lamented before anything had been shot. No one but Margaret Mitchell, who cared the most, was prepared to wait and see.

It was not surprising that George Cukor joined up with SIP, just as he had come along to MGM with David. (Actually, I can't think of anyone, except perhaps Ingrid Bergman, on whose career David had more influence.) He was part of *GWTW* practically from the time the book was bought until he was fired a couple of weeks after shooting began.

I've never before or since felt as bad about anyone losing a job as I did about George and *GWTW*. His association with the movie had gone on so long that he and it seemed to me indivisible. He hadn't been particularly useful on the script, but then David had never found him so. He compensated in other ways. I feel he made a real contribution to the picture by his influence on casting and on the total visual conception. But from the start of shooting David was disappointed in the results he was getting.

I couldn't accept the fact that he was actually going to change directors. His dissatisfaction was born with the first rushes, and his dissatisfaction grew. I pleaded George's case and won him a couple of days' respite at a time—I thought things would get better when everyone got less nervous. They didn't. Finally David called it quits. George was coming to the house that evening after dinner and David was going to have to break the news.

It was awful. David and I sat upstairs waiting in loud silence. When I heard the bell, then a voice in the downstairs hall, I flew down to greet him. (I thought of the stairs as "the last mile.") As George came around the bend halfway up the staircase, he guessed from the look on my face (as he later told me) that the verdict was in. I ran down and flung myself on him, weeping. He comforted me as far as David's room and I disappeared until I heard his car leave. I ached for them both.

The truth was, George's work was simply not up to David's expectations, and he said he had to trust his instincts, right or wrong. Everything was riding on him; he told George that if he was going to fail, it had to be on his own mistakes. At least he had already arranged an MGM contract for George and the much-desired opportunity to direct The Women.

A few years ago George phoned me to ask if I knew why he had been fired from Gone With the Wind. He had just told a man writing a book about him that he didn't know. Did I? I said I did. He didn't press me for the reason, so perhaps he didn't really want to know it. It pained him through the years, I am sure, because he appeared to be taking increasing credit for the film. He had such a distinguished record, he didn't need it.

THE SUCCESS of Gone With the Wind was not luck, just slogging. Apart from securing Clark and Vivien, the good luck of the picture was in not having bad luck. When the stakes are unbearably high, one thinks of the possibility of illness or accident. It was important not to let David know that I shared that suspense, most seriously about whether he would last. If not, the intricately wrought edifice would come tumbling down.

GWTW had become so complex that from the time it started shooting, there wasn't a prayer for anyone to pull it out but him.

David never drove anyone as he drove himself. His was a superhuman task, almost an endurance test. He would work all out to the last ounce, then home for repairs, and he needed support in proportion to the demands made upon him. "Pressure" was the key word and it was contagious. There was no way of sparing me.

The hours were the most punishing. They were insane and only made possible by Benzedrine, in increasing amounts. If he left a note at four A.M. for Farr to wake him at seven-thirty, he would add: "Regardless of what I may say." Several nights he did without sleep. We so adjusted to each stage that without our realizing it the new stress became the norm, but the strain was cumulative. I wondered whether anything was worth it. Perhaps it was only a movie, but on the home front it was more real than life. It was hard to keep a perspective—that movie had priority.

Contractually, he started on time and he got through on time. In the last month of production, five units were shooting simultaneously. David must have read my thoughts. "I assure you I haven't gone crazy. I know what I'm doing." Speed it up . . . get it done before an essential element conks out.

After shooting began, it was like being under siege. We were in a war and we were in it together. I had the house organized "for the duration." Breakfast was earlier, dinner was later, and the children were neglected. So were the amenities. His burden was formidable. He had to lay it off on someone; it would have been intolerable to carry it alone. I didn't know what a beating I was taking until David told me what guilt he felt when he looked at me.

He promised to make it up to me and the children, the poor children. For relief, he painted a picture of the most glorious trip ever undertaken, a year at least and around the world, children included. If he survived the picture—if, if, if the picture was a success—we'd sail away and to hell with it all. Perhaps he wouldn't work again for years. Perhaps he'd never again do movies. Perhaps he'd write. Better still, he would go to Oxford and study. It was "Hold out, hold out!" I could, by clinging to the belief that someday the filming would end. Someday people would be coming into a theatre to see it. That image helped too.

Life was not as grim as it sounds, not for the likes of David. If there was added work and strain, there was all the more need for fun. Perhaps less fun, but better; it was up to me to be choosy. Party-going was rarer and in snatches. I had to find something special for Saturday nights, and our Sunday gatherings were not entirely abandoned. Benzedrine was bad enough for work, but I found it appalling to use it just because a good time missed was lost forever.

The picture took over five months to film and an equal period of hard work until its premiere. In the interim there had to be a preview. That fact led people in Southern California to go to the movies uncommonly often that summer. Previews had always been "sneak," revealed by a modest warning posted outside the theatre. For a couple of months, theatres in adjacent towns, even counties, had taken to advertising a major preview. The more mysterious the signals, the longer the lines and the more resentment from the frustrated movie-goers.

For us, the preview which had been a goal for so long now loomed as a threat. It could spell the end of everything in a few hours. The postponements were many and maddening. Jock was on standby and, finally given the signal, arrived. This was it.

David decided when, but not where—you can't tell if you don't know. That is how the secret of the preview was kept. What a scoop it would have been.

Late one afternoon David, Jock, and I set forth, starting from the house the better to throw "them" off the scent. We pointed ourselves in the general direction of Orange County to find a theatre with the right kind of audience, which depended solely on the kind of film being shown that night. We were trailed by a studio car with Hal Kern, the cutter, and Bobby Keon, the production secretary, and mountains of film cans. The heat was searing, and the further we went, the hotter it became. There was either a dead silence or we were all talking at once. We couldn't sit back properly in the car; one or the other of us was always edging forward until reminded and then pulling back. Eventually we realized that all three of us were sitting on the very edge of the seat. That was the only laugh we had on the way out. Here we were, after more than three years. It was the longest-running emergency on record.

David was afraid we were being followed. I was worried as we passed town after town that it would get too late.

We finally pulled up at a theatre in Riverside, and David, standing on the pavement, sent for the manager. As David introduced himself, the manager obviously jumped to the right conclusion, because he threw out his arms, clearly promising anything, anything. The terms were laid down: he must interrupt the current film, put on a slide announcing the preview of a very long film and stating that after a five-minute intermission the doors would be locked. Anyone could leave, but no one could enter.

Then there was trouble from the least-expected source. Me. What a scene I made! I was unmanageable. Standing in the lobby with David and Jock, I looked into the house. There were a lot of strangers in there—what had they done to deserve to see this picture? I burst into tears and refused to go in. There was no reasoning with me. I wanted them out. When I finally grew calm, David and Jock took me firmly, one on each side, to our seats and sat me down. The three of us solemnly crossed arms and clasped hands. The lights darkened and the studio trademark appeared on the screen. The audience's hopes soared. When the main title came on, the house went mad. I fell apart again and sobbed as though my heart would break. I couldn't bear to see the first scenes. I was crouched down in my seat, protesting wildly. David and Jock took off their jackets and tried to bury me as though they were putting out a fire. I gradually subsided, daring a look now and then. For ten minutes I was the biggest nuisance I have ever been in my life.

The film took over and the hours sped by. The applause was enormous, and when the lights came on, everyone stood up, but most of them didn't move. It was as though something wonderful or terrible had happened. Half an hour later there were still people standing outside. They simply lingered on and on.

There wasn't a bar in sight. We settled for a soda at the corner drugstore while we went through the unusually large batch of preview cards. They were glorious.

We too were reluctant to leave, but at last we drove home in what seemed fifteen minutes. I apologized and David said, "It's all right, darling. You have it out of your system." Calm, controlled Irene. It was not so. Another episode of madness erupted in Atlanta, where I barricaded myself in our suite by moving heavy furniture against the door when David went out. It was all catching up with me.

That was mighty peculiar. At least I gave a decent account of myself at the opening itself; I had hysterics only in the intermission, quite privately. I did better in New York, where I sensibly didn't watch the first scenes. Los Angeles was the easiest and I sat there knowing I need never see the picture again. Several years later, however, I saw a tiny bit in New York. Walking past the Astor Theatre one evening, David had an impulse to pop in. "You're all right by now, aren't you?" We stood in the back. For ten minutes I became part of the rapt audience. Then, without warning, the old familiar pattern returned, and out we went. I hadn't completely healed, and never would.

THE HOTTEST ticket in memory was for the opening of *Gone With the Wind* in Atlanta. Private planes converged. There was press from all over the world—it had become an international event. A state holiday was declared. It was the biggest thing in the South since the Civil War. The crowds and the hospitality were overwhelming. There were processions, receptions, and balls. The good people of Atlanta were celebrating their history, paying tribute to Margaret Mitchell, and honoring their guests, but implicit in all this was the assumption that the film did justice to their book and their past. We had made it thus far, but were all too aware that the results weren't in. The verdict of Atlanta was crucial.

People had come for a good time. Good time? To me, it was momentous, portentous, and a workout. Our suite needed a switchboard. "Darling, I wouldn't dream of bothering David, but would you mind . . . ?" We also needed an administrative staff. I couldn't cope and also attend the festivities, and I wasn't really needed out there. Besides, I didn't want to go, and David said I didn't have to. I did go briefly to something. I felt beset. I needed breathing space. I had to shore myself up for the main event. I had also to brace myself, "in case."

Margaret Mitchell proved to be modest, gentle, but unshakable. She had refused to be involved in any way at all with the film. No money could tempt her. Her restraint was admirable, her behavior impeccable. She had sold the rights and she had agreed to go to the premiere. She and her husband drove with us. The cars inched for miles along streets jam-packed with people. We might have been going to a coronation or a guillotine. Uppermost in David's mind was the hope of her approval.

GWTW opened on December 15, 1939. The response that night was enormous and blessed by Margaret Mitchell's glowing tribute from the stage. We arrived in New York more confident; it was one down and two to go. The film opened at both the Astor and the Capitol, lest there not be sufficient good seats available for those who felt entitled. Names had to be balanced so there was no Class A or Class B theatre.

Things had reached such a pitch that Jock threw open his mother's home, where he lived too, at 972 Fifth Avenue, that lovely Stanford

White house, the contents of the main rooms dust-covered since his father's death ten years before. Jock went all out, as well he might, because he had done himself proud. He had withstood derision and taunts, and had dug himself in ever deeper. It was a fine victory for him that night in his own home town.

There was no hurdle left but Hollywood, the following week. By this time we dared them to differ. A few days before the opening Jock called to ask whether I would mind taking over Mocambo for opening night and inviting the guests in his behalf. At that point, with the finish line in sight, it was a trifle. However, it was no minor matter to take care of the Hollywood audience. It was a question of getting them all in. For once they cared more about admission than location. It was the last lap and all exhilaration. Hollywood seemed to rejoice with us. It was their movie too, and they were the better for it.

Celebrate I did that night. The film was a triumph and my relief equal to the victory. David was bathed in glory, and I thought only of the wonderful peace ahead for us. Our exhaustion was bone-deep. I didn't know how we had survived. Not only the three years but the three openings in less than two weeks, with Christmas thrown in. David awarded me a medal. That year under the tree was a small gold disc, which I attached to my watch bracelet. It was engraved "To the real heroine of GWTW from her Four-Eyed Rhett." I was enchanted. David said, "Heroine, yes, but, alas, the victim." It turned out we were both victims, but David paid a heavier price.

THE WAR in Europe and plans for our future were all secondary to Academy Award night, which was looming, a topic we superstitiously avoided. Despite many nominations, David had never won an Oscar. He had promised me one "someday." This year was surely it.

The build-up to that night was tremendous. We had several tables in the Cocoanut Grove; our guests were the *GWTW* nominees and those who accompanied them. Everyone met at our house first for drinks. When it was time to leave, we spread out in the courtyard. In a flash I saw David get into the first limousine with Clark and Vivien and their escorts and drive away, with nary a look behind. I'd been forgotten. I was dumbfounded. Perhaps "the real heroine" of *GWTW* had better go upstairs and go to bed. I didn't, assuming he'd be back for me any moment. I got the others organized into their respective limousines. David didn't come back for me. After they all had left, I went alone in the remaining car. I could think it over on the way.

When I arrived at the hotel, there was no repentant David at the entrance. I felt numb, but went in, still improvising. At the head of the stairs whoever had been alerted to spot me showed me the room near the Cocoanut Grove which SIP had engaged and where all our nominees and David were happily being photographed. I didn't go in. My only impulse was to flee. If we ever spoke again, he could tell me about it.

I must have changed the seating, because we sat at separate tables.

I couldn't look at David. Denial set in. It hasn't happened. Be reasonable. At least don't leave—see it through and be upset later. Don't think, don't feel; pretend he's not here. It was just a damn shame I couldn't put on an act, exult, and then raise hell when I got home and throw something at him. Too bad for him and too bad for me.

I acted as though it were some other Oscar evening and concentrated on my guests. Not David. He kept reminding me throughout the meal by sending emissaries, who didn't know what was going on, except that I was angry at him. It was hardly an occasion for a wife to be temperamental. He was making me the heavy and broadcasting it besides. But I had made my gesture: I was there and I was behaving. That was not enough. David needed solace. He sent Jock to plead his case. "You're ruining David's evening. For God's sake, nod, smile, anything. He's in misery." "So am I."

The only time I looked at him that evening was when he was on the rostrum. When he spoke, it was directly at me. His glance never wavered, hoping for some sign. I was punishing myself as well as him—it was sick-making. I simply had not been able to rise above my hurt.

He won not only the Oscar, but also the Irving Thalberg Memorial Award for "the most consistent high quality of production," a prize he had dreamed of. He had hit the jackpot.

When we got home, I said, "David, how could you?" The only one who would understand, on whose shoulder I might have sobbed out my misery, was the villain of the piece. It was frightful for both of us. We were robbed of the dream of rejoicing with each other. He thought his behavior was rotten and couldn't forgive himself. I could forgive him only when I pitied him more than I did myself. I had no way to rationalize this one. It hadn't happened for the best. It was five years before David ever spoke of it again. It even cast a pall when the next year he won his second Oscar for *Rebecca*.

I keep realizing that the shooting of *GWTW,* the arrival of Hitchcock, the casting and filming of *Rebecca,* Ingrid's first arrival, and the making of *Intermezzo* all happened in 1939, which seems both preposterous and impossible, except that it happens to be true. It was also the year in which David created his first very own stars, three of them: Vivien, Ingrid, and Joan Fontaine. For that matter, from 1939 to 1944 David's four female stars captured eight Academy nominations, out of which came four Oscars, one for each of them—Vivien, Joan, Jennifer, and Ingrid. An incredible accomplishment.

Intermezzo was made before *GWTW* was finished, and *Rebecca* during its cutting. The film rights of *Rebecca* had been a prize. It was a best-seller at a time when best-sellers had special meaning to David. Daphne du Maurier's novel, while not in the class of *GWTW,* was also a blockbuster with a ready-made audience. The two properties shared the requirement that their romantic leads fulfill the public's imagination. Any story with a good part for Ronald Colman had added appeal for David, and this role was ideal, yet Colman wouldn't commit himself. The next-best choice was Olivier, who had become a movie name with *Wuthering Heights.* As for the girl's role, it was the most desired in many years, apart from Scarlett. The publicity about the competition for it was almost embarrassing in view of the too recent talent search. And Vivien was determined to play opposite Larry. This was a woman obsessively in love. But the qualities which made her the perfect choice for Scarlett made her the worst possible one for this role. David indulged her with a test, to demonstrate that her idea was not feasible. She simply demanded a second test, and she and Larry became resentful.

At any other time *Rebecca* would have monopolized David's attention. I was so passionate about the book that I found myself defending its rights lest it become a neglected stepchild. I needn't have worried; David gave it its just due. However, he seemed uncertain about the *Rebecca* rushes and didn't know what was wrong. When the picture had been shooting some weeks, he phoned in the middle of the day to say that he needed me and to come right over to the studio. There was a vital decision to be made; I was to decide whether the picture should be scrapped. It was either very good or very bad: he had been reacting differently while seeing the same sequences, and he couldn't afford to reveal his fluctuating opinions to anyone else. For the first time he couldn't trust his own judgment. That was a warning I didn't take; it held no significance for me. I just knew that he was over-extended and that for a brief period his objectivity was gone.

He showed me a couple of reels that had been roughly assembled and awaited my verdict. When the lights went on in the projection room, I told him the footage was superb. That evening, dinner was devoted to specifics, which reassured him even more than my enthusiasm.

I was also useful on that picture in the choosing of Fontaine, being the only one who consistently backed her for the part. I had a hand in her appearance as well, backing David's new policy on women's makeup. It had been all too synthetic and too much, and I thought it was destroying credibility and that everyone in Hollywood had lost perspective.

I had begun this crusade when Ingrid arrived. She wore no makeup, which only enhanced her fresh beauty. I agreed with her that she was better off without it. Of course, no one else in town had that skin; perhaps she could be the first actress not to have an artificial look on screen. I promised to help her keep her eyebrows as they were. David saw my point, and the naturalness of her looks proved a great asset.

In David's attempt to spread the overhead, he had bought the remake rights to a Swedish film called *Intermezzo* and then thought he might offer Ingrid Bergman the opportunity to duplicate her role. But Ingrid had not been keen on being "discovered"; she had a nice little career in Sweden well under way, plus a doting husband and a baby girl. She was reluctant. Moreover, she spoke very little English. David had to send Kay Brown to Sweden to persuade her. Then to arrive between *Gone With the Wind* and *Rebecca* was not ideal timing. Even so, she got off to a fairly good start. She lived with us at Summit Drive . . . for a week anyhow. For a house that wouldn't permit a dinner guest for business reasons, having a perfect stranger to stay seems extreme, but Kay in her enthusiasm had rashly suggested it. She assured us that we would have done the same.

When Ingrid arrived, I suggested she might like to freshen up before lunch. Seeing only the one suitcase in her room, I offered to send down for the rest of her luggage. She went crimson and, in her limited English, indicated that this was it. Now we were both embarrassed. Awkwardly, I said I had meant her cosmetics case. Wrong again. She had soap, a toothbrush, and a hairbrush in her suitcase. I tried to gloss the moment over with hospitality: we were giving a party in her honor that weekend. On the defensive, she pointed to the same suitcase and said she had an evening dress. I hastened to explain that wasn't what I meant, as the party was informal. But she was going to wear that dress. I quietly saw to it that everyone dressed.

As David was working that first evening, I took her to a dinner Elsa Maxwell was giving at the Beachcomber, because it was not too large a group. This proved to be a very, very poor idea. The hostess didn't know who she was, and the guests cared even less. It was to be hoped she would fare better at our party. Alas, no. She was being properly introduced, she looked lovely, but she was more or less ignored. The ladies were particularly bitter. Joan Bennett, for one, was heard to mutter in a more than audible tone, "We have enough trouble getting jobs as it is. Do they have to import kitchen maids?" Apparently every new-comer was a threat; a European would have had to have an enormous reputation not to be resented. After dinner, when the party grew relaxed, our guest of honor was suddenly happily engaged. She was sitting on a settee by the fireplace alone with a man whom every actress in the room wanted to be sitting beside, the one whose eye they all coveted, Ernst Lubitsch. He seemed beguiled by Ingrid. By the time the evening was over, it was clear she was a figure to be taken into account.

For someone just learning English, she had a remarkable capacity for communication. One could read her feelings and, despite a nice economy of gesture, she was able to convey her meaning with ease. It is why her charm was always so quickly felt on screen and off. Her lack of affectation was monumental. Simple and direct, she had a totally refreshing quality. In fact, she didn't seem like any other actress I ever knew. I hadn't planned to be more than hospitable to my houseguest, but I immediately took her under my wing and tried to teach her Hollywood. And persuaded her to stay longer than she had intended. After she got her little apartment, she returned often for long evenings of movies to help her English. Much later, when she bought her house, she insisted it be close, not so much to be near us, but because that particular part of Beverly Hills held such meaning for her. She was the only person ever under contract to SIP, apart from George, who was a member of the family.

THE TIME had come for rewards. The most important, success, was already his. This time money could not be far behind. David had at last struck it big. And although the money had not yet come in, he was trying to share it with me; he offered me half, along with extravagant declarations.

I thought he was crazy. I got very upset and backed away. In fact, David had almost as much trouble getting me to take money as my father had had. I was still so old-fashioned I thought it was wrong. I would agree only that what was his was ours and please leave things as they were. He said he couldn't do that because there was a deadline, something to do with a gift tax, which to me sounded pretty silly in a community-property state like California. He sent Morgan Maree to persuade me.

There was indeed such a new law and it was unfeeling of me to deny David the satisfaction that he had longed for, of making me independent. I would be safe, the children would be safe; he could spend, he could gamble without guilt, and if it suited him, he could even "go gloriously broke." I hung my head.

That evening David beamed. He would now have money and freedom both. He thanked me as though I had given *him* the gift. He couldn't wait to make the first installment and was already proclaiming that his wife had money of her own and lived with him for love alone.

The bonus was to be our famous trip, the thought of which had served to see him through. The plan had been to make our home on a fabulous ship and sail around the world with just the children and, I hoped, not too large a retinue. We would take a maid and a tutor and, heaven forbid, a valet, a courier, and a secretary. David would get to know the children. The journey would restore his spirit, his youthful vigor, and give him new horizons. There would be plaudits all along the way, alternating with complete rest on the ship. The voyage was to be punctuated by visits from those he loved best, beginning with Myron and Jock, and by occasional side trips without the children. I didn't remind him that he had no interest in sightseeing or exotic food. His fantasy was of a vivid and luxurious combination of Marco Polo and Omar Khayyám. Jeweled elephants and royalty were not outside his range. There was to be no itinerary except the London premiere, with the King and Queen present. He wanted to see me curtsy. He never once pictured a stormy sea or a cold or rainy day.

The only other thing that had taken David's mind off his movie had been the threatening war in Europe. But even when the Germans invaded Poland a few months before the premiere, our trip continued to be a necessary delusion. He didn't change his plans, he merely postponed them.

He would have had to in any case, because there remained a mountain of unfinished work.

What made things bearable was the fact that studio operations were going to be shut down for a while, a decision David and Jock had reached earlier. As the retrenchment began, a better idea arose: close the company down altogether, take the money and run! It would appear that *GWTW* was so successful it extinguished the company. Some fancy Wall Street lawyers said that if the company were liquidated, the immense profits might possibly be construed as capital gains—just possibly, given certain safeguards. Capital gains were no minor consideration, since all the investors, being millionaires, were in high tax brackets. David owned almost half the company, so liquidation was, not to coin a phrase, his golden opportunity. He could at last get what he considered a real chunk of money.

Prosperity may have done SIP in, but so, I must add, did the state of the world and David's extreme exhaustion. He said he might never want to work again. It suited him to get rid of everything and everybody. He wanted to "be shut of the whole thing." That was understandable, but I thought it madness to talk of simply letting his three new stars go. Their contracts weren't even included among the valuable assets to be sold off. I begged him to reconsider. I was sure he would regret it. He should decide later, meanwhile offer them protection. I predicted he would once again ask me, "How could you let me do it?"

I won that round, but I lost the big one.

David was inundating me with innovative formulas for liquidation. I couldn't abide legalese and had a resistance to a procedure which included a "closing agreement" with the Treasury. I preferred he "net" less and go for the long run. And I didn't approve in principle because there was a chance he might later have to sell his share of *GWTW*. I understood his need of a wad, but it was dead wrong and I couldn't bear for him not to keep some part of that film. That would be like giving up his child. The film was worth more than money. I called it unholy.

Things had come to a pretty pass when *David* was accusing *me* of wanting to gamble. He was astonished at my impracticality, and I found his prudence positively reckless.

It was a very protracted and complicated deal. We had two years of nagging doubts about the liquidation (that gambling losses precluded a choice didn't occur to either of us). It's enough to state that David went through torture reaching a decision. He confessed some years later that he should have listened to me; he considered it the greatest error he ever made, and regretted it increasingly through the rest of his life. It cost him untold millions of dollars, endless struggles, and his peace of mind. Myron had adamantly refused to sell his share to MGM at any price, so to this day, of the Selznicks, only Myron's daughter continues to profit from the millions of tickets sold.

David sold his share of *GWTW* to Jock and Jock's sister, Joan, who in turn sold it to Loew's after a couple of years and made still another capital gain. When SIP was over and the war in Europe had begun, Jock talked to me a lot about "settling down." Hollywood was his last fling. David couldn't understand why I encouraged this idea. He warned me: "You'll see, it will never be the same."

Nothing was the same, nor should it have been. Three months after Pearl Harbor, Jock remarried. Betsey Cushing Roosevelt, daughter of a girlhood hero of mine, Dr. Harvey Cushing, was a happy choice. She had taste and decorum, relieved by humor and, needless to add, beauty.

Liz had mockingly called Jock "The Great Man." Well, that's what he was and then some to Betsey, who absolutely adored him, first, last, and always, and gave him the kind of home he wanted. Seven months later he went overseas.

Apart from his family, David's single strongest emotional tie was to Jock. David called him Strongheart; it suited him in more ways than one, and it pleased him. Then I pointed out that it was also the name of a current star: a dog. When he took offense, I relented. Even in David's last years he referred to Jock by that name, and it never ceased to move me.

After the war the mutual affection between David and Jock remained, but not the intimacy. It was not only the three thousand–mile distance. Jock's life had changed radically, and so had David's. (When David complained to me, I had to tell him that if I were Betsey, I would not have exactly encouraged the relationship; certainly not at the outset of the marriage.)

I was more fortunate than David in this regard, because I was simply more adaptable. Also, I came to live in New York. Jock stuck with me through the years; I didn't have a better friend.

When Betsey's sister Babe Mortimer, just as lovely, married the fellow next door (Bill Paley), the sturdy high wall which separated their estates went down and a connecting road was built. I loved Babe, who had a tender heart and uncommon sensibilities. Bill had made just as felicitous a choice as Jock.

While the Paleys and Whitneys got on extremely well, there were few friends they shared. Increasingly, David and Bill became best friends until David's death, whereupon Bill and Jock became equally devoted. It sounds tangled, but on consideration is logical; everything simply came full circle.

Aftermath

W I T H success and money, life is supposed to get better and more exciting. In our case, it just got bigger and more complex. I found that the more we had, the more I had to cope with. I felt threatened by "things" I had to order, match, insure, protect. I called them all the problems of prosperity. And to hell with them. The responsibilities mounted and the pleasures did not increase in proportion. I was for some consolation. David wanted to expand. The rash broke out—he couldn't wait. He started with the house, which was only just becoming suitable. But he imported the distinguished architect David Adler from Chicago to make sweeping changes and enlargements. I thought the house was perfect—just sell it if he wanted and go build another. I didn't fight the expansion, I didn't participate, and it didn't happen. David shrugged and said he'd had his fun. I felt like a veto board.

Temptation came again. Why not close in the area under the tennis court and build bowling alleys? Because we'd only bowled one weekend years before. Why not build a darkroom for Jeffrey in the garden? Because the boy was not yet interested in photography. There was more to come. He wanted to build a bungalow on the property, with various offices. I thought of the traffic and the lack of privacy. He offered to build a separate driveway. Who would feed them? He'd add a kitchen. I said if the studio was home, we'd have to go out every night. Then he had a diametrically opposite idea: buy hundreds of acres south of Culver City and build a studio city as vast as his father had attempted in Florida.

David didn't build, but buy he did. He gave me jewelry, furs, Georgian silver, porcelains, all on a scale my father couldn't have predicted. While he was at it, he thought we'd better get some paintings, because the walls of our house were still bare, apart from the one picture I had given him. We decided on French Impressionists, even if they seemed a little pretentious.

Hollywood was not yet art-minded (apart from Edward G. Robinson, who had begun to collect), unless one counts the Utrillos by the mile—the symbols of newly acquired status. I was eager but scared. I had to learn, because if you rely on someone else's taste, you may later come to your senses and ask, "Who did that to me?" Some mistakes can be managed, a wrong dress can hang in a closet; but a bad painting is on the wall. I turned again to Dorothy Paley, who knew all the dealers, including one of the world's most important, now a refugee, who had somehow gotten some pictures out of France.

I couldn't believe that this small, wizened man, lacking the customary charm and grand manner, could be the distinguished Paul Rosenberg. Dorothy had warned me not to be put off by his cramped quarters or to be offended by him, as he was inclined to be difficult. Surprisingly, he told Dorothy, "We will get along." We certainly did. He sold me a Cézanne still-life. It was the picture I liked best of everything New York had to offer—an unlikely but promising start for someone groping around. Actually, Rosenberg took over my education where Dorothy left off. I became more a friend than a client. And, possessive though he was, he didn't mind if I dealt elsewhere, which I did. Other pictures followed the Cézanne, too modest to be called a collection, just a small group that were related to each other and to us.

Later, when I moved to New York and my pictures needed cleaning, he made me a gift periodically of his services after business hours. "You get the experts in after I die. While I live, I clean your pictures." He said that in that way I'd miss him when he was gone.

David didn't get on too well with Rosenberg, yet he went on dealing with him. The year after we separated he bought a large Matisse. A year or so later he called to ask me "an enormous favor": he needed some money, and he couldn't afford to let it be known. Would I lend it? (What worried me was that the amount was around $18,000: if he really needed such a modest sum, I wondered how the studio was running.)

I asked no questions but readily agreed; he'd have my check within the hour. There was a catch: he wouldn't take it without giving me some collateral. That offended me; I said that next he'd be offering to pay interest! He was firm, announcing that the only thing of value he owned was the Matisse, for which, not by coincidence, he had paid $18,000. I declined his offer to inspect it. He said, "But suppose you don't like it?" It made no difference: I need never see it. Pay me back and that would be the end of it. He persisted. I said, "Take the money or not." "Well, all right, but if I don't pay you within the year, the picture is yours." I said he should keep it; and any time he wanted to buy it back, the price would be $18,000.

Well over a year later, he called to ask, "What are we going to do about the Matisse?" I told him to worry later. But it bothered him, because it was a reminder that he owed me money. He insisted on sending it to me.

The sorry aspect of all of this was that Danny was there when the man came to remove the picture from the paneling where it was inset. His father had said only, "I'm sending this picture to your mother." I was at home with Danny when the huge crate arrived, and there was David's Matisse. Danny grew very quiet, and a short time later excused himself. When he didn't return, I went to find him. He was lying down and didn't want any supper because he had "a headache." Gradually as we talked he conceded how disturbed he was that I had taken his father's picture. I quickly explained that I hadn't asked for it; I had never even seen it. It was merely part of a business arrangement, and Daddy could have it back whenever he liked.

David had warned me that some people had said it bore a resemblance to me. I could see none, although occasionally a friend did comment. I couldn't figure out whether that was why David had bought it or why he got rid of it.

As David went on admiring "our" Matisse whenever he came to New York, I finally told him that in case he never redeemed it, I had left it to him in my will. He said that wasn't fair; he was only leaving me a Bellows. My answer was that there wasn't anyone in the world who would appreciate that Matisse more than he would, and certainly no one who would appreciate the Bellows more than I!

The saga of the paintings went on and on. A Christmas or two later, my gifts wound up with a large box containing a Vuillard of such irresistible appeal that I needed all my will power to take David aside and protest. I couldn't possibly accept it, certainly not given the financial straits he was in. "Even the boys know; what do I tell them?" He insisted that it wasn't terribly expensive; Rosenberg knew it was for me and so hadn't charged a lot. "He said you'd like it, and I can't tell you the pain it would cause both me and him if you refuse." What I didn't understand —and still don't—is why he hadn't used the Vuillard money to redeem the Matisse!

AFTER *Gone With the Wind,* I wanted to catch my breath, rest, and rejoice. David wanted to celebrate. Accustomed to the lift which crisis and Benzedrine gave him, he wanted to enjoy still more.

Clearly, this was an inconvenient time for me to get pregnant, but it happened. I dreaded telling David. He insisted I was mistaken. Weeks went by; he never mentioned the topic again. When I brought it up, he made clear what he felt by what he didn't say. The most positive response I ever got was, "It's up to you." I ventured that perhaps we were being sent a message: we're supposed to have a baby, not a trip. There was no answer. When I tentatively suggested an abortion, he didn't demur. That settled it. In the hospital there were flowers and endearments and confirmation of what I had suspected when David said, "I hope you won't hold this against me if we don't get to take our trip."

I didn't hold it against him, but I felt guilty at the ease with which I procured the right doctor and the right hospital at a time when the procedure was still so risky and sordid for most women. So much for the law. As for the rest, I tried not to think about it. Clearly, David could not have dealt with another child, and I chose to put his needs first. But I wondered then whether there would be a day of reckoning, and whether we would recognize it when it came.

Having wound down the studio and collected local kudos, we went on to New York as a modest substitute for the big trip. We were feted to a fare-thee-well. *GWTW* was the biggest and the best, and the superlatives went on from there. Hail the conquering hero! The more invitations we accepted, the more we received, and David found he loved loafing. "See, I have talent." I thought things had gotten out of hand when we received an invitation from someone we had never laid eyes on—Mrs. Cornelius Vanderbilt, who wanted us for tea in the big mansion on Fifth Avenue. I said we were being invited like a sideshow. David said that was okay, he had equal curiosity. It would be amusing and good for research. We would be on show, but so would she. David treated our visit as a prank, polite but bold. He told her just why we had come. That amused her, which amused me. The few others present were thrown. She got her money's worth and so did we.

Summer was at hand and we were at an impasse. We couldn't hang around New York, David still couldn't face California, and that war wouldn't go away. It was wretchedly timed. The trip, the trip. He would have unwound and gotten his bearings. As it was, he felt defrauded. History was not discriminating against him, but it did seem that life was out to discipline him.

He was bombarded by conflicting impulses. He wanted peace and quiet, with escape hatches for excitement. He looked at me accusingly, expecting a solution. He said a stopgap would be a place for the summer, something "unique and wonderful."

Like a location scout, I went searching day by day, from dawn to dusk, in the New England I had once not wanted to leave. I found salvation, however temporary: a vast estate with a pool, a court, and a lake. It was in such a distant corner of Connecticut he couldn't face the ride; he would take it sight unseen. "If we don't like it, we can always leave."

A few weeks later we set forth. During the ride I was assailed by doubts: I should have insisted David see the place. "How much further?" He knew perfectly well it was three and a half hours away. What had I done? The suspense was awful.

Stony Batter also boasted a beautifully restored house and pretended to be a farm, with barns and stables and the right animals. David took a look, said it was ideal, but "What is there to do?" What we did was go into New York for a hectic few days every couple of weeks, because a little peace goes a long way unless balanced by gaiety.

And then we had our friends. If you've never had weekend guests in the country and you aren't to the manner born, it's hard to begin with Jock, the Paleys, and the Harrimans. Averell brought an English croquet set, laid out the court, and proceeded to teach me, a panicky pupil who remembered those Honolulu bridge lessons.

Between times I taught Jeff to ride a horse, row a boat, and fish. I was the camp counselor, with Myron a godsend on a brief visit. Late afternoons I drove the family down the country roads in our buggy.

At last David had the leisure to read the mounting stack of books he yearningly had bought over the years, and the luxury of reading from choice. But not working gave him no outlet for his drives, and Cornwall

Bridge, Connecticut, offered no diverting escapes. It was a hell of a place to be for a fellow in terror of feeling low. I found that when I left him alone, he brooded about Hollywood. Mild paranoia set in, reminiscent of his Son-in-Law days. He wasn't getting enough credit because people were envious. "They're stealing my ideas. They're imitating my shots." They would make his movie look hackneyed in no time.

Neither a contemplative life nor bucolic pleasures were for David. The farm didn't rest me or heal him. His standard expression, "I'm a wreck," was more valid than I knew. I can see now that nothing would have been enough. If he'd had the trip, he'd have gotten indigestion. We left before the lease was up, moved to an apartment at the Waldorf, and put the children in school.

I have no idea how many times we shuttled coast to coast during the following year or two. I can't even vouch for the exact sequence of events between 1940 and 1943.

David began to hold minority opinions and seek controversy. Ronald Tree, then a member of Parliament, was in the USA on a propaganda mission and was raising funds for Britain. He was the main speaker at a meeting held at George Cukor's house. As he finished, David jumped to his feet, dissenting and sounding off. Myron rebutted by interrupting him and announcing the first pledge, admittedly more than he had planned. Others followed. I had never before seen David publicly humiliated.

There were little scenes in other people's houses. He had loud arguments leading to bets and threats. He was annoyed when *Gone With the Wind* was brought up, but resentful if it wasn't. He gloried in the praise, but was stung by any hint of criticism; he considered it carping and again spoke of envy. Hollywood was his enemy. The list of people David was willing to see diminished. It was "Get me out of this town." Again we went to New York, but he lost his taste for people there as well; one by one, they irritated him. We finally holed up in the Waldorf and saw no one. He could no longer drown his depression with a drink or outrace it with Benzedrine. Now and then I got out for an hour or so, and when I returned he would look at me as though I were his savior.

His mood deepened and he became really scared. So did I. He confessed he was afraid that he was actually going insane, and told me I'd better get him some help. Dorothy Paley found us a top man, but David couldn't bring himself to go; he wanted the analyst to come to him. Days went by and it was still impossible. I went instead. When he was able, I took him and waited for him. Some days later Dr. Rado sent for me to explain the seriousness of David's condition. He was having a breakdown, and it was urgent that I get him home quickly and into treatment. There were few analysts in Los Angeles then, and the only one he could vouch for was Dr. May Romm. David was as docile as a child, but balked at the preliminaries and sent me in his place. I was getting to be an old hand.

Dr. Romm was a wise little motherly lady, and I envied David the privilege of having her to talk to and told her so. Arranging to see him every day on an emergency basis, she warned me not to let him discuss his sessions or permit him to tell me what he hadn't finished telling her. She would need my cooperation. I was delighted not to share honors with her.

Once I got him there, I felt a burst of freedom; I was out from under! David's treatment went by leaps and bounds—in a matter of weeks he was able to see people. He soon found enough superficial relief to escape into scattered activities. He denied that therapy was at all responsible for his improvement. He became too busy for Romm. He was forty minutes late, if he showed up at all. When he arrived on time, he was often unwakable through the entire session. He recounted these antics as though they were amusing. I implored him. As the months went by, he was missing more appointments than he kept. He wanted her on call, like someone from the studio. It was unfair; she had a waiting list. He misinterpreted her patience as enchantment with him; in fact, he was afraid she was falling in love with him. He rang her doorbell at midnight and, standing outside, demanded to be heard. He found it unreasonable of her to refuse. He was damned if he was going to conform to the restrictions. He resented being forced to halt arbitrarily when his time was up. And, of course, he never got near his real problems.

After close to a year, Romm decided he could not continue "in any way acceptable" to her. He declared that he would resume his analysis later. Meanwhile, he confided to me that he knew more than she did; *he* could analyze *her*.

It was naïve of me to expect David, who had rebelled against conformity all his life, to travel the long, hard road in order to banish his demons. Not when there were shortcuts. Benzedrine, for which there was now no defensible use, was still with us, and for a quick fix he occasionally resorted to a graphologist. I had met her at a party and, finding her skill diverting, I arranged for her to analyze David's handwriting. She didn't stop at that, but felt quite capable of disclosing hidden mysteries about him. This seer was a hearty woman, very Mittel-Europa, who meant no harm, but she was hardly qualified to impart psychological insight to anyone, particularly a troubled personality. I sensed that there was some unhealthy meddling, but he was so reticent about this hocus-pocus that I couldn't probe. Instead, I tried to get him back to the couch—if not Romm, then one of the new, first-rate men. I urged to no avail.

He had to keep awfully busy to justify abandoning Romm. To keep up his spirits, he resorted to momentum. He signed actors he didn't need. He registered titles and used them for trading purposes. Talent commitments and remake rights turned into irresistible commodities. He became devoted to negotiations. He shopped for tempting material, took options, then let them go. Not that he was blaming me, which he did, but if I hadn't insisted he keep his three stars, he wouldn't be having to make deals and arrange loanouts for them and for Hitchcock.

Vivien was another matter.

When Larry returned to England to join the armed forces, Vivien went with him, ignoring her seven-year contract with David. David's appeals went unheeded; she treated them as an imposition. The more time passed, the less she felt inclined to honor her obligations. In the early years I was frankly on her side; I felt she was being courageous and romantic, and that after the war she would make amends. I was wrong. It turned out that I was the romantic one.

F O U R months after the war broke out in Europe, Ingrid had returned with her child to the United States, under contract but unemployed. David had nothing for her. There can't be many people with as much appetite for work as Ingrid. Hard work is not the indulgence most people crave, but to Ingrid it was a necessity, and it was not for glory. The ambition was David's—it was he who was determined to make her a real star. Inasmuch as he considered Vivien ungrateful and found Fontaine difficult, Ingrid gave him an added incentive: she had exactly the attitude a producer doesn't expect to find.

He never had a truer blueprint than his plan for Ingrid's career. When he couldn't get her a proper movie, she'd do a play, or he'd keep her idle, despite her protests. It would have been false economy to let her do something detrimental. Her greatest handicap was her accent, but once she had made *Dr. Jekyll and Mr. Hyde* and *Casablanca,* everything changed. If you become enough of a draw, you don't have an accent!

David's wildest prediction had been that in two years she would play

Maria in *For Whom the Bell Tolls*. Even Ingrid's faith waned after they started shooting with another actress. Two weeks later she sat at my dressing table while David and I carefully watched Sidney Guilaroff (for whom I got the job at MGM) cut her hair off for the role.

Ingrid's husband, Peter Lindstrom, while still a dentist, had begun studying medicine in Sweden. David managed to get Peter a place in the medical school at the University of Rochester, after which they bought a house near us when Peter interned at the County Hospital in Los Angeles. Until they had a pool, ours was at Ingrid's disposal. She would bring little four-year-old Pia over in the morning to teach her to swim; I could hear their laughter as I ate my breakfast. I couldn't understand why Ingrid had such guilt about her child just because she worked. No matter what Ingrid did with her and for her, she never felt it was quite enough. I hadn't known any other woman who had this anxiety, and I believe I comforted her by telling her that more important than the quantity of time she spent was the quality.

Peter Lindstrom was not a subtle man. He was a vigorous, plain-spoken one. Righteous and strict, he was able to dominate his home in Hollywood as he had in Sweden. He had some of my father's old-fashioned ideas, which is why we got along so well. The Lindstroms lived with great simplicity and what even I felt was considerable economy; in fact, I was inclined to scold Peter about it. I tried once to negotiate a new evening dress for Ingrid for an important premiere, but I lost. Peter said he was saving for "the insurances." (I suppose he meant annuities.) It was as well he took care of the finances, because Ingrid knew nothing about money. Throughout her life she was consistently generous and completely non-materialistic.

Because David's resistance to making films continued, I suggested he turn to the theatre; perhaps writing a play might prove stimulating. The nearest I got him to Broadway was Santa Barbara, where in 1941 the studio put on three weeks of plays using some of the people under contract. David had signed John Houseman to help him make the pictures he wasn't going to make, but he let John take time out for this project and imported Broadway producer Alfred de Liagre as well. It had really begun because Ingrid was idle and wanted to play *Anna Christie*. Jennifer Jones, a sweet, eager girl who had recently been signed, appeared in a one-act play and was so promising that she was sent back to New York for a year or more of further dramatic training.

Santa Barbara was the beginning of a long and valued friendship with

John Houseman, whose erudition curiously failed to intimidate me. It also marked my first close contact with the theatre. I was excited by the venture and couldn't understand David's lack of interest.

Between negotiations, David was working on a number of scripts and production set-ups. Each time I was heartened—these were pictures he once would have been eager to make. But he was in no mood for a sustained effort. They were valuable projects and he sold them as packages, using the actors he had under contract. I couldn't understand what there was to be proud of in getting a sum many times these people's salaries and not sharing it with them. He tried to pacify me by saying that half was mine. It was not nice money, not our kind. He signed more actors and boasted that they accepted less to be with him. I thought it unfair unless he told them what he was up to. He made such good deals it became an insidious habit. He did everything but make a picture.

He was Number One. Whatever one inhales at that altitude is addictive. It made it doubly hard to commit himself to making a movie: what movie can you make after *GWTW?* Well, you can't make something piddling. People said David was afraid of competing with himself. He claimed that was untrue. He was only worrying that the banner over his obituary would read "MAKER OF GONE WITH THE WIND."

In late 1941 Mary Pickford and Charlie Chaplin were so eager to get David back that they had invited him to be their partner in United Artists; being short of pictures, they even advanced him a whopping sum "to develop properties." Obviously, they didn't take kindly to his continuing to sell packages to the competition instead of delivering pictures to them. In turn, he so resented their attitude that he started talking of having his own distribution company. He asked my advice—or perhaps it was my permission, because, after all, I was, as he continued to remind me, his partner. In my view, it was a terrible idea. A distribution company is a business of its own. He could form and possibly run one, but not it and the studio both. So he filed that idea away, I hoped permanently.

BEFORE too long we again went to New York. But we weren't quite in New York, because someone was trying to serve David in a lawsuit; we were in Atlantic City, waiting for the all-clear signal. Window-shopping along the boardwalk, David spotted spectacular diamonds. Ridiculous, in a shop that held a daily auction of its shoddy, bazaar-type merchandise. However, I admired an enamel coffee set, antique, exquisite, small enough to sit in the palm of my hand. David took that excuse to go in.

The little set proved to be tagged at $700, a laughable price. In standard fashion, David said yes and I said no. So, now to the mystery of the diamonds. Suddenly a knowledgeable gentleman materialized who seemed as out of place there as the diamonds. He led us to a small showcase in the back with still more diamonds. I thought David was just whiling away an hour, but our salesman knew better. However unlikely, he knew he had a customer right there in Atlantic City for a square-cut diamond ring, probably pretty big.

He confided that this was an experimental outlet for Harry Winston, America's foremost dealer in diamonds, who arrived the following day to take over the proceedings in our sitting room. Winston, suave and persuasive, produced a dozen more gems, ranging from thirty to forty carats. David was mesmerized. Needless to say, I not only resisted, I panicked. Not yet and not here. As David's eyes grew bigger, so did the size of the stones he was ready to buy. I wanted to buy time. "Let's think it over."

Winston left behind David's favorites for consideration. Suddenly all else in life was pushed aside. David had long yearned for me to have what he considered "proper jewelry." He spoke of his mother's jewels and what pleasure they had given his father. Fate had brought us to Atlantic City. "This is the time."

If it was, I was going to protect us by seeing what the competition had. At one point we had three emissaries sitting in the lobby, from Winston, Cartier, and Tiffany, their wares spread out on our bed. These weren't diamonds, they were rocks. I wouldn't be able to lift my hand; it wouldn't be woman wearing ring, it would be ring with woman attached. The game was exhausting us. I promised David that if he'd get rid of them all, I'd settle on something when I went to New York in a few days.

When I got back, I had on my finger the only ring I was prepared to own. David took one look: I had come through. "It's beautiful, it's perfect. Aren't you glad you listened to me!" Tiffany had won out, with the one stone David had refused to consider, despite its quality, because it was too small. After a three-day interval and nothing to compare it with, eighteen and a half carats looked exactly as large as the thirty-five carats which had been David's preference. David was consoled by the fact that Pop always said you could only trust Tiffany. Mr. Winston had lost his sale, but, unbeknownst to me, had gained a future customer.

I actually got the miniature coffee set too—twenty years later! It was a Christmas present from David, years after we were divorced. That he had tracked it down after so long a time seemed to me a very endearing gesture, but he denied everything. "I just happened to pick it up—it seemed like something you would like." I told him I had *always* liked it, but he remained bewildered by my talk of Atlantic City; yes, he had recently been there, but he didn't see the connection. Then I described the shop itself, but he preferred to remain unconvinced—perhaps because I remarked that a sucker like him only comes along every twenty years.

Many years later all my splendid jewelry was stolen, but the coffee set remains, a sentimental reminder of what David called the Diamond as Big as the Ritz.

That diamond had family ramifications too. Poor Bill Goetz; we'd done it again, just as our first Impressionists had started Edie and Bill off collecting. My father took the hint as well, and Mother also got a big new solitaire.

W E   W E R E at Manhasset with the Paleys the Sunday Pearl Harbor was struck. Bill promptly left for the office and we almost as quickly left for home.

David was going into the Army. He was going to be a soldier. A private. His reasons were complex, but they did include patriotism. His spirit was fine, his idea impractical—he was nearsighted, slewfooted, overweight, overage. He didn't need an enemy, he'd kill himself. "You'll put someone's eye out in your first salute and trip over your rifle."

An ordinary tool was a lethal weapon in his hands. I carefully didn't remind him of the occasion in the Waldorf bedroom when he wounded himself just looking in the mirror. Standing by the bureau in his birthday suit, he was peering nearsightedly at his face, unaware that the most sensitive part of his anatomy was dangling over a drawer, open at a dangerous height. As he leaned forward, the weight of his body closed the drawer with himself inside. Too late I screamed out. It was one awful moment. Then, howling with pain, holding on to his precious parts, he hopped around in a circle on one leg, looking like a stork. I fell apart with laughter. He was indignant. "Why didn't you warn me?" Actually, the worst hurt was to his feelings, and the memory of my laughter rankled long. Not that it squared things, but I did tell him that it couldn't have happened to anyone else. Surviving intact was the neatest trick of the year.

I don't think I do him an injustice by assuming he couldn't have survived the first week of officers' training camp. For one thing, how could they wake him?

He balked at wearing a uniform at a desk job in Washington, because someone with a higher rank could overrule him. He hungered for a post in Washington, and was ashamed to say how big a post he expected. He was upset they didn't ask him—others not as qualified were being named. Actually, he needed Washington and Washington needed him, but he couldn't put it together. I warned him to keep a low profile or they'd take a lesser man in order to have breathing space. The thing to do was to start small and build: his humility would take everyone by surprise; they would compete for him.

Instead, he tried to dazzle them. There was too much effort, too much of him altogether. He swamped them. His Washington friends, all big brass in the cabinet and subcabinet, were stimulated by his ideas, but they didn't have the time for his memos. He had one big job after another lined up, but he blew them. They couldn't deal with him and war both.

In the spring of '42 he made a final stab. For the first time he didn't want me with him. I stayed in New York and cooled my heels; perhaps my very presence might inhibit him. He never did come clean. I think he laid siege. We went home to await developments. Nary a beckon.

David knew what everybody else should be doing, but he couldn't find a horse for himself or get up on it. He wasn't doing what he wanted, nor was he sure what that was. He was simultaneously reaching for the war job and digging in deeper at the studio. He temporized, couldn't undertake planning. "Suppose they send for me?"

"Pictures at this time? What kind?" It was impossible to undertake anything tremendous. Audiences didn't want war; escape was too trivial. But if David wasn't going to help run the war, I felt he'd better do what he could do well—make a movie—or soon he wouldn't be able to. Some of the best talent was off fighting, but pictures were so in demand that even junk made money. It was all the more reason to get back to work. I was as hung up on the picture business as ever, and talked foolishly of our lofty youthful notion of paying our debt to Hollywood. Now was the time to implement old ideals. I thought he should make masterpieces in miniature, as he had once longed to do. The only way he could surpass himself was in quality. If he set a trend, others would follow.

Between my pleadings and his obligation to UA, he yielded and made a picture about the home front, called *Since You Went Away.* Given his status, and having waited four years to make a picture, it was hard to keep it small and simple. That idea got away from him, though by his standards the film was modest, even if it cost twice its budget. He not only largely wrote (and rewrote) the script, he was more compulsive than ever about the tiniest detail, yet seemed to lack his usual confidence and enthusiasm. Still, he gave it his all. It was well received, but he had expected a greater success critically, and he was disappointed in the financial returns. He blamed UA. But David had not met their expectations either. He gave them only one Bergman film, *Spellbound,* and one picture made by a hired producer; in all, not much for five years of partnership.

LUCKILY, thanks to David's wanting me to feel free, I was never the studio widow I might have been. I often went out when he was working. I told my favorite hostesses to try me if they needed an extra woman at the last moment, I just might be available. I also would go out for dinner with a man. Armed with my father's assurance that my good reputation would last forever, I felt there was nothing I could do, however unconventional, which would affect it. All women flirt on occasion, consciously or not, but I'm opposed when one's husband is working; there are plenty of chances to kick up one's heels at a party. My occasional evenings out were for interesting talk.

Apart from old friends like George Cukor, I liked writers best, particularly playwrights, and they had come to Hollywood increasingly since sound pictures began. The most successful wouldn't sign term contracts, they came on individual assignments for a limited time. S. N. Behrman came first in my affection and lasted longest. The one I admired most was Sidney Howard. But the one I came to know best was Clifford Odets, an anti-establishment man if ever I saw one.

We became friends in 1942 because he was lonely and in some peculiar way found me an antidote to Hollywood. The only involvements he seemed to have were his work and Clovis, a huge brown poodle. I would go to his little place up in the hills because that left his rhythm undisturbed. I had never before seen a man cook, and it amused me that he cooked dinner for me. Had some other woman gone to Clifford's house like that, I would have questioned the propriety. David didn't think it odd, nor did I.

Clifford talked better than he listened; he was a fiery talker. What he didn't say, he acted out. He gave bravura performances freely. He had been an actor with the Group Theatre before he became a playwright and, having found his voice, used it. There was a message in most of his plays, because he was a man filled with anger as well as love. Being away from the theatre was punishment for him; it lowered his self-esteem to be grubbing for money in Hollywood.

He bought me copies of all his plays. When there were no more to read, in an unprecedented gesture of trust he offered me his famous journals, which no one had ever seen. And no wonder. The journals held more drama than he ever dared put in a play. His life lay open on the page, and so did the Group Theatre. The leading characters were Lee Strasberg, Harold Clurman, and of course Elia Kazan, all of whom, however cherished, were victims of his ambivalence. Also featured was his agent, Harold Freedman, who all by himself was the formidable theatre department of Brandt and Brandt. He was the one I had heard David do long-distance battle with over the services of reluctant playwrights. Clifford was in good company; Harold's clients included Sam Behrman, Sidney Howard, Bob Sherwood, and Phil Barry.

All in all, Clifford unwittingly gave me quite an education in the theatre. Neither of us could know I would ever have any use for it.

Clifford liked Hollywood better two years later when he returned to make his debut as the director of *None But the Lonely Heart,* starring Cary Grant and Ethel Barrymore. Cary had chosen him because of the script Clifford had written. It was a double gamble; playing a dark role was a radical departure for the debonair Cary.

Clifford had this wonderful new friend he wanted to share with me. Having casually encountered Cary a few times in the twelve years since he was Archie Leach, I felt they were a wildly improbable combination, but Clifford insisted I come to the set and he would prove otherwise. It was unlike me to go to a studio, even more so to spend hours on someone's set. But there was time to watch and time to talk, and I found Clifford was right. Cary's serious side had depth; his charm was just a lovely bonus.

I think perhaps Cary was the best present Clifford gave me.

Two years earlier there had been a present I refused to accept: a do-it-yourself analysis. Clifford was at odds with himself, but feared that an analyst would rob him of creativity. He had found a book by Karen Horney through which he could better understand his nature and risk neither his talent nor his money. I wasn't tempted, because privately I thought I was on the verge of the real article.

At the period of David's worst stalling with Dr. Romm, I told him I was in danger of becoming the Elizabeth Barrett of Beverly Hills and did not fancy myself as a cherished invalid. He thought it hilariously funny. I didn't. Despite my rugged health, I had acquired a string of minor ailments. Sam Hirshfeld, advanced as always, decided that practically everything that didn't require surgery was psychosomatic. I didn't believe that talking to someone was going to make my allergies and such go away, but Sam's various specialists hadn't cured me either.

David didn't mind at all if I took his place with Dr. Romm—I'd be better able to understand him. Of course, as I told Romm, I didn't need analysis. I assumed that was equally evident to her. I was level-headed and objective, strong and solid. I was happy and had a wonderful marriage. The only problems I had were those of other people. Apart from friends, I had to help my poor mother, and my father's situation was difficult. I was very concerned about the children, and, as she knew, David was in bad shape. Myron's drinking was having a terrible effect on his health and business, to say nothing of his mother, who also relied on me, as did some other Selznicks, whose names I would skip.

I was a specialist in responsibilities. Having had a head start, I found them easy to acquire. Romm said most people have a healthy disinclination for more than is necessary. Not me, I was a glutton. She added that I was trying to make myself indispensable. Well, I already was; what would they do without me? She figured that without me they'd have to deal with some of their own problems. As it was, their dependence gave me a sense of purpose. I resented that response. She said that if I dealt with myself first, I'd be more useful. I thought just the opposite. First things first: help me get them straightened out; I wouldn't waste her valuable time on healthy, responsible me. Back then I considered that humility.

Romm said I was using these people as a device to escape facing myself. She called that neurotic. It was a condemnation I couldn't accept. I conceded that David was, but not me. When she said neurotics choose neurotics, I was downright offended.

Well, if she'd see me more often, I promised to talk faster, be more concise, and have some time left over from everyone else's problems to talk about myself.

Being on the analyst's couch brought up deep feelings of disloyalty. I was trained to "protect the family." Romm noticed my hesitation. I told her I was dickering: divulging things about my parents and sister couldn't help me that much, it just wasn't worth it. All right, I would try. When I talked about them, I inevitably gave myself away, because it was easier to take blame than to accuse. I justified the family's behavior in just about everything. In explaining things the way I did, I finally began to suspect my motives. I always had got more than was coming to me—clearly, I was afraid my luck would run out. I seemed to be working off that possibility like a sentence. It was ludicrous.

I had retained everything ever instilled in me, layer upon layer of rules, orders, and laws. Any admonition of my parents had been engraved on what I assumed was my conscience. I hadn't had the wit to phase out what was obsolete, superstitions included. And as if this weren't enough, I had added oaths of allegiance to the flag and the Scouts, all to the tune of the Ten Commandments.

I didn't notice that my stutter was almost gone and the ills and allergies were disappearing, just that the more I talked, the more I had to say. I was apology itself that I couldn't get it out faster. I shouldn't have felt guilty—she said that through me she touched many lives, because my therapy had a ripple effect.

Being constructive *and* self-serving, I conspired and got Edie to the same couch. Soon Romm told me she was not a good candidate: Edie preferred not to separate reality from wishful thinking, therefore Romm was willing to give her only supportive therapy, and briefly at that. Edie, unaware, soon announced that she was fully analyzed. She spread her superiority and pity around: "Poor Irene, she's so complicated, she'll be at it forever." What smarted was the violation of my privacy. (In those days few people let it be known they were in therapy. It was certainly hush-hush with me.)

One of the major things analysis did was to relieve me of the feeling of responsibility for Edie; at last I could ignore the Eleventh Commandment: thou shalt protect thy sister. Edie didn't have trouble, she caused it. I had appeased her as a child, as a girl, as a woman. I should have had it out with her long ago—a lot of people would have been better off. It was cowardly of me: peace at any price. But even when I became wiser,

I was still afraid of her. I never did get bold enough to have that confrontation.

During treatment there had been a brief spell of resentment that my parents had let me delude myself that I had no temper. Romm had to teach me to recognize anger and to realize I had the same right to it as anybody else. The trouble was that recognition came so late, I didn't know how to express the anger when it surfaced.

In the end it had to be faced that I was not being put upon—I was doing it to myself. Less would be more; I had to learn the difference between duty and inclination. But I was stuck preferring to do things for other people, and I came by this preference honestly. My father had the most power over me—but Mother the most influence, and the most lasting.

I was stunned one day to learn that at the outset of our sessions Dr. Romm had not fully believed me. Despite the ring of truth, she had found much of what I had been telling her highly improbable. However, "no one could make it up." Ah, for once my painful accuracy was not a disadvantage. Eventually she said I was the most rewarding patient she had ever had, and as a final accolade she asked me to be the executor of her will.

When Romm considered me nearly finished, I protested. I had expected to emerge quite a different person; gradual changes were not enough, I was waiting for a great revelation. Perhaps there was a shameful secret locked in Pandora's box! If I could pry the lid open, I might be transformed. Not too much later, life did exactly that to me and I scarcely noticed.

I S A W no connection between Romm and the strange chapter in my life which followed. It is not very plausible, but I became a Juvenile Probation officer.

David's war job was not going to materialize, so I had to get going. My search was fruitless; like him, I could find nothing suitable. There were enough gracious matrons and charming starlets to smile at the servicemen in canteens. What the Red Cross offered could be done by any willing pair of hands. I wanted something more demanding, what my mother used to call "worthwhile." Many jobs were going undone, yet lots of us were unemployed. I was at the end of my rope. Why not start a Central Casting for volunteers? "Unlikely people for unlikely jobs." David endorsed it, but nothing modest, mind you: I must write to Eleanor Roosevelt. I couldn't imagine doing such a thing, so David wrote me a first draft.

I grew embarrassed as weeks went by without an answer. Then I was disposed of by an invitation to a luncheon meeting downtown, as if to tell me that my kind of agency already existed. It was even sponsored by Mrs. Roosevelt. I could hardly argue back that the Civilian Defense Corps was far from what I had in mind.

I faced the huge board, consisting of representatives of government, labor, women's clubs, Red Cross, and such. Each of them already had something else important to do, and if they noticed me at all, they probably wondered what I was doing there. I was pleasantly received, but otherwise ignored—except by a man next to me, Captain Andrew, who was only from the county sheriff's office. I told him my sad little tale. He was a man good at sizing up a situation. He shook his head and said, "This is nothing for you." However, he wanted to talk to me himself. To me, the sheriff was like the police; my curiosity was greater than my resistance, so I drove over to his office. Look where my wild-goose chase had landed me! Before I said no, there was someone he wanted me to meet, "a great girl, her name is Bess. She works for me." I didn't know there were women sheriffs. If I liked her, I was to ride around in her car with her for a couple of days and then report to him.

Unknowingly, I made a crucial decision. Bess was a husky, good-looking girl who was sent out into the field as a trouble-shooter. She dealt only with women who were in minor difficulty with the law. With her I encountered situations more vivid than a movie, vérité with a vengeance. I admired her and the remarkable climate she established. She made contact instantly with those women and got on with the problem at hand through cheerily veiled competence. And she made me feel indispensable; I still don't know how she could have managed to get that particular family into the car and the children booked into Juvenile Hall without me.

I was hooked. The catch was that each episode was abruptly terminated. I told Captain Andrew I longed for the next chapter about the children. Well then, he had just the thing for me—the Juvenile Probation Department, which dealt with these children and determined their future after they left the detention center. My heart sank when he said that Bess was not in Probation because she only had a high-school diploma. At that rate, I didn't have a chance; how sad—my mother had been right about college. But the department was short-handed because of the war, and most of the officers with post-graduate degrees in social work had joined the WAAC's and WAVE's. Therefore Captain Andrew was willing to recommend me. He would get me an interview, but then I'd be on my own.

I shuttled downtown more times that week than I would have otherwise in a year. Despite the dingy quarters, my meeting with the chief of Probation was a big occasion. I'd never had an interview, let alone an intensive one. My composure was only external. I had been told the agency was considered enlightened; nevertheless, I was surprised by their philosophy: the child is never at fault. But if that was the attitude expected of an officer, it didn't throw me, for who *would* be to blame? Me. That was familiar ground, exactly the attitude I had assumed all my life. Whatever was wrong—the home, the neighbors, the school—the officer should have anticipated. Foresight. That was Old Home Week too.

The chief decided to take me on. Perhaps my eagerness for the job helped as much as the fact that Juvenile Hall was overcrowded. Then, too, I would cost them nothing. He furnished me with a new name for myself —Irene Sells—plus gas rationing coupons and the most remarkable supervisor and mentor, a darling girl by the name of Alice McElheney. She was patient, gentle, and wise, and I loved her. Only she and the chief knew my identity; if it got out, I was done for. I bought a secondhand jalopy, a couple of cotton dresses, and what were known then as serviceable stockings and shoes. I worked three days a week, from nine to four, and I fitted right into the slot, unobtrusively at that. If my central clearing office for volunteers had actually existed and they'd given me this job, I'd have been tickled pink.

Alice started my on-the-job training with huge folders of case histories for me to study. At that time Marilyn Monroe's might well have been among them. The run-of-the-mill were to teach me procedure and how to write up an investigation, but there was more to learn from the others. Apparently she graded my competence on my questions about the successful cases and suggestions about the failures. She started me off on simple ones and then stepped up the pace. She supervised me and I supervised my girls.

Not all of them were delinquent, and it was up to me to decide whether a girl stayed with her family. If she didn't, and was under twelve, I chose a foster mother, to whom the county paid $30 a month. If she was over twelve, she went as a mother's helper and earned the $30 herself, in what was called a work home. Wherever the girls were, one had to visit, except when they went off to reform school, mild, medium, or severe. To me, the awful responsibility was to send a girl away: I would be making a drastic disposition of her life. Such a situation came my way all too soon and required my appearing before a judge in Juvenile Court. The training school I recommended was mild and the girl was eager to go, but I prepared for the trial—I mean the hearing—as though my life were at stake. When I finally got before the bench, the judge, a fat old lady, scarcely glanced at my carefully prepared papers and nodded off as I took the floor. Her approval was hardly an achievement. What an anticlimax! Alice was sorry she hadn't warned me about the judge. "That's why she's not in a different court." The reformer in me burned. Let me not come before *that* judge again!

Those mornings, when I got to First and Broadway, my concentration and enthusiasm were total, and I discovered a capacity in myself which astonished me. Privilege may be great, but anonymity was a relief. I thrived. Pinned down at a cramped desk, I found a freedom I had never known. It is an understatement to say that I carried a slim caseload, but no cases ever had such custom work. Everything I did, however alien, seemed perfectly natural. On the other hand, it was bizarre to sit in my luxurious bedroom behind locked doors and do the special telephoning that I didn't have time for downtown.

The job siphoned off my excessive sense of obligation and helped me reduce the non-essential demands on me. I was no longer the first court of appeal for everyone I knew, or the best telephone directory in town. With some set hours and a new focus, my energies became channeled. I was no busier, just less accessible. I actually had more time. The chief beneficiaries were my sons, whose mother became infinitely more tolerant. I stopped coping with my children, I enjoyed them.

Mrs. Sells, like most of the other ladies, had a husband and children. I often ate my lunch at the cafeteria down the block with the other workers. Here I was careful. "Yes, I have two little boys, but they're at school all day. No, my husband isn't in the service." His work? "Oh, he works about twenty minutes from where we live." The truth as ever, but not all of it, as usual. I must have assumed a protective coloration because I certainly didn't pique curiosity.

My work wasn't a secret, but to broadcast it was risky because it might appear as an item in a column. "A job with the county" didn't sound intriguing enough for follow-up questions. I talked the most freely to Mother, who cared about each girl and was proud of whatever I did. My father just hoped it wasn't dangerous. I tried to discuss it with my sister, who said, "Darling, it is so sordid. It is a side of you I can't bear to think about. It disturbs me even to listen."

David was willing to listen, but I didn't indulge myself much. I am sure he thought my little job pretty inglorious. I synopsized unless my story was really fascinating. He was a little on the defensive, perhaps because when I left in the morning he would still be in bed. One morning he said, "Are you trying to reproach me?"

Then something equally improbable happened. I became a student at USC. The Probation Department chose Alice and somehow me to attend a three-week seminar in the School of Social Work. The idea was bliss, but the very first day I disgraced myself. The lecturer was a sociology professor. Between the incongruity of my being there and the eccentricity of his mannerisms, I lost control and was overtaken by giggles. After class I was summoned to the dean's office and hauled on the carpet. Oh, the shame. Dr. Arlien Johnson, a woman of considerable distinction, questioned my suitability. Not for long, because we struck common ground. Then I confessed I was an impostor. We talked at length. She hoped when my job was over I would serve on some boards in which she was interested. I could be "very effective." She asked me to forget what had brought me to her office and to stay in touch with her. I don't know who was most surprised, the dean, Alice, or me.

I was briefly in charge of two little girls, about seven and nine, who were being held in Juvenile Hall as protection against their father, who was facing a charge of incest. The father made a good living, but the mother, an energetic woman, attracted by wartime wages, had taken a factory job on the swing shift in order, she confessed, to buy a Persian lamb coat she couldn't otherwise afford. Arriving home at midnight, she had caught him at it, called the police, and now regretted it, because her rash act could break up the home and lose both salaries. She explained to me that incest wasn't all that bad. It kept a man at home—he didn't get drunk or spend his money on other women. "It isn't going to hurt that little girl any. My pappy did it to me, I'm all right, and my mother told me her pappy did it to her." The only thing she was mad at was that he had broken his promise not to touch the second child.

What was so incongruous was that on our way to the courthouse the conversation was devoted to good housekeeping. She encouraged her girls to describe how they fixed the Thanksgiving turkey and the baking they did. The girls gave me the impression of being wholesome and joyous children, which only went to prove I didn't know as much about the world as I thought I did.

I'm not sure whether I was there more or less than six months, but, as it happened, I left on a high note. There was this nice fourteen-year-old girl, Betty, stuck in Juvenile Hall because no one knew what to do about her. She was afflicted with nystagmus, a condition which resembled a St. Vitus's dance of the eyes. She was the daughter of Salvation Army parents, in whose steps she dreamed of following. Her mother was dead, and an old man in her building was taking small liberties with her for the sum of twenty-five cents.

Alice asked me to help and I agreed to try, but there seemed no solution. I didn't know how dreadful her eye problem was until I saw her, but she seemed as unaware of this as of the facts of life. A work home didn't seem likely; she was hung up on God and all his creatures and was eager to serve them. When she looked at me, she lit up with hope. She was so open and trusting I couldn't bear it. Listening closely to her gave me a clue. Searching outside our usual avenues, I discovered a job as an assistant to a woman who ran a home for the kind of children who are most often hidden away. She was a teacher, a registered nurse, and a saint. She wouldn't listen about Betty's handicap or discuss the job's requirements, I must just come and visit in order to understand, and please bring the girl along. As I drove Betty from Juvenile Hall to the modest house with its improvised extensions, I cautioned her that the children were not as healthy or average as those she had known. Her anticipation grew; the more she was needed, the more she wanted the job. Would Mrs. Brown really take her?

There was room after room of unfortunate children—Mongoloid, imbecile, syphilitic blind, and severely spastic. I found it unendurable, but Mrs. Brown called each child by name and touched them tenderly. Betty, overjoyed, reached out to them. She no more noticed anything wrong with them than Mrs. Brown did with her. It was a match made in heaven. Betty had a calling and had found it. She just settled in.

But I couldn't absorb the shock of what I had seen. I lingered, trying to show them I was unaffected. It took all my control. Hours went by. It got dark. I tore home, trying to outrace the frightful screaming that was following me. I could hear nothing but "No!" over and over. It took me fully ten minutes to realize it was my own voice.

The experience had shaken me badly, but, as it turned out, I was already at the end of the line, because just about then my cover was blown. I didn't know both my worlds would be present at a large meeting where I was introduced. Mrs. David O. Selznick stood up and took a bow and the same thing happened to Irene Sells. I turned in my resignation and Arlien Johnson had her board member. In any case, I couldn't ever have topped that placement. Years later Alice told me Mrs. Brown felt that Betty would be able to carry on after she was gone.

Arlien put me on the board of the one agency she headed, the important psychiatric clinic. I protested, but she overruled me. It was such a high-power group that I sat meekly by. She advised patience and gave counsel. Gradually I was able to accomplish some things she wanted done, and she had added work for me elsewhere. I was not reluctant to join the board of the Child Guidance Clinic. I had a score to settle there. Arlien knew that the year before I had tried to use their psychiatric service for a girl of mine; I had even braved doing a psychiatric social history. I hated waste, in whatever form, and I thought this place a prime example.

If I say so myself, I did yeoman service on both those boards, and Arlien was proud of me. I told her that when my boys got older I wanted two foster homes of my own, one for boys and one for girls. I suppose it was a way of balancing my life with David. It would be good use for our newfound prosperity. For beyond what we could afford, I'd pass the hat. Arlien felt I wouldn't have trouble getting approval "downtown."

I intended to have a resident married couple and eight or ten children in each house, for either temporary or indefinite care. Pretty imposing for someone without ambition.

I was filled with this idea of my future, and told a few friends. I remember only David's reaction—he seemed not at all daunted. I might be called the old woman who lived in a shoe, but I felt assured that as my boys grew up, it would give them an added sense of freedom.

My first casework, however, had started right in the family, and did not follow quite so successful a course.

I had always found Myron a fascinating fellow, which was fortunate, as he was part of the fabric of our life. To David, he was Peck's Bad Boy and beloved. He was a Pied Piper to his nighttime companions, but to the studios he was a thorn in their flesh, because he had a virtual monopoly on the top talent—it was he who created the talent-agency business in

Hollywood. He was the first and for ten years he was the biggest and the best, and being his client gave instant prestige. David ostensibly had a powerful ally, but Myron didn't discriminate. My father felt he did, most particularly against MGM. But then, each company in turn felt that way.

Sober, Myron was a concise, subtle man of quiet charm. With a drink or two he became quixotic, provocative, and even more engaging. But I didn't like him when he got drunk. Then he was truculent and unpredictable, and boasted of his vendetta against the studios. Myron was inordinately proud of David's accomplishments, which he envied, because producing was what he wanted and had been trained to do. He was an instinctive picture man and a superb executive, and he maintained that being an agent was temporary. But he didn't extricate himself, possibly because of the power and the money. More likely it was the drinking. Myron claimed that despising what he did caused him to drink more. Sad waste, and he knew it.

For a long time, drinking didn't seem to affect his business or his personal popularity. Then it became excessive and began to ruin his health, his business, and his life. Marjorie divorced him. Valuable clients began to desert.

David was heartsick, but he didn't face up until I butted in and said the unmentionable: "He's an alcoholic." Not that I ever dared say it to his mother.

By 1941 I had, understandably, acquired a library on the topic. Had David and I listened to drunks, they might have led us to Alcoholics Anonymous, recently under way, but we listened to doctors. He must go away. The best advice was a large institution in Hartford, Connecticut. There was no one to take him. I stepped right up and began to woo Myron. Good intentions can take you far afield—you can even find yourself shut up in a mental hospital. There was no one to blame but myself.

The day of departure was chaotic. I couldn't get Myron into the car until he saw it was too late to make the plane. He didn't know, however, that David was somehow having it held. I found I had on one blue shoe and one brown, but I did have a quart flask of whiskey on me and the use of a private compartment called the Skyroom.

We broke the journey in New York so Myron wouldn't feel he was being railroaded. A few nights later, just before the train pulled into Hartford, he really panicked. "What the hell is going on? What am I letting myself in for? Jesus, if you double-cross me!" When the institution sent an attendant to the station along with the limousine, Myron asked did they think he was going to bolt? He almost did when we got there, because the reception hall was dim and there was a momentary illusion of figures moving in on us from both sides. I knew they were only there to greet us, but it scared the daylights out of Myron.

The doctor on duty took us up to our suite and offered Myron a drink with "Say when." When he reached the half-pint, Myron said, "That's it."

The doctor told him he could have more whenever he liked, for the time being.

"I said that's it and that's what I mean. I wouldn't have this except for the reception you gave me. I thought your boys were going to jump me." He went cold-turkey and no complaints.

You convince someone, then you deliver him. A step further, you stay overnight. First thing you know, you're providing the case history. Day after day I went over to see the head man, but other than that I was stuck in that sitting room with Myron, who paced the floor relentlessly. He never sat down except to eat the required meals and to play a marathon of gin rummy, the cards trembling in his hands.

So intent was I on my mission that I denied reality, even the screams I heard at night from the big buildings. When Sunday came, I looked out and saw groups of visitors carrying flowers on this sunny spring day. That wasn't all I saw; there was sudden illumination. I wheeled around accusingly. "Myron, there are bars on the windows! It's Easter Sunday, and I'm cooped up in a booby hatch!" Said flat out, oddly enough, it made us laugh.

The next day I told the big doctor I had a family at home and would he please take over the patient. In due time Myron gallantly insisted on escorting me to the train in a limousine. That evening the institution called me at the Waldorf to ask if I knew where the patient was. He had flown the coop, as it were. David's advice was to stay put for the time being. In for a penny, in for weeks away from home. I cooled my heels.

A week later, in strolled Myron, looking fit as a fiddle, casually inquiring, "Where shall we have dinner?" He had been in New Haven and Boston, attending his clients Florence Eldridge and Freddy March, who were trying out a play. The Marches were flabbergasted by Myron's unprecedented consideration. He informed me that their loyalty was restored. What a fine fellow he was!

Well, he was, because the poor thing was still sober and willing. I took steps, and when I got him safely into other hands, I went home. He got help and possibly it bought him some time. However, it didn't reform him, just me (a little, anyway) from interfering.

He died just three years later, at the age of forty-five, of complications resulting from liver damage, leaving millions of dollars and none of the glory which might have been his. On Myron's death, his daughter, Joan, became an heiress. A few years later she changed her name and, to all intents and purposes, disappeared. She was thought, however, to have made a fleeting appearance at Mother Selznick's funeral.

One person in whose eyes I had never been able to do wrong was Mother Selznick. I used to say, "No wonder, no wonder. I make you look good. Look how you behave to your other daughters-in-law—I save your reputation." She thought that was so funny she repeated it everywhere. She didn't even mind when I said, "Of course you're fond of me —I've taken David off your hands. You can give your all to Myron."

She and David were devoted to each other, but they didn't have a lot to talk about. When she came to dinner, usually at my instigation, David regularly fell asleep on the sofa after dinner, the way Pop used to. She didn't mind David's sleeping. She and I really enjoyed each other's company, and she'd learn more than if he'd been awake. I would rouse David in time to bid her goodnight. Otherwise he was infinitely considerate.

She had a way of sighing on a prolonged, descending scale. In the months following Myron's death the habit got worse. One evening, waiting for dinner to be announced, she interrupted the conversation with a lament longer and stronger than ever before. Naturally, David asked what was wrong. Out it came: "Myron is gone. I have nothing to live for." Afterward I told her she must never say that again in front of David, not in our house. She hadn't carried on that way when Pop died.

Apart from that, I never protested about anything to her; that is, until all was over. When David and I separated, I came clean on everything because I thought she was entitled to know. By the same token, I discussed it with no one else, then or since. She was an admirable lady, and we got on to the end of her days, which were long.

I T   W A S around this time that I entered into combat with Sam Goldwyn. He was the only person I ever laid a hand on in my life.

There were no two-way streets with Sam, which made even reasonable arguments difficult. Like most people, he wanted his own way, except Sam wanted his more. For instance, he insisted on winning. He was known to nudge the ball in croquet, he didn't always count correctly at backgammon, and he wouldn't leave the card table while he was losing. Even those fondest of him agreed he was impossible.

I had my own experience with Sam and games because Saturday-night parties were scarce during the war. Leland Hayward came up with a substitute. Boasting that his wife, Margaret Sullavan, was the best hearts player in the USA, he proposed a cutthroat game, the point of which was to "get Maggie." She took that as tribute.

Although we ganged up on her, she won most of the time. She proved to be a scrappy, gleeful player who crowed with triumph.

When word reached Sam Goldwyn that we were having fun, he wanted in. We warned him that team play was needed because of Maggie.

One night, with Maggie well ahead, I made a sacrifice gesture. Sam ignored it and, intent on protecting himself, defiantly played the one card he shouldn't. There were roars of outrage from Maggie, Leland, and David. Egged on by cries of "Kill him, kill him!" I kicked him in the shins and kicked him still again. He screamed blue murder for Frances, who was reading up in David's room. She came tearing down to see what mortal injuries Sam had sustained.

I think his dignity hurt more than his leg. In any case, Frances didn't think it was funny. Naturally, it didn't deter Sam from further playing. He just didn't sit next to me for a couple of sessions.

I can't remember Frances ever again disapproving of me. In fact, as the years went on, she let me feel I could do no wrong.

To say I was a friend of the family is an oversimplification. Sam Junior entered my life when he married a girl I was very fond of, the daughter of my old friend Sidney Howard. I didn't stop at the second generation, because I became godmother to Jennifer and Sammy's second son, John Howard.

WITHOUT investors, there was no one to chide David for rolling up overhead, and no reason for him, like his father before him, not to have, if he wanted, a common purse with the studio. I didn't like the new company, David O. Selznick Productions, being financed out of our money; David pooh-poohed me. In 1944, talking big, he estimated that the new company was worth between six and eight million dollars. I doubted that, so when he played with the idea of selling, I dared him to do it; if he settled for even half, I'd cheer. Some years later I was bought out for $80,000, which spared me the red ink I was afraid lay ahead.

I believed in good deals, not tough ones. David had an arrangement with Alexander Korda under which they exchanged certain foreign rights. Alex, both charming and talented, was clever in business and, not by chance, usually wound up with the edge. The deal with David was an exception: Alex got the short end. When it became clear that David had too good a deal, I wanted him to sweeten it. David said that had never been done, but to me that seemed all the more reason to do it. It would help David's reputation and set an example to others. There had been a time in our lives when he would have eagerly agreed.

When David's goal had not been money, he had gotten Ingrid *Jekyll and Hyde* and *For Whom the Bell Tolls,* and gotten Jennifer *The Song of Bernadette,* which made her a star. As his deals grew more outrageous, I couldn't grasp what it was all about, particularly as the waste in the studio became monumental.

Operating from the house, David would glance toward me for credit, though he knew perfectly well I deplored this wheeling and dealing. Even when he returned to picture-making, it still went on, and after Myron died in 1944, it seemed to get worse, almost as though he were apologizing to Myron for being a producer. One evening he went too far. In the middle of our already late dinner, he paced up and down the dining room, telephone in hand, for half an hour of tough trading. When he sat down, I told him that Myron was having his revenge from the grave. "You didn't steal his mess of pottage, but he is turning you into a flesh-peddler." I was sorry, because it stung badly. Yet he was still not sharing the spoils with the people he was loaning out.

I stopped trying to stop him and took to changing the subject to avoid hearing about his transactions. This hurt his feelings. I was willing to shut up, but not to admire. He didn't want me to "yes" him, but he *did* want me to agree; he was as eager as ever for my approval. "Either don't care so much what I think or don't ask me." He knew more than I did—a lot more—but I was more sensible.

Habits that seemed justifiable when studio operations were at an ungodly pitch didn't go down as well in a slack period. There was no reason to make allowances, but I did, as long as there was a chance of his continuing with Romm. He did see more of the children, but not without letting them know how tired he was and that he was sparing them the time despite what he really ought to be doing.

He left for the studio later than ever. When he finally did get home, he came trailing telephone calls behind him. It was one thing to have the phone on the table during *Gone With the Wind;* it was quite another matter when it came to long calls about loan-outs while the food got cold.

I heard him giving orders in a tone that was unbecoming. Reading something aloud, he asked whether he sounded pompous. Statement or question? "God, don't let me pontificate." Unfairly, perhaps, I blame Pop for the grandiosity which was to follow.

He was not indecisive, but there were mood swings which caused him to change his mind more than was reasonable, be it about a story or a deal. Due to what I called "contingency clauses," his contracts grew as long as his memos, which had become relentless in length. He could have disposed of the subjects of many of them in half the time it took to dictate.

D A V I D had delegated renewal of Ingrid's contract to Dan O'Shea, a charming Irishman whose legal training made him seem an artful negotiator. Peter, who handled Ingrid's business for her, couldn't get the matter resolved, although it had been going on for a year or so. David complained and blamed Peter for the delay, ignoring the fact that his own constant revisions of the contract were responsible.

In desperation, Peter resorted to an unconventional approach. A month before I parted from David, he decided to talk business with *me!* Since I already knew I was leaving David shortly, it was unfortunate timing. I said I never talked business. That didn't stop him, he was at the end of his rope. Saying he trusted me completely, he made a proposal: "If you sit down with me, I guarantee I will accept any terms you offer for a contract." I was dumbfounded. "What on earth makes you think I could do a thing like that?" He said he had looked into the set-up of the Selznick company; as a fifty-percent partner, I was empowered to make a deal. (Wow! I wasn't even going to check on that.) He was going to this extreme because, despite everything, Ingrid loved David and wanted to stay with him. I thanked him for his faith, but told him I never mixed into the business; I would find it inappropriate. But I urged him to persevere because, since each side wanted the other, it was bound to come out right.

I believed Peter and didn't think it a stratagem. David's approach was folly. I'd already warned him. Now I'd have to redouble my efforts, for he mustn't lose her. Ingrid was worth all his other people put together and was one of his deeper professional satisfactions. He said she was an angel. I inquired again how "the Ingrid thing" was coming. Just fine, but Peter was being stubborn and suspicious. I said, with good cause—he wasn't a lawyer and he had an obligation. Besides, David had made big money on her without sharing it. I urged him to take the matter on himself lest it become a war of attrition. Time could run out. David said not a chance, she was too devoted and would never leave him. I told him not to be too sure. David said if she did, she'd regret it. "She has good instincts, but wrong judgments. She'll rue the day."

And thus began the list of things I could never tell David.

The second-biggest secret concerned J. Arthur Rank. In 1945 the British film world was of great importance. The Rank company loomed very large and every American company wanted to make a deal with them. During this period their top men came to California for that purpose and were widely entertained. David said we wouldn't; a decision wasn't going to be based on hospitality. I recall meeting them at an evening at the Sam Goldwyns', where an executive named Woodham-Smith, who was with the group, singled me out. I saw him next in England in 1948, when we became friends. He confided in me that the group, after careful consideration, had selected David for their partner. However, when they had learned of our separation, they had pulled out.

I was baffled by David's decision to make *Duel in the Sun*—his talents were least suited to a Western. But he was determined to do something undemanding which was also bound to be commercial. When it was ostensibly finished, "except for a few pick-up shots," he showed it to me ("I'm not sure you're going to like it"). My notes on cutting were so copious I hoped it wouldn't be evident that I had avoided appraising the picture. But then I wasn't sure he liked it either, because he said it needed "an awful lot of work."

When I was no longer around, he gave it more than that. He was profligate in time and money; he was still at that movie a year later. It grew mammoth—also offensive, so much so that UA refused to distribute it. David therefore very suddenly formed the Selznick Releasing Organization, and didn't choose to tell his partner (me) anything about it until after the fact. He spent still more millions exploiting *Duel,* determined to turn it into a high grosser at any cost. The greatest cost was to his reputation.

He never let on to me about that chain of events, nor did he explain how he and his companies wound up ten million in the red.

Throughout the rest of his life, the twenty years that followed, David actually made only three pictures, partially produced three or four others, and kibitzed on several more. Primarily, he continued to be involved in endless negotiations, because he had to battle his way out of debt.

T H E   O N L Y people apart from myself with power over David were Myron and Jock. I hadn't realized the extent of their influence until it wasn't there any longer; I did a much better job when I had them. When Myron died, it left a terrible hole. David was devastated. In addition, it brought back the pain of losing Pop. David was never prepared for death except, strangely, his own.

Jock's absence in the Army was bad enough. Now six months after Myron's death came news that Jock had been captured by the Germans. In the weeks he was held prisoner before his harrowing escape, David alternated between hope and despair, because, as he said, Jock was both stalwart and foolhardy. Me, I turned to prayer.

We were not spared much that year. It was also in 1944 that my parents' troubles reached a climax.

Mother, always unassuming and undemanding, found orthodox medicine intimidating, so she was never sick—which of course was not true; she merely didn't admit she was. If she had, she'd have had to go to a proper doctor. Doctors pried. She preferred her own remedies, and her privacy. She was as secretive and stubborn about her health as she had been about the relatives. My father pleaded with her about quacks, but there were miracles to be had that doctors knew nothing about. She believed in "treatments," and we never found out if, why, or where.

Toward the end of 1933, when Mother was forty-eight, control of her health had been taken out of her hands; she required a hysterectomy. She had not been in a hospital since Edie and I were born, and I'm not sure that yielding her autonomy was not more frightening than the prospect of surgery. The operation was routine, but nothing again was ever the same. Overall, it was the worst calamity that ever hit our family.

It can't be said for certain what determined the sad aftermath. Mother suffered a breakdown which was termed involutional melancholia, a condition which then, before hormone therapy, was often associated with a hysterectomy. The first sign came immediately after the operation, when my mother complained of pain for the very first time in her life. In fact, she moaned and wept. My father found this incomprehensible unless something had gone drastically wrong. He became highly distraught and was unsparing in his blame, beginning with the surgeon. She grew worse. The more specialists he sought, the more varied were her symptoms. Her pain and the depression deepened and there was clear evidence of hypochondria. The doctors moved her to a tiny house close to where Edie and I lived, there attended by nurses. No psychological factors were mentioned other than hypochondria. She couldn't tolerate more than a fifteen-minute visit a day from Edie or me or even my father. When after many, many months Mother didn't improve, it was decided to send her, with her maid and favorite nurse, to the Riggs Sanatorium in Stockbridge, Massachusetts.

Nothing could persuade Mother that her physical symptoms had anything to do with emotions. To voice inner thoughts and feelings might reflect on her family, and that would be heresy. Her only complaint was pain. Her improvement was slow. It seemed endlessly extended.

My father was lost. In their thirty years together he had spent very few nights apart from my mother. He wandered around brooding, homeless and bereft. We didn't know what to do about him, nor was anyone else able to console him.

I felt for both my parents when the time came for Mother's return. Home was not quite the way she had left it. Nor was she. My father too had changed. I had urged Mother to begin with a moderate schedule, but she, sensitive to what people might have been whispering about her, made inordinate demands on herself. The strain was too much, and after a few months even she thought it best to return to the institution for a while.

Actually, she returned several times, usually spending time at the Waldorf on her way home. She even attempted a trip or two to Europe with my father. She spent probably two-thirds of the following ten years at home, but she could never quite pick up the threads of her life.

There is more about my mother's illness than this, but it is too close to the heart and, above all, would be too great a violation of her privacy. What is pertinent to my story, though, is the effect her health and problems had on me. They were like an ominous cloud over my life for the rest of her years. One of the worst aspects was that, try as I would, I could not solve things for her. Yet I labored under the misapprehension that I could and should.

One thing which I managed to fend off temporarily, but at which I ultimately failed, was keeping my parents technically together.

My father had always practiced the stern morality he preached. Even approaching fifty, he was probably the most unsophisticated, straitlaced man in town. Only gradually did he turn to diversion. He began to go dancing, although never with less than eight or ten in a group. Women came later. Of his personal life I saw and knew little, but prudish he remained. For ten years he was neither married nor unmarried, had neither his freedom nor a home. Though he had his business to distract him, he had a painful time of it. I had, perhaps unfairly, expected him to endure, no matter what. I believe he easily could have, had he been a more worldly man.

Finally in 1944 he made a definite decision to separate from my mother. He broke the news to me first. It was overdue, yet it came as a blow. Whatever he had been through, I ached for my mother. I heard him out quietly, but could not give him the support he possibly had hoped for. On the other hand, I didn't give him the response he dreaded. But then he wasn't asking me. My only answer was that permission was not mine either to grant or to deny.

There was, however, something I had to add. If my words were affectionate, the message hurt and left no doubt about my feelings. "I want to thank you from the bottom of my heart for picking the mother for me that you did. It is the thing in the world for which I will always be the most grateful to you. I would not like to be me without her."

My father had never contemplated divorce. He didn't now, but thought it likely in a couple of years. When the time came for a financial settlement, he was prepared to be generous, but he wanted matters handled informally. I disagreed, because I thought it would be bad for Mother's morale; I thought she should be represented by a lawyer of her own, so I bravely engaged one. I selected the most distinguished man in town. My mother left everything in my hands and I left her in relative ignorance. Had she known I was having a hard time of it, she would have acceded to anything. The prime stumbling block was my father's unwillingness to make an arrangement for her that was completely without restrictions. He pointed out to me how readily she might be exploited. I agreed that this was so, but if he was to have his freedom, I wanted her to have hers. He suggested a compromise which guaranteed Mother a very considerable income—a trust fund, the principle of which would go to Edie and me on her death. But I pointed out that this kind of trust fund would inevitably be connected to him, and I wanted her to have a feeling of independence. I conceded that his plan was eminently practical and that I was unreasonable in turning it down. But I didn't care if she gave money away. She had always wanted to . . . it was high time she did. I wanted her money to be hers outright and hers alone.

Eventually I prevailed. She spent as she pleased. She gave money away to charities on a scale she had never dared to dream of. I cannot know whether or not I was wise, but she did, after all, live out her last ten years with an increasing serenity, one my father never achieved. It was, ironically, my own serenity that was going fast.

Break-up

EDIE'S nemesis, that easy sleeper from Ocean Front, had disappeared. I didn't connect my insomnia to David, but a couple of years after we were married I began to take pills. The champion sleeper, who could conk off as his head hit the pillow, was highly critical. He wished I wouldn't —"It just isn't right." But he never explored why I couldn't sleep, or did anything to lessen my need. I usually would sneak a pill after he fell asleep, and, if need be, two; as time went on, occasionally more. One night, in February 1945, as I made a move in the dark for another pill, he, suddenly awake, said, "Aren't you asleep yet?" Out he went again, but when I reached for the drawer, he whipped around and said, "Why aren't you asleep? What's the matter?" I said, "Nothing. I was just thinking." "What are you thinking about?" "Nothing." Pause. Then out of nowhere came my voice. "The jig's up." "What do you mean?" "I want out." Inelegant but apt. Right to the point. "You can't do this to me! My God, explain!" "I can't, it's late." With that I did a David O. —turned on my side and was out cold. For once, the insomnia was his.

I hadn't known the thought existed until I spoke it. Having heard it out loud, it became a fact that was almost tangible. In the morning, frightened, I begged off and said, "Let me speak to Romm." As I walked in, I said, "My marriage is over." She said, "No, your marriage is in trouble. I've known for some time. I've been waiting for you to reach it."

I had reached it all right, in one fell swoop at the wrong time and in the wrong place. Why now, I charged her, after hundreds of hours on the couch? "Just think—I said, 'I want out' and fell asleep!" It was a shocking statement from someone who didn't say what she didn't mean. What's more, it had been *said to David!* "The marriage can never be the same." Romm counseled restraint and reason: a patient doesn't make vital decisions in the midst of analysis. Then why had she said I was almost finished? I accused her of trying to protect her reputation. I was mad at her. How could this happen to people who had been so certain of their marriage? Until then I hadn't been upset with David, only about him. Inequities and resentments had not occurred to me. My darling had lost his way, and I had been in despair over my inability to restore him to himself. He hadn't healed and I had resumed my role of supporting him through his confusions. I had been so intent on each tree that I never saw the forest. Perhaps I had refused to look. But there was a tiny kernel of outrage buried deep which had shot up in the dark of the night. Now it had escaped, long overdue and upside down. It had caught me as unawares as I had caught David.

David was stunned. My revolt had been sudden and without provocation. No threat, not even a warning. I felt for him. But that was not the way out. That evening what I told him was distilled and all too civilized. It sounded more like dialogue than logic. Only the tone was reasonable. "I must leave you while I love you." What was equally on the level but more simply put was, "Let me go." A curious note of servitude I didn't notice at the time. "You've trusted my instincts till now when they were about you. Trust them now for *me*. If you love me too, don't make it difficult."

Millions of words followed and they changed nothing. I found it unimaginable. So did he. I still do. He didn't believe me because he couldn't afford to. He wanted to know the real reasons as much as he didn't want to hear them. Hurt and angry, he blamed Romm—she had put ideas in my head. Well, all right then, not Romm but Freud. He accused me of misdirected anger, a reaction against my father leaving my mother. Did I still have a grievance about the Academy Awards night in 1940? He brooded again about Dr. David Levy, who had been so unfair to him about Jeffrey.

How could I ruin our lives over a couple of sleeping pills? I said it was equally over a picnic basket—lots of them, none used. The last from Fortnum & Mason, very grand, was a kind of mockery. He decided he had spoiled me. I didn't let on how lopsided the charge was. How did I know I was right? "I'm unhappy and I've never been before. I don't have to be happy, just not unhappy and afraid to look ahead."

When he couldn't figure it out, he took a risky plunge and confessed he was having an affair. No, I hadn't heard, and please not to tell me about it; an affair is a symptom, not a cause. But that I hadn't sensed an affair was in itself proof that we were finished. That I was faithful goes without saying, but what seems so improbable is that I assumed as much of all other wives. Days later he said his girl was Jennifer Jones, and if he gave her up and I still walked out on him, he wouldn't have anyone; hardly a persuasive tactic. Then he did give her up and wanted sympathy for the hard time she was giving him. He thought me unfeeling not to listen. That got us nowhere, because Jennifer hadn't caused our situation. If it hadn't been her, it would have been someone else; there was something deeply wrong with the marriage.

Our talks went on. The drama was pitched very low. I tried my best not to be too emotional because it would upset him further; I saved the *Sturm und Drang* for the poor analyst. I leveled with David as always, but was measured in what I said. I tried not to give offense. I dwelt with tender remembrance on how remarkable our marriage had been. I wanted us to keep that memory—that it was over took nothing away from the past. It was clearly downhill from here, and I wanted to quit while we were ahead. I had been his biggest fan—we must part before I became his biggest critic. "I haven't sacrificed. If you think so, you under-rate yourself." I'd had more than anyone deserved. There was no blame. It takes two to lose the knack of making it go. "From the start you've asked how I put up with you. I did it happily. And now I don't want to. I don't think I 'like' you any more." As time went on, inevitably the talks grew more impassioned. It should have descended to loud voices and harsh words, but it didn't. Romm said a bit of yelling would have been healthier. But we had always prided ourselves on not fighting like other people. There was no substitute for good behavior and it counted now more than ever. I wanted no shabby remnants. David was in turn desperate, tender, unreasonable, appealing, defiant. If it was over, well, in that case he had some complaints to make too. I wasn't perfect. When he finished his inventory, he apologized; he said he'd been petty. I had to persuade him that he wasn't a heel. He said I had changed. I had, but not in the things we stood for, only in what I would tolerate. He wanted me as I used to be, and for me to want him however he was. I tried to avoid repeating, "You can't have your cake," etc. I said it once too often and he turned on me with "Why not? Who said so?" ending that session.

"What are you going to do?" "Nothing." Just get out. It wasn't stop the world, I only wanted to get off David's merry-go-round. I faced an uncertain future, obviously a socially inconvenient one in Beverly Hills. I was resigned to that fact; it mustn't be a determining factor. I didn't want more out of life, I wanted less. Less of excess. I wanted more only of reliability and stability, and a change in priorities. "It's all so wonderful and I'm so sick of it." I felt down-deep tired and hoped it wasn't permanent. I was not yet thirty-eight.

At bedtime I couldn't read more than three minutes before my eyelids closed. This was a more powerful and persuasive argument than anything David or Romm could mount. David was the habit I had to break. I put Romm through some turbulent months. She tried to stem the tide by stepping me up to five times a week, often in double session. I reminded her that she had told me no one can save you but yourself. All we can do is help people help themselves.

David suggested I take a little trip. That was not the kind of running away I had in mind. Eventually, in desperation, he proposed a compromise—that we make it temporary. I wanted no part of that. Any separation would be as final as a decree. I wanted to do my reconsideration now, carefully, however long it would take, and be dead certain. I felt were we to part impetuously, there would have been high drama, romantic goings-on, reconciliation, surely followed by an unhappier split.

Until now there had never been rules, but I had to warn him that, once separated, I would have to seal myself off from him for quite a while except for emergency with the children. There could be no access, no letters, no telephone calls. Not even at a decent hour. If he were free to phone me, I would then have the worst of both worlds. He must have mercy on me . . . he must leave me alone. I knew that would be really hard, but it would be all I asked of him.

He couldn't see how I could do this to the children—most families stay together because of children. I told him that in our case I might have stayed if we hadn't had any; my priorities would have been different. "You'll see more of them this way than you have." It made a dent, because later he told them this as consolation without being aware that it was a confession.

The die was not yet cast. I was not yet determined. What I wanted most was for him to go back to therapy, but that had long since become a sensitive issue. On the other hand, just being on time would be a step in the right direction, which might lead to another, such as a new kind of father or the old David where his work was concerned. I didn't want to tell him what to do, I wanted to respect what he did. Well, my heart wasn't with him if I set terms. I hadn't, not one. Nevertheless, after weeks and weeks of discussion he claimed he didn't have a chance in that climate. He urged me to give him one last chance, to pretend I hadn't taken a stand, to suspend judgment, try it his way for a bit. If I would bear with him—again that hated phrase—perhaps he could change things. ". . . The best is yet to be." Our fifteenth wedding anniversary was coming up on April 29. We must celebrate, have a party; it would all work out. On the morning of our anniversary he gave me a bracelet, the handsomest I'd ever seen, which he had had in work for a year. I couldn't accept it. Then would I grant him "the modest request" of wearing it for the party? I had been praised by word and gift, but they had lost meaning for me. I needed deeds more than sentiment, but I wore the diamond Band-Aid, $60,000 worth, that evening.

The truce, if such it was, lasted a month or so. There had been a rash of near-promptness and some games with the boys, but nothing fundamental changed. I could see the drift clearly, and the shape of things to come. David cared. He would have liked to find commitment for himself as well as for me. He simply couldn't. What was left of my patience ran out, and so it resolved itself. I only hoped for his sake and the boys' that something would make him want to grow and reach again. For me, it was now or never, while I still had the courage. I couldn't bring up three Selznicks; I would go under, and then heaven help us all. It was time for him to leave the nest and find his own way.

Now it was no longer if, but when. It seemed to me that late summer would be natural timing. The war was drawing to a close, lots of lives would be upended—I could mix in the rearrangements. Also, Jeffrey was going to boarding school for the first time. I picked a date halfway between the time he would return from camp and when he would leave for school. I could take him East and stay out of town for a while. I told David the date would be Wednesday, August 15, and that I wouldn't mention it again. I would make the public announcement. For the very first time, I took my life into my own hands.

I don't know whether David believed me. He had no reason not to. I also don't know if he took up with Jennifer again at the time or kept her on a back burner until we actually parted.

Life went amiably on. We were neither grave nor gay. We deflected anything that reminded us of what lay ahead. When I was alone, my feelings of hostility and sorrow overwhelmed me. However, we still enjoyed one another's company. When we dined alone, the talk flowed, but it was of other things. We used our usual phrases, "Darling, would you like . . . ?" or "How would you feel about . . . ?" Granted, it seems unnatural. Obviously, it suited us both.

When I first told Romm, I had thought only of the relief: imagine not to have the responsibility for him! No one had appointed me to preside over his enlightenment. The problem of David was not mine, it was his—let him solve it. But I hadn't yet faced up to the significance of this decision, or the penalties. My life was wrapped up in David. I wasn't looking for independence or freedom. I preferred protection; I had had it all my life. This was disruption at the very roots of my being, and, indeed, part of me kept saying, "I wouldn't do this if I were you." If you love each other and never quarrel and have a wonderful past, surely that is more than enough; one should be able to settle for a tenth of that. Most people do. I told not a soul. I didn't want to explain. I had things most women wanted; I would be disbelieved. Besides, I was afraid someone would try to stop me.

However, in early August I took the precaution of going out with Dad. He was looking forward to a pleasant evening of dancing at Mocambo. I, on the other hand, had something to confide, providing he would promise not to intervene. He listened with genuine regret, but if I had given up, surely there was no chance and he would have to accept it. I started an arduous explanation and he cut in with, "Enough, enough. Don't make it so complicated. It went to his head." That was an oversimplification, but I let it go. I expected a lot of philosophy; instead, he extended me the dignity of not discussing it further. I made him promise that under no circumstances would he see David in the immediate future, even if David sought him out, and he agreed. It made sense to use MGM for my announcement.

I dreaded breaking the news to my mother, again East, who delighted in David. He was perfect, and in return he thought the world of her. He had often said, "Thank God for your mother." I presented my situation as something natural which happens in many families. She, mystified but loving, wept, "My poor baby." I emphasized how good it was for me and the children, and how affectionate everything was, including his feelings about her, and that she would never lose him. Indeed, she never did. Many years later they chanced to meet in a doctor's office. Mother couldn't get over his greeting. "Imagine, he shouted, 'Mommy,' picked me up in front of all those people, held me high in the air and twirled me around. Why would he do that?"

Outwardly, we behaved as we always had. No one guessed anything was amiss; that was emphasized when George Cukor told me with evident embarrassment that he had an invitation for me and hoped I wouldn't be too cross if he extended it. It seemed that Somerset Maugham, whom we knew through George, was giving a party and wanted me but not David. I couldn't imagine a thing like that happening, but without batting an eye I said I'd love to come. It wasn't very nice of me, but perhaps unconsciously I was beginning to strike out and make friends outside my circle with David. When David found out where I had been, he said, "Oh, that's a pity, you should have told me. I'd love to have gone." I spared him the lowdown. Mr. Maugham never knew what he did for my morale.

I braced myself for what was coming. I intended to lean on plans, so I made them carefully. I was scared to improvise. For the first Saturday night I was to be on my own, I arranged a dinner party, weighing each name, three tables of six. Heaven knows what my guests would think when they read the announcement. I scheduled the 15th painstakingly, making certain the boys would be conveniently engaged, and setting a morning appointment at MGM for myself . . . to get a permanent wave. Meanwhile, I indulged in a fantasy: if I could maintain a decent amount of self-control to the very end, I would be entitled to a reward—a kicker, as it were, to punctuate the proceedings. I could see David out graciously, and as he made his exit out the big front door, I would kick over the traces along with the restraints of a lifetime and give him a good swift one in the behind. The thought kept me vertical.

After breakfast on the fateful Wednesday, I told David, "The terrible day has come. This is it." Sad but true, he must leave. He wasn't prepared. He had said it couldn't happen and had been hoping that no news was good news. He had made no plans, he had no place to go, he hadn't even told his mother. I thought that would be a good place to start; it would be harder on her than anyone else. Perhaps he should move to the Beverly Wilshire, where she still lived. I felt bad about her. I asked him to give her my love and say I'd see her within the week. I didn't intend to lose her ever.

I said I had to leave for my appointment at MGM and I'd phone in a couple of hours to see how he was doing. Having had my wave and given my news release, I kept calling, but he wasn't getting anywhere at all. "When will you be home?" My program was going awry. It was a stalemate, so I came back to ease his way out. I found him sitting helplessly in his room.

Nothing was packed. He was, as he said, "unable to move." "What do you want me to do?" He almost broke my heart. There was Pop's little boy, the David who had always prevailed. "Not like this." He'd thought we would talk it over again. He wanted one more day. I said he'd had six months. He'd hoped for a reprieve; he'd always been saved before and was certain he'd be saved this time. Did he mean a special dispensation, like his Scarlett appearing at deadline? Was he relying on his luck? He said, "Frankly, yes. I had no other choice."

Our news would be on the stands within hours. What! I'd made the announcement? Would I let publicity stand in our way? It could be easily handled, he said. But I had paced myself to manage it and I had gotten this far. I mustn't crack.

After an hour of pleading I suggested he ring for Farr to pack a few belongings; I would send the rest on to him. I went to my dressing room and told my maid. Hildur was shaken. She said it wasn't possible. "I have boasted to my friends that I work in the only happy home in Beverly Hills." Looking back, her view seems mighty odd.

The dreaded task of telling the children remained. Jeffrey came first, then Danny. David started bravely, but couldn't go on. I had to finish. He made things no easier for me by saying that the situation was temporary and that it was against his will.

I persuaded him to the top of the stairs. There we took our stand. Each had a valedictory. His concerned marriage. He said he would be wed only once in his life: I would be his wife forever even if either of us remarried. He begged me to get a divorce only if I wanted to remarry, and he hoped I wouldn't, but he would never stand in my way. I must give him my word I would do it in a California court because that took a year to become final and would serve as a protection for both of us.

I said I was proud of his career and jealous of his reputation. If it ever began to slip, I couldn't leave. I said it had already happened, but only in my eyes. In the future, however, it was bound to appear that he had been at his peak when we were together and, the time lag being what it was, I might get false credit. If it happened, he could quote me. I was trying to tell him that I wasn't so wonderful. With not total sincerity

I added, "For all you know, this is what you need. Maybe I am your problem."

The atmosphere was fraught. David wanted to say everything that had gone unsaid in the preceding months. The farewell was taking on marathon proportions. I reminded him that we had married to end the conversation. That seemed to save the situation. He started down the stairs. In a desperate attempt to keep it light and to disclaim pity, I came up with an odd variation of an old chestnut to cover the remaining steps: "I've had the best years of your life." That tore it. David broke down. He said it was all too true—they were over, done for, he was finished. I was appalled. I couldn't possibly have said a thing like that if I had meant it. I went to pieces. I had only been trying to make it easier. With my arms around him I led him down the stairs into the courtyard. I gave him a final embrace. It is still the hardest thing I ever did.

I watched the car pull away. The family was cut down.

After David left Summit Drive, he made a crazy visit to the florist, phoned my father, and both men did exactly what I didn't want them to. And did it immediately. They were closeted for hours in my father's office. David crowned that day by losing $30,000 to Sam Goldwyn at gin rummy. It was fiendishly fitting. (Two years later, when I was discussing a financial matter in Morgan Maree's office, the ledger was opened for me at the wrong page. In that brief moment my eye caught a set of figures I shouldn't have seen. David had gambled away, in the year after our separation, one million dollars. Pop's magical sum.)

I learned of the gin game the next day when I phoned Frances to thank her for some flowers. Apparently David had telephoned as they were retiring, asking them to take pity on him. It was late, he was hungry. "Irene has kicked me out." Actually, that morning I had received three baskets of flowers, each from the wife of a leading producer: Sam Goldwyn, Hal Wallis, and Darryl Zanuck. One wife I didn't even know. Make what you will of it.

I HAD naïvely expected the papers to print the given facts about our separation, but my announcement only served to alert the columnists, who, giving us much space, quoted David's optimistic and sentimental view. Regardless, it was a bombshell.

David was taking the boys off for the Labor Day weekend, so I chartered a boat and invited Katharine Hepburn and Spencer Tracy to go to Catalina, whereupon David also decided to go to Catalina, on John Huston's boat. I discovered this when he came to call on us where we were peacefully anchored out in the bay. I said it wasn't fair and fled to my cabin. (Kate wouldn't let him on board.) It was time to get to New York.

Spence was returning to the Broadway stage, a tremendous hurdle for him, in a play by Bob Sherwood, with Garson Kanin directing. Kate said she'd see me next at the first out-of-town opening. "Second opening?" She said, "Better still." That was a date. I was thrilled at the prospect.

The only pang I had when I finally got on the Santa Fe with Jeff was over poor Danny, despite the many arrangements to insulate him. I looked forward to this New York visit and others like it to compensate for what surely would be a less interesting life in California. I intended to have a fling before I settled down again and remarried, which is what I most definitely had in mind. The only talent I had was for being a wife; I was finely honed, and I came highly recommended. Meanwhile, I needed both old friends and new faces.

It was about eight months before this that Kate Hepburn really came into my life. I had met her briefly a couple of times in her RKO days and not at all after she moved to MGM. I knew her primarily through George Cukor's anecdotes and my father's admiration. I used to enjoy hearing my father talk about Hepburn: he called her Katharine; she called him Mr. Mayer. To him, she was proof that one could have talent without temperament. "Now there's someone I like to do business with. She gives you her word, that's enough, you don't need a contract." Nor did they ever have one; they just relied on a handshake and pretended there was nothing unusual in that. She found my father the most reasonable of men. He praised her character and her manners and her intelligence. His regard for her was total. Had she wanted, he would have let her direct or produce any picture.

He never saw her outside the studio, but wondered why I never did, particularly as we were both so close to George. (George had a firm grasp on us, one in each hand and never the twain shall meet.)

Nevertheless, it was at George's house that I got to know her. One night in 1944 we got stuck next to each other. (Heaven knows what she was doing at a dinner party, as she never went out.) Unlike George's usual well-chosen group, this was a motley gathering. There was no way of seating that table. George began by demoting Kate and me from the seats next to him, saying, "You girls see me all the time." He improvised from there, and we wound up in the last two seats at the wrong end of the table.

Kate made immediate capital of it. Did I realize we were seated below the salt? She sparkled as she took off on George. "What a nerve he has! Look where he puts the people he cares for."

Our friendship began in the first five minutes. We entered a lifelong conspiracy which we haven't yet either defined or implemented.

Instead of giving George credit for bringing us together, we heckled him for having kept us apart, as though it had been his fault. My father was pleased. From then on, though knowing the answer perfectly well, he would ask periodically, "Do you still see Katharine?" Nodding his head, he would say, "That figures."

O N T H E train heading East I was touched by Jeff's efforts to be brave. I also was worried about myself. At least Dorothy Paley could protect me—she had assured me of a warm welcome. Bill was back from the war and I felt their home would soon again be a gathering place. I also relied on the George Kaufman home, which always held fascinating people. I was particularly fond of Beatrice Kaufman, a woman with a rich personality and a flair for relationships.

I went first to Boston, as Jeff's school was nearby. To cushion the shock of separation, we spent a few days exploring the city, with time out to show him where I had lived in Brookline and for a pilgrimage to Haverhill. I then faced up to the big city.

New York, September 1945, was an exciting place to be. Fresh currents, people back from the war, a new order was beginning; there was a certain ferment in the air. But to be in New York alone on a trip was one thing; to be really on my own, another. I was about to place my foot on the ice and see whether it would hold me. Unattached women past their bloom are not at a premium.

Before I could find out how I was going to fare, Beatrice Kaufman very suddenly died. With equal suddenness the Paleys separated—the very night, awkwardly enough, that Bill took me to see *Carousel*. Naturally, I was deeply upset by these events, but I found myself so busy that at least there was no time to be afraid. I had more friends than I had dared to hope for, and that made me feel part of the scene. There even seemed to be interesting, attractive men. It was the first time in my life I was without responsibility, with no one to account to. I couldn't believe it would ever happen again.

Broadway

AFTER the brief scene in Catalina, David kept his word and left me alone, but he was heard from in New York by way of deputies offering gifts. Adam Gimbel called me from Saks about a Russian Crown sable coat David had ordered. He apologized, but said he had no choice but to follow David's instructions. Harry Winston was more persistent. He behaved as though it had just been a lovers' quarrel: all would be well if I would let him send over the anniversary bracelet I had long since returned to David. Understandably, he didn't tell me he already had underway a diamond necklace for Christmas. He had really taken David's measure in Atlantic City.

I didn't want to discuss anything with these two men. I found it awkward and whatever I said wrong. It was an impossible situation.

At a dinner party I ran into my friend George Backer, who told me he was going to the Washington opening of Bob Sherwood's play *The Rugged Path*. Well, I was going to the second opening. George said Washington *was* the second opening. I was delighted to have him as an escort.

In Washington there was a message from Kate saying she would call in the morning and to save lots of time, including lunch. Obviously, there'd be none of Kate that evening. I thought, however, I might possibly see Spence, and certainly director Garson Kanin, in the Sherwoods' suite after the performance.

I expected we'd have a quick drink and leave them to the all-important conference. There was no Spence. That Kanin didn't show was ominous. Curiously, there seemed to be a party going on; several of Bob's friends, Washington celebrities of that period, were on hand—all very interesting, except that nothing constructive was happening. The play had problems, but not anything that couldn't be solved, and I thought it had a great chance. It was being produced by the Playwrights' Company, and I watched Maxwell Anderson and Elmer Rice, along with designer Jo Mielziner, twiddling their thumbs, waiting to confer. I was indignant on their behalf. Geared as I was to the importance of immediate consultations following a preview, I was at a loss to understand how they were going to get down to work. I muttered to George that it wasn't very professional. "Shouldn't we get out and take the others with us, so they can start?" George said, "Too late now, Bob is singing 'Red, Red Robin,'" a familiar turn and a sure sign that Bob was enjoying a party very much indeed.

These were precious hours and I was shocked. We left, and to cool me down, George took me for a long walk while I got it off my chest. We thrashed everything over and George said it was a pity there hadn't been a meeting at which I could have been heard. Little did he know me.

The next morning Kate called and said, "I long to see you. I'm going to drive you out to Mount Vernon. It's perfectly lovely. We'll have lunch out there." I was surprised that she had so much time.

Kate was an admirable guide. We had a glorious, leisurely day, and talked of many things. One could speak freely because of her remarkable discretion. Late in the afternoon there was suddenly an abrupt change. With a great laugh, and stepping on the accelerator, she said, "That's it, we're going back. Spence told me not to dare come back until I'd done it." "Done what?" "Got you to open your mouth and talk. He said, 'Keep her out all day if you have to. There's a lot going on in that head I'd like to know!'" She would remember every word of mine to repeat to Spence. "I think what you said is just great, but then I ought to, because you happen to think exactly what I do."

On the train back to New York I told George Backer how flattered I was that Spence wanted my views and that my thinking coincided with Kate's. I wouldn't presume to believe that my ideas about a play might be considered words of wisdom. George said, "You know, I think Kate's right. Have you ever thought of going into the theatre?" "How could

I? I live in California." But that Kate had invested her day to get opinions from me and found them worthwhile absolutely went to my head. A seed was planted.

It was a ridiculous idea. Impractical if not impossible. I would never leave California, even if my foster homes were no longer feasible. I wasn't going to work. Yet if I did, and I found something linked to the theatre, I could come to New York for set periods. There was a big world out there not made up entirely of movies. But then what of Danny? It wouldn't be fair to him. I already felt guilty about him, despite steady reassurances.

Yet I extended my stay. I went more and more often to the theatre, and found that I was no longer merely a seat-holder. I watched and I wondered. I didn't confess my motives—scarcely even to myself—although I saw every show in town. However, it became significant when in my last week I went to New Haven to see Ethel Barrymore in a Phil Barry play, in such a blizzard that I caught only the last act. All I proved was that I'd been kidding myself; back home where I belonged, I'd regain my perspective and not entertain foolish notions. In case I was serious, though, I had to know my qualifications. The only one who could tell me was David—the one person I didn't want to see.

David seemed pleasantly surprised by my call. I said I had to see him. It was nothing personal. "I need some advice." I asked whether he could come at ten-thirty to the house. Danny would be asleep, the servants would have retired. "Let's not have any speculation. I'll leave the front door open." He stole into the darkened house and came upstairs. I could hardly trot him down to the living room like a visitor. *His* room would have been tactless, *my* room too personal. Idiotically, we settled in the upstairs hall, and I realized later I didn't even offer him a drink.

I came to the point quickly. I had a mad notion I might like to do something in the theatre. "Tell me where I begin and end." I urgently had to know. No superlatives. "If you're not accurate, you'll cause me untold trouble." He burst out, "What! *Now* you'll do it! I've begged you." (Not that he had, or perhaps I hadn't listened.) "After all these years, why now?" "I was used up. I didn't know I was tired. I'm not tired any more." "You'd be marvelous, but why not films? My God, I'll back you. I won't get in your way. I promise you I'll get you . . ."

"David, I don't want films—to be at the mercy of all those department heads and intercoms. I want theatre." He said, "Well, in that case you must have your own theatre." "I wouldn't dream of it. And that's the wrong end. Let's start over." He had the answer for that too. "I have a very interesting proposition for you. Only today, strangely enough, Margaret Webster came to see me. She's bringing over the Old Vic. I'm sure she'd be delighted to have you. This would be a very prestigious start." "That's all wrong. I have no grounding in the classics. I don't share your love of Shakespeare." "Well, you don't want a theatre, you won't listen to me about the Old Vic—I have something better, far more worthy of your talents. I'll buy you a magazine." "But I don't want a magazine, David." He was princely in his offers. "I'll buy you a newspaper." "I don't want a newspaper, David. If I want a newspaper, I'll buy it myself." Neither one of us was in a position to buy a newspaper, but that was beside the point. I couldn't stop him. He outlined what I could accomplish with a magazine or newspaper, how important I would be and the power I would wield. Power? I wanted to operate out of a hat. He seemed suddenly to have forgotten what I was like.

Back to my question: what were my shortcomings? None—I could do anything! What's more, do it brilliantly. Optimum, maximum, etc. A wave of genuine relief swept over me. I couldn't thank him enough; now I didn't have to do it at all. He was appalled. That was the opposite of what he intended—what had he done wrong? Nothing at all. I said he had spared me a great deal of effort—I would only have made a damn fool of myself. In despair, he insisted I explain what had brought on this reaction. I thought hard and figured it out. "You always praise me so much that the only place I can go is down."

Having ducked the grandeur that was not to be mine, I went back to my board meetings and returned to the possibility of establishing a small coed school patterned after one I admired in New York. The impracticality seemed not to have dawned on me. Danny would be past the age for the school by the time it was running efficiently.

Then came Christmas. David was no guest; he was the family. Christmas Eve and Christmas Day as promised. George Cukor was there to make a list of all the presents. It was as of yore. Well, almost. There was a new avalanche of gifts, climaxed by the diamond necklace. His explanation for the jewelry, and the sables as well, was that time had run out on him. These were things he had always had in mind and I hadn't let him finish. It was something he had to do. He would be deeply obliged if I would accept them, as otherwise he would find it humiliating. The following Christmas there were reckless diamond ear-rings. I resisted, but didn't argue; I had become philosophical. I could no more cure David of gifts than of gambling.

(Later, David—remarried and with a daughter he adored—neverthe-less continued to spend Christmas with us wherever we were. He was a creature of habit—example: even five years after we parted, David, after bringing the boys back to Summit Drive and lingering for a chat, would start up the stairs when he got sleepy. Or perhaps it was guilt. He did after all occasionally sign a gift card "Bigamist." After the little girl's second birthday I told him he mustn't have Christmas with us any more. I don't know how Jennifer put up with it.)

I T   T O O K   about a month for me to recover from David's enthusi-asm. I took to reading published plays. I had once read a book by Joseph Verner Reed, *The Curtain Falls.* Reed was a high-minded, well-heeled man, whose book described his disastrous experience as a neophyte pro-ducer. I re-read it to dampen my ardor. At the same time I went seeking information and advice from friends of mine—George Cukor, who to me epitomized theatre, and Rouben Mamoulian, whose experience was wider and more recent. And, naturally, Hepburn. Each one told me I needed a general manager—I, who didn't know the difference between that, a company manager, and a stage manager. I now had lists from my advisors, and, oddly enough, I later employed a candidate from each list in some capacity. But at that point a general manager was years ahead of my needs, if, indeed, I ever was to need one at all.

George's choice was a fellow named Irving Schneider, whom he had met in the service through *Winged Victory,* and who happened to be in Los Angeles because he was being demobilized there. He could surely answer questions no one else had. There would be no obliga-tions.

Mr. Schneider, a modest, pleasant young man, knew a surprising amount. I was insatiable; he was patience itself. I kept apologizing, but went right on cross-examining him. I didn't reveal anything except my ignorance and my gratitude. If he was an example, there'd be plenty in New York to choose from, should the need arise.

I vaguely mentioned to my father that I had a notion about the theatre. Why would anyone want to do that? "If you want to work, then come to the studio. I'll give you anything you like." I could be an assistant to him, as I was at ease with creative people and yet "you speak my language." I was just what he needed. But I was disinclined, so he suggested a position of more importance, for which I was certainly unqualified. He would be accused of real nepotism. Nettled, he went to the other extreme and proposed a job at a very low level. That was equally inappropriate because I knew too much.

He said, "What is it you *do* want?" I said I wanted to get out of town. So he offered me a plum: I could have Carol Brandt's job of finding material for MGM. "You want travel? She travels. She goes to California, New York, Paris, London. She sees people all over the world. She entertains them; they entertain her." All expenses, wonderful contacts, a very pleasant life. "You could learn a lot and make great contributions to the studio." Carol, a literary agent, was the wife of the head of Brandt and Brandt. I knew she had a fascinating job and was successful at it. Why should I rob her? Besides, at MGM I would never feel that anything I achieved was of my own doing. It would give me neither confidence nor satisfaction. I told Dad I thought New York was better for me, better for a woman. Danny would be in a good school; we'd be closer to Jeff. We'd all be out of the Hollywood atmosphere for a while.

I wanted something personal and small; most particularly, I wanted to go "on foot." "What you call simplicity, Dad. I need an antidote." I was talking nonsense. "Why do you think people are in the theatre? I'm surprised anyone as intelligent as you can't figure it out. They're there in order to get what you already have, which is position and opportunity in Hollywood. You have friends, you're well known, you're respected. You've got everything right here. Name me one person that didn't wind up broke in the theatre." I ventured that there were some. He denied it. "It's just a question of time. I tell you, they all go broke. The only reason they stick with it is to get the opportunities you are turning down."

He finally said what was really on his mind—that he needed me, that he was alone and I was alone and my companionship meant a great deal. He would move heaven and earth to keep me in Los Angeles, just to know I was there to turn to.

He had a further proposal. He was not happy with his rented house and wondered how I would feel if he moved into mine; it was a lovely house, beautifully run. What a terrible idea! I merely said I thought it

Arthur Segal, Tennessee Williams, Irene and Irving Schneider
inspecting the set design for *A Streetcar Named Desire*

A Streetcar Named Desire: Kim Hunter, Nick Dennis, Marlon Brando, Rudy Bon

Discussing the script of
Flight into Egypt with George
Tabori and Elia Kazan

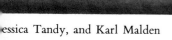

...essica Tandy, and Karl Malden

Irene with Cary Grant, welcoming
Siobhan McKenna to New York

The Chalk Garden : Percy Waram, Marie Paxton, Gladys Cooper,
Siobhan McKenna, Fritz Weaver

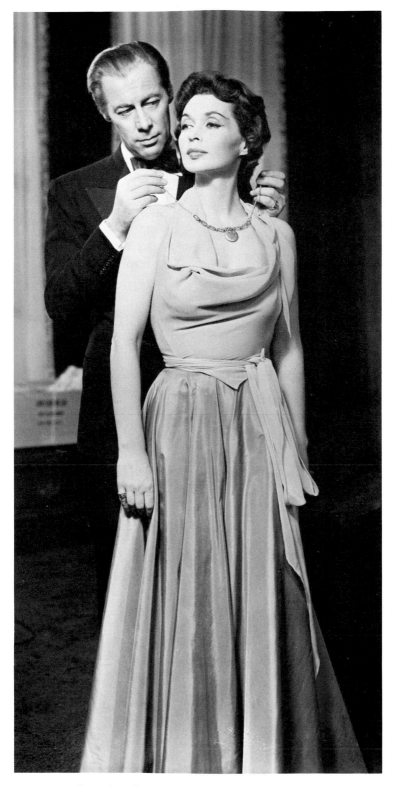

Bell, Book and Candle: Rex Harrison and Lili Palmer

Tennessee Williams, Irene, Oliver Evans, Capri, 1949

Irene, Ingrid Bergman, and Robertino Rossellini, Porto Fino, 1952

Katharine Hepburn and Irene, Montego Bay, Jamaica, 1951

impractical, as neither he nor I would have freedom. On the contrary, he assured me of privacy and independence; I could have him as an escort when I chose and on occasion go with him where he was going. I could act as his hostess, but he would never force his company on me. And it would be good for the boys to have a man in the house.

I tried to be gentle in refusing him. Apart from everything else, I said, it would not be fair to Mother. She must have complete access to my house. Furthermore, I had to learn to live alone. I understood, I sympathized, but I stood firm. "I'm no good to anyone if I don't do what is right for myself. Everyone else's interests have always come first. I must try things my way."

Spring found me back in New York, in a different frame of mind and with an altered purpose. I sought out my good friend Moss Hart, not—this once—for his charm and humor, but for his wisdom, because never was talent better combined with common sense than in Moss.

Moss liked what I had to say. He tackled my situation with his unique gusto and raised my sights considerably. And my courage. I asked about a general manager. I knew exactly what I wanted: a young man with taste as well as business sense, who knew his way around but was not so experienced as to intimidate me. Moss had just the fellow, had known him from his days with the producer Sam Harris and had used him as secretary for his *Winged Victory*. Naturally, it was Irving Schneider. But I already had his name! Moss found that in his favor. Yes, yes, but now he had a contract at Fox studios. Who else had been suggested? I mentioned Max Siegel. He said, "For heaven's sakes, that's Irving's brother. They just have different fathers. He helped bring Irving up." They both had worked for Sam Harris, apparently the ideal reference. Max had gotten Irving the job.

I felt my starting point had to be literary agents (actually, they were play-brokers). Rouben Mamoulian had urged me to meet an up-and-coming one named Audrey Wood, because he knew she nurtured young writers. He even wrote to her about me.

I found Audrey Wood resolute but gentle. She was so receptive I went further than I meant to and poured out how I felt I could be useful to a young playwright. I just didn't tell her that I was going to apply the principles of the Juvenile Probation Department, but control the environment I would. I learned I hadn't sounded foolish after all; she wrote Rouben a letter of appreciation.

Carol Brandt said I must meet Harold Freedman, the dean of them all.

I thought it was premature; anyhow, his clients were out of my league. She claimed the privilege of introducing us—the appropriate thing would be a luncheon in her home. A straightforward meeting would have been better, but she overruled me; clearly, she wanted to do something for the boss's daughter. (I wonder what she would have done for me if she knew I'd saved her job!) It seemed a rather grand occasion for a workaday lunch. Fine food and wine and Mr. Brandt as host. I scarcely got a word in edgewise, so I was relieved that, in parting, Harold suggested we meet and talk.

Before I went a step further, I had to have a place for the children for the summer, so I applied to two of the best summer-stock theatres in New England. Dick Aldrich had the Playhouse at Dennis on Cape Cod and was more than willing. However, Westport was closer to New York and seemed more practical. John C. Wilson, who ran the theatre there along with Lawrence Langner of the Theatre Guild, was equally willing. Alas, Langner was delighted only because of the Hollywood stars he hoped I would lure to Westport.

Moss asked me to lunch. How lovely. I could give him a progress report.

Not a chance. Had I looked for an office? Anyone can see agents. Why hadn't I been seeing general managers? He made me feel I'd let him down. I tried to tell him I instinctively knew that those available were not right for me. He went on: the theatre was no place for pussyfooters. There were enough people on the fringes. I must be professional.

But I had a job! I was amateur enough to think he'd be impressed by my news of Westport. That wasn't his idea of experience. "But they're expecting me." He said they wouldn't care if I showed or not. If I insisted, then do both, just stop dabbling and hang out my shingle. It was put up or shut up. If I was afraid, it was better to find it out sooner rather than later. (He hit a nerve there.) Even his scorn had warmth and insight, but I could hardly believe that darling Moss could be so tough. I wasn't undone, because the cutting edge of truth can be reviving. Furthermore, destiny in the form of Gilbert Miller, who was sitting at the next table, played into Moss's hands. Did Moss know anyone who wanted to rent his old office in the Henry Miller Theatre? As a playwright, Moss of course would have dismissed such a device as too pat. But he was not above using it on me. Presto. "See, there you are!" It was his peak moment.

But I was still not convinced. I was a beginner and wanted something small. He answered that this was only $150 a month, furnished! That was suspiciously cheap. The catch was that the place had no heat. Moss said Gilbert had no intention of heating the whole damn theatre just for those cubbyholes.

It was a fateful day when I first consulted Moss Hart. I didn't "go" into the theatre, I was shoved! The Colony was long deserted before Moss was through with me. By then I had promised to take Gilbert's office and to get Irving Schneider out of my system.

Mr. Schneider liked his job, but missed the theatre. He agreed to come to New York for a weekend "to talk." This time I left the questions to him. I found myself speaking so openly that I realized I had already decided he was it. I tried not to be persuasive, as I was aware of my obligation to him if he gave up his job. However, I assured him it was a steady job, not seasonal like most offices. On the other hand, I warned him I was a stickler for detail. Fortunately, he was too. I wanted a tightly run ship, with all that implied. That suited him; he was as opposed to graft as I was. I was hoping to practice excellence in a small way. If nothing else, simply courtesy—just enough to raise the average on Broadway. He said he'd think it over and find out about his contract as well.

"Wed., May 1. Dear Mrs. Selznick: After I talked to Moss on Monday, my first impulse was to drop everything and run for the next Constellation. I have had a two-day cooling-off period since, and my impulse at the moment is to drop everything and run for the next Constellation. . . . I admire your rock-bound determination, which—and I will be honest—I questioned before."

I questioned Irving's judgment only when he decided to join me. He was with me from my first to my last day in the theatre. In all those years there was not a cross word between us. He was either a saint or a superman, I suspect a little of both.

Irving always hired the secretaries and I had some remarkable girls work for me. The fact that they easily pleased me should have tipped me off that they were over-qualified. At least it proves that my office was a good place to be on the way up: Jacqueline Babbin wound up as a major producer at one of the networks; Ethel Winant is an important TV executive; and when last heard from, Mary Ann Goldsmith was Dean of Admissions at Radcliffe. Babbin stayed the longest, worked the hardest, became indispensable. She was a wunderkind.

Most people start with big ideas and then get realistic. Obviously, not me. I was not out to make my mark. When I had begun to think of working, I'd have jumped at a chance with a company like the Playwrights as some kind of assistant, someone to run interference and do odd jobs. I progressed to the hope of finding a play. Off-off-Broadway, had it existed, would have given me a focus and courage. I didn't aspire to established names any more than I envisioned myself an actual Broadway producer. I wanted neglected playwrights or, better still, fledglings. I fantasized making possible someone's dream. The inevitability of Broadway came by degrees.

A L S O on my agenda at the end of that May was a new school for Jeffrey. Enough of recommendation. There were three in New England that I was going to inspect: Putney, Deerfield, and another still more inconvenient. Between their locations and the train schedules, there seemed a conspiracy against me. I was in for three days of travel and two dreary nights in country inns.

The night before my trip found me, Babe Mortimer (later Paley), Cary Grant, Eddy Duchin, and Howard Hughes sitting in El Morocco. Cary had come east with Howard, and they were flying back the next day. Hearing my proposed itinerary, he groaned. He thought I was foolish—so foolish, in fact, that ten minutes later he told me that Howard ("loving Sam," as Cary called him) had postponed his departure a day and would personally fly me. I'd be back in New York in time for dinner. It was out of the question. Unsuitable besides.

Cary and Howard and some girl picked me up the next morning at eight-thirty. It was not very reassuring to learn that Howard had had no sleep; Cary said he'd been up the entire night routing the trip and securing airfields of sufficient size for the huge plane he was flying. It seems he had also seen to it that a car and a driver were at my disposal at each stop.

The various headmasters were solicitous about accommodations and transportation, but curious as to how I had got where I was at that particular hour. Howard was then an aviation hero and I was nervous that he would be recognized at one of the landing strips and word reach the school that a prospective mother had arrived accompanied by Howard Hughes and Cary Grant. If I'd been the headmaster, I'd have taken a dim view of both mother and son. I just hoped it wouldn't get out until Jeffrey was accepted at Deerfield. . . .

Obviously, I also had to find a house.

Sheer luck turned up a place in Stamford, rustic but unlovely. There was no time to be fussy. It had woods, a brook, a lake, and a sort of pool; a pathetic little version of Stony Batter. Conveniently, it was midway between Westport and the office. I divided my time amongst the three.

Moss was right about Westport. They didn't care. I was downcast when I discovered they had no duties in mind. However, Madam, with a theatrical office and a general manager, had never seen a rehearsal in her whole life. At least I could sit and absorb.

There *was* work if they'd only give it to me. Their star was in trouble. My old friend Jean Pierre Aumont, although skilled on the French stage, could not be understood in a Noël Coward comedy. Jean Pierre tapped me and, with Jack Wilson's permission, I worked for hours a day on his English. (I had done no less with my grandmother at the age of eight.) Jack was so pleased with my results that he turned the ingenue over to me next. This pretty girl, on stage via minor nepotism, was not qualified for more than a walk-on; most important, she couldn't be heard ten feet away. Jack asked me to do something—he didn't care what, but something.

The girl and I went out together, which made two of us who didn't know anything. I gave her some lines and told her to keep walking backward until I signaled, then to inch forward and start talking. When she was barely visible, I yelled, "Louder, I can't hear!" The poor thing shouted her lungs out until at fifty yards' distance we rehearsed her dialogue in ringing tones. I rushed her back to the rehearsal and on she went. Metamorphosis! I was too ashamed to tell Jack how I had done it.

Luckily, I happened to come through for Lawrence with my good friend Olivia de Havilland, whose chance decision changed her life. In the few weeks she was East, she met and married the writer Marcus Goodrich and had her wedding in the Langners' garden in Westport.

Thus my first contributions to the American theatre.

It was only four or five years later that Lawrence Langner's partner, Theresa Helburn, whom I scarcely knew, asked me to lunch. She was firm that lunch be at her apartment. Out of the blue, she offered me a partnership in the Theatre Guild, then at the peak of its importance. She said she wanted to look ahead and preserve the Guild. She was getting old, but still had, she thought, a few good years left. I was the ideal person to take her place and, beyond that, the place of Lawrence. No investment was required, I would be an equal partner.

I was floored. I could only blurt out that I felt honored. I wanted to say, "You people had me when! I'd have settled for a pittance and slaved away for you." Instead, I hedged and said I had my own methods and, besides, there was Irving. They would expect Irving as well. If I chose, I could work in my own painstaking way. I would have first crack at everything.

I managed to leave without giving a definite answer. I ran back to the office and told Irving I had been so carried away I almost gave up my freedom. The next day I declined as delicately as I knew how.

I was fascinated that through the years that followed, my friend Lawrence never once mentioned any of this to me. Possibly Terry had never mentioned it to him!

MY FATHER felt my professional name should be Mayer; David had thought Selznick. I thought either name okay, the combination fatal; it would look as though I had nothing else to recommend me. I reserved the right to use both by starting out as Irene M. Selznick. Whichever name I used, I felt I had an unfair edge, apart from being solvent; but until I proved otherwise, I remained L.B.'s daughter or David's wife.

There was also disadvantage. I learned that there was a theatrical lawyer among the powers-that-be, Bill Fitelson, whom I should know; his clients were valuable and strongly guided by him. My impulse was to go and see him, but I was advised (not too wisely) to invite him to my office.

He came and denounced me. I had a hell of a nerve. By what right did I expect him to come to me? Moreover, he had no use for Hollywood or its people. Most particularly, he was anti-MGM, at whose hands he had recently had a bad experience. He had come over just to tell me that no client of his would ever work for me. I apologized for presuming and assured him I wouldn't bother him again. Of course, I didn't know that a Kazan lay in my future.

E V E R Y T H I N G was in short supply in late 1946. I was taking the boys home for Christmas, and travel accommodations were unobtainable. Once again Cary stepped in and rashly promised to obtain them. But I needed a drawing room, a compartment, and two berths! "How? Just how?" "I'll talk to my good friend Howard Hughes." Plane reservations were scarcer than train reservations. All Howard had to do was exchange plane for train. "Name the day and consider it done."

It was. But I found that the tickets were round-trip and paid for. I mailed a check to Howard Hughes, which was promptly returned. Twice. I was grateful for the favor, but uncomfortable being in Howard's debt. Naturally, I appealed to Cary, who told me to leave it alone. "You'll only offend Howard." Finally I proceeded in my own way. Howard had provided something that couldn't be bought. I would do the same for him.

There was some priceless wine in my cellar, so I selected dozens and dozens of the best, vintages which were no longer available. My florist provided a four-foot-square planter, atop which was a glistening white tree, decorated with tiny planes tied on with red and green velvet ribbons and strips of film. After we filled the base, it appeared almost as though the tree were planted in bottles. I wondered how they were going to lift it. There would be no more stubbornness out of Howard Hughes.

Early Christmas morning there was a shy voice on the phone: "Irene, this is Howard." "Who?" "Howard. Howard Hughes. The tree is the most beautiful thing I've ever seen. I'm overwhelmed." He said he was in tears; he claimed it was the first time anyone had ever done anything special for him on Christmas.

Actually, I hadn't been as thoughtful as I appeared. My gesture was intended to say, "Don't largess me around." Well, he wasn't stung at all. For the next ten years I received four dozen red roses very late every Christmas night. If I was in California, they were air-expressed from New York. If I was in New York, they were air-expressed from California. Much later, during the Clifford Irving scandal, his handwriting was published. I realized, to my astonishment, that the reorder had not been automatic, because his thank-you letter and each year's flower card had all been written by the unfathomable Mr. Hughes himself.

The one thing Howard Hughes couldn't be, to his sorrow, was Cary

Grant. There was no reason, however, that he couldn't have some things Cary had.

A year or so after the Christmas wine, Howard was heard from again. He'd like to have dinner with me, according to Cary. I couldn't imagine why. With a perfectly straight face Cary told me that Howard wanted a woman friend; in this instance, he wanted a woman friend like me. In fact, he wanted me—I was a tested product.

I said no. Cary said I'd have to tell Howard myself. In that case, I'd accept, but I compromised and made it lunch (still that old "How does it look?"). Besides, I was curious.

I suggested "21," where it might seem to be a business lunch. Howard said he was glad I had picked it, because the room had so much wood it enabled him to hear better.

He came right to the point. It was like a proposal. He really needed me. "Why should Cary have a woman friend and not I?" I told him he had a lot of women friends, which is not what he meant and we both knew it. He said he was a very lonely man. He told me the greatest mistake of his life was failing to persuade Katharine Hepburn to marry him. He pleaded on in a shy and earnest way, and apparently he didn't hold my tacit refusal against me, because still later he tried to hire me as a producer for RKO.

MY CAREER in summer stock came to an abrupt end when I found a play. From then on I had to learn on the job.

I had been clear about what I liked. No blank verse or mythological gods; no flashing swords or shining armor. And, incidentally, no farce. None of my strictures to the agents stopped the flow. Oh Zeus! Damn Aphrodite! I wanted plays about just people in the here and now. They didn't exactly pour in. I had to resort to hunches.

I read a play called *Home of the Brave* which had failed the previous season but had received favorable attention. I was struck by the young writer's talent and tracked him down. His name was Arthur Laurents and he had a new play, *Heartsong*. He liked me and I liked him.

Producers rarely back their own shows because they automatically own half without investing. I had no intention of ever being an angel, but since this was a play with a small cast and one set, I decided I could afford to lose the money more than the confidence of friends eager to invest. I told them "next time around," when it would be less risky.

The play needed work—I doubt I'd have gotten it otherwise. It was about a young married couple who had to learn to grow up. Arthur agreed that his central characters had unfair competition from a secondary character who had all the good scenes. If I could just get him Shirley Booth for that part, he could make the necessary revisions.

Arthur had a lively mind and a willing ear, and he was currently being analyzed, so he welcomed discussion about motivation. I stepped right in. The early rewrites were encouraging, and then Arthur ran aground. I sensed a third voice, and indeed there was—that of his analyst, Theodore Reik. I got the feeling that he was treating the play and the patient simultaneously. If so, I had best hear him direct and not once removed. Fresh enough from the couch myself to be unafraid of his scrutiny, and willing to pay for the hour, with Arthur's blessing I went to see the doctor. I thought we'd better get the roles—in and out of the script—defined. It was all very unorthodox, but it cleared the air. I can't remember whether Reik was taking Arthur on credit or had a share of his royalties. In any case, when months later we opened in New Haven, he chose to come to the Saturday matinee. He came, he saw, and he charged. He sent me a whopping bill, which even included traveling time. P.S.: I wouldn't pay.

Arthur worked very hard, and even though the young couple was still not convincing, he had improved the script so much that he was understandably impatient. If I would set rehearsals for January, he would definitely be ready. I broke my neck giving him everything he wanted: four and a half weeks out of town, the Booth Theatre, and, best of all, Shirley Booth.

My heart was with the playwright. Writers in Hollywood forfeited their authority for money; the producer had the last word. On Broadway the author was king and no change could be made, nor anyone engaged, without his approval.

Playwrights had to be a hardy breed because there were no salaries for writers in the theatre. For $500 one could tie up a writer's work for three months; an option for a year might cost $2,000. (In fact, the minimum hasn't gone up that much since.) Certainly a playwright was entitled to be involved in every phase of production and to have his intentions respected.

I hired Irving's brother, Max Siegel, to be our company manager. When the League of New York Theatres approved our opening-night

date, it all became real. I was downright pathetic: "They recognized us!"
Irving said it was automatic, didn't mean a thing.

I had expected the casting agents to be as painstaking as we were, but
they found us resistible after the first couple of weeks. When it came to
the small parts, they even took to ducking my calls. The only one who
called me was Bill Liebling, who had a joint office with his wife, Audrey
Wood. His persistence restored my dignity.

For the set we picked Donald Oenslager, a nice man and a good
designer. When he submitted his ground plan, I felt insulted, because he
couldn't have read the script. There was no playing area for the main
scenes. I dismissed him. How dare I? Well, how dare *he?*

The real letdown came when rehearsals began and it was clear that
Arthur hadn't licked his main difficulty. If he was bored with the young
couple, I asked, how could he expect an audience to stay interested? (In
a moment of truth I told him he should have gotten rid of the young
couple altogether. It's a pity I hadn't perceived that originally.) I had gone
ahead prematurely and it served me right.

If there was script trouble, David was certain he could put his finger
on it if I let him come to Boston. (I hoped he had a better solution for
the play's matrimonial problem than he had for his own. A few weeks
before, Jennifer Jones had gotten me out of a rehearsal on the pretext of
being Dorothy Paley. I had refused the first summons to the telephone.
Summoned again, I was told it was a matter of life and death. When I
got to the phone it was Jennifer. She still said it was life and death, and
she had to see me. Then she waited hours for me outside the theatre. There
was no ducking it. I told my driver to take us through Central Park. She
was distraught about David's unhappiness—he claimed his life was ruined
and she blamed herself. She was bad for him. His career was over. He
didn't love her, he loved me. He didn't want her sons, he wanted his. If
only I would take him back I could restore him. She talked as though
I were responsible. She grew hysterical and tried to throw herself out of
the car—I only just managed to pull her back. We drove round and
round the park. As I quieted her down, I told her David was bad for
himself and nothing she did or didn't do could change that. It was a
dramatic episode, and saddening.) In my suite after the show David began
to discuss the play but soon switched subjects, because something more
pressing was on his mind. In the play the young wife had an abortion,
which came as a revelation to David in the middle of the performance,
although he had read the play in October. He decided that it was that

alone which had caused me to do the play, and, further, that my similar experience had contributed to my leaving him.

He went on and on through the night. I never got him back on the track. He knew I should go to bed, but he hadn't had my ear for eighteen months. I begged him to leave. He agreed that he would, and he did— as soon as room service opened and brought him breakfast. At least there was no mention of Jennifer.

When we hadn't been able to get a name director, Arthur had come up with a woman he thought was ideal for the job. They became thicker than thieves, but fell out in New Haven. So Arthur briefly took over in Boston until, thanks to David, Mel Ferrer arrived, fresh from a recent success as a stage director. Somehow hit shows rarely have replacements out of town; any change is ominous and any statement issued sounds cosmetic. We issued plenty. Not counting Oenslager, our leading lady, Nancy Coleman, went first, then the director, followed by our new leading lady and Lloyd Bridges, our leading man. The saving grace was that, contrary to precedent, I managed to upgrade the names and the skills. By the time we opened in Philadelphia, we had Phyllis Thaxter and Barry Nelson as the principals in a re-staged, re-written play, and we were almost respectable.

However, not good enough for Broadway. The central story was still tedious; the audience coughed as though on cue. But Shirley Booth was superb; her scenes played so brilliantly they could almost carry the show. Arthur was encouraged to try anew. I had to gamble he could come through. He went back to New York for a few days, full of confidence and promises. It was a familiar tale: high hopes, gallant company still rehearsing. The only variations were that the playwright never showed up—he became totally unreachable—and the producer took down the closing notice and played the second week in Philadelphia even after New York was canceled.

The incentive had been Arthur's return. But the momentum for improving the play had taken on a life of its own. We rehearsed right up to the last Saturday matinee. It would have been prudent to close in New Haven. Had I had investors, I would have had to close in Boston. I squandered the money for that last week because the company deserved to be seen. The word spread and theatre people turned up from New York. Their response was the company's reward. Harold Freedman, whom I had persuaded by then to become Arthur's agent, naturally came. He clasped my hands warmly and shook his head as if to say, "If only . . ." Bill Liebling, who had come to New Haven and Boston, surprisingly came again, each time with Audrey, whom I liked so much. She very nicely said to be sure to call her when I got back to town.

It might have seemed then that my commitment to the play was more enduring than Arthur Laurents'. That proved not to be true. He went back to it some years later, changed the setting to Venice, and, retaining her best lines, made it into a starring vehicle for Shirley Booth called *The Time of the Cuckoo,* his first big hit. With further changes it became Hepburn's successful movie *Summertime.* As it turned out, *Heartsong* had served Arthur as "a work in progress." It also had served as my initiation and led me right to the gates of bigger and better things.

To me, the most memorable moment occurred opening night in New Haven. Standing at the back of the Shubert, just before the curtain rose, I heard myself say to Irving, "This has been a cinch compared to Summit Drive."

O N M Y return to New York there was word from Audrey. And then another message. It was kind of her, but I was too busy for sympathy calls until I had cleared up the remains of *Heartsong.* Audrey tried once more: "Third and last call, my girl. Have you lost your manners?" Hers were business calls and I should attend to them, or had I given up the theatre so quickly? She had to see me on an important matter; it couldn't be discussed on the telephone. How quickly could I see her? "You can't be that busy. What about this afternoon?" I couldn't imagine what she wanted.

When she arrived, there were none of the usual pleasantries; she was all business. She had come to offer me "a very important property." I sat there dumbfounded. All I could say was, why? I reminded her that I was not only a novice, I had just had a failure. True enough, the play was a failure, but she felt I had been a success. I could have been faulted only if I had brought the show in. "I know more about you than you realize. Did you know your company manager, Max Siegel, is our closest friend?" I hadn't had a clue. At least that explained Bill Liebling's casting efforts. Apparently Max had called Audrey early in the *Heartsong* period to say, "This is a dame to watch. It's like the old Sam Harris days." Max had been keeping her posted ever since. "You may think you've been trying out a play. Actually, you've been on tryout for me. It's you I'm interested in. I've been waiting for you to become available."

There was a pause; then with a distinct formality she announced: "My most cherished and important client has a play I would like to put in your hands. It is his best play yet. His name is Tennessee Williams."

I was speechless, dazed with disbelief. Finally I managed to get a few words out: "What would your author say?" He already knew; anyway, he always left it up to her. I was beside myself with panic. I repeated, "Why me? Why me?" Her answer was, "Find me someone else."

Obviously, she must have weighed every possible management. Nevertheless, I stupidly plunged ahead. I proposed the Theatre Guild, the most logical choice, not knowing that they had done his first play, *Battle of Angels.* It had been a fiasco in Boston, and Tennessee had published his version of the Guild's treatment of him. My next suggestion, Guthrie McClintic, was equally logical and equally uninformed. He had done Tennessee's last play, *You Touched Me!,* and had frozen him out of rehearsals. Audrey reminded me of the high-minded intentions I'd voiced at our first meeting, emphasizing the value I placed on a writer's participation. She wanted no more, no less, than I had given Arthur Laurents. "The only difference is, this is a bigger production." It had been a hard decision to make and she acknowledged it was a gamble, but she thought I was up to it. She believed that protection and understanding in this case were more important than routine expertise.

I told her I couldn't conceivably tackle anything like that—I would only let her down. She told me to sleep on it and we'd talk further. Meanwhile, she'd send the script.

It arrived at my apartment late the next day. It was my birthday and I had a date with an ardent admirer. The necessity of reading the play that night was greater than going to the theatre and night-clubbing afterward. I couldn't do all three. I offered my beau a choice and we reached an impasse. The temporary solution was to let Irving read the play on the early shift.

I went to the theatre and never heard a line. Furtively, I phoned Irving during the intermission for an interim bulletin and to be sure he'd get the script back to me—I'd be home by eleven. The showdown came outside my apartment door. My friend's last words were, "Choose it or me." I said, "Forgive me," and closed the door behind me.

I shut out everything but the script and my qualms until the dawn came up. When I wasn't reading the play, I was walking the floor. I was as overwhelmed by its power and beauty as by my sense of inadequacy. It was pearls before . . . well, a mouse. I was thoroughly miserable.

I called Audrey at the earliest permissible hour and sadly said, "It's beyond me." She was not put off. She told me to read it still again and we'd meet the following day.

Irving was thrilled it had been offered, shocked I was turning it down; he said Audrey was a better judge than I of what it would take. But in my view he and Audrey were over-rating me—I needed a few more plays under my belt. Besides, this thing had fallen in my lap, I hadn't earned it. Nobody wants bad luck, but sometimes luck can be too good. I'd had my share of that and it scared me, just as it always had. The play was bigger than I wanted, earlier than I wanted. I couldn't swallow it and I couldn't spit it out. If I didn't do it, I was washed up; take my marbles and go home; fraidy-cat. Suddenly I wondered what I was doing so far away from home. I felt like my mother's tiny little girl.

I certainly knew my own mind, but Audrey knew better. She was patient and waited me out. It took days. She chose to call it deliberation and to view my lack of courage as modesty. I didn't know where she got *her* courage; she had more to lose than I did.

I began to waver. But I couldn't have her author buying a pig in a poke. In a last attempt to disqualify myself, I proposed that Tennessee hear me out. Audrey said that in that case we'd go to New Orleans, where he was living. "What, 'swoop down on him?' He'd be cornered; the poor man would have no choice!" Then she'd have him come to New York. "Oh, no!" I cried out, betraying myself. "But then *I* wouldn't have a chance. I'd lose it." Then what would suit me? A happy medium. Audrey picked up a map from my desk and said, "Close your eyes and put your finger down halfway between here and there."

That is how the three of us turned up in Charleston, South Carolina.

I have to admit now that my behavior seems extreme, even irrational, but at the time I thought it quite reasonable. I don't see how Audrey put up with me. She didn't tell me till ages later that Tennessee had said, "This woman better be good!"

Tennessee was in the hotel lobby when we arrived. Our meeting was perfunctory. He was as shy as predicted, but quickly invited me to go for a walk. Having been cautioned not to be thrown if he turned his head away when I spoke (he had a tiny cast in one eye), I walked looking straight ahead. The closest we came to a contact was at the crossings, when, as a Southern gentleman, he took my arm. Neither the play itself nor my relation to it was mentioned, so I could hardly hold forth, although he did ask if I liked the original title, *Poker Night.* Or did I prefer the alternative, *Streetcar?* Did I think it ought to be "Called" or "Named" *Desire?* My answers scarcely proved my mettle. I was wondering when I'd be sitting for my exam.

I hoped that at dinner Audrey would take charge. The moment didn't come. Tennessee talked of possible directors, still without giving a hint of my status. The only time he seemed impressed was when he found out John Huston was a friend of mine. I couldn't tell how I was doing, because he *did* turn away whenever I spoke to him.

As coffee arrived, Tennessee suddenly stood up and said, "Enough. This is a waste of time. Come on, Audrey," and walked away. Maybe well deserved, but he didn't have to do it so bluntly. I was mortified.

Audrey followed him from the table. I sat like lead. Then she looked back and called, "Come on, Irene." Trailing behind, I overheard him say, "Let's get this over with."

Audrey led the way to my room. From nowhere she produced the contracts. Tennessee signed, and then looked straight at me with a great big smile. I was prepared for anything but this.

If there was to be no sentiment, the moment demanded some ceremony. In my toilet case there was a miniature bottle of whiskey left over from *Heartsong.* I got some glasses from the bathroom and poured a thimble each. We shook hands, clinked glasses, and said, "Good luck," and they left. It was mind-boggling. I was now a big-time producer.

Irving couldn't be reached by phone, so I sent him a wire. As if Western Union were the Town Crier, I guardedly said, "BLANCHE HAS COME TO LIVE WITH US. HOORAY AND LOVE."

There was one Freudian note: on the train I left a lovely gold-ribbed cigarette case given me by my ardent admirer.

"Streetcar"

IMMEDIATELY on getting back to New York I took preliminary steps about a director, because time was short. When Tennessee arrived a few weeks later, he did some steady theatre-going. When he saw *All My Sons,* he made up his mind. He told me to forget any previous preferences for a director, he was absolutely certain he had found our man: Elia Kazan.

Gadge, as he was known, was born in Turkey of Greek parents. He had made his first impact on the world of Broadway in Clifford Odets' *Waiting for Lefty* in 1935. I can still recall his explosive performance. He was an absolutely brilliant actor who had turned to directing, and his reputation had continued to build. Now, at thirty-eight, he was poised for the top.

I sent Kazan the play even though he would bring a two-month delay. He read it and turned us down flat, but, surprisingly, a few days later he paid me a visit at home, "because we ought to know one another anyhow." I told him I already knew him from Clifford's journals.

When Gadge wanted to be liked or was exploring someone, he was shameless in his charm. I was aware of what he was doing, but I didn't care, because I was fascinated. And he stayed so long I began to get the feeling that he was changing his mind about the play. I even believed he liked *me.* I turned out to be only partially right.

Gadge *had* grown enthusiastic about *Streetcar.* Between his refusal and our meeting, his wife, Molly Thacher, had read it. Gadge found he had been hasty. (Molly, when a play-reader for the Group Theatre, had been a judge in a contest which had given Tennessee a special award in 1939. The $100 meant a lot, but so did this first professional recognition. Several agents wrote to him. Taking Molly's advice, he chose Audrey.)

I soon learned that before coming to see me, Gadge had sought Tennessee out; Tennessee found him enthralling. Gadge told him he had no commitments beyond filming *Gentleman's Agreement* that summer, and he very much wanted to direct his play, provided Tennessee got rid of me; he freely predicted that Louis B. Mayer and David O. Selznick would be sitting in the front row during rehearsals. He considered himself a producer because he had co-produced *All My Sons*.

As much as Tennessee wanted him, he said no. Nor did he ever mention it to me. I don't know whether it was out of principle or conviction, but he stood firm.

Then the situation changed still further. I found myself negotiating with Gadge's lawyer. I had no choice but to overlook Gadge's behavior and consider what Tennessee wanted and the play needed; I was out to win the war, not the battle.

Naturally, Bill Fitelson was not going to come to my office again. He was "very, very busy." Evenings would suit him better. He said he'd come to my apartment.

I was then living in a rather grand furnished apartment on Fifth Avenue, which could only have further inflamed him. Over-privileged. It was clear he was not benevolently disposed; furthermore, he was in the driver's seat, and he was emphatic in his demands: quite apart from Gadge's usual fee and top percentage of the gross, he must co-produce and own a chunk of the show. It was more an ultimatum than a negotiation. I had never heard of such terms. The only concession he made that evening was to permit my name to come first.

Fitelson would yield nothing in the meetings which followed. However, rather than cost Tennessee his director, I gave up one-fifth of the half I was entitled to as producer, and although it would make it harder to raise money, I took away a like amount from the investors, giving Gadge twenty percent of the show. Beyond that we were stalemated. If Fitelson was trying to provoke me, he succeeded. As co-producer, Gadge would share in my authority, but not my responsibility; there could be no clear lines of jurisdiction. Besides, he'd be unavailable: I couldn't see how he would have time for producing if he was to direct a film all summer and the play all fall. It would be misrepresentation, and I was not going to knuckle under; no good could come of it. I told Fitelson that under those conditions I was prepared to step aside.

Apparently that was more than he wanted. In the end he invented a satisfactory compromise: to give Gadge a second credit, "An Elia Kazan Production."

Tennessee, Gadge, and I set to work as though there'd been no detours. The wonders of working with Jo Mielziner, our designer, brought us quickly together. When the three of us first talked of casting, we decided that the leads would have to sign two-season contracts. Bette Davis being unavailable, there was no hands-down choice for Blanche. Each of us came up with a possible candidate. I proposed Margaret Sullavan, Tennessee suggested Pamela Brown, and Gadge offered Mary Martin. We looked askance at one another. However implausible all three seem now, each had a certain logic then.

I couldn't ask a star of Sullavan's stature to audition, so I invited her to my apartment "to meet Tennessee." During her visit she was persuaded, not unexpectedly, to read a few of Blanche's speeches informally. Although claiming indifference, she read on a second occasion. Nothing came of it, any more than came of Pamela Brown's reading under similar circumstances. Somehow Mary Martin never got past discussion.

There was, however, a natural for Stanley. As with most stage folk in Hollywood, John Garfield constantly vowed to return to the theatre. He loved the play, he loved the part, and he loved Gadge from their days in the Group Theatre. We were delighted. Gadge said it would be a neat trick if I could get him. We were even prepared to settle for one season.

About this time the Music Box Theatre rejected us. Irving Berlin, who owned it with the Shuberts but made the final decisions, thought the play too risky; he was hoping for a nice comedy. The Shuberts said we were "artistic, all right, but not commercial, y'know." A star name would greatly influence which theatre they would give us.

Garfield was not yet ready to commit himself, so we went on searching. I was certainly fighting the lure of filmland, because the only other prospect was the relatively unknown Burt Lancaster, who had had one Broadway success. When he came to see me, his agent, Harold Hecht, came along to run interference . . . for good reason: he wanted to go to Hollywood to become a producer and make his client a star. His plans were already under way; and he chose to explain the movie business to me. Years later Burt told me how he had yearned to do the part. That had been clear all along.

These were precious weeks, because we wouldn't be together again, at least in New York, until September. We settled everything which could be settled. Rehearsals would begin October 6; we would open December 3 after four and a half weeks out of town.

Then, thanks to Gadge's film, the base of operations shifted to Hollywood. With school about to be out, that suited me admirably. There I could make a deal with Garfield and we would find a Blanche. Tennessee came along a few weeks later and settled in for a month. Happily, there was no work to be done on the script apart from cutting. (The cuts were confined to Blanche's departure, which was not only over-long but too harrowing.)

I stayed out of Tennessee's conferences with Gadge, but occasionally he came to my tennis house to work. It was there one day that I fished the play's most famous line out of the wastebasket. Tennessee scoffed, paused, then conceded I was probably right. I don't claim "I have always depended on the kindness of strangers" would not otherwise have survived, but for me right then it was a big moment.

Tennessee was riddled with anxieties. He had morbid fears about his health and was convinced he wouldn't live long. Also he dreaded ever being penniless again; if he were, he wouldn't be able to write. So great was his fear that at the peak of our success he confessed that he would waive all income, present and future, in return for a guaranteed $250 a week for life. He didn't want to hear that, right then, he could easily buy himself a handsome annuity, with a lot left over. In truth, his primary need was for acceptance of his work, and it was that which accounted for the desperation within him. I believe his demons were quieted only during the daily swim he found essential. He needed not only the protection Audrey asked for him, but whatever security that devotion could bring. I grew increasingly fond of him.

After we began to know each other a little, I made bold and asked Tennessee to consider something I'd been longing to bring up—a change at the end of one critical scene. The change involved no dialogue and involved only a few seconds, but voicing it took nerve, because it altered the playwright's intention.

This was the scene in which Stanley makes advances to Blanche, hell-bent on having her. Blanche puts up a fight, falters, and he carries her to bed. I felt she would be destroyed more completely if, after resisting, she began to respond and then he changed course and repulsed her. It would be her fatal humiliation. I would have him fling her across the stage and just stand there, laughing savagely. I thought it would make the last act more valid.

Since Tennessee had never ruled out my idea, I offered it again during rehearsal. Surprisingly, he was excited and insisted that I hadn't suggested it before. He thought it dramatically sound and urged me to tell Gadge. I had already done so, and Gadge hated it. I left it to Tennessee.

Gadge vetoed it once more, in language ripe enough to shock me and amuse Tennessee. He tried to get a rise out of me by accusing me of cleaning up the play to protect the movie rights. He claimed I'd be depriving him and the audience of a nice juicy rape, or words to that effect.

Tennessee persisted, so Gadge persuaded him to wait for second night in New Haven. Then he promised him to try it out second night in Boston. There he told him not to trifle with good luck. And so it went. Tennessee wanted me to try it in London. By then I had given up.

It was Tennessee who by chance had led us to our leading lady. Some years before, he had anticipated Blanche in a one-act play, *Portrait of a Madonna*. Jessica Tandy's husband, Hume Cronyn, an early supporter of Tennessee's, astutely arranged to have this playlet put on at the Actors' Lab while we were all in California. Hume directed, and Jessica's performance was so superb that we practically handed her Blanche then and there. As it happened, the mildest adjective Jessica attracted as Blanche was "brilliant."

Meanwhile, I was negotiating with Garfield's agent, Lew Wasserman, now the biggest agent in town. He assured me of two things: he would negotiate in good faith, however long it took; and in his opinion Garfield would not do the play. We were at it all summer. In August, after I thought I really had him, came his demand to be guaranteed the movie role, along with his refusal to play more than a few months.

A month before rehearsal we still had no Stanley Kowalski. I was in despair. Gadge, calling from New York, said we'd better forget about names and types and go for talent. He proposed Marlon Brando, whom we had turned down as too young, being all of twenty-four. In fact, we'd seen him playing a fourteen-year-old only three years before, in *I Remember Mama*. However, more recently I had seen him as the poetic lover in *Candida* and, more to the point, I'd watched him bring the curtain down to cheers in *A Flag is Born*. I remembered being galvanized by his power. I did some quick re-thinking: his special qualities, combined with the impact of Kazan, just might make Brando a more dimensional Stanley than Garfield. Gadge said that, however risky, he was bound to be interesting and wanted to send him to Provincetown to meet Tennessee. The arrangement was almost as unconventional as the people involved.

Marlon, notorious for bad readings, and out of work for seven months, showed up days late, claiming he was so broke he'd had to hitchhike. Obviously, he had blown his travel money. Tennessee's place had the advantage of not only being bohemian, but having the plumbing broken down and the electricity out. The situation was made to order for Marlon's quirky sense of humor. He put everything right—the plumbing, the electricity, and his future. Tennessee's enthusiasm was the best possible news, although it appeared I was going to have my hands full, because Marlon, however gifted, was considered moody, restless, unpredictable.

On my return to New York from California a few days later, Marlon came to see me. He didn't behave like someone to whom something wonderful has just happened, nor did he try to make an impression; he was too busy assessing me. Whatever he expected, I wasn't it. He seemed wary and at a loss how to classify me. He was wayward one moment, playful the next, volunteering that he had been expelled from school, then grinning provocatively at me. I didn't take the bait. It was easy going after that. He sat up in his chair and turned forthright, earnest, even polite.

One thing he wanted me to know was that he'd never make a movie. This may have been his way of assuring me that he would serve his time —the price of success would be a twenty-month sentence. Even so, given his reputation, it would be a feather in my cap if I could keep him.

Casting the part of Mitch was easy. Karl Malden was the first and last to read for it and he was wonderful.

Kim Hunter was the only one whose job I secured and saved. When I first read the script, Kim, who hadn't quite made it in Hollywood, flashed in my mind, but she had dropped out of sight and was only Hollywood anyhow.

We sat through an endless lot of girls. Then I happened to spot three lines in *Variety* mentioning that Kim was touring in a small stock company upstate. She was such a long shot I didn't mention her to anyone but Irving, who went off to assess her.

As the pickings got slimmer and slimmer, I dared to propose her. She must have been overwhelmed by her luck, because she got less promising

with every day of rehearsal. Gadge talked of replacing her, but I had a
hunch that a quiet talk and some constructive attention from the master
would restore her confidence. Gadge cooperated; the next day her progress began.

Gadge had an uncanny way with actors. He really proved it with
Marlon.

The first week Marlon seemed under pressure and scarcely bothered
with his lines. Then he began to arrive late—one morning very late and
very pale. He slunk onto the stage. Gadge went over to him. I held my
breath. But there was no scene. As Gadge listened, he put his arms around
Marlon. It was extraordinary to see so tough a man as Gadge be tender.
Gadge gave him some money and sent him out to eat; he hadn't slept
either. Lest I be critical of Marlon, Gadge told me there had been no
misbehavior; that Marlon was having a terrible struggle with his role.

In the next couple of days I watched Gadge put Marlon back together
and saw Stanley emerge. It was hard on the other actors, but Gadge in
his infinite wisdom let Marlon get away with just muttered snatches of
his speeches. His performance was becoming so powerful that Tennessee
remained unruffled. Gadge teased me about my uneasiness and warned
that I might not actually hear Marlon until New Haven. He began to
speak up at our final runthrough, but it wasn't until Philadelphia that I
fully heard him in the part. For me, not only Marlon but a part of Gadge
himself remains forever in that role of Stanley.

I didn't permit one extraneous thing to distract me in these weeks of
rehearsal. I'd had personal disturbances to spare in California late in
August. Danny had been scheduled for surgery, and on the morning of
the operation I got to the Santa Monica Hospital at 7:30. By 11:30 David
had neither shown nor phoned. When I got home I tried to reach him
but was told he could not be disturbed, he was still asleep. His Danny!
It was the last straw. Later that day he turned up and I told him I had
gone along with him for two years but would protect him no longer:
I was suing for divorce immediately. While I was at it, face to face, I
inquired whether a blind item in a column I had recently read about a
wife standing in the way of her husband's re-marriage referred to me.
Well, it was possible. Of course he had never *said* such a thing, but owned
up that recently he had been desperate and may just have let that impression prevail. He was deeply ashamed. He tried to explain, but I was
disgusted and refused to listen to his problem. The room crackled with

hostility. The only help I offered was to repeat my earlier promise to get the decree in California, which would grant him a further year's grace.

He thereupon launched into the question of custody. I couldn't believe my ears. Custody? We had settled that early, late, and in the middle. True, but he had changed his mind. He conceded I had been fair about the amount of time he had seen the boys, but he was going to fight. He was, was he? Well, so was I! But I advised him not to, as I would have his mother as my only witness. I heard myself shout, "To the highest court in the land!"

Fight we did, and hard—for hours every day on the phone. Finally he called in a different tone of voice, with a compromise to offer. He said he might have caused the original trouble, but claimed to have come up with a solution. The line or two he read to me referred to a continuation of the satisfactory manner that now prevailed. Contrition had pushed him to the other extreme. His rationale for the conflict was that he didn't want the boys in later years to feel he hadn't cared.

The next hurdle was the division of property, customarily a burial ground for illusions. After a pleasant dinner with Morgan Maree and our lawyer in David's office, it took us an hour to settle everything but the child support. That had to be whittled down because it was double what I would accept. Had there been a settlement or alimony, it's likely the result would have been similar. Then he offered to let me buy his half-share of our paintings at their purchase cost. When I questioned this as being unfair to him, David said the increase in value was surely equal to what I had lost by not taking a share of income-tax deductions and low brackets in the years of my 20th Century dividends. He had noticed that behavior and it was time he acknowledged it. I insisted on buying his half of my jewelry. I kept the house and half the new company and gave him all of our life insurance, among other things. No money changed hands, we simply "traded off." The two businessmen were dumbfounded.

Before my departure, even though I couldn't wait for the hearing, I filed for divorce. The decree became final in January 1949. David married Jennifer in Italy that July, practically four years after he and I had parted. I knew before the news was printed, because of a cable he sent me. The text had been omitted, so I called the cable company. There was no error: it consisted of one word, the signature, "DAVID." I assume he wrote and rewrote the cable until he was at a loss for words. In any case, the message was clear.

RAISING money is a talent I didn't have, and I dreaded the prospect. I'd never asked anyone for more than a dime in my life, and now I needed $100,000. I didn't know why anyone would want to invest in a show, and in a drama, to boot. If I accepted nothing less than one unit, which cost $5,000, I thought I could make it seem a privilege. I bought two units myself to reassure prospective investors.

I had a seasoned angel at hand in Jock, although he had sworn off the theatre; nevertheless, he bought one unit and put it in Betsey's name. Joan Payson came along, and one other rich friend, and so did Cary. And that took care of volunteers.

I resorted to writing letters like everybody else. How does one ask people if they'd welcome a chance to lose money? Or to expect less of a return because of Gadge's share? I labored over endless drafts. I didn't ask—I "offered the opportunity." I concentrated on those who could afford to write it off; I had less compunction about them.

My letters turned up only a few takers, and I was forced to let Irving and Bill Liebling make up a couple of syndicates of people I had spurned because they wouldn't go for the whole five grand; I just looked the other way. We went into rehearsal still $10,000 short, quite embarrassing at that date. Rather than go hat in hand, I quietly picked up the last two units, feeling more a coward than a sport.

That spring we had reserved the New Amsterdam Roof Theatre for rehearsals. Although it was located at 42nd Street and Broadway, it seemed utterly removed from the world—a huge, spooky place, private and silent the way Gadge wanted it. The rehearsals were mesmerizing. I enjoyed the process almost as much as the result, and as I watched, I forgave Gadge bit by bit for the past and, indeed, for the future. He was worth whatever he got. He could sit motionless and silent, totally focused on his actors. There was radar between them. From time to time he would leap effortlessly to the stage, where his economy of gesture and phrase to convey his precise meaning was magical. He imposed nothing on them, but drew out of them whatever was needed. I couldn't tear myself away, and paid in midnight oil for the undue time I spent there. (I took such pleasure that Gadge let me sit in as an observer on his next show.)

As soon as the show opened, however, Gadge left the actors in the lurch. He just walked away; they were all orphaned—or do I mean jilted? I had to urge him to pay a few visits, then taper off. He was getting ready to entrance a new group. The only revenge I took on Gadge for the trouble he had given me was to tease him about Clifford's journals. He longed to know their contents, but I wouldn't ever tell him. (Or anyone else, except Fay Wray. After Clifford's death, I felt she was entitled to know that she had been the love of his life, and how bitterly he regretted not marrying her.)

I enjoyed my father's occasional visits to New York until one of them coincided with the *Streetcar* rehearsals. Even then I made time I didn't have—and hoped my preoccupation didn't show, and that he'd go home quickly. But when his business was finished, he lingered—in fact, asked me if I didn't think he should stay on. He was so oblique, I didn't know he had the New Haven opening in mind. He was yearning to be invited, but kept backing into the subject by using the familiar refrain "How would it look?" if he departed right then. I told him no one would notice. To be frank, I wanted no distractions; I needed my wits about me. I couldn't afford to have either "Louis B." or Dad on hand. Above all, he would be shocked by the play and I was afraid of the scene he was bound to make. I had to keep him away at all costs.

He proved equally determined. Ignoring my lack of enthusiasm, he told me to think it over. Days later he called to say he had reached a decision: he was going to wait and go to New Haven. I was desperate.

In a last attempt to discourage him, I made an outrageous request. If he was so full of paternal feeling and suddenly had all this leisure time, why not run up to Massachusetts and visit Jeffrey at his new school? ("Go there and do what?" he asked.) From Deerfield it would be just a few hours to New Haven.

I found it unreasonable of him to consent so easily. I had miscalculated, so while I was at it, I tacked on a little more to the price of admission. All summer Danny had hugged a secret—a mass of yellow lined paper which turned out to be a play that the Dalton School felt deserved a presentation in their auditorium. However, the date was the morning after my New Haven opening, the one time I couldn't be there—there was a meeting automatically scheduled. My father floored me by agreeing to go to Dalton too. He didn't bat an eye.

In return, he firmed up New Haven; he wanted to know where to meet me. What kind of question was that? I couldn't possibly answer. "No matter what, you have to eat. At that point of the day there's nothing else you can do. Where do you eat?" Fine. He said he'd meet me at Kaysee's at six-thirty and not to worry if I was late.

When I got there, he was already on intimate terms with Kaysee. He had taken over and was so out of character that his first concern was for me to have a drink. I didn't want one. He told Kaysee to listen to him. And no mixed drinks—"Bring her a shot of whiskey and water on the side." He ordered my dinner and he even lit my cigarette.

Halfway through my meal he said I'd had enough and sent me on my way; he'd see me later. I promptly forgot about him.

As the house lights dimmed, a crisis in miniature threatened—a replay of the never-to-be-forgotten first preview of *Gone With the Wind*. I became hostile to this audience too; they didn't know what we'd been through. Ridiculous! This was martyrdom and self-indulgence; I'd better lean up against the back wall and swallow hard. Be grateful we had gotten this far.

The show was a technical mess, but I felt it played very well, although I got a rude jolt in the first act. I thought something had gone wrong when the house unexpectedly rocked with laughter. If I'd ever had a bottle of beer in my life, I'd have gotten the point of Mitch's line on his second trip to the bathroom, "We've been drinking beer." Irving calmed me by whispering an explanation in my ear.

In case we had wanted a full and impressive-looking house, it was there. And all too many familiar faces amongst them. By the time I got to my sitting room in the dingy old Taft Hotel, it was jammed with people who felt they had a right to come up for a drink. Yet there was none of the real excitement I had expected from that group; no out-and-out superlatives. The word "artistic" caught up with us again. It was a fine production, it was distinguished, my courage was commendable; *that* alarmed me. There was too much respect floating around and not enough enthusiasm. The exception was a film scout I knew, who thought it was so wonderful he asked my lawyer to sell him his share then and there; he even offered him a profit. What frightened me was that my lawyer seemed to pause and consider.

My father had yet to speak. He asked me to step into the bedroom for a moment. He said that all those people were goddamn fools. "They don't know anything. You don't have a hit, you've got a smash. You wait and see. Now get back and don't listen to them."

A little later it occurred to me to wonder where Kazan was. I found out. Marching up and down the corridor was the most surprising pair I ever saw—two rather short figures, my father's arm draped around Kazan's shoulders. When I caught up with them, I discovered a mutual-admiration society. Apologies had been in order. They repeated them for my benefit. "Just think, I had this remarkable fellow on the lot and never met him. Can you imagine anything like that? I'm making up for it now. This is a wonderful fellow." Gadge felt terrible that *The Sea of Grass,* his one MGM picture, was a flop, even with Tracy and Hepburn. My father reassured him and called him Ee-lye-ah. Gadge even liked that new pronunciation. Extravagant feelings abounded. "I don't know what to say, Mr. Mayer." For the moment, he was so enamored of my father that he actually sang my praises. Dad glowed. Gadge understood. Not for the first time, I thought, "Greeks are not goys." I left them in the corridor, still marching.

As I was going over my notes late that night, I realized I could finish them with Babbin just as well on the train to New York. Our meeting had been changed to afternoon, and there was more than one play in the family that week. I dictated up to the door of Dalton. There on the sidewalk stood my father and Danny. Dad said, "See, I told you she'd make it." I had, with five minutes to spare. Danny covered himself with glory. I had to hand it to the old man too. I managed to get back, notes and all, in time for that meeting; nobody even knew I'd been gone. That was not, however, the last of my father. He finally did go home, but, incredibly, showed up again in Philadelphia three weeks later.

The local papers ran from fair to poor; our only rave was in the *Yale Daily News.* But we sold out, and the audience response was unmistakable. With success in sight, on Saturday night some of our people and a few of Gadge's pals celebrated and made a night of it. The evening wound up with a rowdy group dancing down the middle of a New Haven street, with Gadge in the lead like a Pied Piper. They must have blown off a lot of steam, because we had quite a few destroyed people on the train the next day.

Apparently not enough steam, because mischief was afoot. In Boston I noticed a change in the atmosphere backstage. I was greeted differently. So were Irving and Babbin. The crew fell silent when we came around. I couldn't put my finger on it, but there was a mounting sense of Them versus Us. I felt I was being undermined. Gadge was so wonderful I couldn't bear to think he was involved; still, it seemed he was at the heart of it. I didn't yet know he had it in for producers as a class: producers exploited the artists. Meanwhile, our endless technical rehearsals went on and on, which somehow added fuel.

That week Jock, who happened to be in town, came to see the play. He had a strange encounter with Gadge, who walked up to him and said, "Jock Whitney, what are you doing here?" Jock explained that I was an old and dear friend, and that his wife had a piece of the play. Gadge claimed not to know it, and Jock wondered how that was possible. It wasn't, because I had just that day learned that Gadge was telling the boys backstage, "Never mind what anything costs. The Whitney millions are backing this show."

That was merely an ancient resentment, but surely it represented the tip of an iceberg. There had to be plenty more, and, whatever there was, I couldn't afford to recognize it right then. I hoped it would go away by itself; if not, I'd worry later. The show had priority.

I never did make an issue of it and chose never to explore it. I just stopped it—unexpectedly, inadvertently, and, strangely enough, without a battle.

The second week in Boston I took time out to visit Jeff at Deerfield. A friend of mine, Dede Ehrlich, Frances Goldwyn's sister, offered to drive me. On our way back that afternoon we had a near-fatal motor accident. Despite the impact of the collision and the shattered glass, Dede was unhurt. I knew I was injured, but I was so stunned, there was no pain. I managed to get to a telephone at the roadside and call Massachusetts General Hospital. Meanwhile, a crowd gathered, and a woman came up on my left side and asked whether I knew what had happened and where the injured were. She went away thinking I was a curiosity-seeker like herself, because she didn't see the torn clothing and the blood pouring from the right side of my head and my knee. The windshield and dashboard had done their work.

At ten o'clock that night I left the hospital against orders—necessarily with Hildur's help. (Hildur was very good to me indeed. She always pretended it was because my mother had once asked her to "take care of my baby.") I was cut up, but, after all, I only had a concussion. However unwise it might prove, I wanted to sleep at the hotel and go quickly home in the morning. But before leaving, I had to see Gadge. I hadn't faced up to "the insurrection," and if I just vanished, he'd think I'd chickened out. Besides, I felt that my notes, even if unwelcome, were essential before Philadelphia.

The scene wasn't staged, it only looked it. I was flat on my back in my room and done up like a stretcher case. Aware of the spectacle I presented, I quickly said I was okay, "just ignore the bandages."

I had no taste for the big topic and little time, so I synopsized. I told him I knew a lot of what had been going on, and that in spite of everything else he might have been up to, he was not as black a villain as he probably felt he was. My note of forgiveness without accusation apparently did him in. He looked stricken. He put his face in his hands and wept. I was so astonished I blurted out a brand-new view of myself, new even to me: "I've survived Louis B. Mayer and I've survived David O. Selznick. It's no use. You better lay off."

We never had a bad moment after that. In no time at all I got through notes that would have been declarations of war on any other occasion.

Gadge obviously didn't forget. A few years later, as he accepted another play from me, he said, "I gave you a bad shake on *Streetcar*. I didn't treat you right. This time we'll be as one." But by then he was almost as fond of me as I was of him.

LIKE a fool, I showed up in Philadelphia on Monday, not as stalwart as I looked. Babbin stood two feet away in case I keeled. The manager of the theatre (where I had closed *Heartsong*) greeted me with the news that tickets were at a premium. The night my father came, the manager was waiting in the lobby, bravely prepared to make good his boast that they were old friends. I felt terrible watching him. Well, they hugged each other on sight. "Louis!" "Leon!" We never know it all. Mr. Leopold, who happened to be the brother of Ed Wynn, had been at the Walnut Street Theatre when my father had it under lease back in Haverhill days.

The show was frozen. I went back to New York, taking my having been hit on the head as a sign that nothing was going to go wrong. I had been the lightning rod; the show was safe. I just had to seat the house right on opening night. The responsibility was mine alone, but I couldn't even start until we wrested from the Shuberts, then all-powerful, the undue quota they claimed. (There had already been skirmishes and trade-offs with them over broker allotments and house seats.) We worked from Irving's huge chart on which was printed the floor plan of the Ethel Barrymore Theatre.

In the middle of my ticket problem David showed up in New York.

I didn't want him at the opening, but he didn't believe that there were no more tickets. He tried me every day. He didn't care where he sat, he just wanted to be an onlooker. "Don't deprive me." I wouldn't even know he was there. He finally confessed that he had come specifically for the opening. "Did you expect me to stay away?" I gave him a medium seat.

I was seated in the last row on the side aisle, closest to the lobby, making me readily available. I gave the signal and the house lights dimmed. As the curtain rose, I felt that singular, familiar wallop, as though one's solar plexus is turning over. The world was held in the balance. Sure, it's only a show . . .

Within minutes a wracking cough devastated the air. Again and again. The source was a white-haired gent, six seats away and two rows in front. He was choking, trying to stop. "Who?" No matter who. It was a Shubert single, a big-wig from City Hall. Out! Through a relay of lateral taps and a beckoning finger, he and I met just outside. For the sake of his health and the show, would he please go home! Two weeks later he was my guest in third row center.

There was absolute silence for a moment when the final curtain fell. It was spooky. Then the applause rang out. In those days people stood only for the national anthem. That night was the first time I ever saw an audience get to its feet. And the first time I saw the Shuberts stay for a final curtain. There was Mr. Lee, the big bad wolf, standing with his hands over his head, applauding with the best of them. Round after round, curtain after curtain, until Tennessee took a bow on the stage to bravos. Everything was so heightened I saw everyone, both on stage and off, curiously ringed with light. I fell back into my seat transfixed.

What I couldn't have foreseen even at that moment of glory was that the play would completely alter the lives of its four leads. Indeed, it fixed the pattern of mine and made Gadge a king. Most suitably, it gave Tennessee enduring glory.

AGAIN I was superstitious. However, not having an opening-night party doesn't ensure a success—everyone just gets gypped. People had been asking should they "make plans." A party was in order and I would be remiss if there wasn't one. I thought for me to give it would be too splashy, besides not wanting to offend those I didn't invite. I needed a front, so I asked George Cukor, who was going to be my escort, to come East a few days early. I informed him that he was giving a party at "21" and all the arrangements were up to him. He'd get the credit and I'd get the bill.

I felt Marlon was up to something when he arrived, neatly attired. He was flanked by a tall, handsome pair he tried to pass off as his parents. They couldn't be, because they were eminently respectable and Marlon had told me otherwise; if I fell for it, he'd tease me forever. To be safe, I greeted them pleasantly but very briefly. Then I rushed off to find out if they were genuine, came back full of apologies, and started over.

Tennessee's mother was there, and so were Gadge's mother and father. It was a great night for parents.

And about-to-be ex-husbands. I had already filed for divorce.

David had kept his word. I had seen him go down the aisle as inconspicuously as though he were folded up, looking neither right nor left. Nor was he visible during the intermissions. Then came "21." By the time I got there, the party was going full tilt. George may have been the host, I may have been picking up the tab, but David, jubilant, did the honors. He was greeting all the guests, crowding George out. I retired him to the rank of a guest, though not too successfully.

In spite of the ovation and the congratulations, I refused to concede success, even when my press agent phoned that the word was good, in fact, excellent. I stayed contained until the notices arrived. I could scarcely read Brooks Atkinson for the tears. It was over. We wouldn't have to make a fight for it, we were in. Oh, how I wept. I embraced everyone right and left. I wanted the evening never to end.

The party went gloriously on. George, who liked to get to bed early, had been sent off by David, who said he'd take me home—he hoped I didn't mind. He said I had to stay, and I did, until the bitter end. He said that only he knew how tired I was. It was one of the few times that David really took care of me. When I reached home, the adrenaline just drained out of me. I fell in a heap on the floor and couldn't move. I was clearly not yet an impresario. He was as tender with me as though I were a child. He undressed me and put me to bed. I had shot my bolt. I felt I would never rise again. Little did I know what awaited me.

At the office, apart from the expected pandemonium, was the bad news I had been spared the previous night. The musicians' union, Local 802, out of the blue had notified us that we must add three musicians to the five we already had, and pay everyone musical-comedy rates. (Obviously, the gravy train was in. The second night the stagehands' union came around and declared us a two-set show. We made their agent stay and dared him to find a second set.)

My lawyer, Howard Reinheimer, who was also Rodgers and Hammerstein's lawyer, was able to speak from bitter experience. He said he would write the customary letter, even though any protest was an exercise in futility. That sounded defeatist to me; he said it was realistic. Be that as it may, it wouldn't do. Apart from my concern about my investors' money, I was being asked to pay three superfluous musicians to sit in the basement and play cards. I, who had been indignant through the years that Hollywood condoned featherbedding, now had it in my own back yard. I was obliged to fight.

The League of New York Theatres, a group made up of theatre-owners and producers, decided to do just that on my behalf. They called an emergency meeting without consulting me. Having invited me, they ignored me. In the midst of arguments and their naming a committee, someone called out, "Hey, what does *she* think?" What I thought was that I stood a better chance alone, but I was grateful knowing they were "there to help if I fail." (Actually, I was aware of the bad blood between them and the union, and I could ill afford them. Besides, their sound and fury was not for me. I intended to speak softly.)

The union added insult to injury: the higher salaries were because "the men must stay alert during the performance to respond to cues." (As opposed to what? I wondered.) Furthermore, no matter how much I reduced the music, the verdict would stand. Worst of all, they said I was lying (". . . totally false and misleading . . .").

I resisted doing battle in the press, refusing to be lured into controversial statements even after my appeal was turned down. I appeared before various union committees anyhow, but my determination didn't impress them. I might just as well have sent my manager. I lost consistently.

This was such a big effort that, while I was at it, I enlarged my goal. If there were a formula by which producers could determine musical costs in advance instead of suffering arbitrary decisions after the fact, it would help both the union and the theatre. A situation like mine could only be a warning for plays to avoid music. While still dealing with "the boys," I took out insurance by going higher.

James Petrillo, the president of the American Federation of Musicians, was the best-known labor boss in the country, and at that time the most hated. Due to a strike, there hadn't been a recording made in six months.

He was a czar as inaccessible as he was powerful. I found someone who knew someone who knew someone Petrillo trusted. And there I was at headquarters, good and scared. This was a hell of a way to be celebrating a hit.

Security was heavy. One door after another opened and I was finally ushered into the sanctum sanctorum. Pathological about germs, Petrillo was known never to shake hands. But as he rose to greet me, to my surprise he extended his hand. That let me know I was being honored.

He put me further at ease by proudly pointing to a wall plastered with hostile cartoons of himself. I confessed I found his unpopularity convenient, because our other unions wouldn't honor his picket line if a strike were to be called; if necessary, we could run the show without music.

I asked no favors, made only one request. I wanted him to see the show.

I stood in the back the night he came and never took my eyes off that seat. At the closing lines he shot up the aisle, and I chased after him. Assuming he wouldn't care to recognize me right there, I crossed the street and beckoned him to follow. That put us right in front of the Hotel Edison. I whisked him into the bar.

He thought the show was wonderful and humored me by saying he wouldn't have known there was music in it if I hadn't told him. That called for a second round of drinks. Instead, I thought we ought to leave. I wanted to really talk.

We each had a limousine outside. Mine was without a bodyguard. We let his follow. I took him to my apartment. What we had in common right then was that nothing like this had ever happened to either of us before.

I talked about my world, he talked about his. It was difficult for him to intervene in local matters, but new policies might be considered at the union's national convention in June. We talked on and on. He reminisced; it was very late when Jimmy left. I thanked him for a lovely evening; he did the same. The last thing he said was, "Have faith; have patience."

Naturally, I kept my mouth shut. Meanwhile, I battled on, but no hostile statements. Six months later I got a telegram: "CONGRATULATIONS. HOW WOULD YOU LIKE TO BE MY LAWYER?" It was signed "HOWARD REINHEIMER." I'd won not only a reversal, but the overall formula I'd been fighting for.

I was a heroine to the League. At a meeting I was hailed and told, "You are what we need." In no time I was elected to the Board of Governors. Actually, this was no great shakes, but I didn't know that then. I was amused at the occasional apology for the mild profanity at meetings. I asked mercy only on dead cigars.

And so began my life with the big boys. I didn't suspect that one day I'd turn down the presidency.

WE HAD so hoped Tennessee might win the Pulitzer Prize that we scarcely dared speak of it. It was a golden day when that dream came true. The Drama Critics Circle Award came his way as well. The play was to be honored with a Sunday radio broadcast. Gadge would talk and the cast present a scene; that was the good news. The bad news was that I was expected to speak on the program.

I simply couldn't. Not possibly. I became stubborn.

Some people who stutter just get up and stutter. Closet stutterers go through a different kind of torment. Their efforts at concealment can be understood only by a fellow sufferer. I could face the world, but not a microphone.

I had tried once and it was a disaster. It was during the war, at a banquet at the Waldorf on behalf of China Relief. I was seated prominently on the dais. A man carrying a microphone for a coast-to-coast broadcast traveled down the table, introducing the guests, each of whom said a few words. He bore down on me. I was trapped. Methodically he introduced me—once, twice, three times. I tried. I opened my mouth; not a sound came out. He moved on. I sat mortified.

Well, I had since done other things I'd thought I couldn't do. In short, I was persuaded into it against my better judgment. But free-floating anxiety had turned into panic by Saturday night. Rational thinking didn't help: I'd been sentenced to public humiliation.

Perhaps I did have a use after all for that newfangled machine David had given me, which he hoped would "somehow be helpful in your work." It was a tape recorder that resembled a small coffin and weighed a ton.

It would have been too shaming to be overheard, so once Danny was asleep, I locked my bedroom door and took microphone in one hand, text in the other. Nothing came out but some strangled sounds. Contempt for myself was mixed with self-pity. It took until midnight to master the first two sentences. I did trial runs through the night. By six A.M. I had two perfect takes. Rarely has effort been so out of proportion to a task. Before

I left I showed Danny how to run the machine, without telling him how scared I was. In case I got through okay, I wanted proof.

The presence of the *Streetcar* people compounded my terror, so I had myself smuggled into the studio. I stood in a remote corner, facing a blank wall. On cue, my fifty-five seconds of speech flowed, without apparent effort. It was a damned miracle. Now my only concern was whether Danny had pushed the right buttons.

I have hoarded the tape that Danny made and play it now and again, very privately. Smooth as silk, but I've never faced a microphone since.

David heard about the broadcast and was relieved I was getting my due. Ever upset about a producer's credit, he had been prepared from the start to fight for mine. To begin with, he took on Harry Luce—in my house, of all places, three weeks after the play opened.

Clare and Harry came to Summit Drive in 1947 for Christmas dinner, not for the first time. David of course was on hand and behaving as though he were still in residence. (This may have raised false hopes in Clare, who had been the only friend to say I must go back to David, either for my sake or his—I wasn't sure—or because she had become a Catholic.) In the middle of our meal, he assailed Harry as though it was his fault that *Time* magazine's review of *Streetcar* was our least favorable. And while he was at it, he also reproached Harry because *Time* hadn't saluted me as producer. I begged him to stop; it was awful, especially at Christmas. Clare interrupted to say that I had to expect such treatment as Harry's friend. Complaining that Time-Life always did their worst by her, she began to enumerate her grievances against them (by now ever so familiar to me. Clare was never less than interesting except on this topic). Harry told her to stick to the subject, which was me, but he was out of luck.

Clare didn't much like women, but I think she was fond of me. I was useful and—here I go again—dependable. I enjoyed her, but she was unpredictable. From time to time she would declare her devotion to me, sending me any number of affectionately inscribed photographs of herself in silver frames. She said I was one of the three women she loved. (As I didn't much admire the other two, may they rest in peace, I was unmoved.) She would occasionally even present me as "the woman I love," but the next time I saw her she could give me a very cool "How do you do?"

With Harry I knew where I stood, undemonstrative as he was. For a time there, Harry gave me birthday presents (he remembered because our birthdays were a day apart). Not a big, splashy present, but he did go and buy it himself. I was delighted. But Clare scoffed at my pleasure. She knew that, whatever the gift, I wouldn't be able to use it. True or not, that was beside the point; Clare was just being a killjoy. I found it rather touching that he had no talent for picking a gift.

Harry stayed a good friend until his death. In the thirty-odd years I knew him, he changed quite a lot. For one thing, in his last years he didn't stutter even on TV, so serene was he.

MY FATHER, not a great one for backing down, had never reversed himself about a daughter of his working, but he was bursting with pride and delight over *Streetcar,* though he couldn't find quite the proper words. Nothing was more alien to his nature than lavish presents, but they were what he now chose as a means of expression. I said there was nothing I wanted for my birthday. When pressed, I gave him a practical suggestion: I could use new luggage. "Luggage you can buy yourself." He wanted something super. I wound up with a five-piece set in cherry-red alligator, far more suitable for display than use.

That hardly satisfied him. My next birthday brought a work of art worthy of Cellini. He had Van Cleef & Arpels create a gold compact with a scene from *Streetcar* etched on the lid, the figure encrusted with diamonds. This was followed, a few months later, by a lavish dinner-dance when the road company of *Streetcar* arrived in California. My father had always frowned at Hollywood gestures such as flamboyant figures carved in ice, but there in his own home, when the dining-room doors opened, was an enormous streetcar melting its heart out. My father thought it was lovely, and so did I.

Edie was at her nicest to me after *Streetcar.* What maddened me was her amnesia. In talking of our recent tryout in Boston, I mentioned my favorite relatives, Fay and Anita, daughters of my mother's brother Victor. Edie said, "Who? Where?" "Fay and Anita, our cousins." She looked perplexed, then indulgent: "Oh, darling, I'd forgotten. You always *were* a family girl." Her praise always had a putdown tucked away. A few years earlier, Edie told me I had had looks, in fact still had, but in her view I did nothing with them; if I took pains I could still look marvelous. "Do me a favor, darling. While I want you to look beautiful for yourself, actually I'm being selfish. Everyone thinks I'm years younger than you, but there are some people from way back who remember. So take care of yourself for my sake, because you make me years older than I appear." Jean Kerr recently reminded me of my response to her question "How old is your sister?" "She used to be two years older than me." I believe I added, "She is younger than springtime."

Edie re-created her past as she went along. Her exaggerations were many and they snowballed. There was no keeping up with them. Her confusions were also many; she was known to have suggested that her charms were so great, her father was jealous of Bill. In her late years she went so overboard in a printed interview that she attributed to Bill one of the highlights of David's career.

MY CURRENT status, however unexpected, was nothing compared to the vision of me producing in London.

In the first years after the war there wasn't much theatrical traffic between London and New York. English plays didn't do too badly here, but something seemed to happen to ours in mid-Atlantic. American playwrights found themselves not as protected in England, where the producer's role was mainly management. (Actually, directors were called producers there.) Therefore, instead of the customary sale of the English rights, Tennessee and Audrey wanted me to pick a management and co-produce in the American sense. At last I'd be doing something with real experience to back me up.

Although American plays were not in great demand, every management in London wanted *Streetcar*. There were thirteen offers in all, including one from Laurence Olivier, who asked to direct it for the Old Vic, saying: "Tremendously enthusiastic about prospect and hope it will fructify." That sounded pretty exotic. But the first and most persistent bidder was Hugh Beaumont, known as Binkie, of H. M. Tennent, Ltd. Apparently in London "Binkie" was a magic name, a password; not to know its meaning was to be illiterate.

I sought advice from Harold Freedman, who knew the English theatre well. He reduced my list to a handful. Why did people say Beaumont was the best, *but*? But what? Well, he was shrewd, he was clever, he had charm. They all sounded like indictments. Was he honest? "Well, yes." But? I'd have to read the fine print. "Why have you used him so often?" "He gets the job done and is good at it." Coming from Harold, that understatement amounted to a considerable endorsement. (Years later he put it differently to his client Jean Kerr. He told her not to be deceived by Binkie's charm: there was real ability behind it.)

Nevertheless, I sailed with the slogan in mind: "Beware of Beaumont." I was definitely looking forward to some comparison shopping.

Before they let the passengers off at Southampton, we stood at the rail watching the luggage slowly slide down to the dock. When Louis B.'s cherry-red came into view, there was a low whistle, followed by "Who?" "Who do you think?" Seeing my new luggage like that, I didn't really blame them. I gaped with the others before heading for the boat train.

Lined up at Waterloo Station, it seemed more appropriate. Waiting for me were three limousines, three chauffeurs, and a man from Claridge's. Dressed in Valentina's simplest, than which there was no grander, and trailed by Hildur, the impression I conveyed was as close as I ever came to seeming a princess.

The scene was joined by a young man who had been watching from a distance. He was immaculately groomed, impassive, and had an air of anonymity. "Mrs. Selznick? My name is Beaumont."

My instant reaction was that I hadn't heard right, and that the great man had sent some self-effacing deputy. He repeated, "My name is Beaumont." I said, "What? Oh! *Really?*" and put out my hand. He smiled. All I could think was Peter Pan.

He asked if I was ready to leave. Not quite. Rather than detain him, I thanked him for coming—it was very kind. (Which was not what I was thinking. I thought, "How enterprising, getting the jump on his rivals.")

Mr. Beaumont preferred to wait for me; he had plenty of time. After dismissing the car I'd ordered and organizing Hildur in the car from Claridge's, I went along with him. As the car pulled away, his personality emerged. Here was Binkie, good-looking, spirited, charming. I redoubled my guard and listened with care.

By the time we reached Claridge's, I was swept with admiration. Without rushing, he had gotten to the point in a hurry. His adroitness outweighed all the apprehension I had stored up; whatever his strategy, the campaign was over before the battle had barely begun. We had been together less than an hour, but I had found out what I needed to know. I'd be a fool not to have his skill operating on my behalf, and it made no sense to hold out on him. I owned up to "Beware of Beaumont" and said I was going to risk the fine print. He was unprepared for so quick a victory. It was almost an anticlimax. He had planned to put in the next day and the days after until he won.

Still sitting in the car, we actually talked casting. I mentioned Vivien. Oh, a very great friend! He happened to know she adored the play. The Oliviers were in Australia, but he could practically guarantee her, if I was prepared to wait a year. Larry? Well, that might be managed. I detected less enthusiasm and no intimacy.

Again and again he said, "Let me keep you a few more minutes." When I finally left his car, he asked whether, if I wasn't too tired, he could come up for a tiny drink. Two hours later he was still there. We were both having a splendid time. He proposed dinner. Lovely, but I had to change: "I'll be back in ten minutes." His face fell. After a lifetime of prima donnas, he wondered if any restaurant would still be open by the time I was ready.

I returned, as advertised, in ten minutes. He exclaimed, "I don't believe it." Now we surely were going to hit it off; he had known that in Waterloo Station. I had my priorities straight. We stayed late enough to close the restaurant. There was an affinity between us out of which grew a deep affection and a friendship which lasted until he died twenty-five years later.

Before that evening was over, he made another offer. He suggested I come each day and watch him in his office. It wouldn't bother him, in fact he'd enjoy it, and it would be the best way for me to learn about him and about English theatre. I never asked him whether it was my remark about the fine print which prompted the invitation, but he did let me listen to his phone calls and read his mail.

A few years later, in *Queen* magazine, Kenneth Tynan painted an interesting picture: "The ruling managers of the London Theatre . . . have been awakening to the fact that the balance of power is not what it used to be. The truth is that they have a Richelieu in their midst, and most of their thrones are in his shadow. By an exercise of flair, diligence and supreme business cuteness which it would be unfair to call stealth, Hugh Beaumont . . . has more power . . . than any comparable association in the history of the English legitimate stage. . . ." Nonetheless, I found he kept a low profile and low overhead. The secret of his success was that he seemed not to sense his power, but tried as hard each time out as though he were starting from scratch.

The London production was now postponed for a year. Meanwhile I had my work cut out for me. What faced me in New York was the mounting of a road company.

The powerful Chicago critic Claudia Cassidy made it clear that Chicago might be the second city, but would not take second best. Uta Hagen was giving an extraordinary performance in a revival of *Angel Street,* and she became our unanimous choice for Blanche. She had the right looks, was the right age; she just wasn't the right size. A tall cast was the solution, beginning with a hefty Stanley in the person of Anthony Quinn, to tower over her. What we couldn't find was an understudy for Quinn. Our staff was instructed to stick to 44th and 45th streets during lunch hour, to stop any man over 6'2" and ask if he was an actor (he would not be offended). That is how we got the hitherto-unknown Jack Palance. (That job brought luck: Richard Kiley, also then unknown, followed Jack.)

When Jessica's contract was up, she was ready to relinquish the role, having served Tennessee nobly for two seasons. Uta scored such a triumph on the road for nearly a year that she took over on Broadway with Tony Quinn, while Judith Evelyn succeeded her. Judith at least had the excitement of playing Los Angeles.

I didn't have two homes of foster children, but I did have two companies for which I had the responsibility, and people need attention. I went to Chicago, where we played twenty-three weeks; Madison; Indianapolis; Kansas City and other points west.

I was back in London the following May to settle the casting of Blanche. Although Tennessee felt that the prestige of an Olivier production would be enormous, he didn't share my confidence that Vivien could handle the role. I insisted he come from Rome to see for himself. Vivien was making her initial appearance with Larry on the London stage, where they were playing in three Old Vic productions, *The School for Scandal, Richard III,* and *Antigone.* Tennessee asked, "Why do you make me do these things?" "Because I don't have the courage to make the decision myself."

If it wasn't one Selznick, it was another who held the key to the role of a Southern belle (and, as it turned out, two Oscars). Vivien in essence did an audition for three nights running, and she was all too aware of it. By the third evening the matter was settled, so we all had a quiet supper at Binkie's. By this time I had learned that he and Vivien were thick as thieves and it had been Binkie who had helped plot Vivien's path to Scarlett O'Hara. Here he was again getting her her heart's desire.

At the table Larry asked for freedom to cut the play, and Tennessee gently refused, explaining that it had already been cut to the bone for New York. That was that.

Then the Oliviers gave a party, a buffet supper, in Tennessee's honor. Tennessee rose to the occasion by uncharacteristically ordering a limousine. The driver got hopelessly lost and we arrived more than half an hour late. By then our host had disappeared, although his presence was evident overhead. We heard his footsteps back and forth, back and forth, throughout the evening. Tennessee was not the only one disconcerted.

Nevertheless, Larry was charm itself when I went to Notley Abbey, their country place, for the weekend. His only reference to the party was, "How sorry I am, darling, that I was deprived of seeing you."

Tennessee chose to come out on Sunday, so I blithely arranged for Larry to confer with him, since this was to be Tennessee's only visit in connection with the production. Gadge had greatly profited from consultation with Tennessee, and I assumed—well, I assumed too much. The two of them were together about fifteen minutes. All they exchanged were compliments and expressions of good will. Tennessee had an enjoyable day, but wondered what had made me think Larry wanted to talk to him. That was a Sunday we were all to remember.

The first part of the summer of 1948 I was busy with Judith Evelyn in California. The rest of the time I spent with the boys on their long-awaited European tour. We saved London for last, where I had people put by, like Sidney Bernstein, whom I had come to know well since my honeymoon. Also living there then were my old friends Mary Lee and Douglas Fairbanks; and Marietta Fitzgerald, who had recently married Ronald Tree; and, of course, the spellbinder, Alexander Korda.

I had now been immersed in *Streetcar* for two and a half years and had been through three Blanches, each singularly different, the last two without Gadge. Tennessee and Audrey were certain that whoever did the play in England, Larry included, was bound to find me useful.

Aware of the oft-repeated claim that Larry had a dreadful time staging *Streetcar* in England, I can only say that so did I! I had forgotten *how* dreadful until recently, when I re-read a stack of letters I had written Irving during rehearsal. I saved my sanity by unburdening myself on paper at shameless length.

The primary cause of the trouble is revealed in a letter I wrote on September 20, just before we opened out of town: "A great deal has come to light. . . . It wasn't affectation on Larry's part, he really scarcely knew

Streetcar in May and in any case was not terribly keen about it; he thought there were a lot of boring and repetitious passages. He consented to direct it only because Vivien talked him into it."

When I arrived in England this time, the Oliviers greeted me with flowers and "Darling, how divine." But there was nothing professional. The closest I got was to remind Larry that there could be no cuts without Tennessee's permission. He said, "Oh, the old boy won't mind. Why should he? Surely it is a director's prerogative to take out anything he wants to and rearrange as he sees fit. Who's going to stop me?" When I protested, he said that was why he preferred dead authors. I tried to talk to him about it. He said he was too busy—"Later, later." Actually, he *was* busy; he was busy cutting. Whatever his eminence, it was unbecoming. It was also unfair to the play. On top of which, it violated my contract with Binkie.

But Binkie couldn't help me at that point. He and Larry were not on the best of terms; their cordiality was only surface. Besides, Larry was unlikely to consult a producer, and an American one at that. Binkie advised patience. His understanding of talent and temperament was such that he instinctively knew when to pamper and when to assert himself. Meanwhile, he let Larry have his head. Larry took it as his due.

Hardly ever had Larry directed for a commercial management or done a modern play; his reputation as a director had been built on Shakespeare and the classics. As one of the ruling heads of the Old Vic, his word had been law. However, he had recently been dismissed from that kingdom. It was unfortunate that *Streetcar* was the first undertaking to follow.

Our actors, apart from the four leads, were cast in a single session. There were no auditions, even for accents. Larry summoned whom he chose and interviewed them in Binkie's own office, while Binkie and I sat in the next room. Binkie didn't bat an eye. Nor was there any kind of pre-production meeting. I didn't think anyone's position in the theatre was that high and mighty.

I kept Irving fully informed. He edited me to Audrey, who told Tennessee the necessary minimum. Tennessee was on a job in California; however, he had written me: "I place it, like Pilate, in your hands. . . . See that everything possible is done to protect *us* and the *play* as distinct from Sir Laurence and his Lady."

Binkie and I were permitted to go to the first reading and not invited to rehearsals thereafter. The cuts were given to the actors, but not to me. It was a hard week's work getting them. And no wonder—they were horrifying. Vivien later asked, "How could Tennessee object to the cuts unless he knew about them? How did Irene find out? Where did she get them?"

I knew Tennessee would be very upset. In my letter enclosing the cuts, I spared him so much that I misled him. I began: "I know well enough how understanding and generous you will be to Larry's need for expression and individuality."

But I could do nothing until Tennessee answered my letter or Larry sent for me. I was miserable and sat immobilized, waiting, hoping, to be called. After two weeks, on September 12, I ventured into rehearsal. It was soon evident that Larry was taking pains to avoid copying Kazan. He resisted and resented the stage directions in the script without bothering to find out whether they were Williams or Kazan. Exasperated at having to use certain moves that were unavoidable, he told me he felt "like just a stage manager." His only inquiry was about the color of stockings two characters were to wear. I sensed I was holding up the rehearsal and left. I was clearly an unwelcome chaperone. After my meteoric rise up the ladder, this was quite a come-uppance. I reported: "The people surrounding them are all scared and desperately respectful. Mind you, it's all polite, charming. . . . (My, I would not mind hearing some of Gadge's four-letter words.)"

I couldn't stand it. I was better off waiting in Paris, where *Streetcar* was also in rehearsal. There the situation was reversed. I hadn't planned to go, but they had been eager to have me and were grateful for whatever I had to give. I didn't think it was much; they thought it was a lot. They embraced me.

I came back to London a few days later, but it took until the 19th to discover that Tennessee had long since cabled a reply; on the 12th, in fact. I tracked Binkie down. It's a miracle our friendship survived the phone call which followed. The cable had been withheld on the basis that it was from Audrey, since it originated in Connecticut, where she had a country house. Binkie and Larry discounted it as double-talk—Audrey making agent noises. Binkie said I spoiled playwrights. I answered that he hadn't permitted cuts in Priestley or any other author Harold Freedman represented. I reminded him of the clause in our contract to that effect. I said that protecting playwrights was my strength, not my weakness. Larry had not only challenged the source of the cable, he had convinced Binkie that Tennessee had granted him full license that famous Sunday at Notley Abbey.

The content of the cable was hard to come by; I had fairly to drill for it. But the words were as clearly Tennessee's as the signature: "DEEPLY DISTRESSED OVER PROPOSED CUTS IN SCRIPT SINCE ALL MATERIAL NOT CUT HAS PROVEN ESSENTIAL TO CHARACTER DEVELOPMENT AND QUALITY OF PLAY. . . ."

It was outrageous. However, going to the runthrough was worse. I was kept out that day, but I damn well got in the next morning. High time. There was one week left until the Manchester opening.

I said little, got into my car, and had hysterics. It wasn't Tennessee Williams and it wasn't good; it was Olivier versus Kazan, and it was a disaster. Larry had simply gotten off on the wrong foot. I summed it up in a cable: ". . . CUTS LEAST HEARTACHE. AM WRETCHEDLY SICK ABOUT EVERYTHING . . . PARTICULARLY INTERPRETATION. APPALLED LACK OF COMPREHENSION."

I sent for Binkie. Binkie sensed crisis in my voice. However quietly I was speaking, he heard me loud and clear. It was one thing to humor Larry about cuts, but quite another if the show was in jeopardy.

Quickly I got his skulduggery over the cable out of the way. No matter how good the cause, it was no way to deal with me, particularly after I had leveled with him about Beware of Beaumont. (Fortunately, that proved to be the only time I ever found him skating on fine print.)

Then I got down to real business. The show did not ring true. Tennessee's meanings had consistently been misconstrued. Furthermore, stripping the play of its lyricism had led to a misconception of Blanche and left the piece merely lurid. My concern with the cuts now was simply that they compounded the problems.

I talked for two hours, scarcely drawing breath. I held forth with a heat and a sweep I never reached again in my life. I wound up by saying that I wanted nothing more radical than a meeting with Larry. Restraint had gotten me nowhere. A showdown was in order. If so, I had better be specific, tactful if possible, and at all costs not emotional. I was scared to death. But the alternative was unbearable.

We met that night at Binkie's house. Unforeseen was Vivien's presence. As the director's wife she had no right to be there, less still as the star. But she was adamant. So be it.

Miraculously, Binkie had delivered a Sir Laurence willing to listen. I begged Larry's indulgence. He told me to say it all. It was such a relief to get a hearing that I was able to keep my feelings out of it. Luckily, I spoke my piece with less eloquence than earlier in the day, and more briefly. Scene by scene, I outlined the play's intentions as opposed to what I had seen that morning. Larry protested just once; he got to his feet and waved a letter from Tennessee, claiming it gave him carte blanche (which, incidentally, was wishful thinking). He said, "Let's not waste time discussing cuts." I hadn't and I wouldn't, because Binkie had warned me I was doomed if I did. Besides, I had too much else to say. The most difficult part was pretending that Vivien was not there when I discussed her characterization.

It was a bruising experience for one and all, yet, perversely enough, there was a better climate when we finished than when we began. But apparently not chez Olivier. They were up until six in the morning, arguing. I hoped they might have been rehearsing as well. When I saw the show next, in Manchester, I was so relieved I cabled: ". . . MUCH BETTER. MANY CHANGES. IF ONLY A FEW MORE. . . . HOWEVER MOST VITAL ONES ACCOMPLISHED." Some of the cuts were actually restored. Far more surprising was the fact that on the second night Larry met with me till five A.M.

Our stay in Manchester was punctuated by an overnight visit from David, who couldn't resist the temptation. Breathing good will and advice, he took over the hotel dining room at supper. Whether Larry and Viv liked him or not, they respected his opinion and hung on his words.

David had chartered a luxurious plane for the round trip. Binkie was dumbfounded, but we rode back to London with him in style. I told Binkie it wasn't his wealth, just his extravagance. Binkie's feelings got hurt. He said David made him feel shut out. "I thought you people were divorced." I told him he should have seen us in the old days.

I found more and more lines restored when I went back to Manchester a week later. Larry had also given me trouble about the music but I now let him use any tune he liked, any place. You can't win them all. Anyway, by then the music was relatively unimportant to me.

Larry came to my room the last morning, "just to visit." He was warm, even cozy; held my hand while we talked. I told him I was no longer afraid of London; I felt we would get by.

Streetcar in London wasn't what it might have been, either artistically or critically. Kenneth Tynan said it showed the way "in which a good play can be scarred by unsympathetic and clumsy direction." However, we did good business for the eight months Vivien lasted.

Binkie wrote that we'd have to replace her soon or shut down. She was "tired." (He had not yet confided in me about her periodic spells.

The gods had given Vivien every possible gift; at her best, there never was exquisite beauty and charm so combined. Then, as if they had gone too far, they added a flaw, tiny but lethal—a recurrent emotional disturbance, which brought her tragic years.)

In the spring, when I returned, Binkie said it was imperative I see the matinee that very day, as Vivien had been anxiously awaiting my opinion on her present performance. I didn't believe that, but when I went backstage, it seemed dramatically true. She held on to me for dear life. I was moved by her reaction, and could honestly tell her she was wonderful.

When eventually Gadge undertook the movie, I readily contributed a vote for Vivien. Unlike Larry, by the way, Gadge was usually willing to listen and often willing to concede error. He was the earthiest man I ever knew, and in those days, perhaps as a carry-over from his radical days, the height of inelegance. (As Vivien put it, "He sends his clothes out to be cleaned and rumpled.") Most important, of course, he was a very great director, with a visceral response to actors-at-work and to the dynamics of a scene. I have to admit that in post-England retrospect he looked even greater.

A Hit and a Flop

T H E R E were no more excuses, I simply had to have a play for the 1950 fall season. I longed for something uncomplicated and remembered envying Alfred de Liagre the previous season when he announced a romantic comedy about a witch—*Bell, Book and Candle,* by John van Druten.

I called John's agent, Monica McCall, to ask why no more had been heard of it. I was told it had been canceled because Margaret Sullavan and Lilli Palmer had both turned it down. For some reason, van Druten had then withdrawn it and had forbidden anyone to read it. I pleaded. Monica gave in, but strictly off the record.

Two hours after I got my hands on that script, I was telling Monica I had to do it.

Monica was floored. For two years she had tried in vain to sell me a play and now she had me pleading for a discard. She was afraid at first to tell John in California that she had disobeyed him, but when she did, his response was to take the next plane to New York.

Was I sure I wanted to do it? Courageously he showed me a letter from the man whose opinion he most valued, Oscar Hammerstein, who had advised him to shelve it because there was something sinister in the witchcraft. I couldn't see that. I took the witchcraft for romantic magic. Girl wins boy via a spell, girl loses boy when he finds out, girl gets boy back. I went merrily ahead, unaware that witchcraft was still believed in and practiced and that John had employed its methods literally. When I caught on, I read up on the subject and paled. John said he had warned me, and offered to let me withdraw. In a last-ditch attempt, I suggested that we comb out everything unhealthy (which John called "the smell of sulfur") and, lo, the play was better than ever. Claudette Colbert said no, Margaret Sullavan said no again, but Lilli Palmer took a second look and decided she wanted to play it. Now all we needed was a leading man. (The ideal one, of course, was Rex Harrison—Lilli's husband.)

The first five I approached turned me down because it was the girl's play. I tried to encourage John, back in California, by saying that I would be arriving for the summer, and that there were plenty of actors out there.

When, to our consternation, the next five declined, I went back to the script, studied it again. Then I assumed the perspective of the five men and told John why I, as an actor, was turning down the part. I didn't enjoy just feeding lines to the leading lady, and pointed out place after place where my part could be strengthened. After each five new refusals I became the actor again.

That summer, in my tennis house, John wrote three drafts with me at his side. I gave advice and John gave me an education in playwriting and claimed he had trained my ear. The play got better, the actors got worse. There were twenty-two in all. We had scraped the bottom of the barrel a dozen actors earlier.

I kept writing to Lilli through the summer, despairing about the search for our leading man and truthfully telling her how the play was improving. I finally wrote to say that I was now sending her the final script and wondered whether anyone in her house was taking the hint. I had already said to John, no more offering this part around, because "if we're not careful, it's going to get so good Rex might agree to play it."

I confided in Binkie, who had been trying to help, that we now had a hundred-to-one chance of getting Rex. He wished me luck, but said not to bank on him. "If for any reason Rex doesn't do his movie, there is something of mine he wishes to do." Binkie went on believing that right up to the day Rex decided on us.

Our news was an absolute bombshell on Broadway, and no less a one in poor Binkie's office. Rex Harrison?? Oh, what must have gone on, with twenty-two leading men accusing their agents, and vice versa!

It may have been a great coup, but once I had achieved it, I went into shock. I was scared to death of Rex Harrison, who had a reputation for being difficult. I wasn't up to this; once again my luck had been too good. Van Druten, as the director, was fairly uneasy himself. I told him to be careful of what he prayed for next.

Rehearsals didn't take off at a great clip. Everybody was intimidated by Rex, John included. Rex, meanwhile, groped around as though he had never read the play. It took John a few days to figure out what he was up to. Rex would worry a single line over and over, writhing and shuddering, oblivious to everything else, until he got it just right. It was the purest concentration John had ever seen, and the results were brilliant. John may have been finicky, but Rex was meticulous. It became obvious that these two urbane Englishmen understood theatre the same way.

But John couldn't accommodate himself as easily to Lilli, who had been trained in Berlin and was primarily a dramatic actress. As Rex was conceded to be the absolute master of light comedy, it wasn't possible for her to compete against him, but it was essential that she hold her own. John, not in tune with her, just couldn't give her the help she needed.

Her confidence lessened. By the time we got to New Haven, an explosion was overdue. Instead, she went into spasm. The day of dress rehearsal she came to me with pain written all over her. She couldn't turn her head or raise her arm. Hot packs didn't help. She begged me to advise her what to do.

Surely a quick fix from a local doctor would be risky, but, as it happened, Lilli had walked right into my specialty. The only real talent I ever had was in my fingers; they had many a healing to their credit. I offered my services. For once I had real faith in myself, though I hardly expected Lilli to share it. John said that there was a risk either way and was willing to gamble on me. Rex stayed out of it. Lilli submitted and it worked out extremely well, though *she* didn't think it at all remarkable.

That evening an unscheduled drama took place on our stage. Rex, ticking like a time bomb, kept his temper hour by hour during a catastrophic lighting rehearsal. At midnight I fled to a phone.

The only one who could advise was Eddie Kook. Kookie was a powerhouse quite apart from his company (best known by the program credit "Century Lighting"). He told me we had all the wrong lamps, that it was too late to hire a lighting man, and that he was down with a 102° temperature. Solving my problem was strictly outside his province but well within his expertise. Despite everything, he pitched in. The mighty

Kookie literally rolled up his sleeves and did the job himself. He jammed my car full of equipment, commandeered the rest from Yale, and worked around the clock.

A compact fellow, Kookie fitted neatly along the back seat of my car. I tucked him in tenderly for the ride back. He had been a hero, plus.

We found out the first night in New Haven that we almost had a lovely show. Alas, we let the audience down with a thud at, of all places, the end of the second act. Rex, defying the spell Lilli has cast, has stormed out, leaving her to play a big dramatic scene by herself. The scene didn't work, but we had no curtain without it. John had no notion how to solve the problem, I had no notion, nor did any of our friends. We hoped for a brainstorm by Boston.

The first week there went by. John listened to all comers. Then, with only one week left, we froze the show, telling ourselves that if we went on polishing what we had, we might just get by. Down deep, we knew it was a near miss.

Sunday was piled high with postponed work. I began early with Irving, who had to return to town. Midway through our agenda there was a call from a friendly Rex, asking to see me. I tried to deal with it on the phone and be done. He said that was impossible, but he would wait—an unexpected patience.

After Irving left, I was still tied up. When Rex next phoned, I offered to see him then if it could be brief. No. He didn't care how long he waited, provided he eventually had my undivided attention and unlimited time. He was sweet as pie.

I worked all day. Whatever Rex was doing, he didn't leave the ground floor of the Ritz and he kept on calling. Then, at around eleven, when I was finally finished, I pleaded that I was shot and, what's more, was looking a mess; it was too late to make myself presentable, couldn't it wait till morning? No, he had to see me then, never mind how I looked. But I had on a woolly nightgown and a robe! He was coming up anyhow. I brushed my hair.

Rex's determination of the morning was intact. He had come to say that the show was nearly a hit, but something was wrong. He couldn't put his finger on it, and was asking me for a solution. He made it sound as simple as if something had merely been mislaid.

He went over and over the problem. Relentlessly. Rex is not the most articulate of men, but he can be the most persistent. He traced the play from the audience's viewpoint, then from the actors'. On and on he went.

I thought he would never leave. My mind closed down for the night.

Suddenly I jumped to my feet with a whoop, and then fell back in the chair. I'd had an idea, but it was shame-making. Rex insisted I tell him. I refused. He said I was being unfair. I told him I didn't dare. "You're a big star, you'd find it insulting." Yes, it involved him, but it was corny, in fact almost slapstick; not exactly his line of work. Well, it was only something visual, but it *was* graphic. (Not incidentally, it eliminated Lilli's dramatic solo.) It was as follows: Rex slams out and, faster than it would take him to reach the street, is propelled—magically—back; the door flies open and there he stands, calling for a taxi. Freeze. Curtain. It was a sight gag, pure and simple. "I say, I say, that's rather good." He thought he'd like to take a crack at it. He would consult Lilli, I would consult John, both of us uneasily.

The change, though minute, was radical and affected many other scenes. I set to work, not daring to look at the clock. If I went to bed, I was sunk; it was easier to stay up than to get up. John was an early riser. The better to face him, I mapped everything out and had it all left under his door. To save time, I used scratch dialogue to illustrate what had to be done.

John was pleased but incredulous. Had Rex really consented? Who would break it to Lilli? How could it all be accomplished in the few remaining days? John as director was needed at the theatre. It was agreed that if I could keep going on the script, he'd give me what time he could. Afraid that my participation be misconstrued, I made John promise, as I had Rex, not to implicate me. I had the courage of desperation, but the caution of a lifetime. (John chose to forget the promise.)

I used one secretary by day and the other by night. I sat propped up in the sitting room, and there I stayed. No distractions, no interruptions, not even meals. Hildur stocked the room with cold milk, hot coffee, pitchers of orange juice, and a bottle of whiskey. With a silent apology to David, I added Benzedrine to that menu. My senses were so heightened, my lines seemed masterly to me. Actually, they were at best serviceable. Oh well, John was going to refine them. But in the end he didn't bother.

I could think, but by Tuesday I couldn't stand. Anyone who assumes that being a producer is glamorous should have seen me crawling to the bathroom on my hands and knees. It was a long night, the one that ended Wednesday morning. I was okay when I finally got to bed, but when I woke up I was like a beached whale.

Rex had been practicing his new exit privately for days, and only unveiled his efforts on the Thursday evening, an hour before the doors to the theatre opened. He was dazzling. That, and all the other changes, went in that night. The audience reaction was monumental. They were still laughing as they walked up the aisles. I was intoxicated.

There was a further dividend. Relieved of the burden of her big dramatic solo, the tone of Lilli's performance lightened and took on a shimmer.

We had made it, we were safe. But not safe enough to give a proper opening-night party. Just about twenty or so friends for supper at my apartment. When I walked into the living room, George Kaufman was huddled on the sofa by the fireplace. He gave me a dour look and shrugged. Oh dear! When the notices came in, I sat by him while he read Brooks Atkinson. A rave. He was indignant. What was the theatre coming to!

I forgave him ten days later on the night *Guys and Dolls,* which he had directed, opened. The notices were smash, but he was even more morose. This time he denounced the critics *and* his show.

Bell, Book and Candle ran from November to June of '51. I am still asked why I closed it at capacity. A provision of Lilli's signing allowed her to leave in June, when the house she and Rex were building in Portofino would be ready. I'd given a solemn promise not to beg for more time, and I'd have gotten nowhere if I had—and broken my word as well. As it was, there was good will and the likelihood of London; Binkie would have Rex back at last. And meanwhile Rosalind Russell played it on tour.

And then, of course, there was the movie. That came less easily. For someone with an inside track, I seemed to be jinxed in selling movie rights. The property was a natural, but till the summer of 1953 there was nary a nibble. (I did receive an offer from Howard Hughes' lawyer, but that didn't count because it involved my services as producer.) Then Otto Preminger made John a bid—a percentage deal with no cash up front. John felt that a bad deal was better than none, but, fortunately, the Dramatists' Guild then gave a producer, if dissatisfied with an offer, five days to top it.

David knew the market and, naturally, was overflowing with opinions. He named all the possible customers and gave me all the proper selling points, but before I could put them to use, he called back. "How would your author feel about a flat hundred thousand?" That sounded glorious.

"You've got a customer. Me." He had bought his own sales pitch—he'd found it irresistible. I asked him how he was going to pay. Well, he was going to borrow the money to buy it, and then make money reselling it. He did. And so did the next purchaser, who eventually sold it to Columbia Pictures.

I'D ALWAYS believed nothing comes easy. In November 1951 a play came along to contradict this notion—*Flight into Egypt,* by George Tabori. It was about a Viennese couple waiting for visas to America, which the man is denied because of ill health. I accepted it, and got my director as well, in a matter of days—thrilled to have secured no less than my old friend Kazan, now top of the heap. (I was pretty hot stuff myself, after two hits. I not only had to ration investors, I had a waiting list.) Given my nature and my feelings about luck, I had to pray that if this show too was a hit, the good Lord would make sure that nothing happened to my children; things were going far too well.

As it happened, the blow landed squarely on Gadge. I refer, alas, to the House Committee on Un-American Activities, which had been grabbing headlines with its show of rooting out Communists in Hollywood.

At our first meeting Molly Kazan turned up with Gadge. This surprised me, because they had a firm agreement that she would never involve herself in a play of his. She had come along, Gadge said, to tell me the play was politically safe. I was as astonished to learn that the play might be considered political at all as to learn that Molly was an expert on politics.

I found out what it was all about the next morning when Gadge walked in and said he had something to tell me: I was his friend and he owed it to me. "I was a Communist." There are very few answers to that. I chose, "I assumed as much," which I hadn't at all. I'd never known a Communist—leftist, yes, but no Communist. (Well, perhaps two or three.) This was a fine thing to be telling someone whose political activities had been limited to joining the League of Women Voters on her twenty-first birthday and never turning Jock down when he was raising money for a liberal Republican. Gadge told me that his fling with the Party had been youthful and brief; he had proved a stormy petrel and they had tossed him out.

I mistakenly assured him that he ran little risk. After all, the witch-hunt had been confined to films, radio, and TV, and I saw no way it could succeed in the theatre. Besides, by now he had so much prestige as a Hollywood director that they wouldn't touch him. That was not so naïve as it sounds. I just over-estimated the combined power of Warner Brothers and Fox, which had millions tied up in his two most recent films.

By coincidence, our author, who lived in Rome, was also having visa trouble. Due to a mix-up, he didn't arrive until the day before rehearsals began, so Gadge and I had been working alone for a couple of months. Gadge had suggested that I book only two weeks out of town, because the production was uncomplicated and the script was solid. However, the climate of fear being what it was, he wanted a couple of ambiguous lines changed. He wrote to Tabori: "Maybe you don't know how extremely ticklish the situation is here . . . they are just waiting to misunderstand!!!!"

Gadge and I were a cozy twosome, together practically every day. He talked to me a great deal about "the problem." I had a frame of reference from Hollywood friends who were left-of-center. Because I believed they were alarmists, Gadge tried to make me more realistic. "Read the *Daily Compass*." It was the only honest newspaper; I. F. Stone was a giant. He showed me a picture from its front page of an internment camp surrounded by barbed wire, in readiness for political dissidents and subversives.

Eventually I sampled the *Compass* in a way that seemed logical. Every night for a week I spread the *Times*, the *Journal-American*, the *Daily Compass*, and the *Daily Worker* on the floor, and went on hands and knees from one to the other, comparing. Gadge found this a novel approach and was curious as to where I got the *Daily Worker*. Perfectly simple: Michael, the chauffeur, slipped it to me along with the *Compass* in a plain brown envelope.

The *Compass* didn't echo the *Daily Worker*, but it didn't resemble the *Times* either. It was not for me, however much it did reflect Gadge, and there was no doubt about where he stood. If he was called by the Committee, he was prepared to tell them to go to hell and then some, to put it delicately.

It was common knowledge that if one was called, there were three courses open, outside of ducking the subpoena before one's passport was lifted: the respectable route, to resist the Committee by taking the Fifth Amendment, even though that resulted in being blacklisted; to defy them and risk a jail sentence for contempt of Congress; to turn informer and go through the ritual of naming names. Praise the Committee and pass the ammunition.

If they wouldn't let him make movies, he always had the theatre. If that got tough, he could work in Europe. He would never knuckle under.

That was brave talk, and I admired him for it. To those in comparable trouble, some bigshots included, he gave advice and strength.

This was Gadge's first play since *Death of a Salesman,* and there was a rush of actors to climb aboard. While the Actors' Studio might monopolize his time when he wasn't making movies, I wasn't going to let Studio members monopolize our casting, although not to use any would be reverse discrimination. Then we got to the hot topic of actors who were blacklisted by publications like *Red Channels.* I figured I had political respectability to spare and could afford to employ a few in a cast of eighteen; it would help everybody's morale.

The line formed to the left. We wound up with four, two of whom would not have made it had times been normal.

When we couldn't find a fat, suave Englishman for the Cairo innkeeper, Gadge insisted on Zero Mostel, who at least was fat, but was more entertainer than actor and who gave a perfectly terrible reading. Gadge promised me he'd be wonderful, but here his sympathy outweighed his judgment. Nor was Paul Mann right for the role of an attractive young Austrian. I had to tell Gadge that he was at fault for having told Paul the part was his; also, that being under a cloud didn't justify a higher salary than he'd ever had before—we weren't paying according to how long someone had been out of work. In the end, however, I was pushed into paying more than he was worth.

We settled on Paul Lukas and Gusti Huber, a lovely actress from Vienna, to play the leads. (David had called immediately to say Jennifer could play it. The next day, taking no chances, Jennifer called herself.) Inadvertently, Gusti caused us a different kind of political trouble. Instead of censure coming from the Right, midway through rehearsal I found myself attacked in anonymous letters as a fascist and anti-Semite and was threatened with picketing for using Gusti, who was denounced as a Nazi sympathizer. Rumor was widespread, and our theatre parties began defecting.

It turned out this campaign was being waged by a lone woman, a European actress who thought she deserved the lead and failed to get even the understudy role. We managed to keep this from poor Gusti until her husband was able to furnish the theatre-party people with official proof that her record was spotless.

Rehearsals were otherwise uneventful, but the fact that Molly came along on the road should have tipped me off that something was afoot. Bit by bit, the script began to be sanitized. I made little protest, because Tabori had arrived with a case of hero-worship and did whatever Kazan wanted. These changes, though, were apparently what *Molly* wanted; I didn't know what to think when one day Gadge made me take his place, arguing with Molly against further changes.

The constant fiddling with the script, with only two weeks on the road, made it difficult to get an overall view of the show. It was not till I saw a runthrough in New York that I realized that this was not the play we had set out to do. I felt sick about it, for, no matter how the changes had come about, it was up to me to have seen before this that the play had gone wrong. In the wee hours I wrote Gadge a letter that he found in the morning slipped under his door. I begged him, in a way that makes me cringe to remember, to agree to postpone the opening for five days in order to restore the play to what it had been. I pledged—a little too nobly—to pay personally whatever losses the postponement would involve.

Unfortunately, the deadline for decision was noon. Early that morning I had locked Gadge into my living room with a now unfamiliar script, the one we had agreed to do. I then asked Tabori to come over.

Gadge reluctantly conceded that the original was superior. Hearing this, Tabori at long last made an eloquent plea. Gadge seemed torn, then to my relief opted for postponement. He might change the play back; on the other hand, he might not. Would I forgive him if he took the five days and didn't restore the play? Time was running out. I had to take the chance.

By opening night he had polished the performances, but had left the play alone. I will never know whether we'd have had a success if Gadge had accepted my challenge, nor can I know how much his personal plight was responsible for all that had happened with the play.

Offstage, a bigger drama was unfolding. One evening during our brief run I was approached in a restaurant by Gadge's movie agent, who told me that Gadge was a hero and I would be proud of him; all I had to do was pick up the bulldog edition of the *Times*.

I read the paper with total disbelief. My head reeled. The unimaginable was there in print: Gadge had done an about-face politically. He had caved in and named names. He also had bought a quarter-page for an ad, defending what he had done and exhorting others to follow his lead.

When a devastated Tabori called the next morning, he insisted that our place was backstage during the matinee that day; the actors would need us. At the theatre, their stricken faces told it all. It was not necessary for anyone to say a thing. We stationed ourselves in the wings, lending moral and occasional physical support to the poor cast.

Gadge was such a number-one prize he had been permitted to testify in private session. With him, the Committee had hit the jackpot. Après lui le déluge.

However much he had wanted to stick to his principles, he simply didn't. He let down those who believed in him. I was the least of his victims, I only lost some illusions.

I made no effort to get in touch. From then on, when we met, Molly cut me dead. Gadge was tentative. For years his action estranged him from a lot of people he cared about, and I include myself among them. Some never forgave him. He was, on the whole, the man who was least forgiven, because he had been the epitome of courage and strength. After Molly died, he and I drifted back together and we're friends today—I think.

SIX MONTHS later I went political myself.

My father and I were both Republicans, but we never agreed politically. In addition, he was informed and I was not. In 1952 Jock got his last money from me to help Eisenhower against Mr. Taft, obviously my father's choice (although I'm not sure he wouldn't have preferred General MacArthur). When Taft lost out, Dad and I had a candidate in common. Not for long. When I saw Adlai Stevenson on television my immunity to politics ran out. My friend Marietta Tree, a hard-working Democrat and a great friend of Adlai's, was astounded when I joined the ranks. My father learned of my defection when he found my photograph on the front page of the *Herald Tribune,* in the very good company of Ethel Barrymore, Richard Rodgers, and Robert Sherwood.

What I lacked in experience I made up in passion. I turned my office and everyone in it—and a lot of money besides—over to the cause. We worked seven days a week. I was indefatigable. Nothing was too minor.

But nothing was too major either. George W. Ball, who ran Stevenson's campaign, has confirmed the fact that I even tackled Senator Wayne Morse, that bastion of Republicanism, and got him to come out of the closet and declare for Stevenson. Not only that, I persuaded him to head the list of Republicans who were switching parties, in a full-page ad we took in the *New York Times*.

We sent entertainers to political rallies; we had a speakers' bureau; we pitched in on various odd jobs. And we closed the campaign with a Madison Square Garden rally, with the added assistance of George Abbott and Joe Mankiewicz.

After that baptism I stayed a Democrat, but more important, a reasonably informed citizen. And none the worse for wear—better, in fact, because out of the campaign I made two wonderful friends, Clayton Fritchey, second in command, and Alan Jay Lerner, who with Bob Sherwood was the backbone of the Arts Committee.

"The Chalk Garden"

HAROLD FREEDMAN had just received a new script from London —*The Chalk Garden,* by Enid Bagnold—that was right up my alley. He was giving me first crack, so he needed a quick answer. He sounded excited, very unlike him.

I read it immediately. It made no sense at all. It had some wonderful dialogue, but was simply not a play. Harold argued in vain. He said I'd be sorry.

That didn't stop him sending me other plays. In rejecting them, I occasionally teased him by saying, "I'd rather do *Chalk Garden* than *that!*" "It's curious you keep bringing up *Chalk Garden.*" He insisted I have another look. "How come such a gem is lying on your shelf all these months?" It had my initials on it; in fact, no one else had seen it, which told me a great deal.

It improved on second reading. It had possibilities, but there was too much wrong with it. Also, I was suspicious. Why first to an American, and why the hard sell for something so in need of work? Harold was forced to confess it had been turned down by everyone in England, beginning with Binkie, but he still had faith in the piece. He asked what I *really* thought about it. Having heard me out, he led me to believe that my notions were peerless. Wouldn't I repeat them to Enid in a letter? Of course not, it would be presumptuous. She was a noted writer, and an old lady besides (at least to me then; she was all of sixty-four!). Harold didn't tell me she'd been at it for years and was in torment, and that my letter would give him a breather. He said it would be of great assistance to him. And to her; she needed another voice. I would not get involved. That's how it all began.

As a compromise, I wrote the letter to Harold and made it clear he was free to reveal as much as he saw fit. I criticized, analyzed, suggested; the play had intriguing passages, but didn't hang together; it was over-written and yet incomplete. It was a two-thousand-word letter, and I worked as hard on it as though I were dying to land the play. Harold sent it to Enid in toto. By return mail I got a letter more than twice its length, which she later confessed had been "intended to hook" me into helping her rework the play. I thought it would take a few months. Naturally, if I had known, etc., etc.

Before we were through, hundreds of letters had flowed between us and I had made countless trips to England. By then London had become, as New York once had been, my home away from home, so it was far from a hardship to go oftener and stay longer. I soon told Binkie what I was up to. He, her real god, said: "Oh, not her! She's a demon-lady." She had peppered him with calls and notes for years. When the first act was final, I eagerly handed it to Binkie. He was pale when he gave back the pages. It seemed unchanged to him! He begged me for my sake not to go on; if I agreed, I could have any production of his, current or future. Anything I wanted, anything. I was ruffled, but stubborn.

Enid had produced four children, a volume of verse, and several novels, being best known in America for *National Velvet* and *Serena Blandish*. When her husband, Sir Roderick Jones, had been chairman of Reuters, they had entertained on a fashionable scale in their house in Hyde Park Gate in London. Now they lived modestly in the village of Rottingdean, a few miles from Brighton. Sir Roderick, at seventy-six long retired, had dwindling interests; Enid was still flaming forward. Parties and people had faded away. Their life would be whatever Enid brought to it.

Enid found novels a long and solitary pursuit. The theatre offered contacts and intimacy. Greedy for praise, affection, and the last crumb on the plate, she was also shamelessly stagestruck. I have known no one else in my life as eager for laurels as Enid still was at sixty-four. One felt that no triumph—social or artistic—could have sufficed. Compliments intox-icated her; if necessary, she settled for flattery. In short, she craved celebrity.

Enid towered over her husband, but Roderick, diminutive as he was, ruled the roost. This roost, called North End House, had originally been two cottages put together. The Joneses added an adjacent boardinghouse, with its rabbit warren of rooms. The result was a very strange shape indeed, haphazard and higgledy-poo. Enid worked in what she called her tower. It was many flights up and hard to find, because the staircases weren't related. I never did figure out on which of the cottages the tower room actually perched. It was an attic, bare except for a work table and two chairs. It was bare of heat as well. "Ah, these thin-blooded Americans." She closed the window. I was still cold. She furnished me with a portable heater before she ever admitted she had an electric pad tucked into a blanket, unseen by me, that was wrapped around her legs.

I put up with an incredible mattress, which I privately named the Bumpy Road to Broadway; but I did complain that I couldn't read with a fifteen-watt bulb. She replied that I'd be with her earlier in the morning if I didn't read at night. When I tried that, she said I was leaving her no thinking time.

At first it was an adventure. I had nothing to lose. I'd catch the Brighton Belle on Friday at noon and take the train back after lunch on Monday, as delighted to get out as Enid was to see me go. She, however, had her work cut out and would have to face me again on Friday.

When we began, her attention was more on me than on the play. My background and life excited her curiosity. She was certain there was lots of drama and hidden romance and thought of me as living in satins and jewels, which she found when she poked through my closets in London. "Why so simple in Rottingdean?" I had never before been regarded as an exotic.

Enid didn't tangle with the word "Jewish." "Do Hebrews . . ." I explained that people like me were customarily called Jews. I should have said, "Why not Israelites?" I told her I didn't like talking about myself, we'd better get back to work.

Her gift for language was not confined to the written page, it spilled out in her conversation. She was a remarkable raconteur and, being a novelist, was inventive. I, particularly, was made highly colorful. With the children there for Sunday lunch, she described what she imagined was the luster of my Hollywood position and Broadway successes. "Enid, please, *no.*" She wanted me to shine by entertaining the family with extravagant reminiscences. To the children, skeptical of her theatrical skills, I was a trophy, the living proof that she was to be taken seriously.

At the same time, she exaggerated the rigors of her work and her martyrdom at my hands. Roderick, being factual, knew better, but he was glad to have me there for her sake, and honored me nightly with his best claret.

Enid's plays were not thought out in advance. A random line would start her off, and then the piece would take on a life of its own, a practice not conducive to structure. Enid's first grandchild, Annabel, had come to stay one summer. Enid thought she required a governess and, accordingly, she placed an ad in the Brighton paper. One young woman who applied both intrigued and appalled Enid. Interviewing her, she thought: "What am I taking into my house? How do I know this woman is not a murderess or perhaps out of a lunatic asylum?" She didn't engage her, but she put that on paper, and *Chalk Garden* began. The two leads were Miss Madrigal, the governess, and Mrs. St. Maugham, an elegant old lady living in the country, who says: "I lower my net and who knows what treasure comes up in it?"

A great many years later Enid placed an ad in a London paper, saying, "I am lonely." She signed it, "Lady Jones (Enid Bagnold)" and added: "Enquiries will be encouraged." Coming from anyone else, this might be considered brazen or pathetic. I'm sure it was neither, just Enid in search of material. Had publicity resulted, she wouldn't have minded; she always loved a spotlight.

Her energy was boundless—she insulted it by taking a handful of Benzedrine every morning. She was heroic in her resolve as well as her build, and had the courage of a lion. When it came to determination, I was fluff compared to Enid. If she couldn't be young, she made a weapon of her years. "At my age one knows these things." More often she blackmailed me with how long she'd worked on the play, how old she was, and how little time Roderick had left. When other strategies failed, she resorted to flattery. There she went too far. I told her that if I were all that clever, I'd write a play myself.

She wooed me as much as she fought me; there were times she was loving and grateful. She was also resentful, not of my contribution, but of her dependence. If only my gift (or my trick, as she often called it) were contagious, she could dispense with me. Fortunately, we never quarreled, but there were tense moments: "My dear girl, how do you think I've been writing all these years?" She quickly added, "Although admittedly you're helpful."

Guilt rose readily and often in Enid. When we'd have a good morning, she'd confess to having harbored black thoughts and beg forgiveness. At lunch she'd retract to Roderick what she had told him the previous night. Nevertheless, I grew increasingly fond of her, she was so admirable and touching in her reach. I had taken no option on the play and had no obligation, but I got in deeper and deeper and so did she. Apparently Harold telephoned her frequently: "He says it's you or nobody, so I suppose I must." She admitted that he had also reminded her "the bird is not yet caught." When the correspondence grew a burden, I'd fly to England. The reverse would find me back in New York.

Enid was long on felicitous prose and short on logic. She tended to build up to key scenes and then shirk them. Because she felt she couldn't write them, she denied the need, with a stubbornness born of desperation. Defiance was thrown out at a luncheon guest: "Irene thinks I'll do it, but I shan't." Eventually she did, with muffled anger and an occasional tear of self-pity.

Her satisfaction once a scene was right sustained her faith in me. A structured story emerged. It was there, all of it; it had to be, because I couldn't create it. She was the artist, I was the carpenter and the school-marm. Generously, Enid said of me in her autobiography: "Nobody has ever got so near writing without writing."

She also wrote: " . . . none of [Irene's] questions was as simple as it looked." At our first session I had disconcerted her by asking, "What is the story?" Her reply disconcerted me in return: "Whatever you want it to be." The truth was, she didn't know (at least consciously), because she kept changing the focus as she went along. Motivations pointed like arrows in all directions. That meant a lot of hacking away and rearranging. No scene remained untouched. Lines were shifted not only from one act to another, but often from one character to another. Yet with luck the play would not seem different, only better (the way unsuspected alterations can make a dress becoming). There would be no fingerprints, I would impose nothing. But then I always worked best behind someone else.

She would try to get lines by me as though smuggling them through customs. "Oh, I knew you'd catch me out." Or she'd ask me to rate stuff according to her effort. "I suppose you think I came by this lightly." Some days not one line was achieved. Other days she'd say, "How can I write with you sitting there?" Then practically in the same breath, "Ah, I have it." As she handed it to me, she'd sniff, throw her head back, and say, "There you are. Nothing to it."

When a word wasn't in the dictionary, I told her it couldn't be in the play. When Enid couldn't explain what a sentence meant, she called it elliptical. I said if the audience was busy weighing the meaning, they'd miss the next line. Words alone were not enough, nor mellifluous, cascading sentences; we wouldn't get actors to speak those lines, or audiences to sit still for them.

She was so wedded to her bon mots, she would make a hash of a scene for the sake of a line she adored. She called them plums, as in Christmas pudding, but they came in such clumps it gave one indigestion. The only solution was redistribution. I took them away by the dozen. I didn't rob her, just hoarded them in a box like pieces from a jigsaw puzzle, then used them to fill spaces for which they seemed perfectly designed. A plum would come into its own.

There was no longer a manuscript, just heaps of pages, the approved along with the discarded. I couldn't think for the disorder. I sent for Babbin, who could solve just about anything. While she was at it, I landed her with my box of plums to classify.

With about six months yet to go on the script, I told Harold I thought we had a play. In that case, he wanted to talk terms. I assumed them to be "standard." Not at all, he wanted top terms for Enid. From *me!* I couldn't believe it. He said he could get them from quite a few producers around town. "How dare you do this? You couldn't even show the play!" He said: "I couldn't then; I can now." Harold, having had his fun, compromised with me.

The play had a special style which would be hard to bring off, so I thought George Cukor wonderfully suited to it. Although twenty-five years away from the theatre, he was still considered stage-oriented. He found the prospect amusing. It was quite a coup when he agreed to do it. And with George as an added inducement, I could hardly fail to get our mutual friend Kate as Madrigal. She was the only one I could see in the part, and my heart was set on it. I had always longed to do a play with Kate.

When Hepburn first turned us down, I didn't take it too seriously. She would change her mind just as I had; if I held to the hope and worked hard enough, I'd win out. The trouble with my theory was, she didn't like the play. But I was certain she would. I tried once again with the next draft. I kept at it. Well, the best-laid schemes . . .

(Kate didn't much like *Chalk Garden* even when she saw it, yet there was something in that play that made me think she and Enid were a natural; I was determined to get them together someday. I made one attempt. Kate was going to London and I gave her Enid's phone number and address, saying "Lady Jones, Rottingdean" was sufficient. "One needn't put North End House." Kate chose to phone. "Hello, Lady North . . ." "Who?" "Lady North." "Come again." "Lady Jones." "There, that's better." They didn't meet then, but it was the beginning of a relationship which resulted in Kate's doing Enid's last play, *A Matter of Gravity,* twenty years later. My idea was right; my calendar was wrong.)

Failing Kate, there was no list of ladies to turn me down, apart from Wendy Hiller, who didn't want to leave England. Nor did any agent come up with a valid suggestion. I began to feel the part could not be cast and I would have to consider postponement.

At about that time I was sitting in a London night club when a woman passed by who suited the part perfectly if only she were an actress; she had that indefinable quality Madrigal needed. The woman turned out to be Siobhan McKenna, Ireland's noted star.

Siobhan was almost impossible to land, for the simple reason that after accepting the role she vanished without signing a contract. It didn't bode well; for all I knew, she had changed her mind. I was dying to tell her to go to hell, but instead tracked her down to a remote little island off the Irish coast and had then to send a man far out in a rowboat to reach her. In the end she was worth any effort.

She proved the most dedicated of our actors, the one to whom Enid was a heroine. She was a true believer and understood every line Enid had written. All the praise she was given was well deserved.

Fortunately, Mrs. St. Maugham was easier to cast. The most obvious choice for the role was Gladys Cooper, except, of course, for Edith Evans. (Enid had so worshiped Dame Edith that at an early stage of the play, years before I came on the scene, she had cycled seventeen miles to drop a copy at her house and, according to Binkie, had "blotted her copybook" with the Dame.)

Gladys was known to take three months to reach a decision, but this time she cabled in three days: ". . . THRILLED TO PLAY THE PART. LOVE GLADYS." Those words were to come back to haunt her.

Gladys had had fifty years in the theatre, a star both in London and in New York. She arrived jaunty and still beautiful, a woman of considerable charm who when crossed was sharp, icy. She was as tough as Enid and imperious as well. As experts on the English, Enid and Gladys were a stand-off. Nor could either exercise the authority of age, as they were only a year apart.

I kept sending George copies of my Enid correspondence, but he didn't have time to read them. He was involved with preparations for a movie called *Bhowani Junction,* but I was not to worry.

He was still behind schedule when he got to New York and hadn't yet caught up with our script, so to help him along I had a scale model of the set ready for him in his suite. "Whatever for?" So he could block his scenes, for heaven's sake! A tiny doubt crossed my mind.

It should have been an ideal situation for him. He and Enid got along famously, Gladys was a pal of many years, and Cecil Beaton, the designer, was then still a friend. There was also Irving, whom he had originally sent to me. I thought George would be in his element, and he was—until rehearsals began. He said: "Now let me see . . . " Gladys said, "Suppose I just stand here," and placed herself stage center. She became the hub of the wheel and the other actors the spokes. George seemed to like all her suggestions. She got the major part of his attention, and Siobhan suffered benign neglect without a murmur. It was all I could do to keep Enid in her seat.

The staging was as professional as Gladys could make it. She had the bit in her teeth and George in the palm of her hand. Well, she may have been an actor-manager, but she was no director.

George, alas, was no longer stage-wise by 1955. Looking straight on from the center of the house, he naturally could see everyone, but that wasn't the case from the sides, so I spoke to him about the sight-lines. (Technicalities were always his short suit.) Still concerned a few days later, I asked him to stand with me to one side to see what I meant. He didn't know what I was talking about and blew up. "Sight-lines! God-dammit, where'd you pick up that word?" He told me it was an affectation and to stop using it. I could hardly answer that sight-lines were older than Broadway, and that he had simply forgotten both the principle and the term. I really began to worry.

That was not all. While I couldn't blame him for taking *Bhowani Junction* as seriously as I took my play, from the time he arrived he had been on the phone to Culver City about whether he really should go back for retakes. And indeed he left in the middle of rehearsals, when every hour counted. It was unsettling, to say the least.

It was agreed that Enid take over in his absence. She not only had the courage, she had the urge as well, having been sitting out front fit to burst. Enid had been crestfallen to learn that the playwright must not comment to actors, only to her director. When she couldn't contain herself, I invoked Harold, and she reformed. Now the stage was hers; at last she could have at the actors. With the assistance of our stage manager, she "unblocked" George's scenes, to the relief of everybody but Gladys. A few days later, as lunch hour began, I could hear backstage voices growing louder and louder. They were unmistakably Enid and Gladys. I heard Enid: "See here, I know what's intended!" Gladys' voice shrilled out: "Novelist! Amateur!" I may as well say it—the two old girls were going at each other.

It had begun with the first rehearsal when George, having heard Enid read her play aloud, insisted she do so for the entire cast, because he admired her tone and inflection. Enid, proud and all a-tingle, did it superbly, obviously at her best as Mrs. St. Maugham. Gladys took against her then and there, and started calling her Miss Bagnold. After this set-to, she took to calling her Lady Jones.

The matter of dentures also came between them. Gladys, in her day the reigning beauty of England, didn't much fancy making her first entrance saying, "You can't fit false teeth to a woman of character," having just slipped something into her mouth—a lower plate, to be precise. She got her own back at Enid opening night in New York. She simply omitted the line.

A lot was accomplished in George's absence, and on his return he was understandably upset about Enid's restaging, but he took over where she had left off. He still didn't really know the script. The tension was awful. I watched and watched, and at last I decided. Darling George or not, he would have to be replaced—once again. If it wasn't one Selznick, it was another. I've mercifully forgotten the details, but I fired him at the back of the theatre in the middle of a rehearsal. To his credit, he carried on as though nothing had happened—and magnanimously offered to stay on until I found someone or, if need be, even till New Haven, which he did. It was very stylish of him. If he had hard feelings, he contained them. The day he left we had a sentimental breakfast. In other words, I wept.

Meanwhile, I had set about the awkward task of finding another director. No one quite bought my story that George had been called back by the studio; I just appeared to have a show in trouble. After a handful of directors begged off, I appealed to Harold. To him, it was elementary: never mind who you want, who can you get?

A director, Albert Marre, due back from London on Sunday, had asked Harold to look out for something for him. Mr. Marre, having made some money on a big musical geared to mass appeal, wanted, Harold said, "to do something 'high-class.' I think you can grab him." He was no sooner off the plane than he had a script. Enid, Irving, and I waited in my apartment all that afternoon for his call. Instead, he showed up without warning and handed me the script as I opened the door. He wouldn't come in. Quite briefly, quite bluntly, he didn't care for it. "It's too *o-blike.*"

I dragged him inside and somehow got him pinned to a seat in the living room. I brought Enid in, whether to woo him or have him break the news to her gently, I know not—probably both. However, I had first taken the precaution of *obleeking* him twice. Irving and I sat in the study and speculated on what was taking so long. What could it mean?

It meant only that Mr. Marre had been running her play down. When Enid rejoined us, she said: "What a common young man. It's just as well. *O-blike!* What was Harold thinking of!"

I next saw Mr. Marre twelve days later in New Haven. Harold had sent him there to see the show for the simple reason that we hadn't yet got anyone else. I had found the prospect embarrassing, but Harold told me to ignore his presence unless he lingered as the house emptied; I should take that as my cue.

Well, there he was! No mention was made of our previous meeting, we just spoke as though the matter were settled. He couldn't join us until Tuesday in Boston. I could let George off the hook then.

There was plenty of work before the opening there, so George called a rehearsal for Boston on Sunday afternoon. When the company assembled at four o'clock, Gladys was not present, nor had she reached her hotel. George was certain there was a misunderstanding; I feared an accident on the road; Irving was plain suspicious.

My first phone call found her cheerily at home in Mount Kisco. Gladys, who didn't know her lines, was taking the day off. I told her to get going, I'd be waiting for her. She arrived past midnight, then took her own good time and a long, hot bath. She stalled until one-fifteen.

I had a mighty good case against Gladys, but said I was not going to give her the luxury of being fired, which would have suited her perfectly. I pointed out the enormity of her behavior—the best she could hope for was not being brought up on charges before Equity. She again called Enid "nothing but a novelist," which scarcely served as a defense. Thereupon she panned both Enid and the play to me. I had to remind her that she had used the word "thrilled" in her cable of acceptance. I had a further grievance: that very evening I had learned we had a Cassandra in our midst. Gladys had been sending forecasts of doom everywhere. I told her not to rely on her predictions, as we were going into New York and she with us, so she might just as well become as good as she possibly could.

To end on a friendlier note, I decided to take her into my confidence by telling her we were "losing" George. She voiced no regret, gave him not even lip-service, but made an instant reappraisal: "Ah, yes, I see." Receiving this exclusive news somewhat restored her dignity. She took her leave like a fellow conspirator and thereafter buckled down to work. I gave her a success in spite of herself.

Apart from seeing the play produced, Enid had most set her heart on having her friend Cecil Beaton design the show. ("You mustn't mind him. He's malicious, but he's amusing and a darling.") Enid had once loaned him her next-door cottage, and he had brought her all the color and gossip of his life. They would be friends forever; she counted on him as the companion of her old age.

They had in common their skill with a brush, their love of gardening, a taste for the great world, and Diana Cooper as friend. And, undeniably, the theatre. Cecil fancied himself a playwright and felt as entitled to a production as Enid.

Second only to having a play of his own done, Cecil wanted to design *Chalk Garden*. I, however, had a strong reason not to use him. In 1938 he had illustrated an article for *Vogue* which lamented the intrusion of show people into the ranks of Long Island society. There was nothing racial in the piece, but on the opening two-page spread, garlanded with Cecil's illustrations of country versus café society, amongst the flowers and gift cards were the names of Mrs. Mayer, Mrs. Goldwyn, and, most clearly, Mrs. Selznick. Nearby, in tiny but just visible print, there appeared twice a nasty four-letter word for Jew.

There was a great uproar. The matter reached the press, and in New York it even made the front page. *Vogue* advertisers, many of whom were Jewish, pulled out in droves. The edition had to be reprinted, and Condé Nast's friends feared the magazine might go under. Beaton's *Vogue* contract was canceled, and he didn't return to America for many years.

Enid's dream of Cecil cosseting, admiring, designing seemed doomed. My attitude was: no feud, but no hiring. However, his offense was long since past and amply paid for. It was small-minded of me to deny her something that meant so much. Besides, he was right for the production. In the end, I yielded.

The set, all white, cream, and ivory, was lovely, but the actors' faces against it went blank. Once again Kookie came to the rescue. ("Where were you when I needed you?" He was a telephone call away.) He arrived in New Haven and announced that it wasn't the lights; the set had the wrong tones of white and must be repainted to bring it down a couple of shades. He added that I must warn Cecil. Cecil took it well enough to show up Monday morning in Boston with a smock and brushes to supervise and add his own touches, and, to our relief, that night the actors' expressions could be seen. However, as Enid and I reached the exit, Cecil slithered past and hissed at her, "You'll be glad to know your show went better, my dear, but you have completely ruined my set." Enid stood as though struck by lightning. She claimed he was seething, might never forgive her. I thought it was momentary and that he'd come round, because she could grant him the London production. Her fear was almost palpable.

After Albie Marre got to Boston the next day, he had little time for the actors, and Enid had even less for me. Despite their inauspicious beginning, she stayed closeted with her new mentor as precious days went by. I let them be. Abruptly Albie came to me, saying, "Keep that woman away from me!" By then he loathed her. But not as much as she loathed him.

Enid showed up drenched in tears of remorse, calling herself disloyal, ungrateful, and a fool to have taken the bait. Vanity had done her in. Apparently Albie had asked if she had a copy of the original script. After studying it for a day, he had asked why, when it was so good, had she changed it? She had drunk in his praise and turned to putty. He had then given her his own ideas of script. She tried, but he didn't get any new scenes, and I believe they wound up insulting each other. She was utterly ashamed of the whole episode.

One big happy family we were not. Poor Enid. First Gladys no talkee. Then Cecil. And Albie made three.

They were easily kept apart. I became the go-between and he never knew whether the notes I gave him came from me or from Enid. What I didn't give him were the alterations in the set he suddenly wanted. The set was fine; it was the actors who needed the work.

Mr. Marre didn't much like any of us. Nor, it seemed, did he want us to like one another. While having a bite of supper with me late in the Philadelphia run, he saw Gladys and Siobhan come in together and said, "This is something new. I'll have to break it up." It was a miracle we made it into New York. Fortunately, the cast didn't leave their first really good performance behind in Philadelphia. They saved it for opening night.

We played the Barrymore for five months. In that period the play opened in London. Binkie hadn't wasted time on humble pie. He cabled immediately after our opening, full of congratulations, enthusiasm, and anticipation. He got Edith Evans and Peggy Ashcroft for Enid, with John Gielgud directing. The notices were superb, dazzling. While Brooks Atkinson and Walter Kerr had been flattering, Kenneth Tynan went overboard. He said: " . . . a wonder happened: the West End theatre justified its existence. . . . The occasion of its triumph . . . may well be the finest artificial comedy to have flowed from an English . . . pen since the death of Congreve. . . . "

The show packed the Haymarket Theatre for twenty-three months, a glorious twenty-three months for Enid. That success shaped the rest of her days. She had everything but honors from the Queen, and that too came in time. But the one thing she had wanted most was to have Cecil back, and he, alas, was not that easily had. He had surfaced for one day in Philadelphia and for opening night in New York, but Enid saw him only at a distance; he didn't choose to see her either in America or in England.

Some time later, still lonely for him, she sent him an expensive set of fire tools with rock-crystal handles. By then he had the grievance of the successful London production. (Our London set was so terrible it should have given him sufficient revenge.) He didn't return the gift, but he didn't thank her either. She just went on yearning for him. He nearly broke her heart. In her memoirs, almost fifteen years later, she was still hoping he would come back: "I have suffered—if that's any joy to him." No doubt it was.

THE WRITER who came into my life after Bagnold was no less than Graham Greene. Apart from being novelists-turned-occasional-playwrights, all that these two had in common was nationality and the connection to me. They were diametrically opposed in everything else, including theatrical wisdom. Furthermore, Enid was drenched in words, while Graham was born edited.

In the spring of '59, Binkie handed me a new Greene play, *The Complaisant Lover,* which he was about to put into rehearsal. It was mine for New York if I liked it.

I simply loved it, but Binkie suggested I not commit myself until I saw it out of town. I agreed, but assured him I would do it anyhow, because if it didn't go well in Liverpool, it would not be the fault of the play.

I had already met Graham Greene in the home of a mutual friend, Peter Glenville, and he had seemed the least pretentious of men. Now, faced with doing his play, I was suddenly intimidated by his body of work. However, in working with him I found him cozy rather than thorny, patient rather than unpredictable. I even thought him a little shy, until I discovered the gleam in his eye whenever he was about to say something wicked. He was, on the whole, just delightful. Nevertheless, I was always afraid of Graham Greene, except of course when I was with him.

Graham's patience was tested during the two years it took me to get *The Complaisant Lover* on. When a play has casting troubles, I figure there's something wrong either with the play or with the producer. There was nothing wrong with this play; I simply couldn't cast it. I worried that the unconscionable delay might reflect on the play, but Graham, who should have objected, was the least critical.

We knew whom we wanted, but Ralph Richardson, who was superb in England, wouldn't repeat his role, and Alec Guinness refused it. We refused everyone else.

I next began on Americans. Freddy March, then Robert Preston turned it down, followed by Ralph Bellamy. No one wanted to compete with Sir Ralph. We reverted to the English. A suggestion of Graham's that I thought interesting but extreme was Robert Morley. He happened to be in New York, and was delighted to come and see me. When he left my office, I wrote to Graham:

November 24, 1959

. . . Morley came to see me late yesterday, all of him. I found it very easygoing. I didn't turn out to be at all as tongue-tied as I had feared, as he is the most outgoing creature alive and brimming over with zest and recklessness. He started off by saying he hoped I had a play for him. I had. He hoped I had more than one, all new, and to be done in England. He could act in one and produce the others—the more the merrier! His face fell when he heard New York, and the room bounced with refusals before I could even tell him what the project was. [Eventually he listened and "went straight" long enough to make a conservative speech about being deeply flattered.] He has not seen the play, but refused even to read it lest he lead me down the garden path. He said he was too old to have any role tempt him, but even if it did, he would get back to England and somehow get out of it. . . .

All in all he was quite an enjoyable experience—apart from refusals which I loathe—he has without doubt the most extravagant personality I've ever encountered. He confided to me that he adores disasters, particularly on stage, and neat planning is anathema to him. Goodness Gracious!

I'd never been as frustrated. I offered to withdraw. Months later it was Graham's turn. He cabled: "LET'S GIVE UP. NO FUN IN RAGBAG." And he followed it up with a gallant letter: "I sent you a cable of despair, but I really think we shouldn't bother [with the ragbag] but call it a day. I'd naturally pay back the advance. . . . Let's wait for another play." I redoubled my efforts.

The play was a smash in London and what I would call a failure in New York. We ran only three months. I made my initial error by casting Michael Redgrave. Not that it was Michael's fault, but he simply was not a good, stout fellow who happened to be a dentist—not remotely. Regardless of who proposed Michael or who agreed, ultimately it was my responsibility and I was therefore to blame.

Graham let me off easy. He wrote: ". . . I have many bad memories of the theatre, but you—and all our grim and funny efforts with TCL —are some of the really good memories." I read the play over not long ago and found it as delicious as ever. Oh dear.

I have one footnote: There was a piece of casting for which I did take credit. Kazan, who wanted me to take an interest in the Actors' Studio, had, as a rare privilege, let me attend an entrance audition. I certainly didn't go hoping to find an actor for an English comedy; however, one young applicant was so appealing that I asked him to read for a role he couldn't conceivably fill, a Dutchman, for which he was twenty years too young and forty pounds too light. No part was ever more quickly redefined. And thus Gene Wilder made his debut, making a very large dent in not so big a part.

THE FIRST hint that I should stop producing plays came when I misjudged *Look Back in Anger* and *A Taste of Honey*. The theatre was changing, but I wasn't changing with it. Perhaps more important, I felt that I just hadn't done what I'd set out to do—it had turned into something much grander than helping out a few struggling playwrights; I certainly had never planned on a career or a life work! And the obligations had grown with the success of the whole operation. As usual, I had been over-conscientious—about my little company, about the theatre itself. I resented being a prisoner of my office and felt guilty if I wasn't there. I had been on call—to my family, to David, to my work —since I was tiny. Now I wanted options and, luckily, I could afford them. Once again I was quitting while I was ahead, and with my reputation intact. In my mid-fifties I took early (but not premature) retirement.

My Father

IN 1938 my father had found a new interest which helped fill his life: he lost his head, not over women, but over horses. This was as sudden as it was implausible. I had thought he never quite approved of racetracks. Anyhow, he threw himself into it as though he were creating a studio, and used some of the same methods. He aimed for quality and looked for talent.

The racing fraternity viewed him as a Johnny-come-lately, as indeed he was. When a newcomer to racing begins to really buy, there is lots of curiosity and lots of criticism. My father earned his share by an incredible turnover of trainers. Then, when he got a man who suited him, it all changed; he began to be a big winner. The papers stopped making cracks and my Eastern racing friends stopped baiting me.

He bought still more horses, but changed his focus. Believing as he did in bloodlines, he found that the thrill lay in breeding rather than racing. To prove that California was as good a place to breed horses as Kentucky, he bought five hundred acres seventy miles from town and created a place not only ideal to breed and train horses, but also to shine as a grandfather.

His rise in this new field was more spectacular than the rise of MGM in the Twenties. In 1945 he was the country's leading money winner and, beginning in 1945, for three years running, the country's leading breeder of stakes winners.

Then in the late Forties he began a series of dispersal sales which apparently were without precedent in their magnitude and prices. I didn't know why he was forced to do this, nor did I question him. One reason certainly was the time and concentration diverted from his job, but I believe the settlement on my mother and possibly tax problems played their part.

Four years after my parents' separation, my father married Lorena Danker, a vivacious widow, between Edie and me in age, who made it her business not to be on bad terms with anyone. She had a bright, earnest daughter, Suzanne, about twelve, whom my father later adopted. I had a pleasant relationship with Lorena, but my heart was with the child. Suzie found her situation confusing. Her mother, inclined to flatter, kept telling her to do as she herself did—say yes to my father, always smile and be affectionate. My father told her to pattern herself after me. I told her to be herself and never to say what she didn't mean. Suzie leaned on me, Lorena on Edie. But the important thing was that my father had companionship again, and a home.

In 1950 my father's dream of breeding a Kentucky Derby winner almost came true. He was inordinately proud that he had bred the favorite. The horse, Your Host, was raced under Bill Goetz's colors, but I have forgotten the precise details of the ownership and the reason for the mystery thereof. Bill, although relatively new to racing, refused, in the weeks prior to the race, to take my father's advice about when and where the horse should run, thereby making, in my father's opinion, a series of unsound decisions.

After listening to my father and then to Edie, nothing could have induced me to attend. By Derby Day, Edie was filled with visions of triumph, and my father with dire predictions. Father and daughter were so hostile that they didn't even sit together. Your Host went to the post at eight to five, led for the first mile, and then finished ninth. My father felt the race had been needlessly lost and was thoroughly incensed.

Back at the hotel, he called Bill and sailed into him, which outraged Edie. She grabbed the phone and blasted Dad, who thereupon lit into her. It was the first real collision of those terrible tempers since 1923. Dad gave her some down-home truths, and there was nothing Edie minded so much as being reminded. She slammed the phone down on him.

Edie was so aggrieved she no longer felt indebted to him. She vowed to get even; she didn't want peace, she wanted victory. My father bitterly weighed the Goetzes' ingratitude. He felt victimized.

What he and Edie had said to each other that day in Lexington stung so badly that they proceeded to denounce each other right and left. It was inconceivable that such a thing could happen in my family. I still believed we cared about unity. I begged them to stop broadcasting. I refused to hear them out because neither one could be reasoned with. That I wouldn't take sides upset them both. I was grateful I lived in New York.

By 1952 it had somewhat simmered down, but there was no real healing. My father could still have been reached with a mea culpa. Then, during the political campaign, Bill co-hosted a cocktail party for Adlai Stevenson with Dore Schary (who had helped oust Dad from MGM the previous year). Bill said that had been unavoidable, but my father viewed it as betrayal. Edie said her political freedom and loyalty to her husband were at stake. She gloried in her defiance and said it was forever. Bill took to making obscene jokes about my father. It was doubly offensive because once at a dinner party I was sitting at the table. I stared straight ahead, and it is to my eternal shame that I did not get up and leave. I was still avoiding conflict.

The battle assumed epic proportions. My father must have felt that the alienation was permanent, because two years later he removed Edie from the board of his foundation and apparently made a new will. I never again heard him mention her name. When he said "my daughter," he referred to me.

Now, decades later, I have a new perspective. I find there was a pattern of divide-and-rule established by Edie when she came back from her honeymoon. By turning her back on Mother and me, by refusing to listen to us, she had permitted the first family split.

The year his daughters were married, my father, still smarting from that confrontation in his office, had needled me by saying, "You'll see, I can make somebody out of anybody." He had, with Edie's help. And he had made, with Bill's help, a somebody out of Edie—somebody who also became a formidable enemy, one in his own image. All along David had said there would be a day of reckoning. Now the birds had come home to roost.

It got worse in 1957 when my father died. His will caused a scandal. One clause read:

"I make no bequest to my daughter Edith Goetz nor to her children nor to any other member of the Goetz family, as I have given them extremely substantial assistance during my lifetime, through gifts and financial assistance to my daughter's husband, William Goetz, and through the advancement of his career (as distinguished from that of my former son-in-law, David Selznick, who never requested nor accepted assistance from me) in the motion picture industry."

Because of the Goetz clause, the will hit the front pages.

But my father didn't have the last word. The will did anything but settle the score. It reminded Edie once again of things she most wanted to forget; it made her angrier still, and long after his death she was still having her revenge by what she said of him—to friends, to acquaintances, and, I'm afraid, to biographers.

I attributed my father's vigor at seventy-two to good genes and good habits. He, on the other hand, felt he owed his health to vigilance. Each year he reported that the doctors were astounded. "I am as fit as a man of forty." The only menace he acknowledged was cancer, which he felt could be defeated by early detection. However, in later years, having gotten tests and a clean bill of health in one city, he would repeat the procedure elsewhere, without revealing how much X-ray he had already received. When he took ill in the summer of 1957, he called his stay in the hospital "a check-up." Nevertheless, I began to phone his doctors as the weeks went by. But I learned nothing.

Suddenly he wanted to involve me. "Never mind all those other specialists. There's only one man to call, this fellow from Boston." Dr. Sidney Farber was worth the whole lot. I found that Dad had told him all about me.

Farber seemed glad to have me in the picture and talked of various blood disorders; the diagnosis was not yet certain. If I went to California right then, I would alarm Dad. I must be patient. He suggested that meanwhile I avoid emotionalism on the phone.

A few weeks later he gave me the green light, so I called Dad to say nonchalantly that I might be paying him a visit, that he was probably bored and things were slow in New York.

My real troubles with Edie began on that trip. It never dawned on me that if Dad were really sick, she wouldn't bend. She welcomed me with flowers, aquavit, and a calendar of social events, something for every night. That was the first indication I had of what her attitude to Dad's illness was to be. When she phoned to greet me, she was cordiality itself. And which invitations would I accept? None, for the moment; I wasn't planning on any going out. She found that unreasonable and was clearly annoyed.

When I arrived at the UCLA hospital, I was shaken to find Dad having a blood transfusion. He assured me he'd be home in a day or two.

However, the next morning was quite a different story. He was depending on me to find out what this was all about; he had to know, because his affairs were not in order. Dr. Lawrence, the head of the hospital, was expecting me. "If it's going to go on like this, you get me the pills and I'll take care of it."

Dr. Lawrence used the customary euphemisms. I finally asked him whether this could be a forerunner of leukemia. Deceived by my apparent calm, he announced that it *was* leukemia, and terminal. I wept uncontrollably. He put cold cloths on my face and drops in my eyes, and said I had better get back, Dad was waiting. I couldn't stand up. He gave me smelling salts and put me in a wheelchair, telling a nurse to rush me back.

I sat outside Dad's room a few minutes, wondering how to say what. I had never lied to him. However, I had never told him the entire truth. This was no time to start.

I pulled myself together and gave the acting performance of my life. As I sprang through the door, the light from the windows full upon me, I confronted my father angrily and told him there was going to be an end to nonsense and he was going to have to reform. He had to use the nurses he was employing, and the servants must go home. He was to stop bothering the technicians about the blood tests. There was going to be a whole new order.

My prologue sufficed. He was docile as a child and didn't ask me a question, then or ever again. That told me more than I had told him.

Lorena and Jessie Marmorsten, a devoted friend who was his local doctor, were disappointed in me because I hadn't told him the actual facts. I was relieved that I hadn't had to, and amazed that they hadn't prepared me. There was a great deal I didn't understand. And still don't.

My father's remark about his affairs not being in order hung in the air. He didn't retract it or repeat it. I didn't know whether it was a worry to him or a directive to me. I was remiss if I ignored it, insensitive if I pursued it. To mention his will would be tantamount to suggesting death. The only thing more indelicate would be to call his lawyer to ask about his will, which is exactly what I did.

I was aware that my father had promised bequests to Myron Fox, his bookkeeper, and Howard Strickling, a faithful friend. While I didn't want to trespass, I had to make certain they were remembered. Yes, they were, I was told by the lawyer, whom I knew. (Actually, my father had got him through me.)

My ears should have pricked up at what followed. Was there anything else I wanted to know? No, I was satisfied. Was I sure I didn't want to see the will? Of course I didn't! He offered to come to the hospital parking lot so I might read it!! He was a high-minded man and an upright citizen, and he was trying to tell me something, but in my condition I failed to pick up the signal. Had I known he was sitting on a tinderbox, I would have acted differently.

Meanwhile Edith was giving me a hard time. She was aloof when I called with my hospital bulletins and displeased when I continued to refuse invitations, which were veiled ultimatums. She insisted I was dramatizing Dad's condition. I had been dreading telling her about the leukemia and was shocked to discover she already knew. We were at cross-purposes. Although the hospital was five minutes from Edie's house, she made no move to see me throughout my entire stay. If I wasn't with her, I was against her.

I was at the hospital all day, every day, and so were the ladies, Lorena and Jessie. Exhaustion overtook me at night when I crept back to George Cukor's house, where I was staying.

Attuned to Dad as I was those weeks, I abided by the climate he established. In an unstated collaboration, we stayed away from anything provocative. He closed his mind to all else but getting well, and conserved his energies to better endure the necessary therapies. Specialists were called in to manage various complications resulting from the treatments and from the disease itself, and so he lived on a day-to-day basis. High-strung though he was, he demonstrated a self-control that I found extraordinary.

Suddenly his fever shot up to 105°. The situation became critical. I alerted Edith, who got angry. Dad wanted Dr. Farber, but I didn't dare summon him just like that from Boston. My father insisted. "Tell Farber I need him badly. He will come, I assure you." I repeated his words to Farber, who asked only that a car meet him at the airport that evening. Not until I hung up did Jessie tell me Farber would not take money.

Waiting through that long day, Jessie said that Farber's visit could be an opportunity for my father to learn that his illness was fatal; Farber was noted for his skill in breaking such news. Would I please ask him to do this. I refused because I felt Dad had made it clear he didn't want to know.

Preparations went on the entire day. People came and went to get my father into what he considered a presentable condition. Anything for

Farber. He even insisted on having himself packed in ice to lower his temperature.

Dad was uplifted by Farber's presence. Farber was his symbol of hope, and Dad attributed godlike qualities to him. That evening I spent hours with the doctor. He was a quiet man with a rare inner quality, a truly inspiring human being.

I apologized for having urged him to come when he couldn't be paid. He said he didn't accept fees because he couldn't have both freedom and money. He earned a modest salary from Harvard Medical School and from the children's cancer hospital he ran; he treated whom he pleased and where. All hospitals welcomed him because they acquired his advanced techniques and many donations for research from his grateful patients.

The next day Farber asked if I agreed with the ladies that he tell my father he was dying; he wouldn't do it without my consent. I said it was up to the patient, not the family. If Farber had been with him for the hours he had and my father hadn't questioned him, obviously Dad could best accept the reality by not acknowledging it. Anyhow, if he had to face up, he would also have to make a new will, and I didn't want him to do that either. I knew he intended to increase the amount he was leaving me, and I didn't need "more"; it was enough that he wanted me to have more. I certainly didn't want any extra via a deathbed will.

My father, in the next room, sent me a message through Farber—he didn't trust himself to discuss it directly. Would I please "not pull any surprises"; it was too late, and the possibility was making him uneasy. I would understand what he meant.

He needn't have worried. Edie had given me neither hint nor opening for such an undertaking. Perhaps it was bravado, or perhaps she had gone too far to do an about-face. I prefer to think she was "hoping to be sent for." (Later she was known to have said she had pleaded to see him, but had been refused.)

Then we came to what Farber wanted: I must go back to New York. "The only thing that could convince your father that he is not mortally ill is your leaving. He trusts you completely. If you mean what you say, you must go or your very presence will be telling him." He added that, judging by how I looked, I wasn't going to last anyhow. I must promise.

I said I couldn't do it. He said, "I don't mean right now." We agreed on a time limit.

What might have been a period of candor was one of indirection. Dad talked of few matters close to his heart. I had dreamed that someday my father and I would have an ultimate conversation, a chance for everything left unsaid and unasked. Now there was a sad realization that the occasion would never take place.

I brought him messages from the outside world. "David sends his love and is sorry you can't have visitors." My father said, "Why not? Did he really ask to come?" They must have had a great time, because the next day, when David left, my father said, "He's a fine fellow." A similar message from Kate resulted in another visitor. Hadn't he always told me she was a wonderful girl? He was glad we were such friends.

One day when my father was feeling comfortable, I remarked that I didn't know why I was hanging around—"I really think I ought to get out of here in a few days." The following day I mentioned, "I'm leaving day after tomorrow." Each time he ignored the information. He had chosen also not to recognize my departure, so the final day presented an added hurdle. He was in no condition for drama. There would be none if I could help it. Not one tear. Not the word "goodbye."

The day of departure he kept putting his hand out for me to hold. He said there were things he wanted to talk about. He made a plan for the next day. I finally had to remind him I was leaving. I began to thank him—he'd been through hell and had behaved wonderfully; I wanted him to know I appreciated it. I said it one way, then another. I was afraid to stop. It was a perilous moment.

His tears welled. He tried to talk, but could get no further than, "Tell Danny . . . tell Danny . . ." I didn't know what, but I said I would. I added quickly that I was off. "Let me know if you want me" was tossed over my shoulder. I fled the room without looking back. I wasn't sure he had heard me, but I had gotten it out. It broke my heart to leave him.

I later learned that he had heard me. He had heard me loud and clear.

I stayed in touch with Farber and with California. There was not as yet any remission. Lorena told me she had known I was smart, but not *that* smart—I had timed my visit brilliantly! Dad had been impossible, but I managed to get there just when his mood was changing and was shrewd enough to get out just before he grew difficult again. I felt that no ill-will was intended, that she was at her wits' end, but she conveyed more than she realized.

I found the long-distance vigil harder on me than attendance in the hospital. I couldn't work, I couldn't play. Distractions depressed me. I couldn't stand being with people. I was alone in the country on weekends. One Sunday I could bear it no longer. I had no premonition; I simply had to be in Los Angeles. I thought I'd hole up in a small hotel, making my presence known only to Dr. Lawrence. Hildur packed for me that afternoon.

Very early the next morning, as I was about to leave for the airport, the phone rang. It was Dr. Lawrence, asking if I could possibly come at once. My father had had a major setback and had been saying something repeatedly during the night, which the doctor hadn't been able to understand; just now he had realized it was "Send for my daughter. She said she would come." Dad was "in poor condition." He would be alive. Did I care if he was conscious? I told him to say I was on my way, in precisely those words, and to do what he thought best.

When I arrived, my father was unconscious. Dr. Lawrence told me the last words Dad had heard were "Your daughter is on her way." Around midnight Dr. Lawrence sent me home with Lorena to wait. He called an hour later to say the end had come.

I called Edie. She cut me off with: "I already know. I have my own sources." That was all, and it was the last straw. It was also the last word spoken between us for many years.

Next I phoned David, who arrived at once and took charge. Howard Strickling came, and so did Dad's great friend Clarence Brown. With Lorena and me sitting in, they settled the who, when, and where. When the most important decisions were out of the way, David said that they would finish up—I'd better go to bed, I looked terrible. I discovered that I couldn't make it. Once again he took care of me and carried me up the stairs.

The next morning I received from David masses of orchids and a letter I can quote only in part, because he paid me tribute beyond any woman's worth.

Afterwards

Dear Irene,

How strange, this vacuum he has left. It is not love that has been lost, nor tenderness, nor even paternal protection. Rather it is as though we had all lived fearfully in the shadow of a magnificent, forbidding Vesuvius, which is now suddenly removed: no more the little arbors huddled on its slopes, no more the threatening lava. . . . You, above all others, know that I never ate of the grapes nor feared the eruptions. Yet I could stand in awe. And I can feel that the world this day is different than all the days of our lives before....

Even this vein of writing is so foreign to me that I am amazed: what power the man had, even over those free of the best and the worst of him alike. . . .

You know the little religion that I have clung to—that what matters most is the continuity of life, and its improvement from one generation to another. Never has there been a greater example of its potential than in you. What are you going to do about it?

You remember too that I've always felt that every set-back or calamity has its purpose, if we but have the patience and perspicacity to find it. Because I have been so unexpectedly shaken by your father's death, I have sought its meaning. I think I have found it. The strange finish of your father's bizarre life can have meaning if, and only if, your own life is the fulfillment of what his might and could have been, if only he had had your character. . . .

David

David had summoned Jeff from Europe and advised Danny to stay put at Harvard. Jeffrey and I were to go to the funeral in the car with Lorena and Suzie. Then, suddenly, it appeared that Edie had decided to go to the funeral. Moreover, she wanted to go with us. Lorena asked if I minded. I told her I thought we should stick to our arrangement. However cruel, the fact was that Edie had made it impossible for me to ride with her on that occasion. Anything but that.

Edith went with her older daughter. The morning of the funeral there was an item in the *Hollywood Reporter* saying that Edith had had a deathbed reconciliation with her father. She didn't choose the family entrance, nor did she, I believe, go to the cemetery, but at least she was at the funeral.

As we waited in a side street for the procession, a remark of my father's came back to me. Some twenty years before, not far from the studio gate, he had said to Sam Behrman: "See that girl?" pointing to my retreating figure. "She will walk behind my coffin to the grave."

Just then Suzie claimed that she saw David across the street. "Hiding behind the bushes!" Sure enough. When the photographers dispersed, I beckoned. He came, explaining that he was standing there to make sure nothing went wrong until we were under way. I silently thanked him; I had never known such protection.

T W O - T H I R D S of my father's estate went to his foundation. Lorena, who was uninterested in foundations, felt that her share was insufficient and was unwilling to sign the waiver necessary for probate. For days she was behind locked doors on the telephone. She told me she was getting advice and considering going to court about the will. I didn't know whom she was talking to. It seemed the better part of valor not to find out. I was astonished that she thought I had something to do with that much money going to the foundation.

Suzie, who was devoted to my father, was heartsick. Weeping, she came to my room to say that Dad's will was fair and generous. It was a house divided, but there was no clash. Lorena remained pleasant to me, but food was scarce. I didn't want to make waves by moving to a hotel. I lay low until the storm clouds blew over and stayed until Lorena signed the waiver.

Edith's quarrel with my father might have become a closed book with his death, had it not been for the will. Edie set out to make herself a heroine by maligning Dad. She was no heroine and he had not been a villain. And, of course, there was no love lost on me. Years went by without communication. It was just as well.

My son Danny urged me for years after my father's death to end the long estrangement. He talked of sisters, family, and invoked the memory of Granny. He was even more inclined than I to peace at any price. Besides, he was fond of her, in a way.

Because of Danny's persuasions and to stop Edie talking, I agreed to a truce. It was makeshift because of her stipulation that nothing of the past be discussed. After a few years we mercifully drifted apart, may my mother forgive me. Trying to influence her was pointless. Anyhow, I couldn't keep track of her feuds. I frankly didn't give a damn who was top dog in the Beverly Hills social circuit, which is really what everything was about from the beginning.

A few years ago, out of the blue, I was startled to hear from Edith, who said, "What shall we do about our father?" She wanted me to join her in a lawsuit against a company which had portrayed him in a movie: she was concerned about his image. I let her off easy. I just said no.

New York

DESPITE evidence to the contrary, I kept on insisting through the late Forties and early Fifties that my stay in New York was temporary. Each year we went out to California for Christmas and for the summer; then we started skipping Christmas, and the summer trips got shorter. I was no Broadway producer on these periodic trips except for the first couple of weeks, when I would be a welcome guest of honor like all the visiting celebrities I remembered. I had given some of those dinners myself.

As time went by, keeping the house on Summit Drive made less and less sense, though I went on kidding myself that it represented security and continuity for the boys. I suppose the reality was that I couldn't see the future clearly and was acting on my motto: when in doubt, don't. The only ones I was fooling were myself and Uncle Sam, and he had caught up with me. According to Morgan Maree, I was about to face terrible tax trouble.

The boys didn't mind if I sold it. When I found a buyer in 1953, I consoled myself that my being permanently in New York would give my mother an excuse to come East. She liked nothing better than to see a show I'd produced. She gloried in whatever I accomplished (after all, "accomplishment" had always been high on her agenda) and got a tremendous thrill from my life in the big time.

After selling the house, more often than not I stayed with George

Cukor. But some things didn't change. Certain loving friends were always there to pick up where we left off—Janet Gaynor, Cary Grant, Rosalind Russell, of course my beloved Sara Mankiewicz, and the Goldwyns.

My friendship with the Goldwyns continued to grow even after I left California, as did David's. They remained devoted to the Selznicks, together or apart, and the Selznicks to them.

Sam respected achievement, so when my life in the theatre flourished, he paid attention, and when I'd come back to Los Angeles he'd give me the local-girl-makes-good treatment. The whole thing gave Frances vicarious delight; she made that clear by dubbing me "the happy pirate." Frances was a wise and endearing woman. Over the long stretch she was one of my Hollywood friends I most valued.

I took care to time my trips when Hepburn would be there. Kate and I liked to go swimming together when we were in California. Mind you, nothing as convenient as the pool at George's. Kate would bring masses of towels, a huge lunch, and we'd make a day of it. Years before John Cheever's story, we'd swim our way across town, from one pool to another, until we reached the surf at Malibu. We gave our patronage to friends and strangers alike, showing up uninvited, unexpected, but, we assumed, welcome.

This movable swim was a by-product of our habit of driving through the hills to find out what was being built where; we were crazy about exploring new houses. An empty house and a sparkling pool had the effect on us of a formal invitation. The place with the most natural appeal was my old house, and after I sold it, on each trip West our first "drive-about" included 1050 Summit Drive to see how it was faring. The pool now belonged to a house built, alas, right in the middle of what had once been my front lawn; to create another driveway, one wing of my house had been chopped off.

One year it had again changed hands. Judging from the workmen's paraphernalia scattered about, the alterations didn't seem quite finished. Although there were bits of furniture around and some curtains had been hung, clearly no one was in residence. We were dying to get inside to see what still another owner had done, but every door was locked. However, there was one near the pantry that we knew was apt to be left unlocked; it was at the top of the stairs leading from the basement. We knew how to get there through the garage, and that door gave us our chance. We felt like Tom Sawyer and Huck Finn.

For two people so passionate about privacy, this was a hell of a thing to do. We knew better, but somehow felt entitled. Justice was served, because we got caught red-handed—and by the owner, no less. As we were inspecting the bedrooms, we heard a woman's voice, shrill and frightened, from below: "Who's there? Who's there?" I turned to jelly.

Kate, instantly mobilized, called out, "We'll be right down. It's all right, I assure you." She brushed past me down the stairs, all contrition and good manners, hand extended. "My name is Katharine Hepburn," as if it needed telling. "Let me introduce . . . ," etc.

The lady was aware of our history with the house, and the trespassers were made welcome. She had plenty of questions and she got plenty of answers. What I'd really like to hear is the story *she* dined out on!

Looking back, it seems to me that anything unconventional I ever did, I did with Kate. It wouldn't occur to *me* to ask a tugboat captain to give us a ride down the East River and around the bay on a hot Sunday afternoon.

Kate's taste, like her charm, bears the test of time. There's evidence in every room of my apartment of past Christmases. I've caught her checking up on these things, pleased to see them again. She didn't object when I told her that eventually they would be hers. The only bargaining we've ever done is over what we're leaving each other, which was settled ages ago. When I recently told her I'd made a new will, I had to assure her that she still was down for the Bessarabian rug. I asked whether she'd rather have the Bessarabian runner; it was more practical. No, she'd prefer both. I said: "Nothing doing." In that case she'd stick with the big rug; she thought she'd put it in her bedroom; "But what happens if I die before you?" "You're out of luck."

There's different fun for different ages.

Kate had always ducked the press to the point of being rude. They, in turn, were hostile. But after Spence died, Kate did less battle for her privacy. She gradually opened her door and her arms wider—I imagine because there was not so much to lose, or perhaps there was extra to give. I remember when her phone number and address were sacred. Now she doesn't mind being caught shoveling snow in front of her house. Not too long ago a passerby, not up to date on obituaries, called out: "Didn't you used to be Joan Crawford?" "Not any more I'm not!" said she.

Kate sets extraordinary store by her family, so I was deeply moved when she first signed a letter to me "Sister Kate." By then I realized that her close friends became part of her family. I am part of hers and she is part of mine.

She got Spence to speak at my father's funeral, and I asked her to speak at David's. My children called her Aunt Kate. When I gave a party at the house for Jeff on his eighteenth birthday, Kate volunteered her presence because she figured I wouldn't have anyone to talk to. She stood next to me and thereby turned us into a receiving line. With her dainty dress and demure manner, it was Kate in soft focus. I shouldn't have been surprised, because this is as valid a facet of her as the tomboy.

She doesn't seek protection, she gives it. I don't know where her sense of duty ends and her loving heart begins. But when you're in trouble, she's Gibraltar. If I said she was noble, she would kill me. But she has the qualities which, when I was too young to know better, I thought good people ought to have. When Kate first said, "Character is destiny," it seemed so spontaneous and suitable I thought it had originated with her.

Kate got a most unexpected dividend from having invited me to see Spence's play in Washington—she got to live in my house when she was in California. While nothing could have induced me to rent it, I felt guilty that it stood empty. I no longer remember how often or how long she was there, but the first visit was in the autumn of '47.

She not only took wonderful care of the house, she supervised the garden. She taught my old gardener how to paint, whereupon my butler, Farr, suddenly developed an interest too. Kate bought still another set of painting materials.

I hadn't known she painted until she sent me a water color of the house with her in front, a tiny figure, racquet in hand. It was done at the moment of *Streetcar*'s New Haven opening. On the back was written: "From the heart of your 'territory' all hearts are beating for you Thursday the 30th. God bless you and it." It still hangs on my wall.

I let only one other person live in that house—strangely enough, Barbara Hutton. And thereby hangs a tale.

Cary Grant and I took in each other's washing. We didn't keep score, but I was under the impression that I owed him a favor or two. In 1952, when Barbara, his former wife, decided to come to California for two weeks in September, she asked Cary to find a house for her and her son. I refused to rent mine, but, as a favor to Cary, I agreed to lend it to Barbara.

The two weeks stretched into months without so much as a by-your-leave. I had been paying no heed to anything other than the political fortunes of Adlai Stevenson. But after four months I wrote her, with what tact and courtesy (pages of it) I could muster, that I had promised Kate the house on January 12. Barbara's answer, dated January 13, was maddening.

She was really "more than grateful . . . so kindly allowed Lance and me to stay in your beautiful home for so long a time . . . if agreeable to you I will move out in a month. If this does not meet with your approval, please do not hesitate to let me know and I will endeavor to make other plans." In a change of tone, she then said: "There's been a number of fairly costly repairs in the vicinity of $3,000. Naturally I've been very happy to pay this, and will be grateful if you will be kind enough to let me know the balance which is owing, which would cover rental charges."

I bristled. I wired her that I was "SORRY I CANNOT INVITE YOU TO STAY ANOTHER MONTH," as Kate was arriving the following Saturday. "I HAVE NO CHOICE BUT TO ASK YOU TO LEAVE. . . . THERE WAS NEVER A QUESTION OF RENT. . . . YOU OWE ME NO MONEY. ON THE CONTRARY . . . I HAVE INSTRUCTED MR. MAREE TO REFUND THIS . . . ," etc.

Barbara called the next morning and was sweet and apologetic, but disinclined to move out. I had to remind her that I was her hostess, not the landlady. When she plaintively said, "Where shall I go?," for a moment I felt sorry for her, but quickly recovered and said: "People usually go to a hotel." That's exactly what she did three days later, although she left behind an endless number of trunks and crates, as well as some retainers who were peering at Kate from behind closed blinds as she arrived.

I was dismayed to learn that the pale green carpet in my bedroom would have to be replaced; apparently Barbara's dog had used it as a bathroom. That was the injury. The insult came when her lawyer asked me to sign a quit-claim.

But the unkindest cut of all had to do with Farr. Barbara, having appreciated his services, had invited him to leave me and join her staff. Indeed, she had ostensibly thought so highly of Farr's paintings that she had arranged an exhibit in Beverly Hills. As Farr was not quite a Grandma Moses, I was astonished when I heard that the exhibit was a sell-out. Barbara's hangers-on, who had reason to expect a treat from Cartier at Christmas, were rewarded that year with an original James Farr.

ACTUALLY long before I sold the California house, I was firmly settled in New York in an apartment in the Pierre Hotel which I'd gotten by chance. In 1949, the very week I was to buy the apartment I had been subletting, the manager of the Pierre—out of the blue—offered me one of their residential apartments. I couldn't understand it; I knew there was a waiting list, and had been for years. When I hesitated, the manager said he hoped I held no grievance against them. Grievance? I had nothing but fond memories. Not so the Pierre! Out tumbled the explanation of why, for a dozen years, the hotel was full up whenever we had tried to make reservations. Mr. Selznick was a fine gentleman, the manager offered, but they couldn't render service to him and to their other guests simultaneously. David treated the staff as studio employees, swamping the desk, the bellboys, and room service, and, most particularly, tying up the switchboard. I was not offended for more than a moment, for there was a certain sense of fitness: this place had also rebelled! I looked, I rented, then later I bought. I've been here ever since.

The new apartment placed a demand on me for which I was unprepared: Mother in the kitchen. Before, there had always been a full staff; now blessedly there was only Hildur, my hidden weapon, and on weekends only me. The first night of school holiday the boys had room service. Next night, the perennial treat, the Colony, where they had been spoiled from a tender age. When Sunday came, it was pouring rain and they revolted. Well, then, room service again? Nothing doing. "We'll settle for anything. Hildur's left some canned soup, there's some baked beans, there's eggs." However delicious the Pierre food, it wasn't what the other boys at school had in mind as they left for the holiday. My sons seemed to need a new kind of mother and I was at my wits' end.

I explored the fridge. There were provisions I hadn't expected, including a chicken, which Hildur in her unfathomable wisdom had seen fit to order. I had never touched a raw chicken and it filled me with horror. There was this terrible animal and the mandate, but the hour was getting late and they were ravenous. If I hadn't felt guilty at being a working mother, I wouldn't have been so desperate. I recalled I had asked Hildur to buy a pressure cooker. I knew it was a dangerous object, so I dug around for the instruction book. There was a simple recipe for something called spicy chicken, and quite suddenly I had it on the table; and a more aromatic, delicious dish had never passed my children's lips. The boys were filled with amazement; I hid mine.

As a young woman, I had been skilled at chocolate fudge, naturally, and at scrambled eggs, but that was the limit of my repertoire, despite my father and what was called "cooking class" at school. It was just as well, because I had married a man to whom culinary skills were repugnant, although he didn't object to scrambled eggs at midnight. The inside of a refrigerator turned his stomach. I hadn't realized any of this until one night in our little beach house, the first year of marriage, I planned a big surprise. The servants were off, and the little woman cooked dinner for her bridegroom. It took all afternoon and part of the evening. Disaster upon disaster, and insufficient pots and pans despite the growing pile around me as the clock raced on. When the guest of honor made his ever-tardy way home, the battered bride squeaked out, "Welcome." He recoiled and said, "Please, darling, no, I can't stand it. Don't do this to me." Mind you, this was before he had any idea of what lay behind the kitchen door. That was my last attempt for twenty years.

Now, carried away, I turned to the kitchen with a vengeance. Weekends were an orgy; home for meals or not, I cooked up storms. It was all so easy and triumphant; for a while there I couldn't put a foot wrong. How had those cooks over the years so intimidated me? Any time the boys were out of school, they had a proper mother and home-cooked food. I even tried a batch of cookies, which Danny, being David's very own son, found so superlative that I sent him some at school. Months later I was spending a week in an obscure health spa in Florida, and as I ran sheet-draped from the steam bath, a fellow inmate breached my precious anonymity and said, "Are you Mrs. Selznick?" I looked blank. "Mrs. Irene Selznick?" I hesitated. She continued, "The mother of Danny Selznick?" I beamed. She said, "Are you the woman who makes those wonderful cookies? My son is making my life miserable!" That was my high point; a little knowledge is a heady thing.

The Pierre was also the scene of a somewhat more dramatic event than my baking—Ingrid Bergman's return to America in 1956 for the premiere of *Anastasia,* her first trip here after the scandal that had destroyed her Hollywood career. Although given a suite upstairs by the film company, she chose to stay with me, just as—by a wild coincidence—she had left for Italy from my apartment seven years earlier.

Ingrid, who loved the theatre, had always come to New York more than my other Hollywood friends. Late in 1948 she was at loose ends, without a producer and unhappy about her work. Her movies hadn't turned out too well after she left David. She was still the very top star, but none of her many offers included a great director. She told me she didn't care about money; she wanted opportunity. She was prepared to take a real cut for the chance to work with any one of five directors; she named William Wyler, Billy Wilder, George Stevens, Roberto Rossellini, and, I believe, John Huston. She wondered what to do about it.

I came up with a plan that was as simple and direct as Ingrid herself.

The thing to do was to write each one, in her own charming style, asking him to bear her in mind in case the right story came along.

She was unimpressed, in fact dubious. I told her it was a beguiling idea that only she could get away with. I could just imagine the astonishment of a director receiving a handwritten note from Ingrid Bergman asking for a job. I told her how to reach them, including Rossellini, with whom I had recently dined in Paris and whom I had found charming. Some months later, Ingrid told me she'd had a marvelous letter from him. I asked if she'd also heard from the others. She said of course not; she had only written Rossellini. That summer the Lindstroms met him in Paris, and he visited them in the winter.

In March Ingrid was in New York, all set to fly to Italy to make her first Italian picture. Everything considered, it was natural to spend the last evening with me. We wound up at my place for a drink. Ingrid talked and talked. She was not so much exhilarated as fevered. Her spirits were higher than a couple of highballs would account for. I asked no questions, because if something was afoot, I preferred not to know it. It got pretty late, so I got undressed. When she didn't take the hint, I went to bed.

She didn't leave. She sat down beside me and phoned Roberto in Rome. I tried not to listen and I still didn't pry. She didn't want to be alone or go back to the hotel at that hour. I had a great big bed; if I didn't mind, she would sleep right there. I gave her a nightie and a toothbrush, and on the way to the bathroom she slipped on the polished floor and cracked her head on the corner of the air conditioner. She fell so heavily I thought she was a goner. An eighth of an inch in a different direction and she wouldn't have gone to Rome.

She sent a cable on arrival. I have it still: "I AM HERE. INGRID." It didn't say much. On the other hand, it said a lot and left no doubt. Ten days later there was another cable, which said more. It read: "WE DON'T HAVE TIME TO WRITE BECAUSE WE ARE SO HAPPY. BERGELINI." For an awful moment I thought, "What have I done?" Actually, nothing at all. It wasn't my fault she hadn't written the other four directors.

Nonetheless, Ingrid was quite a letter-writer. One letter says: ". . . I was going through my mind about all the things that happened in New York and in Italy a year ago. When I fell flat on the floor in your bedroom, it must have been symbolic! The fallen star! I should have known already then, that the way I felt could not end without disaster."

Her tale needs no retelling here. Every year when I was in Europe I went to Rome and so witnessed some of her happiness and some of her pain. For some years I carried gifts from her to Pia. I was Ingrid's last link to her daughter and the last of the Lindstroms' friends on whom Peter shut the door.

Pia now lives no further from me than her mother had in California. After all the *Sturm und Drang* between her parents, it seems to me remarkable that in Pia's home I see all her younger half-brothers and -sisters—the Lindstroms and the Rossellinis. Even together on occasion. Most important, I found it a relief that Peter and Ingrid were eventually able to share Pia amiably.

Ingrid survived some terrible difficulties and, unlike many others, so did her disposition. When a journalist asked what was her formula for happiness, her response was: "A poor memory."

The person who stood behind her second to none was my old friend and hers, Sidney, now Lord Bernstein, who has a unique talent for friendship. On the weekend of Ingrid's sixtieth birthday, Sidney, a hitherto conservative man (apart from his politics), chartered a super-luxury plane from London that we might spend the day with her in the French countryside, where she was then living. Sidney's wife, Sandra, also came, along with their son David and daughter Jane, who happens to be my godchild. Ingrid was as delighted as we were by our excursion. When we left, she ran alongside our car the length of the driveway waving goodbye and calling out, "My two pillars!" Through the rear window I caught a glimpse of her standing against the gatepost, her arms still stretched toward us. I like to remember that moment.

A F T E R settling into the Pierre and selling the California house, I began to feel that I needed a place in the country for weekends. After two years I found it—in Bedford Village, two miles from the Connecticut border. It was just large enough to wrap around me, yet could open up to accommodate guests with comfort and privacy. Peace, quiet, lots of land, and a little water. I wound up with forty acres, two ponds, two waterfalls and one brook. "Imspond" was a companionable house that took no getting used to. Simplicity was the key, plus a cozy personality that managed to escape being cute.

I learned something about my future while showing a friend around, just before moving in. "I see you're not planning to get married again," she said. I had assumed I was until that moment. But she was right; the layout didn't preclude a husband, but apparently I had no plan for one. It was quite evident that my mind was clearly made up and I didn't even know it. Privately, I concluded that this attitude was less a reflection on the past than satisfaction with the present. The truth was, I had already found a way of life that suited me and a man who made me happy. For close to twenty-five years he and I managed to be together and yet escape attention. Fortunately, he shared my obsession with privacy, to such an extent that no one—not my children, not even Hildur—knew of our relationship.

To David's credit, he never delved into the more personal side of my life, perhaps because he better than anyone knew what my privacy meant to me; perhaps because he knew I was happy. On the other hand, he had a thing or two to say about Imspond. When he heard I was still remodeling after a year, he called to say that if I wasn't satisfied, to sell it. "Write it off and get another one." But when he finally got to see it, he thought it was wonderful. "Why did you ever want to sell it? This is great! It suits you." He did, though, propose a few major additions "which would be fun."

Over the years the Hornblows were my favorite guests at Imspond. I had looked up to Arthur since my earliest David days, and now he had married the engaging Leonora, aka Bubbles, who had ruthlessly wooed him back to New York. (Imspond was about as far as she could comfortably stray from Manhattan.) Inasmuch as Hornblow houses had so helped shape my tastes, it seemed only right and just that Arthur and Bub would take to Imspond so naturally.

But I think the person to whom Imspond meant the most was Kitty Hart. Naturally I cared about Moss a lot—in fact I adored him like everyone else who knew him. Each was his best friend; we all deluded ourselves. When he started squiring Kitty Carlisle, everyone agreed that she was charming. "How nice for Moss, and how lovely for her." But marriage? Usually the bride is the possessive one, or the groom. In this case it was the friends. In no time at all, of course, she had us eating out of her hand. Indeed, Kitty grew on me. She came into my life when she married Moss and under my wing when he died; it was to Imspond that she then found her way and her first healing.

Through the years I'd given a lot of cheap advice to Kitty. (Once she said, "I'm doing great—your head on my shoulders!") The time came for Kitty to turn the tables. When I shut down my office in the mid-sixties, I had to dispose of my papers—I couldn't bear just to toss them out. Eventually they found their way to the Boston University Library, whose Director of Collections not only said that I could come and visit them whenever I liked, but hoped that I'd give a little talk to the Friends of the Library.

Considering my possibly recurrent stutter and my excessive reticence, I don't know what possessed me to consent. Probably because I couldn't have managed otherwise, I minimized this undertaking as much as I had magnified the prospect of that radio broadcast back in 1948. I reduced this speech in my mind to a "conversation" with a few people who were coming to meet me. Kitty, who did a lot of lecturing, knew better.

First, I mustn't take a drink, not even a sip of wine at dinner. If I thought it would relax me, I was wrong—I'd only get muddled. She wondered what I was going to say. I was damned if I was going to read a speech; I thought I would just let them ask me questions. Kitty said it was presumptuous of me to expect people to leave their homes just for that. She told me not to wing it; if I wasn't going to prepare, I'd better just skip the whole thing. The thing to do was memorize a few opening remarks and then use cards. Cards? I was thoroughly mystified. It was inconceivable to Kitty that I didn't know that speakers generally listed their topics on cards, and I should do the same. I resisted her right down the line.

I bought the cards, but they were still blank when I got to Boston. At the last minute I made notes on a dozen or so.

Throughout dinner I resented Kitty every time I looked at my wine-glass, but I didn't dare take a chance. Suddenly I was on, in front of a capacity audience of two hundred. I wasn't the woman behind somebody this time, I was it, the main act, all there was. When my memorized lines came out without a falter, I took heart. Somehow I knew I wasn't going to stutter. I silently blessed Kitty as I turned the first cards.

I didn't need wine to become intoxicated, the first laugh did it. There was no holding me. When I had got behind the lectern, I had laid down my cards and a watch like a pro. Now I was so carried away I felt confined, and moved to open space, leaving behind the cards and my watch and my caution. The most surprising thing is that I leveled. I told things about myself and my family to this group of strangers that I couldn't imagine telling anyone, and yet I felt intact. Oddly enough, what I said there began to give me a perspective on my life and was possibly the first step toward this book.

I talked double the agreed time, but hardly scratched the surface. Had I taken another hour and a half, I might have had time for questions.

At the reception which followed, I accepted the praise as though I were the real article and was delighted I was urged to return.

Back at the hotel, my exhilaration mounted so high that I would have given anything for another audience then and there. What by all rights was a minor event in a crowded life appeared to me as my greatest accomplishment, and in some way it was. I'd shown two of my demons that I wasn't afraid of them. I had had a victory so peculiarly mine that I couldn't believe anyone else could possibly understand.

D A V I D and Jennifer had a baby in the summer of 1954, and Jennifer's two sons by Robert Walker were surely as delighted as mine that it was a girl.

David could hardly wait for me to see her. I happened to be in California, staying at George Cukor's house, when she was about six months old. One morning, when I was still in bed, David burst into my room, followed by a nurse carrying Mary Jennifer.

These surprise visits with the child were repeated in New York and London. It took me a few years to discover what they were about: they were part of a campaign. David felt that if I got to know her, I'd be so charmed I'd consent to bring her up in case he and Jennifer were killed in an accident. He went on to explain that if I agreed, all he then had to do was sell the idea to Jennifer. He considered this a perfectly reasonable approach.

He worried still more about providing for her financially as he was nearing his sixties and she was still a little girl. There was more than a possibility that there wouldn't be enough in his estate to maintain either Jennifer or their child. Although he already was carrying more life insurance than he could afford, he took to buying more, which at his age was increasingly expensive.

As he was having a hard time keeping up a front and still making ends meet, I suggested he not leave money to our sons, because we had already given them some; they both had trust funds from my parents, and they would be my heirs. Besides, they were grown-up. Jeff and Danny agreed with me more readily than did David, who sadly reflected on what his gambling had brought him to. This time it was he who worried how it would look, and he went to great pains in his will to explain why, though he left them his papers and books, he left them no money.

David continued to hope that he could again make a picture or two on his own terms. It was Sam Goldwyn who best understood his professional problems. Sam went to such extreme lengths to get David reestablished and able to function with sufficient freedom that David became really sentimental about him.

David was moved that Sam Spiegel, the only other independent producer making important pictures, also repeatedly made valiant efforts in his behalf. It was the kind of thing David would have been likely to do, but not something he would have expected from colleagues.

He found a different kind of generosity in Bill Paley, from whom he thought he had concealed the extent of his difficulties. He was both touched and astonished to have Bill, without any preliminaries, hand him a check for an enormous amount. Bill didn't want to discuss it, beyond indicating that it was not to be treated as a debt. David told me with satisfaction that it had been repaid. Fortunately he was also able, in the last six months of his life, to sell certain film assets, which eased his burden considerably.

My marriage came and went, but my connection to David lasted until death did us part.

There wasn't a peep out of him from Europe all the summer of '64, which was strange. The day before his return he phoned from Paris to say that he had to see me. It was very important.

It was also pretty terrible. As he walked into the room the following afternoon, he said, "I am dying." Judging from the expression on his face, it was all too true. In France he had invented an ankle injury to account for his immobility, but actually he had had a near-fatal heart attack.

I was very still; had I reacted, I believe he would have broken down completely. He gave me no details, just the verdict. He didn't want anyone else to know, including Jennifer and his children; and if Bill Paley knew, it would cast a pall on their relationship. Anyhow, for business reasons it would have to be kept quiet. He thought he could best dispose of some remaining assets if he stayed in New York. He established himself at the Waldorf Towers with ten-year-old Mary Jennifer and spent most of the next nine months there. Jennifer came from time to time.

Obviously, David didn't comply with his doctor's orders. Only acute discomfort could slow him down. When it struck, he'd lie low, then surface again when he felt better.

What he couldn't always do was to carry out the weekend program he had promised Mary Jennifer. He got in the habit of asking Danny to take his place at the last moment, and this was raising havoc with Danny's life and an important romance he was having. In any case, I thought Danny ought to know the truth. (There was no point in telling Jeffrey, because he was living in Paris and couldn't help.) When David looked to me rather than to his internist to find him a different cardiologist, I agreed, provided that in return Danny be allowed to talk to the new doctor. This great big man couldn't tell his son the truth and wouldn't let me, but saw no contradiction in letting a strange doctor tell him. I now had to comfort a son who was badly shaken. Danny then got an extra telephone line and an answering service so that his father could always reach him.

David put on such a good show that no one guessed, least of all Bill. When David was spending a weekend at the Paleys' that spring, he phoned me on Saturday when he arrived because he had a big problem: his room was on the third floor! Please, what should he do?

I pointed out that there were two landings in the first flight where he'd be able to sit down; and the second flight was enclosed, which made it possible to take one step at a time. I told him he could stay if he went upstairs only once, at bedtime, and left Sunday night.

He called after he got back, greatly pleased with himself. He had pulled it off, and thus had proof that Bill didn't have a clue. (Afterward, Bill found it hard to believe that David could have had heart trouble without his knowing it. Months later he was still haunted by all those stairs on David's last visit. I tried to console him by telling him what a lovely present for David that incident had proved to be.)

David was surprised to reach his sixty-third birthday on the tenth of May (his father had died at sixty-two). He said, "At this rate, I'll live forever." Two weeks later, at a dinner party at the Hornblows', I saw him leave his table and go into Arthur's bedroom. He gave me a signal as he passed. I soon joined him and found him in frightening pain. I called the cardiologist, who gave me simple instructions. He said it was not another attack and to keep him lying flat as long as possible. No fuss was made. Bubbles and I kept an eye on him during the evening; whoever asked was told that David didn't feel well and was just lying down. Only Leland Hayward was suspicious and lingered after the other guests left. He insisted on helping me take David back to the Waldorf and put him to bed.

The next day Bubbles, who loved David dearly, wept as she told me that at one point when she was watching him anxiously, he had said as though to comfort her: "It's all right, Bub; it's not so much fun any more." He died a month later.

We dined together the night before he returned to California. He stretched the evening out by hiring a horse and carriage. We rode through the park a few times and then endlessly up and down Fifth Avenue. Our conversation was as aimless as our route. It got very late. There was a certain poignancy in his inability to say goodbye. I'm not sure I could have managed if he had said it. I waited until I got upstairs before I went to pieces.

After he went back, we spoke a few times; the last call, three days before he died, went on for an hour and a half. He couldn't seem to say what he wanted to say, he just hung on the phone. His death came on June 22.

Jennifer tried to persuade me to come out for the funeral, but I thought better not. She deferred to Jeff and Danny on the arrangements. They consulted me and Bill Paley, who flew out along with Jock. Naturally, Kate presented herself to the boys. When they went to Forest Lawn for the final details, they discovered why she had been determined to go along. She did indeed know all the ropes.

At the funeral Kate read "If," which Danny had chosen because David had always admired Kipling. George Cukor and Joseph Cotten spoke, and Cary Grant read the tribute Bill Paley had written. When Jennifer wrote to thank me for what she felt was my contribution, she said my sons had "managed everything in true Selznick style."

The headline in the *New York Times* said exactly what David had predicted, but the front page was an honor he'd thought he might no longer be granted. *Newsweek* headed its article "Epic Man," and *Time*'s title was "The Producer Prince." I wished I could have told him.

Etcetera

WITH the boys off, my office shut down and Edie off-limits, I was to all intents and purposes on my own. After Louis B., fifteen years of David plus fifteen years of Broadway had taken it out of me. It was time to stop—time to forget the Girl Scouts once and for all.

At last I began doing the things I thought would give me most pleasure rather than fulfilling responsibilities. I could even be frivolous! Clothes? I could shop without guilt. Bridge? Why not! Always I had had to hoard time; now I could spend it. I could read all I wanted—and for pleasure, not work. I could go to the movies—I could even go to the theatre—without having to make a professional judgment. And since I was once more an amateur, I was free to speak up. The relief!

The boys were of course no longer boys; they'd grown up with all the tribulations normal to becoming adult, and went on giving me the delight and worry common to offspring. But they were leading their lives, not mine, and I was sensible enough not to center my existence on them. We did, though, do some happy traveling together when they were still unattached—I saw Russia with Danny; Spain and Israel with Jeffrey; the Orient with them both.

Travel became an increasingly important part of my life, partly because my curiosity was still sharp, partly because at last I could do it my way, on my own time. Every spring I went to Europe. In the winter I often stayed with Marietta and Ronnie Tree in Barbados, and later with

Claudette Colbert. (My friendship with Claudette has survived fifty years, mostly due, I claim, to her scrupulously ignoring the advice she so assiduously demanded of me.) I went to Yugoslavia with her, to England with Kate, and to Italy with Kitty. I spent part of many summers on Sam Spiegel's yacht in the Mediterranean. And wherever the Whitneys went, I was made welcome—at Fisher's Island, at Saratoga, and at the Embassy in London when Jock was ambassador there.

Best of all, at last I had enough time for my friends. Once separated from David, I had spread myself more widely, and friends became the network I trusted; friends are the family I wound up with. Of all the continuing good luck I've encountered, that (apart from health) has been the greatest. I don't mean my friends are better or more to be cherished than anyone else's, it's only that I had been trained not to depend on them. Moreover, contrary to expectations, I acquired some new friends every bit as close to my heart as though they'd been there through the years. My parents had never stopped warning me against strangers; against people trying to gain my affection. People would use me. It's true, I've been used a lot. And well—very well. What could be a better life?

So much that happened to me seems unlikely. I didn't turn out to be what I or anyone expected, not in any possible way. Well, I did get married and have two little boys—but married to a David? And what about the serene and balanced life I was going to have with the perfect second husband? And what happened to the never-to-be-revealed fantasy of becoming a doctor? And how did I ever achieve a *career*?

Actually, I see now that I've had three lives—one as the daughter of my father, another as the wife of my husband. The theatre furnished me with a third act. I suppose this book is a review of all three. I'd have settled for so much less.

With perseverance I've gotten this far; now, with a little more luck, I'd like to grow very old as slowly as possible.

A NOTE ON THE TYPE

The text of this book was set in film in a typeface named Bembo. The roman is a copy of a letter cut for the celebrated Venetian printer Aldus Manutius by Francesco Griffo. It was first used in Cardinal Bembo's DE AETNA of 1495—hence the name of the revival. Griffo's type is now generally recognized, thanks to the research of Stanley Morison, to be the first of the old-face group of types. The companion italic is an adaptation of the chancery script type designed by the Roman calligrapher and printer Lodovico degli Arrighi, called Vincentino, and used by him during the 1520's.

Composed, printed, and bound by
The Haddon Craftsmen, Inc., Scranton, Pennsylvania.

Design by Dorothy Schmiderer